Eastern Africa Series

FOUNDATIONS OF AN AFRICAN CIVILISATION

Eastern Africa Series

Women's Land Rights & Privatization in Eastern Africa
BIRGIT ENGLERT & ELIZABETH DALEY (EDS)

War & the Politics of Identity in Ethiopia KJETIL TRONVOLL

Moving People in Ethiopia
ALULA PANKHURST & FRANÇOIS PIGUET (EDS)

Living Terraces in Ethiopia ELIZABETH E. WATSON

Eritrea GAIM KIBREAB

Borders & Borderlands as Resources in the Horn of Africa
DEREJE FEYISSA & MARKUS VIRGIL HOEHNE (EDS)

After the Comprehensive Peace Agreement in Sudan
ELKE GRAWERT (ED.)

Land, Governance, Conflict & the Nuba of Sudan
GUMA KUNDA KOMEY

Ethiopia JOHN MARKAKIS

Resurrecting Cannibals HEIKE BEHREND

Pastoralism & Politics in Northern Kenya & Southern Ethiopia
GŰNTHER SCHLEE & ADULLAHI A. SHONGOLO

Islam & Ethnicity in Northern Kenya & Southern Ethiopia
GŰNTHER SCHLEE with ADULLAHI A. SHONGOLO

Foundations of an African Civilisation DAVID W. PHILLIPSON

Regional Integration, Identity & Citizenship in the Greater Horn of Africa
KIDANE MENGISTEAB & REDIE BEREKETEAB (EDS)

Dealing with the Government in South Sudan CHERRY LEONARDI

The Quest for Socialist Utopia BAHRU ZEWDE

Disrupting Territories
JÖRG GERTEL, RICHARD ROTTENBURG & SANDRA CALKINS (EDS)

*The African Garrison State**
KJETIL TRONVOLL & DANIEL R. MEKONNEN

*The State of Post-conflict Reconstruction**
NASEEM BADIEY

** forthcoming*

Foundations of an African Civilisation

Aksum & the northern Horn 1000 BC - AD 1300

DAVID W. PHILLIPSON
Litt.D., F.B.A., F.S.A.

Addis Ababa University Press

List of Illustrations

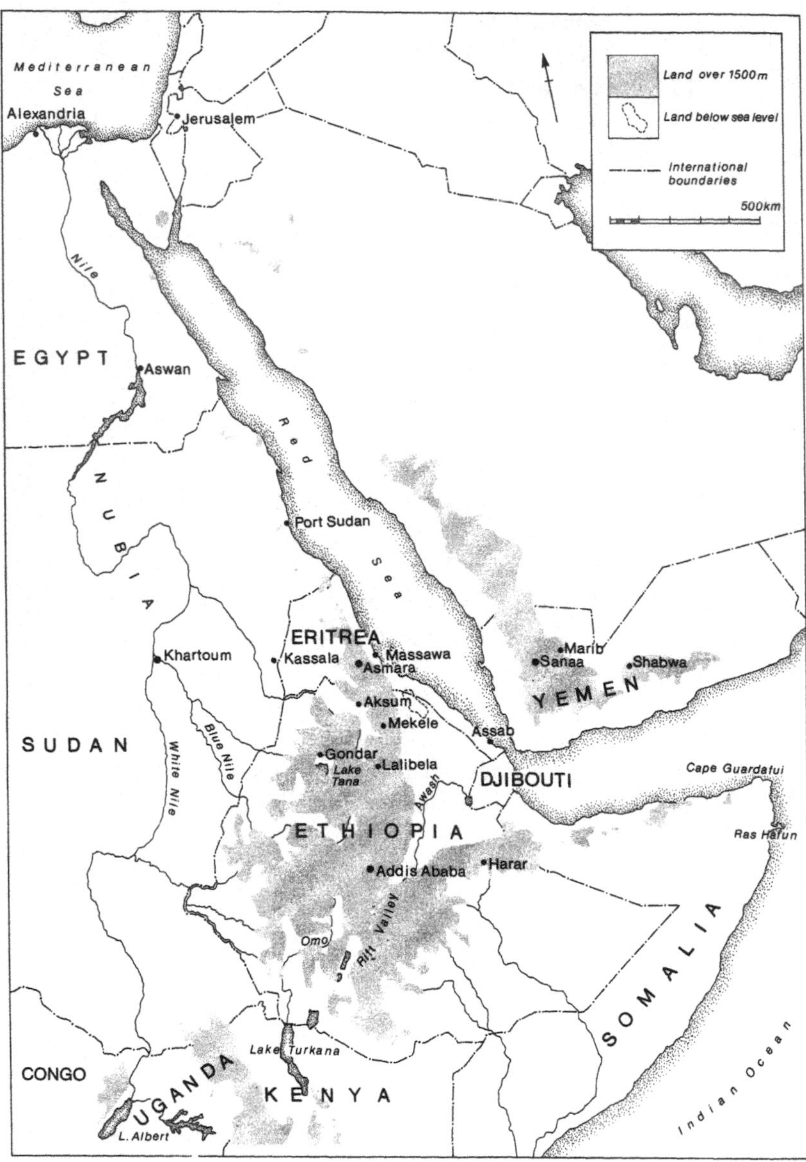

Fig. 1 The northern Horn of Africa and adjacent regions

1

General Introduction

Aims and sources

The aim of this book is to present a critical outline of current knowledge about the peoples who inhabited the highlands of what is now northern Ethiopia and adjacent parts of Eritrea[1] during the period between about 3000 and 700 years ago (Fig. 1). It devotes most detailed attention to the Aksumite civilisation that flourished during the first seven centuries AD but, in order to provide context, it also provides overviews of earlier and later periods within the same general region. The cut-off point at which the book's treatment ends is *c.* AD 1270, when major changes accompanied the establishment of the so-called Solomonic dynasty.[2] Overall, this was the period that saw the gradual development, from a subsistence-farming base established long previously, of a complex literate civilisation whose people erected some of the largest and most elaborate monoliths the world has ever seen, issued a unique coinage in copper, silver and gold, practised sophisticated metallurgy, ivory carving and manuscript illumination, established their rule over extensive surrounding territory including part of the Arabian peninsula, developed trade links extending from the western Mediterranean in one direction to Sri Lanka in the other, and whose Christian rulers were sought as political as well as religious allies by successive Roman and Byzantine emperors, while also maintaining the subsistence-farming, domestic architecture, and stone-tool technological traditions of their local forbears. It is now increasingly recognised that this civilisation in turn gave rise – far more strongly and directly than previously recognised – to the Christian civilisation that flourished in these highlands during more recent centuries.

My discussion focuses primarily – but by no means exclusively – upon the archaeology, but uses this material in conjunction with that derived from numerous other disciplines to compile a composite picture of the past. The beginning of this period represents – very roughly – the time when archaeological evidence ceases to be the dominant source of information that it had been for so-called prehistory, and takes the role sometimes designated as a distinct sub-discipline of historical archaeology.[3]

[1] For clarity, this book will sometimes refer to the region as 'the northern Ethiopian highlands' or as 'the northern Horn'. Except where the context clearly implies otherwise, references to 'Ethiopia' may be assumed to include Eritrea: occasional avoidance of repeated mentions of Eritrea implies no disrespect or disapproval of that nation's separate identity.

[2] I have published recent accounts of Aksumite civilisation's immediate predecessors and successors (D. Phillipson 2009c and 2009a respectively). For the changes that took place *c.* AD 1270, see *idem* 2009a: 22, 197.

[3] Confusingly, the term 'historical archaeology' is used with varying connotations in different parts of the world. In North America, Australia and South Africa, and now – increasingly – elsewhere, it is used to designate the archaeological investigation of European colonialism from the late-fifteenth century onwards. This limited, Eurocentric and unhelpful usage is irrelevant to many other regions and is not followed in this book.

Treatment here is based on the view that archaeology is, first and foremost, a method of learning about the human past. While it can be employed alone – as, indeed, it must be in situations where no other sources of information are available – its full potential for illuminating the past can only be achieved in conjunction with all other available sources of information relating to the period and situation under discussion. Such additional sources may include written materials, whether these were indigenous to the society under study or produced by visitors from elsewhere. Knowledge of ancient languages and their inter-relationships is not derived solely from ancient writings, but may also be reconstructed on the basis of more recent spoken forms; indeed the content of many texts may have been transmitted orally for a long time before being committed to writing. Language itself, as well as the subject-matter of both its written and oral manifestations, is thus a valuable source of information about the past,[4] although establishment of absolute chronologies for pre-literate developments remains problematic and controversial. Ancient populations depended for their food on plants and animals – whether wild or domestic – and these, like the changing environments on which these populations depended, are often the subject of separate studies by specialists working either on fossil or other ancient remains or on more recent evidence including genetics. This book provides numerous examples of the ways such sources of information may complement narrowly defined archaeology in the reconstruction of the past. It includes summaries of established views, but goes into greater detail where new evidence or interpretations require that these be reconsidered.

It is appropriate to compare these sources in terms both of their interpretation and of the information they can yield. Archaeology is based on the recovery and study of tangible remains that can often be dated directly, by comparison, or by reference to the context in which they are preserved. Such material is not restricted to portable artefacts, but may also include buildings or their components, remains of plants and animals whether or not modified or used as food, waste such as ash, slag or dung, or materials illustrative of the human environment. All have it in common that – ideally – they should be demonstrably contemporary with the events or processes under study, and undisturbed since that time. In such circumstances, potential sources of error are largely restricted to the archaeologist's own observations and interpretations. Most of the information gleaned by archaeologists refers impersonally to material aspects of daily existence including economy, technology, diet and perhaps to aspects of funerary customs and political systems, but only by implication to the beliefs on which these were based. Rarely, and exclusively in the context of literate societies, can the names or identities of individual people be ascertained. Acts and their results may be reconstructed, but their reasons only indirectly inferred. Neither thoughts nor the spoken word are preserved directly in the archaeological record unless they are committed to writing. In their different ways, archaeology and the study of orally transmitted or written records can all contribute to an understanding of the past.

Inscriptions preserve only what their writer or instigator wished either to have recorded or to be seen by a particular readership. Many so-called historical texts were originally propaganda, and should be interpreted accordingly.

[4] This is not the place for detailed evaluation of the methodologies by which information about the past can the extracted from linguistic data or from orally transmitted or written texts. For historical linguistics, the reader will find guidance – admittedly sometimes conflicting – in works by Ehret 2000 and Blench 2006, and for oral tradition in Vansina 1985. Written materials are highly diverse, those from Ethiopia giving rise to the additional complication that many texts were transmitted orally for a long time before being committed to writing.

Inscriptions on coinage similarly reflect the views – or at least the prejudices – of those responsible for its issue, although they were presumably intended for a much less narrowly defined readership.

Written documents on less permanent materials are even more difficult to interpret. In most instances, the oldest version extant today was produced long after the period to which it ostensibly relates. This may be because it was copied from an earlier version which itself no longer survives, in which case the possibilities of accidental error, emendation in the light of changed circumstances, explanatory additions which were not necessarily correct, or deliberate falsification all need to be taken into account. Alternatively, the text may initially have been composed a significant time after that period, in which case circumstances of composition and transmission, as well as sources of information, need to be considered. Perhaps information was first handed down orally and subsequently committed to writing, so that evaluation must apply different criteria for each stage. It may well be that a document surviving today combines materials that originated in diverse times and circumstances, each component of which will require appropriate interpretation.

Focus here is on the highlands of Eritrea and those of northern Ethiopia, the latter being today subsumed within the Tigray and the eastern part of the Amhara regional states. It would, however, be highly misleading to treat this area in isolation. National and international boundaries in northeastern Africa are mainly nineteenth- or twentieth-century impositions and do not necessarily have any relevance for earlier times. Furthermore, no community – today or in the past – has been able to exist in total isolation, and it would be misleading to reconstruct its history in such terms. This book will therefore frequently make reference to regions outside – sometimes far beyond – those with which it is primarily concerned. In particular, the highlands and other parts of northern and western Eritrea will sometimes be included, as will more southerly regions of Ethiopia itself and neighbouring Djibouti. Many developments in the northern Horn may only be properly understood through reference to contemporary events or processes in Arabia, the Sudanese Nile Valley, or areas even more distant.

Ambitiously, the book addresses three distinct audiences. I hope that it will prove of interest to my fellow specialists, including those whose prime interests are in areas other than the northern Horn. I have also long been struck by the lack of any reliable textbook suited to the growing numbers of archaeology students at Ethiopian universities and I hope that this work will go some way towards meeting their needs. Likewise, in many other parts of the world, there is increasing interest both in the Ethiopian past and, more generally, in the interdependence of archaeology and other historical disciplines. Finally, there are many less specialised readers – Eritreans, Ethiopians, people originating in those countries but now living elsewhere, foreigners and tourists – who desire a comprehensive account of these topics but may not wish to burden themselves with controversies and minutiae. To facilitate use by this varied readership, all bibliographical references and detailed argument, together with much discussion of disputed interpretations, have been relegated to footnotes. For those who do not wish to consult all the footnotes, I hope that the main text will provide a coherent but concise narrative, with access to detail and further guidance should these be required.

There has long been a tendency for past developments in the northern Horn to be studied in isolation, with inadequate reference to trends or events in other areas, whether neighbouring or distant, with which its inhabitants may have had contact. Equally – if not more – insidious has been the alternative viewpoint that has sought to interpret innovations in the northern Horn as introductions from elsewhere, without adequate evaluation of the possibility of local development. These distinctions are, of course, rarely simple 'either/or' situations, but ones where far more complex interactions were almost certainly at work. Many passages in this book include discussions and evaluations of such problems which – however necessary they may be if we are to obtain a proper understanding of the northern Horn's true place in human history – are rarely conclusive. To take but one example: the Christian religion originated in the lands bordering the eastern Mediterranean and – by whatever means – must have been introduced to the Aksumite kingdom from that area. Its subsequent nurture and eventual florescence in the northern Horn may now, however, be seen as an essentially indigenous process, but one that did not take place in a complete vacuum, without contact or knowledge of trends in Christian communities elsewhere.Confusion not infrequently arises from changing application of names to the territories of the northern Horn. The name 'Ethiopia' was very loosely employed in ancient times, sometimes with particular reference to Nubia, alternatively to any area lying to the south of Egypt. Other writers divided this area between Libya west of the Nile and Ethiopia on the east. Any region east of the Nile, including the northern Horn, could also be regarded as part of India and not clearly differentiated from the peninsular South-Asian sub-continent of that name.[5] The term 'Ethiopia', as used more recently in historical and cultural – as opposed to political – contexts, can be a somewhat artificial construct relating to what is sometimes designated culturally as the *orbis aethiopicus* or, geographically, to the greater part of the northern Horn.[6]

The current state of research

The reader of this book will immediately realise that it is based on incomplete research. In parts of the northern Horn, investigations have been restricted by political[7] or economic factors. Needs to develop infrastructure or tourism facilities may have encouraged or hindered the investigation of ancient remains. Elsewhere such study has not yet even begun. Such research as has been undertaken has had widely varied emphases and project-designs. Epigraphical and numismatic research has sometimes been conducted in virtual isolation, with little attempt at integration with results derived from other methodologies. Results of some important archaeological investigations have remained incompletely published and thus not available either to other scholars or to the wider public. One of the aims of this book is to draw attention to these gaps in our knowledge, whatever their cause, and thus to offer a guide to needs for future research.

Published data relating to this topic are beset by two main problems. First, they are written in a variety of languages and have appeared in a wide range of journals, conference-proceedings and monographs including many whose primary focus is in fields far removed from the study of the northern Horn. Residents of Ethiopia and Eritrea themselves have a particular difficulty, in that a significant proportion of these publications are virtually impossible to

[5] The problem is surveyed in greater detail by D. Phillipson 2009a: 3 and 2009b. See also Dihle 1964; Crone 1987: 31; Mayerson 1993.

[6] For a not dissimilar usage of the term 'Nubia', see Adams 1993.

[7] While political ideologies are not infrequently reflected in archaeological interpretations, related factors may encourage or prevent the conduct of field research. For example, Michels' archaeological survey strategy in 1974 had to be modified in the light of security concerns; the impracticality of excavation in Ethiopia during the 1980s encouraged important research in the adjacent Kassala area of Sudan; and – more recently – researchers from Yemen, at a time of deteriorating conditions there, have turned their attention to Tigray.

obtain in these countries and in some cases employ languages that are not widely understood there. Finally, archaeology in both Ethiopia and Eritrea has suffered disproportionately from excavations – including excellent and important ones – that have been described only in preliminary reports but of which definitive accounts have been excessively delayed, sometimes for several decades. Even more problematic are research projects known only from summaries of their conclusions, with little if any indication of the evidence on which such conclusions are based. For these reasons, this book has been provided with a comprehensive bibliography.

Despite its length, compilation of the bibliography has been selective. For each topic, I have attempted to include the most recent comprehensive account, together with primary works presenting relevant aspects that are not otherwise covered. Preliminary publications have usually been omitted, except where they include important data not subsequently repeated. For the benefit of Ethiopian and Eritrean readers, I have given priority to works published in those countries or to those in English that are likely to be readily available there. Recognising the difficulties in obtaining such African publications elsewhere, the principal foreign publications are also included, despite the duplication that may result. Where background information and comparative material are required, I have – wherever possible – referred to general works containing their own bibliographies. All works cited in this book are in the public domain: I have strictly excluded items such as unpublished university dissertations and conference presentations, reports of limited circulation like those to licensing and funding agencies, and notes in newsletters.

Despite this apparent wealth of published information, any attempt at synthesising knowledge relating to the Ethiopian past is inevitably hampered by its uneven coverage. Many aspects remain unexplored; the distribution of archaeological exploration and excavation is particularly incomplete. Particularly distressing is the amount of research that has been undertaken but of which the full results have never been made public. The account here offered is thus much less coherent than would have been possible if prompt and comprehensive publication had taken place.

Although the book aims to be authoritative, it deals with many areas where the evidence is inadequate to support a firm conclusion, and with others where differing interpretations prevail. While I have not hesitated to indicate my own scepticism and preferences, I have tried to evaluate alternatives. One of the aims of this book is to demonstrate uncertainties and lacunae, thus offering guidelines for future research.

Chronological and territorial division

Several different systems have been proposed for subdividing the period on which this book focuses; on occasion, these systems have been subjected to repeated revision – sometimes without adequate justification of definition. Difficulty has been compounded by the same period-designations being repeated with varied or even contrary definitions. In view both of the confusion to which these schemes have given rise and of the increasing chronometric precision that is now being attained, I have decided not to employ such periodisations in this book, but to set my narrative in the framework of an absolute chronology expressed in terms of years BC or AD.

A number of geographical subdivisions [*e.g.* Akkele Guzay, Agame], relating to parts of Eritrea and northern Ethiopia and dating from before the Italian colonial period are still encountered in historical and archaeological writings. They are no longer in current use and their precise delineations are rarely understood: they are therefore not employed in this book. All distances cited, unless clearly specified otherwise, are approximate straight-line measurements, not those of routes by which it is practicable to travel.

There are no standardised or officially approved transliterations of place-names or personal names from Amharic or Tigrinya into the Roman alphabet, and numerous variants will be encountered in the European-language literature. Here, I have tried to minimise confusion by simply adopting spellings which follow established English usage and give a reasonably clear indication of how the names are pronounced locally. The symbols and diacritical marks used by linguists have been avoided. Citations in text, footnotes or bibliography of works by Ethiopian or Eritrean authors follow the established practice of those countries, using and alphabetising the first name rather than the patronymic.

Acknowledgements

The lengthy process of preparing the text and illustrations for this book has involved the advice and assistance of very many people spread across four continents. Among others, I am particularly grateful to the Australian Association for Byzantine Studies (Dr Andrew Gillett), Dr Ayele Tarekegn, Ms Eleanor Bedlow, Ms Rosalind Bedlow, Nebur'ed Belai Mersa, Dr Robert Bracey, the late Mr David Buxton, Dr Matthew Curtis, Professor Catherine D'Andrea, Dr Richard Duncan-Jones, the Ethiopian Heritage Fund (Ms Blair Priday), Professor Brian Fagan, Professor Rodolfo Fattovich, Professor François-Xavier Fauvelle-Aymar, M. Pierre Ferrand, Ato Fikru Wolde-Giorgis, Dr Niall Finneran, the late Ato Fisseha Zibelo, Ato Gebre Selassie Gebre Medhin, Professor Michael Gervers, Ato Gigar Tesfaye, Professor Wolfgang Hahn, Professor Mark Horton, the late Dr Bent Juel-Jensen, Dr Kassaye Begashaw, Professor David Killick, Professor Michael Knibb, Professor Manfred Kropp, Dr Marlia Mango, Dr Bill Manley, Dr Andrea Manzo, the late Mr Derek Matthews, Dr Jacques Mercier, the late Professor Merid Wolde Aregay, Professor Joseph Michels, the late Dr Stuart Munro-Hay, Dr Claudia Näsr, Mr Gwil Owen, Mr Crispin Paine, Professor Peter Parsons, Dr Jacke Phillips, Dr Tacye Phillipson, Mr Graham Reed, Mr Eric Robson, Dr Delwen Samuel, Professor Peter Schmidt, the late Dr Roger Schneider, the late Dr Sergew Hable Selassie, Dr Luisa Sernicola, Ato Solomon Tekle, Dr Federica Sulas, Abba Tekla Haimonot Asseyahegn, Ato Tekle Hagos, Professor Steffen Wenig, Mr Vincent West, and Dr Pawel Wolf. None of these, of course, carries any responsibility for errors, omissions or other shortcomings.

I have greatly benefited from the help provided at several libraries, notably those at the British Museum (Department of Coins and Medals), Gonville and Caius College (Cambridge), the Institute of Ethiopian Studies at Addis Ababa University, the Royal Numismatic Society, the School of Oriental and African Studies (London), the Society of Antiquaries of London, the University of Cambridge, the Institute of Archaeology at University College London, the Victoria and Albert Museum (National Art Library), and – until early in 2011 – North Yorkshire County Libraries (Skipton).

Funding for the research on which this book is based has, over the years, been generously provided by the British Academy (including a grant from the Chittick Fund), the British Institute in Eastern Africa, the Trustees of the British Museum, the Master and Fellows of Gonville and Caius College, the McDonald Institute for Archaeological Research, the National Geographic Society (USA), the Natural Environment Research Council (UK), the Society of Antiquaries of London, and the University of Cambridge.

Lastly, but most importantly, the book has been immeasurably improved by the criticism and suggestions of Dr Laurel Phillipson who has read repeated drafts of the entire text.

Part One

Before Aksum

2

The Northern Horn 3000 Years Ago

This chapter surveys the lamentably incomplete evidence that is available about the inhabitants of the northern Horn during the period immediately preceding the appearance of literate complex societies early in the first millennium BC. There are indications that at least some sections of the region's population may have practised a farming lifestyle, but much of the evidence is secondary, comprising inferences from later trends. It was not until the 1970s that archaeologists working in the northern Horn began to take an interest in ancient domestic economies, and not until the 1990s that concerted efforts were made to recover materials on which their reconstruction might be based. Economic matters were only rarely recorded in traditional histories, whether transmitted orally or in written form. In the absence of primary information, other sources were perforce emphasised.

Ancient visitors to the region noted relevant details only tangentially, and it was not until the sixteenth century that travellers began to arrive who were interested in recording conditions that prevailed in other than political spheres, and in the day-to-day lifestyles of the rural inhabitants. Such visitors were, in contrast to their predecessors, often particularly concerned with the possibilities of religious conversion, settlement by missionaries or exploitation of natural resources. Plants, animals and foodstuffs were often described by comparison with those about which the visitors were already knowledgeable, and the resultant terminology may be incorrect or difficult to interpret. It is tempting to take the conditions observed between the sixteenth and the twentieth centuries as reflecting those of earlier times, but caution is needed. Many travellers to the northern Horn at this time were seeking opportunities for exploitation and settlement by outsiders; they may thus have tended to exaggerate the favourable aspects of prevailing conditions. There is, however, evidence that the local climate from the sixteenth to the nineteenth centuries was particularly productive, with rainfall and other factors permitting excellent harvests – often more than one per year in some places.[1] An apparent deterioration in productivity during the twentieth century has undoubtedly been linked with the enormous increase in human population brought about by a combination of improved medical facilities and the discouragement of homicidal activities. Caution is thus needed in the application of recent 'ethnoarchaeological' observations to the interpretation of ancient conditions.[2]

[1] See, for example, Beckingham & Huntingford 1954: 45; Barradas 1996: 12, 119.

[2] Studies relevant to this area include those by D'Andrea *et al.* 1999, Lyons & D'Andrea 2003 and Lyons 2007a, 2007b. Such research can indeed provide valuable insights into many areas of ancient life – including, but by no means restricted to, economic and technological practices – but changing circumstances may sometimes invalidate their direct application.

It is inappropriate to consider the exploitation of domestic plants and animals as a unitary phenomenon since these activities occupied distinct – not always interconnected – niches in economic practice; consideration of both under the single rubric 'food-production' is even more misleading as many of the benefits derived from domestic species were in non-dietary areas.[3]

Terrain

The northern Horn of Africa has long formed a distinct cultural area, despite being currently divided by a political frontier that is both disputed and increasingly impermeable. One of its defining characteristics is its separateness, and this is partly due to its physical diversity. A detailed description of physical geography falls outside the scope of this book.[4] It may simply be noted that the region comprises highlands that are bounded on the east by the precipitous escarpment bordering the Danakil lowlands and the Red Sea. To the west, the country descends more gradually to the extensive plains of the Nile Valley but is riven by the rugged valleys of the Takezze and other Nile tributaries. In the north, with decreasing altitude, the terrain becomes progressively more arid as the Sudanese lowlands converge with the Red-Sea coast. It is only to the south that the highlands continue, linking them with the principal mass of the Ethiopian plateau, near the western edge of which lies Lake Tana and the source of the Blue Nile. The greater part of the northern plateau is tilted down towards the west and drains to the Nile, resulting in a network of deeply eroded valleys that still form major impediments to inter-regional communication.

Climatic and environmental conditions in these isolated highlands have for a very long time supported human lifestyles that contrast markedly with those in surrounding areas. Even within the highlands, communication between populations only a few kilometres apart may be so difficult that distinct cultural traditions developed and were maintained. There is thus a danger that incomplete coverage of research may result in underestimated diversity and unjustified generalisations.

People and languages

Most inhabitants of this land have long supported themselves by farming, being both cultivators of crops and herders of livestock, foraging for wild resources – whether animal or vegetable – being of progressively decreasing significance.[5] It is likely, however, that minority peoples of diverse economy – herders and, perhaps, hunter-gatherers – were also present throughout the period here considered. The different languages that are spoken all belong to the extensive family known as Afroasiatic.[6] In the northern Horn, these languages fall

[3] For discussion of these points in a wider African context, see D. Phillipson 2005: 169.

[4] Useful accounts have been published by Abul-Haggag 1961 for the physical geography and by Simoons 1960 for the human, but the best way to appreciate the terrain is to view it from the air. Note that the 'northern Ethiopia' discussed in Abul-Haggag's book is, effectively, the modern Eritrea.

[5] For details, emphasising traditional practices, see Simoons *op. cit.* Innovations that have taken place within recent centuries, while extensive, are not relevant in the context of this book. The possible origins of the domestic plants and animals involved are discussed below and in Chapters 3 and 10.

[6] For a general treatment of African linguistic classification, see Heine & Nurse 2000. The Afroasiatic languages are considered in chapter 4 of that book (Hayward 2000), in historical perspective by Blench (2006: 139–62), and – with more detailed emphasis on the Horn in recent times – by Bender *et al.* 1976.

into two groups: Cushitic and Semitic.[7] The first is today widely distributed in the Horn and adjacent regions of northeastern Africa including Somalia and much of eastern and southern Ethiopia; its local representatives in the northern Horn are usually classed together as Agau. Languages of the Semitic family – which also includes Arabic and Hebrew – are today spoken over wide areas of northern Africa and western Asia. Those of the northern Horn form a distinct Ethio-Semitic linguistic group comprising principally Tigrinya, Tigré and Amharic, together with a number of more southerly languages and the older form – Ge'ez – that survives in liturgical use by the Ethiopian and Eritrean Orthodox Churches. The Ethio-Semitic languages – with others that have been spoken in Arabia – are classified as South Semitic. A glance at a distribution map of these languages (Fig. 2) clearly shows that the Ethio-Semitic ones occupy a large and populous highland area largely surrounded by lower terrain where the sparser populations speak Cushitic languages or – in some areas – Arabic. There are several Agau-speaking enclaves, with indications that they were formerly larger and more numerous, within the predominantly Ethio-Semitic-speaking highlands. The most widely accepted interpretation of these observations has been that South-Semitic-speakers established themselves in territory that had previously been occupied by a Cushitic-speaking population. The former belief that this arrival of South-Semitic-speakers took place in about the second quarter of the first millennium BC can no longer be accepted in view of linguistic indications that these languages were spoken in the northern Horn at a much earlier date.[8]

Technology and subsistence economy

As noted above, the subsistence economy of the northern Horn's inhabitants during the last two millennia BC was largely based on the exploitation of domestic plants and animals. The evidence for this is diverse and largely indirect: very few archaeological excavations on sites of this period have been undertaken and fully reported, while at even fewer have faunal or floral remains been preserved and studied. Rock-shelter sites both in the Aksum region and in Tembien some 90 km to the southeast have revealed evidence for settlement by people who made flaked-stone artefacts and pottery but had no knowledge of metals.[9] Published accounts of artefacts from these sites have largely been restricted to morphological and technological descriptions, with little attention paid to their functions and economic implications. By about the eighth century BC, in both the Asmara and Aksum areas, stone-built houses – often grouped into compounds or villages – were in regular use (Chapter 3; Fig. 4). These closely similar traditions were so well established by that time that they may safely be assumed to have begun at least several centuries earlier, although firm archaeological evidence for this has not yet been recovered. It should not be assumed, however, that all population groups in the northern Horn at this time were cultivators and herders; it is highly probable that non-

[7] It must be emphasised that the terms 'Semitic' and 'Cushitic' have purely linguistic implications; although they are also often loosely applied to peoples whose first languages belong to one of these groups, it is incorrect and potentially misleading to use them as ethnic labels.

[8] For outline surveys, see the works cited above in note 6, also Hudson 1977, 2000; Appleyard 1978; Hayward 2003. See also Chapter 3.

[9] The primary evidence is described by D. Phillipson 1977a; Agazi 1997; Finneran 2000a, 2000b; Amanuel & Shea 2008. For an analogous but undated occurrence near Makalle, see Barnett 1999a. To the south and west, excavations by J. Dombrowski 1970 and by Fernandez *et al.* 2007 should also be noted.

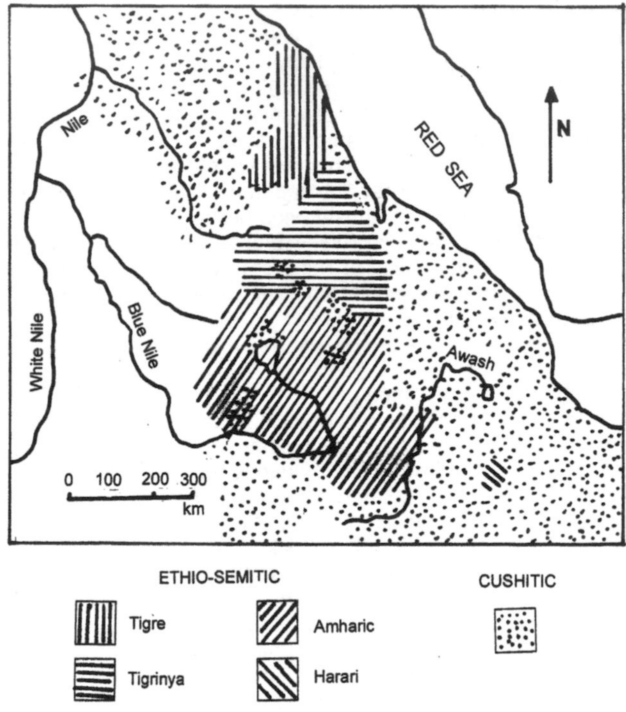

Fig. 2 Distribution of Ethio-Semitic and Cushitic languages in the northern Horn: this sketch map attempts to indicate approximate distributions of first languages prior to the major population-dispersals that have taken place since the mid-twentieth century

cultivators were represented in some areas, including both pastoralists and hunter-gatherers.

The detailed issues surrounding the beginnings of cultivation and herding in Ethiopia and Eritrea fall outside the scope of this book,[10] but it is relevant to note that the plants and animals that were exploited included varieties that seem to have been first brought under human control in the northern Horn itself, as well as others that were introduced directly or indirectly from elsewhere. The relative chronology of these innovations, and the manners in which they were achieved, remain subjects of controversy. There are currently no firmly dated physical remains of cultivated plants or domestic animals in the northern Horn that demonstrably pre-date the first millennium BC, which has led some writers[11] to conclude that they were not exploited there until that period. Such a view, however, ignores the almost total lack of relevant archaeological research and publication at sites in the northern Horn dating from the second and third millennia, when it seems increasingly likely that these crucial developments took place. The following summary of current understanding should be regarded as highly provisional and subject to revision in the light of ongoing research.

The domestic plants that were grown included emmer wheat, barley and – less certainly – teff. The first two are known to have been cultivated in south-western Asia by about the tenth millennium BC.[12] It is very likely that they were introduced from that region into the northern Horn. Whether this introduction was direct or indirect, by what route and at what date are all unknown,[13] but the diversity of varieties[14] that are restricted to the northern Horn suggests that they have been cultivated in this region for several millennia. Emmer is classed as a hulled wheat, *i.e.* one that requires pounding after threshing in order to remove the husk.[15] Teff, a cultivated form of the genus *Eragrostis*, is a highly nutritious cereal that today forms the preferred staple food for most inhabitants of the northern Horn highlands. Until the twentieth century, it was an exclusively Ethiopian/Eritrean crop,[16] so it is reasonable to conclude that it was first brought under cultivation there. It has been argued[17] that the cultivation and processing of teff are so labour-intensive that they are unlikely to have been adopted subsequent to the introduction of wheat and barley; this suggestion ignores the former cereal's numerous advantages and carries little weight, leaving open the question of teff's possible priority as a cultivated crop in the northern Horn.[18]

[10] For overviews of this topic, see Brandt 1984; D. Phillipson 1993; Barnett 1999b; Finneran 2007: 67–108; Lesur 2007; Lesur-Gebremariam 2009.

[11] *e.g.* Hassan 2002.

[12] Barker 2006: 104–48.

[13] They were, however, cultivated in the Nile Delta by the early-fifth millennium (Hassan 1988).

[14] *e.g.* Engels *et al.* 1991.

[15] See Nesbitt & Samuel 1996. It is probably for this reason that more recent Tigray farmers have preferred subsequently-introduced free-threshing wheats (D'Andrea *et al.* 1999; D'Andrea & Mitiku 2002; for further discussion, see Chapter 10).

[16] Impressions on pottery from the southern Arabian site of Hajar bin Humeid, however, suggest that it may have been cultivated – or imported – there at a late date in the first millennium BC (Soderstrom 1969: 399–401). The much older date cited for this material by Finneran (2007: 84) appears to be an error.

[17] *e.g.* by Shaw 1977: 103. For a contrary argument, see Lyons & D'Andrea 2003.

[18] Archaeological evidence for cultivation of teff (see also Chapters 3 and 10) is sparse, partly because of the difficulty in differentiating wild and domestic varieties of *Eragrostis* (D'Andrea 2008), and also because the exceptionally tiny seeds are not easy to recover.

Other crops[19] are of comparatively minor significance and their cultivation in the northern Horn probably did not begin until long after the local establishment of emmer, barley and – possibly – teff. Sorghum and finger millet were both initially cultivated in regions of Africa adjacent to the northern Horn; as discussed in Chapter 10, they were probably introduced to the latter area during the mid-first millennium AD. At roughly the same time, varieties of free-threshing wheat made their appearance alongside emmer.[20] Two oil-yielding crops have been economically important since at least the early centuries AD: linseed and noog, respectively of foreign and local origin,[21] but there is as yet no clear evidence that either was cultivated in the northern Horn at the early date with which this chapter is concerned. Linseed (*Linum usitatissimum*) yields flax fibre as well as oil; in recent times its cultivation in the northern Horn has been almost exclusively for the latter purpose but, as discussed in Chapter 10, this may not always have been the case. Noog (*Guizotia abyssinica*), like teff, is not known ever to have been cultivated beyond the Horn of Africa in pre-modern times; it is attested at Aksum in the fifth-to-sixth centuries AD and – less certainly (Chapter 3) – up to one thousand years earlier.

Sheep and goats are difficult to distinguish on the basis of most of the bones found on archaeological sites. They are both known to have been domesticated in southwestern Asia around the ninth millennium BC[22] and to have been in the northern Horn for long enough to permit the development of many local varieties.[23] Linguistic evidence suggests that sheep and/or goats may have been known to early speakers of Cushitic languages in what is now northern Eritrea and adjacent areas of northeastern Sudan as early as the seventh millennium BC,[24] and this is supported by bones excavated from a cave in the Red Sea Hills of southeasternmost Egypt.[25]

The situation regarding cattle is more complicated. Known in Lower Egypt by the sixth millennium BC, they were once thought to have arrived there from southwestern Asia, but it is now recognised that there was also another centre of early cattle domestication in what is now the Sahara.[26] Their arrival in the northern Horn may have been contemporaneous with, or possibly later than, that of sheep and goats. Humped cattle were almost certainly a later introduction from southern Asia; although their earliest African attestation – in Egypt

19 The probably early cultivation of enset in southern Ethiopia (Simoons 1965; Brandt 1996; Hildebrand 2007) is not considered here, there being no evidence that its area ever extended into the northern Horn. On the other hand, this section does – for the sake of clarity – include mention of most crops traditionally cultivated in the northern Horn, differentiating those which current evidence suggests may date back at least to the beginning of the first millennium BC from those that are considered later introductions.

20 See D'Andrea & Mitiku 2002. Free-threshing wheat is further discussed in Chapter 10.

21 Linen textiles were extensively employed in Egypt throughout the pharaonic period (Vogelsang-Eastwood 2000), long preceding the introduction of cotton which was apparently unknown in the Nile Valley until Ptolemaic times. More recently, noog has been cultivated in India, as a condiment.

22 Barker 2006: 104–48.

23 Hall 2000; Workneh *et al.* 2000.

24 Ehret 2002. The presence of a word for 'donkey' in this context could, however, refer to the wild animal rather than to its domestic counterpart.

25 Vermeersch *et al.* 1994, 1996.

26 Blench & Macdonald 2000; P. Mitchell 2005: 38–42; see also Marshall & Hildebrand 2002. Cattle, presumably from this Saharan source, in the Western Desert of Egypt (Wendorf & Schild 2003) are thus earlier than their counterparts in the Nile Delta that were of Asian origin.

– dates from the second millennium BC,[27] there is no convincing evidence for their presence in the northern Horn before the early centuries AD.[28] Excavations in Djibouti indicate the presence of domestic humpless cattle before the end of the second millennium BC. [29]

Elsewhere, rock-art depictions include numerous figures of cattle – long-horned, short-horned, humped and humpless – as well as less-common camels, equids, and wild animals. The art – in which several styles have been tentatively recognised – was almost certainly executed over a considerable period. Despite the fact that camels appear to have been depicted only in later phases of the rock-art sequence, the information that can be obtained from these images is severely limited by the difficulty in establishing their ages.[30]

The donkey [ass] is the only animal that seems likely to have been domesticated for the first time in northeastern Africa or an area immediately adjacent.[31] It was known in Egypt since Pre-Dynastic times and in southern Arabia since at least the mid-first millennium BC,[32] but has not yet been recognised until significantly later times in the Horn. A figurine from a mid-first-millennium-AD context at Beta Giyorgis near Aksum has been described as representing a horse;[33] this identification, while plausible, is not incontrovertible, and the possibility that some other animal was intended cannot be ruled out. The fact that donkeys were probably kept as pack-animals, rather than as sources of food, may explain why they are only rarely represented in archaeological assemblages or in rock art.[34]

Until very recent times, camels were probably only occasionally brought to the highlands. With the exception of a single tooth from Gobedra rock-shelter near Aksum,[35] the dating of which remains controversial, they have not been recognised archaeologically. As noted above, their appearance in rock art is restricted to styles that are thought to be of late date. Specific mention of camels in a sixth-century Aksumite inscription (RIE 191; *cf.* Chapters 6 and 10) refers to peripheral areas at lower altitude.

This survey serves to emphasise the lamentable paucity of available information concerning the crucial period around the beginning of the first millennium BC, when the economic foundations of Ethiopian civilisation were probably already in place. A minimal interpretation would see farming communities widespread but not necessarily in sole occupation, cultivating emmer and barley, and herding cattle, sheep and goats. Some of these people probably lived in stone-built rectangular houses. Pottery and flaked-stone tools were in regular use, but it is not known whether use of copper and/or its alloys had yet begun.

27 Nicolotti & Guérin 1992.

28 The argument of Schmidt 2010 that humped cattle were present at Ancient Ona sites in the Asmara region earlier in the first millennium BC is not wholly convincing (see Chapter 3).

29 Guérin & Faure 1996; Gutherz *et al.* 1996; Lesur 2007; Cauliez *et al.* 2008.

30 See, for example, Joussaume 1981; D. Phillipson 1993; Calegari 1999; Zelalem 2008; Tekle 2011.

31 Marshall 2007.

32 For southern Arabia see Antonini 2004: fig. 14, tav. 67.

33 Fattovich & Bard 2003: 26 and fig. 3.

34 Marshall 2007.

35 D. Phillipson 1977a.

Extra-regional connections

Despite the difficulties of communication noted above, it is clear that the inhabitants of the northern Horn during the second millennium BC were not totally isolated from those of adjacent regions. One practice that was widespread through northeast Africa at this time was the marking of burials by means of upright stones [stelae].[36] Comparisons between the ceramic and lithic traditions of this period are hampered by the scarcity of data; it must be admitted that they have validity in only the most general terms and that meaningful affinities remain to be demonstrated. Designation of the stone-tool industries of the northern Horn as 'Wilton' implies only that they included significant numbers of small backed tools with steeply backed retouch, as did those of many other parts of the world during the Holocene. Likewise, the similarities that have been proposed between pottery from Gobedra and that from the Kassala region of eastern Sudan can only be accepted as highly general, possibly suggesting common ancestry and parallel development but not necessarily indicative of any direct connection between the inhabitants of the two areas. Typological affinities of pottery and stone tools from a site near Agordat in Eritrea, *c.* 120 km west of Asmara, have also been suggested as providing evidence for contacts with more westerly regions, possibly linked with the introduction of domestic animals to the northern Horn as early as the third millennium BC.[37] However, the admittedly sparse evidence relating to cultivation and herding, noted above, indicates that domestic plants and animals that had originated elsewhere were adopted by the inhabitants of the northern Horn, even though the dates and circumstances of these developments remain effectively unknown. The evidence currently available permits only the tentative observation that such contacts are likely to have been – not necessarily exclusively – with areas lying north and west of the northern Horn.[38]

Although it is a topic that falls well beyond the time-range – and perhaps also the geographical area – covered by this book, pharaonic Egyptians' contacts with the region or regions that they designated 'Punt' are often considered in this context and should be noted briefly. Egyptian records of such contacts, which occur at intervals during the third and second millennia BC, emphasise the exotic nature of Punt, its inhabitants and the materials that the Egyptians obtained there. A sea-voyage was evidently required, presumably on the Red Sea, and there has been much controversy as to the location of Punt, how far south and whether on the western or eastern side of the Red Sea. In so far as any consensus has emerged, it seems to favour a location extending inland from the general area of the present border between Eritrea and Sudan. Little consideration has been given to the possibility that, through the two thousand years of its currency, the term 'Punt' may not always have been applied to the same defined area. A port has recently been investigated at the northern end of the Red Sea whence ships evidently set sail for Punt during much of the second millennium BC. It is noteworthy – but regrettable – that most research

36 Joussaume 2007; D. Phillipson 2010.

37 See, most recently, Fattovich 2010. These arguments place considerable weight on the exiguous Gobedra pottery (D. Phillipson 1977a) on which it is difficult to recognise any defining stylistic characteristics other than those imposed by the available technology. Until a much clearer picture can be obtained from other sites in the northern Horn, and these sites can be more securely dated, such inter-regional comparisons should be regarded as provisional.

38 Arkell 1954; see also D. Phillipson 1977b: 66–7; Brandt 1984. Brief re-investigation in 1994 (Brandt *et al.* 2008) provided a much clearer picture of the artefact assemblages, but their chronology and significance to the archaeology of the northern Horn still require further elucidation.

on the Punt trade has been undertaken from an Egyptological background and perspective.[39]

The state of research

Until recently, interpretations of developments that took place in the northern Horn during the first millennium BC were based on almost total ignorance of the region's inhabitants during earlier times. Statements emphasising the contrast between populations with southern Arabian affinities were thus flawed, in that no comparisons could be made either with their predecessors or with any contemporaries amongst whom such affinities were less dominant. Reconstructions proposed in earlier years[40] took no account of these factors; indeed, they could not do so because the necessary information was simply not available. Today, it must be admitted that the situation has improved only slightly, but the daunting extent of the research that is needed is at least becoming apparent. There is growing realisation that the first millennium BC in the northern Horn was a period of adaptation and continuity from earlier times rather than simply one of abruptly imposed change from elsewhere.

[39] Recent literature on Punt includes Fattovich 1991, 1996b; J. S. Phillips 1996, 1999; Harvey 2003; Meeks 2003; Balanda 2005–06; Kitchen 2004; Bard & Fattovich 2007; Bard *et al.* 2007; Tallet 2009.

[40] *e.g.* Conti Rossini 1928: 91–108; Ullendorff 1960: 5.

3

The First Millennium BC

It is against the background outlined in the previous chapter that we must now view the highly significant developments which took place in the northern Horn during the first half of the first millennium BC. A major reassessment is required as to the degree of local continuity associated with these developments, and of the extent to which they were stimulated by external factors. A recurring theme of this chapter is the need critically to evaluate the view that cultural and political trends in the northern Horn were dominated by contacts with southern Arabia and, more specifically, that colonisation from the latter area was responsible for numerous cultural innovations which, according to the late Professor Edward Ullendorff, contributed to 'a vastly superior civilisation'.[1] This view, first enunciated in detail over 80 years ago by Carlo Conti Rossini,[2] has been widely – if uncritically – accepted and has passed into much popular historical understanding and, for that matter, mythology,[3] despite strong epigraphic counter-indications from the 1970s and, more recently, archaeological evidence that a number of innovations to which Conti Rossini had attributed a southern Arabian origin were in fact indigenous African developments at a significantly earlier date. While it should not be argued that cultural trends east and west of the Red Sea took place completely independently at this time, it now appears that the scale, duration, and overall importance of their interconnections have been significantly exaggerated. As argued in Chapter 2, this has been at least partly due to paucity of information about earlier times in the northern Horn.

Understanding of the diverse materials considered in this chapter is hampered by continued use of a conceptual and terminological framework dating from the 1950s and 60s. No absolute dating was available at that time, but it was clear that the sites concerned were older than those of the Aksumite civilisation which, it had long been recognised, arose during the first century AD or – according to some (see Chapter 7) – slightly before. The earlier materials were accordingly lumped together under the label 'Pre-Aksumite', despite the illogicality of naming something retrospectively – in terms of what it subsequently became or by what it was succeeded. A refinement emphasised the distinctiveness of sites that preserved traces of monumental architecture, inscriptions or sculpture of apparently southern Arabian affinity, and recognised that these affinities were closest with the Sabaean kingdom which was the dominant southern Arabian polity for most of the first millennium BC. The communities in the northern Horn that displayed such features were therefore designated 'Ethio-Sabaean'. Sometimes 'Ethio-

[1] Ullendorff 1960: 5

[2] Conti Rossini 1928: 91–108.

[3] *cf.* Isaac & Felder 1988.

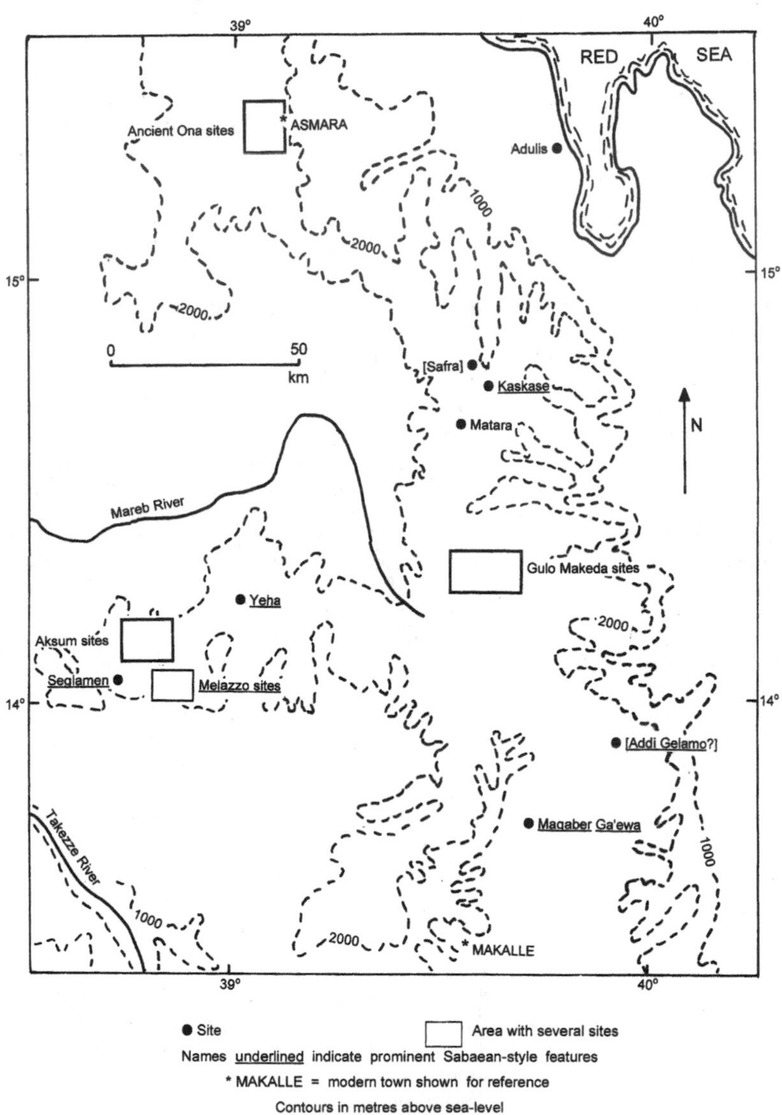

Fig. 3 Location of principal archaeological sites of the first millennium BC in the highlands of the northern Horn.

Sabaean' and 'Pre-Aksumite' were seen as successive stages, but sometimes both were attributed to a 'Pre-Aksumite' period that was divided into two phases, the first being termed 'Ethio-Sabaean' and the second 'Transitional' or 'Intermediate'. In any event, the appearance of the first inscriptions was seen as a watershed – largely, one must suspect, because conceptually it marked the end of prehistory. Inevitably, this led to emphasis on élite elements of ancient society and culture, with concomitant disregard for signs of underlying continuity.[4] Continued use of the term 'Ethio-Sabaean' has served to perpetuate the resultant misunderstanding.

It is clear that these nomenclatures were based on rigid application of periodisation within an ill-defined area, little – if any – allowance being made for the possibility that significant cultural diversity may have occurred in parallel within a defined period. This is a difficulty which has, surprisingly, survived the availability of more precise chronometry and the expanding coverage of archaeological investigation. The problem is particularly relevant to consideration of the so-called 'Transitional' stage, now dated to the last four centuries BC, when developments in a narrowly restricted area around Aksum seem to have followed a course that was significantly different from that attested elsewhere. The term 'Proto-Aksumite', applied to these Aksum-area materials, may be justifiable in the local context, but I argue below that attempts to extend its usage elsewhere have impeded understanding, and I have attempted in this chapter to suggest a less rigid framework based on absolute chronology.

Until the 1990s, the absolute dates proposed for these African materials were based largely on correlation with those proposed on stylistic and linguistic grounds for southern Arabian inscriptions and for the historical developments that they indicated. This southern Arabian chronology has, over the years, seen considerable controversy and differences of opinion. The so-called 'short chronology' eloquently advocated by Jacqueline Pirenne[5] achieved significant support during the 1950s and 60s, and was followed also by the majority of scholars specialising in the northern Horn. This placed most if not all of the materials designated 'Pre-Aksumite' within the second half of the first millennium BC.

Recent research in both Eritrea and Ethiopia is producing much new data, set more firmly in time and within more closely defined spatial parameters, permitting us to view the so-called 'Pre-Aksumite' communities in their chronological and geographical contexts and to recognise their diversity (Fig. 3). Interpretation of radiocarbon dates from sites of the first millennium BC is hampered by the atmospheric fluctuations in the proportion of radioactive carbon that occurred at this time,[6] so our knowledge of absolute chronology remains more than usually imprecise. Overall, indeed, our understanding is still both patchy and incomplete: on both sides of the Red Sea, studies of archaeology and epigraphy have remained poorly integrated and – as is inevitable – much recent research has been quite narrowly focused geographically. Here, while recognising the many lacunae in the available data, I attempt a broader view.

[4] For an early recognition of this problem, see Fattovich 1978a. For a more comprehensive discussion, see D. Phillipson & Schmidt 2009.

[5] Pirenne 1956, 1987.

[6] These problems, which are – of course – not restricted to the geographical areas with which this book is concerned, have been discussed by Killick 2004. For an illustration of the imprecision of radiocarbon dating at sites of the first millennium BC, see D. Phillipson 2009c: fig. 2.

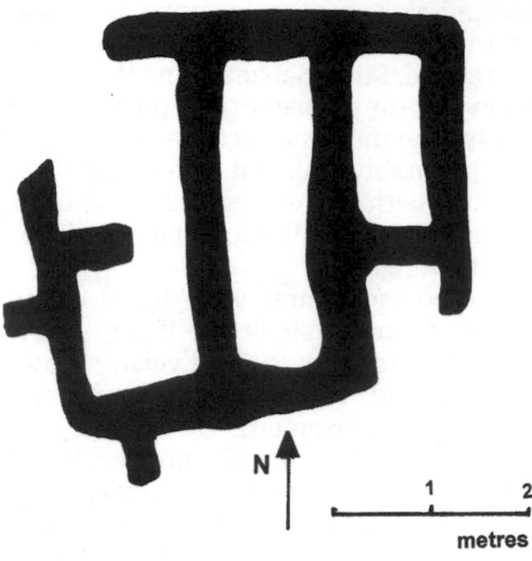

Fig. 4 Plan of an Ancient Ona building at Sembel near Asmara (after Schmidt *et al.* 2008a)

FROM THE NINTH/EIGHTH TO THE FOURTH CENTURIES BC

Until recently, the attention of archaeologists working in the northern Horn – like that of their counterparts across the Red Sea – has been concentrated on sites where monumental architecture and works of art have been preserved; this bias still hinders the validity of historical reconstruction. Epigraphic specialists have also devoted detailed study to the relatively small number of brief inscriptions that are so far known from the northern Horn.[7] Some of this research has been undertaken by scholars whose primary expertise has related to southern Arabian materials and who have tended to apply assumptions based on their understanding of the latter area. By contrast, little attention has been paid on either side of the Red Sea to sites where these élite artefacts were not preserved, with the result that such matters as subsistence economy, everyday material culture, non-élite settlement and domestic architecture have remained largely unknown. With changing emphases since the last quarter of the twentieth century, more information is becoming available that indicates much greater indigenous continuity and emphasises local innovation as well as long-distance contacts as contributors to cultural change.

Comparison between the architecture preserved at religious sites and that of domestic settlements demonstrates an important dichotomy, the

[7] The inscriptions from the northern Horn are less numerous and significantly shorter than their southern Arabian counterparts. In this book, individual inscriptions known prior to 1990 from the former area are designated in the form 'RIE --', following the numbering adopted by the *Recueil des inscriptions de l'Ethiopie des périodes axoumite et pré-axoumite* (Bernand *et al.* 1991–2000). Still in progress (see Leclant 2007, 2008), the *Recueil* provides detailed primary data and a guide to sources; it does not attempt a critical evaluation of interpretations, and it is only for Greek inscriptions of the Aksumite period that translations have so far been made available.

full significance of which remains to be demonstrated by future research. Some houses were rectangular, others circular, both of undressed dry-stone construction; dressed-stone masonry and monumental sculpture were apparently not employed in these domestic contexts.

Non-élite settlements

One of the largest, and apparently earliest, non-élite settlements of this period was discovered by Joseph Michels at Yeha near Adwa, on a low ridge some 1.2 km northeast of the modern village and the Great Temple (see below) for which Yeha is famous.[8] No excavations have yet been conducted there, so the nature of its occupation remains unknown, but comparative ordering of surface-collected pottery suggested that occupation began somewhat earlier than that around the Great Temple. The pottery collections included sherds that resembled those from other parts of Michels' survey area – which extended as far to the southwest as Aksum – but none for which it was necessary to postulate a more distant origin.[9] Michels reasonably interpreted this as indicating the concentration of population whose ancestors had formerly been more widely dispersed in the Aksum-Yeha area. Further investigation is a high priority.

A group of sites on the high plains west and south of Asmara has been known for some years and recently seen detailed investigation and publication.[10] Designated 'Ancient Ona' by their most recent investigators,[11] these sites are now dated to the first millennium BC and seen as peasant[12] settlements of subsistence farmers whose lifestyle and material culture shows little – if any – sign of contact with southern Arabia or with élite communities in more southerly parts of the northern Horn.[13] Of numerous known sites (Fig. 4), those most intensively investigated include Mai Temenai, Sembel, Mai Chiot, Weki Duba, Mai Hutsa and Ona Gudo.[14]

A similar situation prevailed in the Aksum area, where a large farming settlement has been investigated in the deeper levels at Kidane Mehret; it has been shown to be broadly contemporaneous with the Ancient Ona sites and, like them, to lack evidence for significant southern Arabian connections.[15] Materials related to those from Kidane Mehret have also been investigated on nearby Beta Giyorgis hill.[16] Such sites were evidently widely distributed, but only in these few instances are detailed accounts and dating evidence

[8] Michels 2005: 69.

[9] *ibid.*: 66.

[10] Tringali 1965; Munro-Hay & Tringali 1991; Schmidt & Curtis 2001; Schmidt *et al.* 2008d.

[11] *Ona* is a Tigrinya word signifying 'ruin'. While locally comprehensible, the term itself is inadequately specific and potentially confusing.

[12] In Ethiopia and Eritrea this term refers simply to a small-scale traditional farmer and carries no derogatory connotations.

[13] Before detailed study was undertaken and radiocarbon dates obtained, it had been suggested that these Ancient Ona sites might be older than more southerly settlements such as Yeha (see below) where southern Arabian connections are apparent. This now appears not to have been the case although, as discussed above, radiocarbon-based chronologies for much of the first millennium BC are unusually imprecise.

[14] For details, see Schmidt *et al.* 2008a, 2008d.

[15] D. Phillipson 2000b: 267–379; J. S. Phillips 2004.

[16] Bard *et al.* 1997, 2000.

available.[17] Strong continuity is apparent from earlier times, notably in pottery, flaked-stone artefacts and farming economy. A few copper-alloy[18] objects are attested, but none of iron. Although, as noted in Chapter 2, earlier domestic architecture in the northern Horn remains unknown, that of the first millennium BC appears entirely local in its inspiration; monumental architecture and sculpture were restricted to religious and élite contexts, as discussed in greater detail below. It is safe to conclude that peasant communities – almost entirely indigenous in origin – continued to form the majority population in the northern Horn throughout the first half of the first millennium BC. In some parts of the region they may have been the sole inhabitants although – as in earlier times (*cf.* Chapter 2) – one should not rule out the survival of distinct non-cultivating populations, despite the fact that these have not yet been definitively recognised in the archaeological record.

Elite sites, architecture and artworks

The sites where élite features have been preserved seem for the most part to have served a religious function, and to have been located in places of exceptional fertility. Representative examples may now be described.

Yeha[19] in north-central Tigray is a remarkable site, providing clear evidence for the erection of temples that share so many features with southern Arabia that they may safely be described as Sabaean in style. The Great Temple may be discussed first, since it has been known to the outside world for several centuries. Set a short distance from the domestic settlement noted above, on the southern part of a small hill that is still walled to form a sacred precinct, it comprises a well-preserved rectangular structure, 18.6 x 15.0 m, built of large, extremely finely dressed, rectangular blocks of silicified sandstone which survive to a total height exceeding 13 m (Figs 5 and 6). Detailed examination[20] has revealed the former presence of a massive portico of six rectangular pillars as well as the strong resemblance of the original structure to southern Arabian temples of the seventh century BC, notably Sabaean buildings at Marib and Baraqish,[21] although doubts have been expressed as to whether the Yeha building was ever completed. Fragments of neatly inscribed stonework found re-used in later contexts demonstrate dedication to Almaqah, the southern Arabian moon god. It was formerly believed that this stonework had formed part of the temple structure, but the recent discovery of a virtually identical inscription (Fig. 9) at Maqaber Ga'ewa (see below) near Wukro some 100 km southeast of Yeha indicates that it had belonged to a central altar similar to that shown by floor-settings and associated drains to have formerly existed at

[17] Such sites have been recorded, for example by Godet (1977, 1983), although little attempt was made to differentiate them from those of later date. Michels (2005: 55–81) recorded numerous occurrences in his Aksum-Yeha survey area, including an exceptionally extensive one near Yeha; around Aksum itself, a particularly comprehensive picture of changing settlement distributions is emerging through more recent fieldwork (L. Phillipson 2009b; Fattovich 2010). Sites have also been attributed to the first millennium BC in the northeastern highlands of Tigray (D'Andrea *et al.* 2008a), where investigations continue.

[18] Some publications state that these objects were made of bronze but, so far as I am aware, few – if any – metallurgical analyses have been conducted, and a less specific designation is preferable.

[19] Two recently discovered inscriptions (Weninger 2007; Gajda *et al.* 2009; Nebes 2010) demonstrate that the toponym 'Yeha' was already in use by the mid-first millennium BC.

[20] Robin & de Maigret 1998; Japp *et al.* 2011.

[21] Robin & de Maigret 2009; Japp *et al.* 2011.

Fig. 5 The exterior north wall of the Great Temple at Yeha

Fig. 6 The interior of the Great Temple at Yeha, viewed from the southwest

the latter site.[22] Two fragments of a carved stone frieze of facing ibex (*e.g.* Fig. 7), now built into the west wall of the modern church, may have originated in the adjacent temple. The interior of the Great Temple was divided by rows of square pillars into five aisles, those on either side being roofed, while the central nave was open to the sky; the eastern end – furthest from the entrance – was divided into three rooms. While very close parallels for this arrangement are known from southern Arabia (noted above), it is remarkable that the plan was adopted for the earliest Ethiopian Christian churches (*cf.* Chapter 11).[23]

At Yeha, a long succession of occupations is indicated, although no part of it has yet been dated radiometrically. The initial, apparently non-élite, settlement is noted above. There is general agreement that the Great Temple is the oldest feature at Yeha still visible above ground, although it is now recognised[24] that it incorporated materials from an earlier but perhaps broadly analogous structure. This may have stood some 30 m to the north of the Great Temple, on the highest point of the hill occupied by the modern church and its predecessor, since it is otherwise not easy to understand why the Great Temple itself is not on the summit. Epigraphic comparisons tied to the 'short chronology' favoured by southern Arabian specialists in the 1960s suggested a date for the Great Temple no earlier than 500 BC, but more recent views on the chronology of southern Arabian epigraphy and architecture favour an age some three centuries earlier.[25]

The second major structure at Yeha, Grat Be'al Gebri, was excavated in 1971 by Francis Anfray, assisted by Rodolfo Fattovich who undertook a detailed study of the pottery.[26] More detailed investigation and much-needed conservation work, is currently being undertaken.[27] Three phases were originally discerned, of which the earliest was believed to represent low-status settlement preceding erection of the élite building. The second phase was marked by a huge structure of wood and stone, clearly of élite status and covering an area some 44 m square. On its southeast side stood a portico of six massive monolithic square-sectioned stone pillars (Fig. 8), analogous both to that at the western end of the Great Temple, and to a temple at Sirwah in Yemen.[28] Neither the age nor the function of the Grat Be'al Gebri élite building has yet been definitively established, but preliminary indications suggest that it may be almost as old as the Great Temple.

Fattovich's studies of pottery excavated from Yeha in the 1960s and 70s yielded results not inconsistent with those outlined above.[29] It appears safe tentatively to suggest that the Great Temple or its vanished predecessor was

[22] Robin & de Maigret 1998: esp. fig. 22.

[23] Krencker's plan of the Great Temple (Littmann *et al.* 1913, 2: Abb. 166; Finneran 2007: fig. 4.5) has been shown to be incorrect. Finneran (*op. cit.*: 186) was mistaken in attributing its five-aisled layout to a Christian-period remodelling.

[24] Robin & de Maigret 1998: 778, 797; discussed further by Manzo 2009.

[25] A more precise dating of the first (now vanished) temple at Yeha 'before the mid-eighth century BC' has been proposed (Manzo 2009: 292) on the basis of similarity between carving on a re-used fragment found within the surviving Great Temple (Robin & de Maigret 1998; 772–5) and materials from southern Arabia (Antonini 2004; see also Audouin 1996). In the present writer's view, neither the similarities nor the chronology of the southern Arabian materials concerned necessarily support such precision.

[26] Anfray 1972a, 1997; Fattovich 1972a, 1972b, 1976, 1978b, also 2009.

[27] Japp *et al.* 2011.

[28] For the Sirwah building, which had a portico of five pillars rather than six, see Japp *et al.* 2011: fig. 7.

[29] Anfray 1963a. Fattovich (1990, 2009) subsequently published further details.

Fig. 7 Stone-carved frieze of facing ibex, currently built into the west wall of the church at Yeha, perhaps originally at the Great Temple; width of original: c. 40 cm

Fig. 8 Part of the portico at Grat Be'al Gebri, Yeha

Fig. 9 The central altar at the Almaqah temple, Maqaber Ga'ewa (photograph by D. W. P., reproduced by kind permission of Dr Pawel Wolf)

Fig. 10 Statuette (height: 33 cm) and monumental inscription at the Almaqah temple, Maqaber Ga'ewa (photograph by D. W. P., reproduced by kind permission of Dr Pawel Wolf)

the first of the major structures at Yeha, although the presence of older non-élite occupation in the immediate vicinity is now strongly indicated. It was closely followed by the first building-phase of Grat Be'al Gebri, of which the square-pillared portico is the most prominent surviving element. There may have been subsequent alterations to the building behind this portico, details of which are not yet fully clear. While this building remained in use, the focus of non-élite settlement shifted from the eastern ridge to the site of the present-day village. Use of the nearby shaft tombs is discussed below. Later developments at Yeha are not relevant to the present discussion (but *cf.* Chapter 11).

Maqaber Ga'ewa, 6 km south of Wukro, preserves a second Almaqah temple, discovered in 2007;[30] the probable presence of Sabaean-related antiquities in the vicinity had long been indicted by inscribed sculptures preserved in the nearby church of Abba Garima Addi Kaweh.[31] While broadly analogous in overall plan, this temple lacked the finely dressed masonry of Yeha and its southern Arabian *comparanda*; in this respect it more closely resembled the contemporaneous indigenous domestic architecture of the northern Ethiopian highlands. By contrast, exceptionally fine sculpture, much of it inscribed, was preserved in or close to its original location (Figs 9 and 10).[32] Research at Maqaber Ga'ewa is continuing, and the detailed chronology of the site has not yet been established.

Other religious sites, more numerous, more widely distributed and perhaps later in date, continued to feature massive porticos of square-sectioned pillars but were otherwise less dominantly Sabaean in character, as discussed below. Similar pillars are known also at other sites, notably at Hawelti, southeast of Aksum, and at Kaskase near Senafe in Eritrea.

Kaskase in Eritrea, 5 km north of Senafe, has been known since the beginning of the twentieth century. Despite the lack of detailed investigation, the site has achieved some prominence in the literature, perhaps partly due to its ease of access from a principal highway.[33] The site is apparently of limited extent and no excavations have been recorded there, other than one of several graves in close proximity. Several massive square-sectioned stone pillars or stelae are preserved, two of which bear inscriptions (RIE 11, 12) recording names of kings, as further discussed below. Although the date of the site has not been clearly established, the inscribed pillars and pottery exposed on the surface suggest an age in the mid-first millennium BC.

The **Melazzo** sites beside the Mai Agazen river, some 10 km southeast of Aksum, comprise several localities discovered and excavated in the late 1950s by Jean Leclant and by Henri de Contenson.[34] They were revisited in 1974 by Joseph Michels, who has also provided a useful summary of earlier work.[35] The sites are often cited under individual names – *e.g.* Gobochela, Hawelti, Hawelti-Malazzo, Enda Tcherqos, Mazaber – but their relationships are unclear and, since many of the artefacts from these sites were not recovered from primary

[30] Hiluf 2009.

[31] R. Schneider 1973, 1976b; Gajda & Yohannes 2009.

[32] Hiluf 2009; Gajda *et al.* 2009; Wolf & Nowotnick 2010a, 2010b; Nebes 2010.

[33] Conti Rossini 1900; Littmann *et al.* 1913, 2: 143–4; Tringali 1978; Wenig 2006b; Kropp 2006b; Fattovich 2007; Curtis & Daniel 2008.

[34] Leclant 1959a; de Contenson 1961b, 1962, 1963b. For a map of the area, see Pirenne 1970: 123.

[35] Michels 2005, 1979.

contexts and may have been moved from one place to another in ancient times, it seems best to discuss them here as a group.[36] Unfortunately, only preliminary publications are yet available, and they devote more attention to artefacts – particularly art objects – than to the buildings and other contexts or associations; estimates of the age/s of these materials rest exclusively on inter-site comparisons, both within the northern Horn and more widely.

Broadly, remains of stone structures fall into two categories. At Hawelti, a low but extensive mound (Fig. 11) preserves traces of at least twenty square-sectioned monolithic stelae, not dissimilar to those noted above at Kaskase. Although most are clearly no longer in their original position, they do not appear to have come from porticos like those of the Great Temple and Grat Be'al Gebri at Yeha. On the southern slope of the same mound were found the disturbed remains of two rough-stone buildings, each measuring approximately 10 m square. The narrow space between these buildings yielded a quantity of fine stone-carving, much of it fragmented. This material had clearly been collected and placed in this sheltered place, but whether it had originated at Hawelti or elsewhere cannot be demonstrated.[37]

Alongside numerous other items were pieces of a remarkable stone baldachin or canopied throne,[38] 1.4 m high, with fine relief carving on the exterior. The carving on the front edges comprised a frieze of small, stylised profile figures of ibex, while that on each side represented a large bearded male figure wearing a cloak and carrying a paddle- or fan-shaped object and a smaller beardless gowned figure, possibly female, who – in one case – was labelled RFS. Two seated female stone statuettes were also recovered, one of which – 0.8 m high – may originally have been placed within the baldachin. The heads of both statuettes had been broken off, but one was recovered separately. Round and smiling, its hair – like that of the figures depicted on the baldachin – is short and tightly curled. Most commentators have attributed these objects or their inspiration to southern Arabia, but in fact neither the statuettes nor the baldachin show clear affinities with works of demonstrable provenance in that region. Their affinities are far wider and more generalised; the only element with clear parallels in southern Arabia is the ibex decoration on the baldachin.[39] It is unfortunate that the chronology of the Hawelti materials is

[36] Material later than the period with which this chapter is concerned was clearly present, but was not differentiated stratigraphically or in the published descriptions. The older of the two successive churches at Enda Tcherqos incorporated earlier inscriptions but that site is not otherwise considered here: see D. Phillipson (2009a: 43–4) for a re-assessment.

[37] See Pirenne 1967, 1970. The principal pieces, unfortunately re-assembled and restored in such a way that their formerly fragmented condition is no longer apparent, are displayed in the National Museum, Addis Ababa. For detailed descriptions and illustrations of the stone carvings, see de Contenson 1962 and Leclant 1964. Photographs of the principal pieces have been republished on numerous occasions and so are not reproduced here. New excavations at Hawelti have recently commenced (Japp *et al.* 2011).

[38] Some commentators (*e.g.* Manzo 2009) have applied the designation '*naos*' to this object, following the practice of Egyptologists referring to broadly comparable specimens. However, the term is Greek in origin, in which context it can be so widely applied that its use for the Hawelti baldachin is best avoided.

[39] See, in particular, de Contenson 1962; Manzo 2009. The two statuettes share features of posture and dress with somewhat smaller stone carvings – noted elsewhere in this chapter – from Maqaber Ga'ewa (Fig. 10) and from Addi Gelamo. The only other known example was acquired by the Museo Nazionale Romano in the 1930s (Pallottino 1938) as part of a collection assembled in southern Arabia, but has no recorded provenance; Pirenne (1965b) suggested that it may have been brought from Ethiopia in ancient or more recent times. I am grateful to Dr Luisa Sernicola for arranging for me to examine this specimen in Rome.

Fig. 11 The Hawelti site, Melazzo: top – view of the mound; below – two stelae

currently surrounded by so much uncertainty.[40] While a date for the sculptures in the second quarter of the first millennium BC appears perfectly plausible, it must be emphasised that this estimate is based solely on indefinite stylistic comparisons. The objects concerned were recovered in unclearly recorded circumstances that suggested their hasty or careless redeposition following removal from elsewhere; certainly, other items apparently associated with

[40] de Contenson 1963b. This uncertainty is likely to be remedied through renewed excavations begun in 2010 (Japp *et al.* 2011).

them are now thought to range widely in date and to include material of Aksumite age.[41]

Another site in the same complex is Gobochela, where a small building of undressed masonry – interpreted as a temple by the excavator[42] – was associated with several stone altars and incense-burners bearing dedicatory inscriptions to LMQ, the moon-god Almaqah whose worship is well attested in southern Arabia, as well as at Yeha and Maqaber Ga'ewa. Three inscriptions (RIE 3 - 5), found re-used in the walls of the nearby Enda Tcherqos church, are thought to have come originally from Gobochela.

Addi Gelamo. One further locality deserves mention here. Although sometimes treated as a primary site in publications and on distribution maps, it appears to have been a cache containing artefacts – several of which were broken – with religious and/or élite connotations ranging in date for almost a thousand years from the second quarter of the first millennium BC to around the third century AD. Details are not easy to reconstruct but, in 1954, the newly founded Ethiopian Institute of Archaeology received from the government office in Makalle a report that some remarkable archaeological objects had been discovered in eastern Tigray. On prompt investigation,[43] it was ascertained that the objects had been found 'under a stone slab' during construction of a mosque at a place, the name of which is variously given as Addi Gelamo, Hawila Assaraw and Atsbi Dera, located six hours' journey by mule eastwards from Senkata, on the main Adigrat road 60 km north of Wuqro.[44] The ten items recorded[45] were clearly produced at widely different dates. The discovery must thus be interpreted as representing a cache of objects, gathered together and finally buried at a date not earlier than the beginning of the third century AD, this being the approximate age of the most recent item included.

Burials

Knowledge of burials is currently restricted to shaft graves with clear élite associations. Rock-cut examples have been excavated at Yeha, a short distance southeast of the Great Temple, in the 1960s and more recently on the outskirts

[41] A similar situation is clearly demonstrable for the objects found at Addi Gelamo, discussed below.

[42] Leclant 1959a.

[43] Admassou 1955. Unfortunately, the objects concerned were taken to Makalle before they could be examined in detail, and the full circumstances of their discovery could not be ascertained.

[44] Sketch-maps subsequently published suggest that the site lay about 30 km east-southeast of Senkata, rather than due east. No more precise indication of its position appears to be available, but detailed local enquiries – even after half a century – might reasonably be expected to remedy this problem.

[45] Caquot & Drewes 1955; Doresse 1960. For convenience, although the most significant pieces are discussed in greater detail elsewhere, a brief but complete listing is provided here:

1. A stone statuette of a seated female, with head separated, set on an inscribed base (RIE 52). An almost identical specimen has since been discovered at Maqaber Ga'ewa (see Fig. 10).
2. A broken inscribed altar of stone (RIE 8).
3. A copper-alloy sickle-shaped object, inscribed with the name and title of an early Aksumite king (RIE 180; Fig. 23). This is discussed in Chapter 8.
4. Two pieces of an animal figurine carved in white calcareous stone.

5, 6. Two small three-legged round stone altars, both broken and incomplete.

7–10. Four hemispherical copper-alloy bowls. One elaborately decorated example was almost certainly produced in the Nile Valley during the early centuries AD (Doresse 1960; J. S. Phillips 1995; see also below); a broadly similar origin is likely for the others also.

of the settlement.[46] Their details have not been fully published, although it seems that use of the shaft tombs near the Great Temple was continued for several centuries. Similar graves at Beta Giyorgis, Aksum, were set in a large stone-built platform and marked by stelae. Like those at Yeha, they represent an ancient tradition that survived in the northern Horn into significantly later – Christian – times (*cf.* Chapters 2 and 12).

Material culture

Pottery studies have, until recently, been based on broad categorisation of fabric which displayed remarkable similarity across wide regions.[47] More detailed analysis is yielding evidence for greater differentiation. The pottery produced in the northern Horn at this time was exclusively hand-made, the potter's wheel being apparently unknown. Vessels, when described in adequate detail, were mostly small, modestly decorated, and of forms suitable for use in the preparation and consumption of food. Large open-mouthed vessels, usually well-made but undecorated, were probably used for storage of dry foodstuffs. Much attention has been attached to a group of tall, flared-mouthed vessels,[48] representatives of which have been found both in the northern Horn and in southern Arabia. Following the assumption that they had a common origin, and controversy over whether that was located west or east of the Red Sea, it has now been demonstrated that similar vessels were locally made in both regions.[49] They are sufficiently distinctive to be attributable to a shared tradition and to common function, the latter illustrated by analysis of residues from some vessels' interiors.[50] Innovative research on pottery from Maqaber Ga'ewa has demonstrated the presence of wares originating in several different – but not yet positively identifiable – areas.[51] Despite attempts to demonstrate transport of pottery across the Red Sea at this time, no convincing evidence for this – in either direction – has yet been offered;[52] it is safe to conclude that virtually all pottery was locally made, with inter-regional similarities being best attributed to common antecedents, limited contact, or the movement of potters.

[46] Fattovich 1980, 2009. Further investigations at Yeha commenced in 2010 (Japp *et al.* 2011) and resulted in the discovery of further shaft tomb, but detailed results are not yet available.

[47] Fattovich 1980, see also Fattovich 2009. Generalised long-distance pottery comparisons, as opposed to more detailed local ones, have had a chequered history of acceptability whether in African archaeology or elsewhere; too often, similarities have been interpreted with reference to transport of pottery rather than to movement of potters.

[48] These were originally – but inappropriately – designated 'amphorae', despite the fact that they have no handles. Recent literature refers to them as 'torpedo-shaped vessels' or as 'form 4100 jars' (Anfray 1963a: esp. pl. cxxviii; Van Beek 1969: 170; Porter 2004 and references cited, 2010).

[49] Porter 2004. Research on fabric has so far been based on gross composition in comparison with local geology, since examination of clay sources has not yet been undertaken.

[50] Porter *et al.* 2009. The interiors of some of these vessels appear to have been smeared with a beeswax-like substance in order to reduce their porosity when used to hold liquids.

[51] Daszkiewicz *et al.* 2010. This analysis clearly distinguishes between the clay and the added temper. The two largest fabric groups were apparently produced in the Wuqro area and in a part or parts of northern Tigray, perhaps including Yeha. Three other groups, represented by only a few specimens, came from other unidentified localities, but in no case was there reason to suppose that they originated beyond Tigray.

[52] See Fattovich 1996a and, for an overview, Durrani 2005: 107–12.

Stone. Architecture, figurative and non-figurative sculpture, and inscriptions being considered elsewhere in this chapter, this section is restricted to smaller items, mostly in everyday use. Like the pottery, the flaked lithic industries of the first millennium BC show significant regional variation and temporal development, but remain poorly known overall due to the uneven coverage of research and publication.[53] It is clear, however, that they comprise predominantly microlithic artefacts of apparently local 'Late Stone Age' affinity continuing from earlier tradition/s. The diversity of these industries probably represents different populations, cultural traditions and economic practices. Flaked-stone artefacts represent a significant proportion of the archaeological assemblages present on settlement sites although, hardly surprisingly, they are rare on those that were used for religious and/ or administrative – as opposed to domestic – purposes.[54] Locally available materials were widely employed, although the particular flaking qualities of obsidian were clearly recognised. As more obsidian sources are reported, it is becoming clear that the distances over which it was transported were often significantly less that was formerly believed, and that numerous other deposits were exploited in addition to the abundant sources on the Dahlak islands.[55]

Other items of stone include seals, jettons and beads.[56] Prior to the third century BC, beads were rarely of glass, and the majority of these small stone objects were presumably manufactured locally. Seals may have served a function analogous to that of the 'marks of identity' discussed below, their designs being better suited to demonstrate ownership to the non-élite, largely illiterate sectors of the population. Jettons – which were made from fired clay or ground from broken pottery – have been assumed to indicate some degree of centralised administrative authority, but the possibility of an altogether different function – *e.g.* as simple playthings or informal counters – seems not to have been adequately considered.[57]

Metalwork. Sites of this period reveal rare items of copper alloy, although iron was apparently absent, at least initially. Metal was generally rare and items recovered from settlement sites were mainly limited to small objects of copper or copper alloy, most being linked to personal adornment. Iron appears to have been unknown. A characteristic artefact of this period, cast in copper alloy, has usually been termed a 'mark of identity' and probably served as a sort of seal, brand or stamp; the openwork design, often zoomorphic overall,

[53] But *cf.* L. Phillipson 2009b: esp. 109–12.

[54] The question of recovery needs to be kept in mind: some archaeologists specialising in the study of religious structures and artworks may not always have noticed the presence of lithic artefacts.

[55] Zarins (1990) drew attention to the Dahlak source, but also emphasised the presence of numerous other deposits that were – and remain – imperfectly investigated. His reservations have sometimes been ignored by subsequent researchers. Work in other areas (Agazi *et al.* 2011) has amply demonstrated the information that can be obtained through detailed mapping and analysis of obsidians, but comprehensive research along these lines has not yet been undertaken in the northern Horn.

[56] Michael Harlow 2000: figs 296–7; D. Phillipson 2000b: figs 309a, 309b.

[57] It is worth considering how the view that is here criticised seems to have arisen. So far as areas adjacent to the northern Horn are concerned, the suggestion was first tentatively applied to objects excavated at Kassala (Fattovich 1993a; Sackho-Autissier 2002) on the basis of distant *comparanda*. This hypothesis, ignoring the doubts and provisos very properly applied to the original proposal, has subsequently been applied to material from Beta Giyorgis (Fattovich 2010).

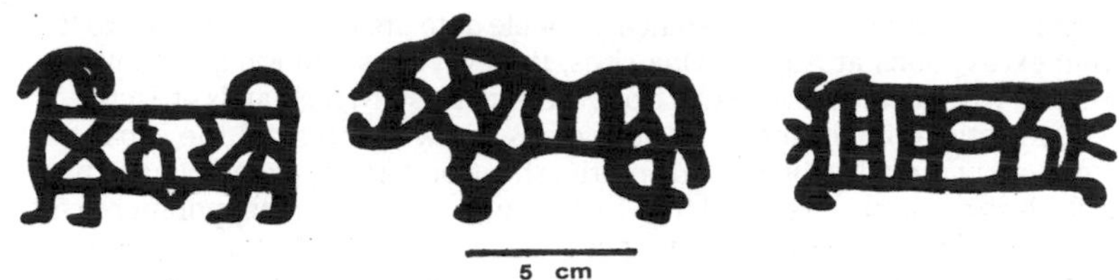

Fig. 12 Copper-alloy 'marks of identity' from the shaft-graves at Yeha (after Anfray 1963a)

can sometimes be recognised as script forming a personal name. These objects (Fig. 12) are best known from tombs at Yeha (RIE 295–307, with others from Sabea (RIE 292), Hawelti (RIE 293–4) and a possibly related fragment (RIE 308) from Matara.[58] Comparable – but significantly less elaborate – objects are known from southern Arabia, where there is evidence that they were used in the sealing of pottery jars.[59] The Ethiopian examples may have provided the means whereby ownership could be indicated to the illiterate as well as to the literate.

Metalwork generally seems to have been largely the prerogative of the élite, and a high proportion of the known material has been recovered from burials. This circumstance may serve to explain the apparent non-functionality of copper-alloy tools resembling sickles and axes, recovered from shaft graves at Yeha.[60] While the objects themselves may have been made for funerary deposition rather than for use, their existence might indicate that those responsible for their manufacture were familiar with the existence, if not the precise form, of iron equivalents. The only remains yet recovered in the northern Horn illustrative of the obtaining or processing of metals during the first millennium BC are at the Ancient Ona site of Hara Hot, north of Asmara,[61] where ancient workings – probably for copper – were reworked for gold during Italian colonial times.

Rock art. As noted in Chapter 2, the rock paintings of the northern Horn are currently of rather little value in elucidating the region's past, because of the difficulty that is almost invariably encountered in establishing their chronology. Naturalistic and schematic images are represented, the former predominating. Domestic animals greatly outnumber wild ones; humans, when shown, appear to be engaged in herding or – rarely – agriculture. Association with *graffiti* suggests that some of the paintings were probably executed during the first millennium BC.

Subsistence economy. Long-distance exchange seems to have played a much smaller part in the economy of the northern Horn at this time than was formerly believed. Evidence for transport of pottery and of obsidian, evaluated above, leads to the conclusion that such activity was on a small and localised scale. Consideration of the economy of the northern Horn's inhabitants at this time

[58] Anfray 1963a; Anfray & Annequin 1965; for further discussion see Anfray 1990; Manzo 2002, 2009.

[59] Costa 1992; Glanzman 2002; Simpson 2002: nos 240–1.

[60] Anfray 1963a: pls cxlviii, cxlix.

[61] Schmidt *et al.* 2008b; D. Phillipson 2008b: 152.

must focus primarily on subsistence. Reliable data are largely restricted to those from excavations at Ancient Ona sites, Beta Giyorgis and Kidane Mehret near Aksum, with preliminary results from the northeastern highlands of Tigray.[62]

Domestic animals and cultivated crops are well attested; the subsistence economy was evidently based on cattle, sheep and goats, emmer wheat, barley and – less certainly – teff and free-threshing wheat.[63] Although draught cattle – perhaps latterly including humped zebu – were employed,[64] evidence for camels and donkeys remains inconclusive.[65] Irrigation – if practised at all – now appears to have played a much less important role in the northern Horn at this time than was formerly believed. The view that irrigation contributed to the prosperity of Yeha during the first millennium BC is not supported by hard evidence, and the dam at Safra near Cohaito, Eritrea, cannot be assumed to date from this period, but in any event now appears to have served principally for the collection of run-off water on a comparatively small scale and not to have been linked to any means of wider distribution.[66]

Languages and inscriptions

It is important to distinguish between languages that were spoken and those that were written. The inscriptions that have been recovered suggest that literacy was not widespread through the population as a whole. Historical linguistic considerations (Chapter 2) indicate that both Cushitic and Semitic languages were spoken in the northern Horn at this time. The inscriptions are, however, exclusively Semitic; the script – like all those used by Semitic-speaking peoples at that time – was unvocalised [indicating only consonants].[67]

The inscriptions may be divided into two groups: monumental and informal. As noted above, their distribution and archaeological context have rarely received significant attention. There has also been a tendency for scholars who are not expert linguists or epigraphers to attribute unwarranted certainty to published translations, and to ignore the extent to which these may be due to doubtful readings or hypothetical reconstructions.

[62] Boardman 2000; Cain 2000; Bard *et al.* 2000; D'Andrea 2008; D'Andrea *et al.* 2008a, 2008b; Shoshani *et al.* 2008. Information has not been published concerning any economic evidence recovered from other excavated sites of this period.

[63] The evidence for teff comes from the Ancient Ona sites (D'Andrea *et al.* 2008b), Beta Giyorgis (Bard *et al.* 2000; D'Andrea 2008) and Kidane Mehret (Boardman 2000; Cain 2000). For teff, compare D'Andrea 2008 with D'Andrea *et al.* 2008b. There are no equivalent data from any of the élite sites. Two grains of free-threshing wheat were recorded from upper levels of the Ancient Ona site at Sembel (D'Andrea *et al.* 2008b; Schmidt *et al.* 2008a), the dating of which is not wholly clear.

[64] Osteological studies having so far proved inconclusive (see Cain 2000), evidence for the presence of humped cattle rests on artistic representations, notably a copper-alloy figurine from Zeban Kutur near Addi Kai [Keyh], Eritrea (Ricci 1959) which, on the basis of an Ethiopic inscription that it bears (Drewes 1962: 27–9; RIE 184) may tentatively be attributed to the last century or two BC. The 'clear' evidence for zebu *c.* 500 BC in the Asmara region cited by Schmidt (2010) is not convincing. It should be noted that, although humped cattle are widely accepted as having originated in India (Marshall 1989), they were known in New Kingdom Egypt where they appear to have been prestigious possessions in a cattle population that was predominantly humpless (Nicolotti & Guérin 1992).

[65] The poor representation of these species in archaeological bone-assemblages may be due to their use as beasts of burden rather than for food.

[66] For Yeha, see Michels 2005: 60–1. The Safra dam has been discussed by Brunner 2006. For broader consideration of this matter, see Sulas *et al.* 2009.

[67] Vocalised and unvocalised scripts are discussed and compared in Chapter 5.

Fig. 13 Types of first-millennium-BC inscription (after Bernand *et al.* 1991–2000): left – monumental; right – *graffiti*

Apart from their literal meanings, inscriptions can yield information in the two largely independent areas of language and script. All those from Eritrea and northern Ethiopia attributed to the first millennium BC are in South Semitic (*cf.* Chapter 2) languages, but they are not all linguistically identical. Unfortunately, many inscriptions are so short or fragmentary that their linguistic affinities cannot be determined with any confidence. A few – designated group I[68] – are in Sabaean, linguistically indistinguishable from that used in southern Arabian inscriptions. True Sabaean inscriptions in the northern Horn are very few, totalling only some 40 words, half of which are personal names. The other inscriptions that are linguistically diagnostic – group II – show signs of specifically African linguistic forms; their language has been designated 'Old Ethiopic', or alternatively 'Proto-Ge'ez',[69] and several of the personal names that they contain are not attested from southern Arabia.[70] Palaeographically, it may be shown that the group-I inscriptions are not invariably the earliest ones.[71]

Scripts also show considerable variation. The classification generally used distinguishes between monumental and cursive forms (Fig. 13), each of which may be subdivided. Confusingly, the first of these broad categories has often been designated 'Epigraphic South Arabian'.[72] As explained in Chapter 5, the term 'Ancient South Arabian Monumental' is here preferred. While this detailed classification is useful, it has yet to be demonstrated that any part of it necessarily has chronological significance.[73] On inscriptions that are sufficiently long – or sufficiently well preserved – the script proceeds boustrophedon [i.e. with lines reading alternately from right to left and from left to right], the individual letters themselves being reversed in alternate lines.[74]

68 Drewes 1959, 1962: 97.

69 R. Schneider 1976c. The former term is here preferred: 'Proto-Ge'ez' carries implications about the origin of the Ge'ez language that are not supported by some recent linguistic research (Weninger 2005).

70 Drewes 1998–99.

71 R. Schneider 1976b.

72 Unfortunately, the term is often used in contexts where language and script may be confused; furthermore its abbreviation 'ESA' is also used by archaeologists to signify 'Early Stone Age'.

73 *contra* Fattovich 2009 and Manzo 2009.

74 Single-line inscriptions – often *graffiti* – are known reading from right to left or from left to right. Boustrophedon likewise predominates in multi-line southern Arabian inscriptions of this period, although some are known where each line reads from right to left.

These considerations emphasise the difficulty of dating the inscriptions independently of the archaeology. They also indicate that script alone is a poor guide to attribution or authorship. Presumably, however, the group-I inscriptions were written by, or at the instigation of, people who maintained strong affinity with southern Arabia, had themselves come from there, or claimed to have done so for reasons of enhanced status. The more numerous group-II examples, on the other hand, would have been produced by members of a local population or possibly one that was dominated by the influence or authority of such indigenes.

Political organisation

Inscriptions[75] are a prime source of detailed, personalised – but not necessarily factual or unbiased – information about political organisation. It has, for example, often been considered that the northern Horn was the setting of a 'Pre-Aksumite' state called D'MT which closely mirrored contemporaneous polities in southern Arabia. The name and, indeed, the very existence of this assumed D'MT polity are inferred exclusively from inscriptions. Despite the prominence accorded them in historical reconstructions, and omitting hypothetical textual amendments, these inscriptions number only seven, all dedicatory, none of which can be claimed as having been recovered from – or recorded in – its original situation. Three of them are inscribed slabs found in the vicinity of Aksum[76] while the other four – closely resembling one another – are altar-like incense-burners from the highlands of eastern Tigray[77] These last, it now appears, may originally have been associated in some way with the temple recently discovered at Maqaber Ga'ewa. Significantly, not one of the inscriptions from Yeha – often suggested[78] as the capital of the proposed polity – mentions D'MT.

The inscriptions indicate that there was within the general area at this time at least one potentate who did not claim suzerainty over D'MT. While it must be emphasised that no other kingdoms are named, and it cannot be assumed that this ruler – whose name is given as WRN HYWT – had no connection with D'MT, two observations may be made: first, that no site in what is now Eritrea has yielded an inscription naming D'MT and, second, that the inscriptions naming non-D'MT rulers are widely distributed – at Seglamen[79] (RIE 1), Yeha (RIE 7) and Kaskase (RIE 11). The data are few, and future discoveries may support a completely different interpretation, but – for the present – one could tentatively suggest that the earliest indications for kingdoms in the northern Horn come from the Aksum-Yeha region, extending into eastern Tigray and the southernmost Eritrean highlands. Whatever the details, it seems safe to conclude that the polities currently known were localised, short-lived and non-inclusive.

[75] As elsewhere in this book, individual inscriptions (other than the most recent discoveries) are here designated 'RIE --' according to the system adopted by Bernand *et al.* 1991–2000 (*cf.* footnote 7, above). Note that numbers with this prefix are those of the catalogued inscriptions, not page numbers.

[76] RIE 2 at Abba Pantalewon monastery, RIE 3 and 5 found re-used at Enda Tcherqos on the Malazzo plateau.

[77] RIE 8 formed part of the cache at Addi Gelamo (see above), while three others are preserved in the church at Addi Kaweh near Wukro. (RIE 9, 10 and one recent discovery published by Gajda & Yohannes 2009.

[78] *e.g.* Munro-Hay 1993.

[79] An illustration of this inscription (Uhlig 2007: 157) was accompanied by a caption that incorrectly and misleadingly associated it with D'MT.

The names of four rulers are preserved. WRN HYWT was described as MLK [= king] on the stone slab from Seglamen,[80] some 10 km southwest of Aksum, that is widely regarded as the oldest inscription currently known from the northern Horn. The same name and title are more roughly carved on one of the pillars at Kaskase (RIE 11) and are recognised also on a stone at Yeha (RIE 7). Two further inscribed seals from Yeha[81] have been less certainly interpreted as recording a similar name, although no title is associated and it should not be assumed that these items belonged to the same person. There is, of course, no reason to assume that all these inscriptions – particularly those where the royal title is absent and to which widely divergent dates are attributed – refer to the same individual. Inscriptions record the names of three people – probably rulers – who appear to have been associated in some way with D'MT – RDM, RBH and LMN – all being specified on occasion both as MLK and as MKRB; there has been much speculation, discussed below, concerning the significance of this latter term. There is some evidence that two lineages may have been represented. At least two inscriptions, from Addi Gelamo (RIE 8) and Addi Kaweh (RIE 10), read MKRB D'MT WSB; the last word has generally been translated 'and Saba'. Although the word MKRB is known from a number of inscriptions in southern Arabia as well as in the northern Horn, no mention of D'MT has been recorded in the former area.

The word MKRB was formerly widely interpreted in both areas as a title carrying connotations of overlord of some sort of federation; this seemed to conform with the indication on some inscriptions in the northern Horn that the person so designated had connections with both D'MT and SB, and seemed to be further confirmed by references to divisions within D'MT specified as 'east and west' or 'red and brown'.[82] More recently, however, A. J. Drewes has argued that MKRB may in fact have signified 'blessed', thus carrying no essential implication of political authority.[83] The former view that use of the word MKRB in the northern Horn simply copied contemporaneous practice in southern Arabia, irrespective of whether or not the rulers of D'MT really exercised any authority over Saba or *vice versa*, has largely given way to the idea that a small number of Sabaeans – perhaps mainly the architects or masons mentioned in inscriptions from Gobochela (RIE 26, 27) and Yeha (RIE 29) – were resident west of the Red Sea. However, interpretation of the inscriptions' use of the word SB in connection with some of these individuals should be evaluated against uncertainties over its meaning and the likelihood that a claimed southern Arabian connection may have served to enhance the status of the person concerned. The detailed evaluation of these arguments and speculations need not concern us here. Of greater relevance is the point that, in contrast with their prominence in historical reconstructions, mentions of D'MT are remarkably few and highly restricted both in geographical distribution and in timespan. In view of the reassessment, noted above, of the connotations of the word MKRB, it could even be questioned whether D'MT actually was the name of a state, as opposed to a simple designation for the area's indigenous

[80] Ricci & Fattovich 1986. The inscription was not recovered from its primary context, but found re-used in a construction of later date.

[81] These comprise a perforated stone example (R. Schneider 1976b; RIE 289) from a third-phase level at Grat Be'al Gebri, and a metal openwork seal or 'mark of identity' (RIE 303, see above) from chamber B of tomb 6 which Fattovich (1990, 2009) has tentatively attributed to a relatively late date in the Yeha sequence.

[82] For the relevant inscriptions from Addi Kaweh, see R. Schneider 1973; Gajda & Yohannes 2009; see also Taddesse 1988.

[83] Drewes 2001. This important contribution has escaped notice from most scholars specialising in the northern Horn (but see R. Schneider 2003; D. Phillipson 2009c; also Gajda 2009: 183–4).

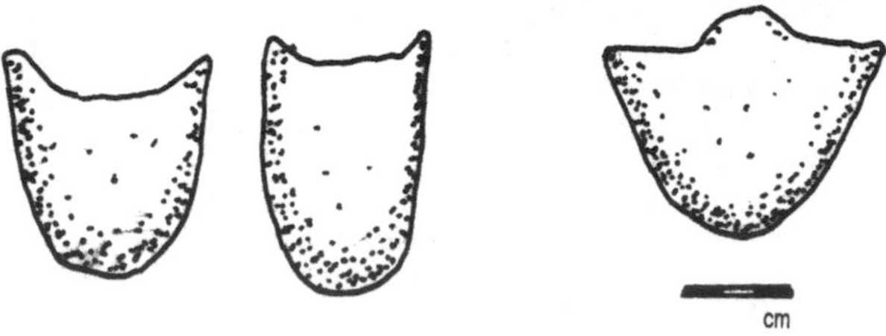

Fig. 14 Bulls' heads from Ancient Ona sites: left and centre – clay, from Sembel Kushet (after Tringali 1987); right – stone, from Sembel (after Schmidt & Naty 2008), claimed to represent a humped beast

population. Even if this interpretation is preferred, there can be no justification for applying the name D'MT as a broad synonym for 'Pre-Aksumite', as has recently been proposed.[84]

Religion

Inscriptions recording dedications to LMQ are clearly attested from several sites, notably Yeha, Maqaber Ga'ewa and Gobochela. There can be no doubt that the recipient was Almaqah, the moon god whose worship is also well attested in southern Arabia. At least one other member of the southern Arabian pantheon – 'Astar – is likewise named in an inscription (RIE 39) from Yeha. Stone incense-burners bearing the crescent-and-disc symbol occur at several sites.

The religious practices and beliefs of the indigenous population are much less easy to recognise, and the extent to which those originating in southern Arabia were adopted remains unknown. Ancient Ona sites have yielded large numbers of stone and clay objects (Fig. 14) that have been interpreted as stylised representations of bulls' heads, and it has been argued that they may be connected with religious practices analogous to those of the recent Kunama in western Eritrea.[85] Archaeological evidence from the Ancient Ona site of Sembel Kushet has been interpreted as representing activity comparable with that continued into modern times at the Masqal celebrations of the Eritrean and Ethiopian Orthodox Churches.[86]

Concluding overview

There can be no doubt that, long before Aksumite civilisation arose, architecture, inscriptions and material culture at several locations in the highlands of the northern Horn attest religious practices of southern Arabian affinity. Most of the relevant sites were investigated during the 1950s and 60s, and detailed stratigraphic and contextual information is rarely available. By their very nature, these sites and artefacts have received disproportionate attention from archaeologists; intensive survey has shown that such sites were very few in number when viewed in the context of overall contemporary settlement. In some instances, most notably at Yeha, the southern Arabian

[84] Finneran 2007: 117–8.

[85] Tringali 1965; Schmidt & Naty 2008.

[86] Schmidt 2009.

affinities are so varied and strong as to permit no reasonable doubt that people from southern Arabia were physically present and contributed significantly to the sites' development, although never forming more than a small minority of its inhabitants. In this chapter it is argued that these Arabians were probably few in number and that their presence as a distinct population element was brief. The extent to which they established political dominance in any area of the northern Horn is extremely doubtful, and it seems that any of their descendants who remained on the western side of the Red Sea were rapidly assimilated by the numerically dominant indigenes. The view that a large area of the northern Horn formed a unitary kingdom – D'MT – at this time, whether or not it closely resembled contemporaneous southern Arabian practice, is now seen as extremely doubtful. The Arabians' contribution to longer-term cultural development in the northern Horn was by no means negligible, being most clearly seen in the fields of architecture, literacy – but not, it now appears, in language – and perhaps also in some elements of religious belief and practice. Such contributions were, however, rapidly passed to the indigenous population and ceased to represent a separate system.

THE LAST FOUR CENTURIES BC

Introduction

In the northern Horn, the period immediately prior to the emergence of the Aksumite kingdom as an extensive polity has long been poorly understood.[87] The chronological re-assessment noted above implies that this period may have begun as early as the fifth or fourth century BC. It is clear that significant socio-political change took place during this interval; although archaeological survey indicates continuity of settlement, it is only at one location – Beta Giyorgis hill adjacent to Aksum – that detailed investigation permits a more comprehensive understanding.[88] No significant inscriptions – other than, perhaps, a few *graffiti* – are attributed to this period in the northern Horn, which is in marked contrast to current interpretations of contemporaneous trends in southern Arabia. If these views are correct, developments on the two sides of the Red Sea would appear to have been largely independent during the last four centuries BC.

Significantly, this was a time which saw increased Egyptian activity on the African Red-Sea coast. The Ptolemaic dynasty of Macedonian-descended kings who ruled Egypt from the end of the fourth century BC actively sought African war elephants, mounting expeditions along the Red Sea for that purpose.[89] Much of this activity concentrated on areas to the north of that with which this book is primarily concerned. An inscription of Ptolemy III was recorded by Cosmas Indicopleustes in the sixth century AD at Adulis,[90]

[87] *cf.* Anfray 1996.

[88] The research at Beta Giyorgis, directed by Rodolfo Fattovich and Kathryn Bard, is discussed below. The excavators' full publication of the research is awaited but several preliminary and specialist reports are available and are cited later in this chapter. The observations and suggestions offered here should be regarded as tentative.

[89] As heirs to Alexander the Great, the Ptolemies were well aware of the military advantages that resulted from the use of elephants. For these Ptolemaic expeditions, see Agatharchides; Burstein 1989, 1996; Casson 1993. Burstein (1996) argued that these expeditions sought ivory as well as live elephants.

[90] *Christian Topography* II, 54, 58–9; Wolska-Conus 1968–73, 1: 364–72. It is now accepted that Adulis lay behind the western shore of the Gulf of Zula [Annesley Bay] on the Eritrean coast some 50 km south of the modern Massawa (Peacock & Blue 2007), although Casson (1981, 1989: 103–6, followed by Burstein 1989: 9, 1998: 145) believed that it was on the Bay of Massawa itself.

but it should not be assumed that this was necessarily the place of its original erection some seven hundred years previously.[91]

Beta Giyorgis

Intensive archaeological research at Ona Negast on Beta Giyorgis has revealed evidence for prolonged occupation through much of the first millennium BC and (as discussed in the relevant chapters below) the first millennium AD. Particular interest, however, attaches to events during the last four centuries BC which are the focus of this section.[92] The local sequence was established primarily on the basis of seriated pottery typology, with chronology based on radiocarbon dates and on the ages of associated imports. The excavators designated this period 'Proto-Aksumite' in accordance with their belief that it represented a significant break with previous trends and greater continuity with the succeeding Aksumite civilisation.[93]

Archaeological manifestations of this period at Beta Giyorgis include funerary and residential structures, both apparently of élite status although lacking the grandeur subsequently attained by their counterparts. The former comprised a massive built platform in which were set rough-hewn stelae marking shaft graves (Fig. 15). Later in the period, the graves were more elaborate, with the stelae larger and more neatly shaped. Nearby buildings and artefact-deposits were interpreted as associated with the burials. The whole funerary area extended over a total area of some 10 ha, over one hundred stelae being visible on the surface, but it is uncertain whether all are attributable to this period. The pottery associated with these features formed a homogeneous assemblage, displaying limited continuity with that produced during earlier periods. Lithics[94] continued and refined the trends previously recognised, finely produced crescentic microliths in several instances being apparently deposited as grave goods.[95] Imported items included glass beads plus, possibly, a copper-alloy seal and a pottery beaker fragment of Meroitic affinity. Iron was limited to an arrowhead and two model axes. There was evidence for the cultivation of barley, emmer wheat, a little free-threshing wheat and – less certainly – teff,[96] also for the herding of cattle and ovicaprids and the presence of dogs. The imported beads raise chronological problems since the *comparanda* cited are

[91] This is a convenient place to note a stone carved stone *cippus* bearing a hieroglyphic inscription, almost certainly originating in Ptolemaic Egypt, noted by James Bruce (1790, 1: 417–8, 3: 496) as having been given to him by the king at Aksum in 1771. No subsequent record of this object appears to have been made until Sternberg-el Hotabi (1994) recognised it in the collections of the Royal Museum of Scotland, to which institution it had apparently been given anonymously some years previously. For illustrations, see D. Phillipson 1998: fig. 8. Dr Bill Manley kindly discussed this object with me. One can only speculate as to whether, how and when it got to Aksum in the first place.

[92] For a comprehensive overview, see Fattovich & Bard 2001.

[93] While the basic observation is not disputed, its interpretation is problematic. The premise that the 'Proto-Aksumite' period marked the demise of the so-called D'MT kingdom (Fattovich & Bard 2001: 4) is incompatible with the conclusion reached above regarding the political status of the northern Horn during the middle centuries of the first millennium BC. In subsequent publications, *e.g.* Fattovich 2010, it has been proposed that the 'Proto-Aksumite' period marked the initial phase of Aksumite civilisation; as discussed in Chapter 7, where an alternative terminology is proposed, this presents difficulties in accommodating a highly localised cultural manifestation with one that was subsequently established over an extremely extensive area.

[94] Usai 1997; L. Phillipson 2009b: 112.

[95] L. Phillipson 2009b: 86.

[96] For the cultivated plants from this period at Beta Giyorgis, see D'Andrea 2008.

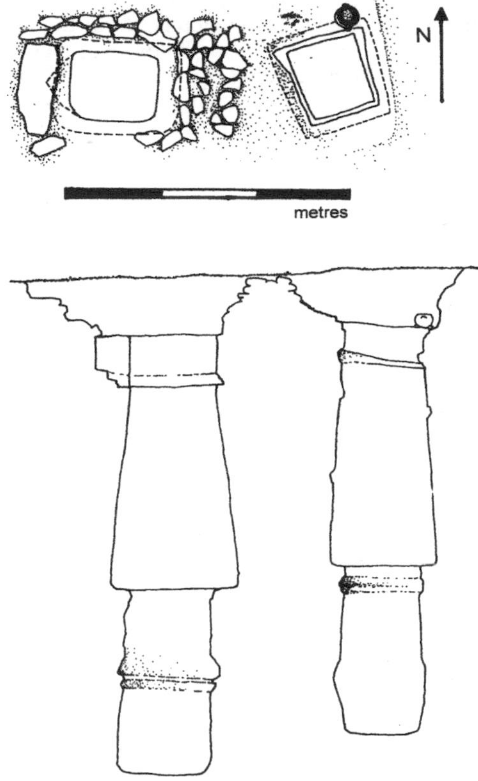

Fig. 15 Plan and section of shaft graves at Ona Enda Aboi Zewge, Beta Giyorgis (after Fattovich & Bard 2001)

thought to date after the mid-second century BC, which is later than the period originally proposed for the 'Proto-Aksumite' period as an entity within the Beta Giyorgis sequence.

There can be little doubt that the occupation of Beta Giyorgis at this time belongs firmly within a local tradition, traits suggesting foreign connections being few. It is, however, noteworthy that the affinities of imported artefacts – and, it is suggested, other features – are predominantly with the Nile Valley rather than with southern Arabia.[97] Proposed similarities with the archaeological sequence at Kassala,[98] in Sudan adjacent to the Eritrean frontier, are potentially misleading in view of the distances – both geographical and chronological – which separate Beta Giyorgis and Kassala, although they confirm that the Beta Giyorgis materials of the last four centuries BC fit clearly

[97] The few fragments of wine amphorae from deposits of this period appear to have originated in the western Mediterranean rather than – as in later times – the eastern. A Nile-Valley route for their importation is more likely than one *via* the Red Sea, and the same is true for the rare artefacts of Nile-Valley origin that have been found in the northern Horn (J. S. Phillips 1995), including the copper-alloy bowls, noted above, from the Addi Gelamo cache.

[98] Fattovich 1989, 1993a; Bard *et al.* 2002.

and neatly within a context that is indigenous to the Horn and its immediate vicinity. Arguments[99] that political developments in the Aksum area at this general time reflected those in the Nile Valley, while demonstrating broad similarities, are potentially misleading in their implication of causality. The perceived similarities and links are too slight to support a hypothesis that political developments in the Aksum region were inspired through contacts with the Nile Valley.

Conclusion

Although there are clear indications[100] that the Beta Giyorgis 'Proto-Aksumite' was a highly localised phenomenon, confusion has arisen through the application of the term to a time-period over a significantly wider area. This has led to the potentially misleading statement that 'No evidence *dating to this period* has been recorded in the other archaeological sites more extensively excavated in Tigray and Eritrea' [present author's emphasis],[101] despite the paucity of precise dating evidence and the fact that no prolonged general hiatus in settlement is attested. Michels' survey of the Yeha area indicated settlement during the last centuries BC by people whose pottery differed from that of their contemporaries closer to Aksum.[102] There are also indications of activity at this time in the Gulo Makeda area on the highlands in eastern Tigray and – less certainly – at Emba Derho near Asmara.[103] These discoveries, however, in no way invalidate the conclusion that the 'Proto-Aksumite' inhabitants of Beta Giyorgis were directly ancestral to those who were subsequently responsible for the establishment and expansion of the Aksumite kingdom, as discussed in Chapter 7.

[99] Fattovich 1993b; Fattovich *et al.* 1998; Bard *et al.* 2002.

[100] See Fattovich & Bard 2001: 21; DiBlasi 2005; Michels 2005: 126.

[101] Fattovich & Bard 2001: 21.

[102] Michels 2005: 103–21.

[103] D'Andrea *et al.* 2008a; Schmidt *et al.* 2008c. The second of these publications is unclear as to the suggested affinities of the tomb at Emba Derho: considerable weight is attached to a single radiocarbon determination – on a shell sample – between the second and fourth centuries AD, but the comparisons cited are with the significantly earlier material at Beta Giyorgis.

Part Two

The Kingdom of Aksum

4

Aksumite Civilisation: An introductory summary

The arrangement of the following twelve chapters is thematic. While Chapter 7, on emergence, and Chapter 16, on decline and transformation, are principally concerned with the earlier and later stages of the period during which Aksumite civilisation flourished, the others follow their themes throughout that time – which inevitably requires much cross-referencing in order to avoid repetition. Sources of written evidence that are relevant to several different chapters are, for convenience, evaluated in Chapter 6. As with many chapters in this book, a high proportion of the relevant data is from Aksum itself, other Tigray areas and much of southern Eritrea having been less well served by research and publication. The Asmara area seems to have been sparsely inhabited during the greater part of this period.

A book such as this, which attempts to set Aksumite civilisation in its context of overall historical development in the northern Horn of Africa, requires that somewhat arbitrary parameters be imposed. While it must be recognised that historical processes may occur at distinct times and with variable form and intensity in different areas, clarity of narrative requires a chronological framework. The difficulties are exacerbated since it appears that, in its earliest phase, the Aksumite kingdom was a geographically restricted entity that subsequently greatly expanded its territory to incorporate diverse previously distinct populations. For reasons discussed more fully in Chapter 7, Aksumite civilisation is first recognised at the time when a major new settlement was established in the valley between Beta Giyorgis and Mai Qoho hills in the highlands of west-central Tigray; this probably took place around the first half of the first century AD. Subsequent developments are better discussed, not in terms of chronological compartments such as 'Classic Aksumite' or 'Late Aksumite', but against an absolute chronology expressed in terms of years or centuries as is attempted in this book (*cf.* Chapter 1).

The kingdom of Aksum flourished during the first seven centuries AD, but its localised formative processes may be traced significantly earlier and its cultural influence extended very much later. It was thus not the isolated phenomenon implied by some previous studies, but one firmly embedded in the continuing development of Ethiopian civilisation. There is little doubt that the origins of the kingdom may be traced directly back to an earlier community on Beta Giyorgis hill (see Chapter 3) and that, following the transfer of its centre to the adjacent valley and plain, both its prosperity and its territorial influence greatly increased. The scant archaeological evidence for the processes by which this was achieved remains poorly understood but, supplemented by a number of monumental inscriptions, probably indicates the incorporation of surrounding polities (Chapter 7) within the hegemony of that centred, from the first century AD, at Aksum.

For much of its history, the boundaries of the territory subject to Aksumite control and/or influence remained – notwithstanding the views, claims or acquisitions of its rulers – ill-defined; they are still poorly understood. At their maximum extent they probably included the area south of Massawa on the Red-Sea coast where the port of Adulis was located, together with the highlands in south-central Eritrea and in the greater part of Ethiopia's Tigray region. The extent of such influence further to the north and west remains to be determined, although it seems likely that one or more incursions were made into the Sudanese Nile Valley early in the fourth century. Aksumite influence in the areas west and south of the Takezze river was probably – at least initially – slight and/or transient. For much of the sixth century, and perhaps also on some earlier occasions, Aksumite rule was exercised – directly or indirectly – over parts of southern Arabia, as is discussed in Chapter 15.

The Aksumite kingdom established far-reaching international trade links (Chapter 15) in which the export of ivory played a major part, adopted Christianity in the second quarter of the fourth century (Chapter 9), and declined some three hundred years later. Our knowledge of Aksumite civilisation comes from diverse sources: archaeology, epigraphy, numismatics, references in Graeco-Roman written works, and Ethiopian traditions – some of which were committed to writing in later times. Interpretation of all these materials is subject to distinct and particular problems, details of which are set out in Chapter 1. Some members of the Aksumite community were literate in the local Semitic language, Ge'ez; there was also a Greek-using minority (Chapter 5). While other languages were almost certainly spoken, there is no evidence that any of them were written. In the past, there has been a tendency to stress overseas connections and to minimise evidence for local continuity and development. However, it is now recognised that, although the Aksumite kingdom brought together many cultural influences of diverse origin, numerous aspects of its basic economy and technology were derived from local developments during the first millennium BC. These elements prevailed – with relatively minor modification – throughout the period when Aksumite civilisation arose, flourished and declined.

The remarkable commemorative monuments (Chapters 11 and 12) illustrate Aksumite technological and organisational capabilities, as well as many aspects of the kingdom's history, including its military expansion and its gradual adoption of Christianity. They are still imperfectly understood, however, and many questions remain unanswered.

As with many ancient societies, much of our knowledge about the Aksumites is derived from the burials of their dead (Chapter 12), those of the élite having received disproportionate attention from archaeologists. While such tombs, in so far as they have escaped subsequent robbing, reveal much information about funerary customs – indirectly reflecting many topics including religion – and material culture, their evidence should not be taken as indicative of conditions prevailing through Aksumite society as a whole. The most elaborate Aksumite tombs are those dated to the third/fourth centuries AD in the so-called Stelae Park at Aksum itself, marked by huge standing monoliths – stelae – each carved in representation of a multi-storey building and originally bearing one or more metal plaques at its apex. It is reasonable to assume, although definitive proof is lacking, that these tombs were those of kings. Be that as it may, they date to the period immediately preceding the conversion of the Aksumite rulers to Christianity. They indicate enormous concentration of resources: the largest stela weighed some 520 tonnes and – had it been successfully erected – would have been 33 m high. Later élite tombs retained some of these architectural features, but the use of stelae was discontinued.

Tombs of apparently sixth-century date were surmounted by funerary chapels of clearly Christian form and had much less space for grave-goods than had been the case in earlier times. It is noteworthy that, although the quarries near Aksum where the large stelae were extracted employed technology for which the closest known parallels are from Roman Egypt, most other aspects of Aksumite architecture show only the most general affinity with that region. Non-élite burials were, of course, much less elaborate, sometimes comprising a simple pit in which the deceased was interred along with few if any artefacts as grave goods, but marked by a small stela of undressed stone. Such burials were usually concentrated in separate areas peripheral to the main conurbations.

The architecture of the living (Chapter 11) likewise varied in accordance with the wealth and status of its users, although it is probable that traces of less substantial structures – such as may have housed the poorest people – have not yet been examined archaeologically. Buildings known from this time were invariably rectangular. Except for roofs, stone was the preferred material, although – particularly initially and for the more prestigious structures – the stone walls incorporated horizontal beams held together by transverse wooden ties with rounded ends called 'monkey-heads', like those represented on the stelae. The largest and most elaborate structures – other than tombs and churches – each included a square central building, perhaps two or three storeys high at the corners, entered by means of a monumental stair central to one or more sides, and standing in a courtyard surrounded by suites of rooms. Such complexes show considerable variation in overall size and elaboration; none has, however, been excavated and published with a view to demonstrating its precise chronology or the uses to which it and its component parts were put. Lower strata of Aksumite society made use of buildings in which dressed-stone masonry was rarely, if ever, employed and in which timber was incorporated more sparingly. Most were rectangular, apparently of one storey and – as in earlier times – set around courtyards. The simplest houses, so far known only from clay models, were likewise of one storey, rectangular, with flat or ridged roofs, the latter apparently covered with thatch.

Buildings of all these types, except perhaps the simplest, occurred in both urban and rural situations. This observation leads to a consideration of the overall nature of settlement in Aksumite times. Although reference is sometimes made to Aksum itself as a city, the term and/or its connotations are inappropriate. During the first seven centuries AD, Aksum comprised a loose conglomeration of buildings and burial areas. It was not clearly demarcated; neither it nor any other analogous place within the Aksumite hegemony was equipped with a surrounding wall or other structural means of defence. The very incomplete information that is available suggests that there may have been some differential between 'town' and 'country' in the activities that were conducted: food production, for example, being for obvious reasons concentrated in rural areas, while some craft activities whose products were a prerogative of the élite were mainly carried out in more urban situations, but the division was rarely rigid.

The subsistence economy (see Chapter 10) remained based on that which had been locally practised during the previous millennium but, as economic and political contacts widened, elements of more distant origin were gradually incorporated. The material culture and technology of the Aksumite kingdom (Chapter 13) shared the diversity noted above. Much research attention has been paid to high-value items – or their containers – that were imported from the Mediterranean world. Imported commodities included wine in amphorae from areas bordering the eastern Mediterranean and the northern Red Sea, pottery and glassware from Egypt and North Africa – both of which were copied by Aksumite craftsmen – and occasional prestige objects such as fine glassware and engraved gemstones. While virtually all metal artefacts appear to have been produced locally, the sources of raw material have not yet been located and some at least may have been imported. Overall, it is important neither to exaggerate the scale of Aksumite overseas trade nor to ignore those elements that are difficult to recognise in the archaeological record. This last point is particularly relevant in connection with Aksumite exports which, it appears, consisted primarily of ivory and other raw materials. Most of this long-distance trade was conducted by way of the Red Sea and the Aksumite port at Adulis; the associated land journey across the plateau and escarpment must have added considerably to transport costs. Movement of commodities and personnel within the Aksumite realm is demonstrated both by commemorative inscriptions and by distributions of artefacts, notably pottery. This discussion of trade should not, however, obscure the fact that the kingdom was largely self-sufficient and that it developed substantial local expertise in metallurgy, ivory carving and the manufacture of glass vessels and other items, while retaining other technological traditions – including potting and stone knapping – which derived directly from the practices of their local predecessors.

The second half of the third century witnessed a rapid increase in the kingdom's material prosperity, concentration of wealth at the political centre, and long-distance trade. Significantly, this was also the time when the issue of Aksumite coins began, and it was at just this time that Aksum was included in a list of the world's major kingdoms. The coinage (Chapter 14), with denominations in gold, silver and copper, initially bore inscriptions in Greek – a feature that was retained for the internationally circulating gold coins until minting was discontinued in the seventh century, although those on silver and copper – which saw mostly local use – were latterly in Ge'ez. The resources at the disposal of the kings were clearly extremely large and well organised, as reflected both by the labour expended on the royal burials and other prestige projects, and by the military operations recorded in grandiloquent and highly detailed inscriptions.

Recognition of this broader picture permits a more meaningful view of events in the early sixth century, when the Aksumites under King Kaleb were militarily involved in southern Arabia (Chapter 15). This operation apparently received some measure of connivance or support from the Byzantine imperial authorities, whose dominant motives were both economic and political, aimed at securing a trade route to the East that was not subject to Persian control. Elsewhere, notably in the northern Horn, the campaign was presented in religious terms, as avenging a persecuted Christian community and liberating it from domination by non-Christian monotheists recalled – probably misleadingly – as Jews. In neither guise was long-term success achieved. This period saw increased church-building activity in regions under Aksumite rule, and illuminated manuscripts appeared; several instances of Byzantine influence may be discerned, although local elements predominated.

As Chapter 16 explains, decline of the Aksum conurbation seems to have resulted in the transfer of the capital to a more easterly location rather than – at least initially – in a broader diminution of the kingdom's prosperity. These complex processes resulted in the gradual transformation of the civilisation formerly centred at Aksum to that which flourished in more easterly and southerly parts of the Ethiopian highlands from the eighth century onwards. Any 'end' of Aksumite civilisation is thus a nebulous and elusive concept; attempts to define it and to establish its date serve only to mask the essential continuity that is now apparent during this crucial period.

5

Aksumite Languages and Literacy

Elucidating the linguistic history of the Aksumite kingdom during the first seven centuries AD is fraught with difficulty. Two very distinct written languages are represented: Ge'ez and Greek, belonging respectively to the Semitic and Indo-European families. The texts that were demonstrably produced during this period were largely limited to inscriptions on stone, less than a score of which have significant length, to those on coins, and to *graffiti*, including very short texts – often only a single word, name or abbreviation – on rocks and also on pottery or other portable objects.[1] Only the last of these – the *graffiti*, which are exclusively in Ge'ez – are likely to reflect at all closely the speech employed in everyday life at any level of Aksumite society; they often record the names of individuals, perhaps as owners or users of land or simply as passers-by.[2] As Chapter 3 makes clear, some sections of the northern Horn's population had been literate during the second quarter of the first millennium BC, but the extent of continuity from this into Aksumite times has not yet been fully demonstrated. Among the Aksumites, it is clear that basic literacy – at least in Ge'ez – was not restricted to an élite and to scribes, perhaps becoming progressively more widely distributed in later centuries.

While most of the more formal stone inscriptions are from Aksum, others are widely distributed geographically (*cf.* Chapter 6). It is clear that there were people both at Aksum and elsewhere in the kingdom, at least between the third and the seventh centuries, who were able to write Ge'ez and/or Greek; it is only reasonable to assume that these languages were also spoken and that some of these speakers could read. The two languages are here considered separately.

Ge'ez

This – doubtless with significant dialectic variation – was almost certainly the everyday vernacular language for most inhabitants of the kingdom's core-area, while other languages or distinct dialects continued to be used, at least in recently subsumed regions. This statement is, however, open to misinterpretation. Ge'ez,[3] having been replaced only within the past two hundred years or so as the principal written language of Eritrea and Ethiopia, survives today as the liturgical language of the Orthodox Church in both countries. Modern

[1] The sole surviving exception, the Abba Garima *Gospels*, is considered below.

[2] The larger numbers of such *graffiti* recorded from parts of Eritrea, in contrast with their scarcity in the eastern highlands of Tigray, is probably attributable to the extent of twentieth-century recording.

[3] Drewes & R. Schneider 1976. For a convenient linguistic survey of its principal features, albeit with out-dated treatment of historical issues, see Gragg 2004.

Tigrinya is descended from Ge'ez; Amharic is a more distant relative. Although subject to strong conservative pressures, Ge'ez has undoubtedly evolved to a significant extent during the centuries that have passed since the decline of the Aksumite kingdom, and it would thus be misleading to assume that ancient everyday Ge'ez was identical to its modern liturgical form. Although it was formerly believed – and is still sometimes repeated[4] – that an early form of Ge'ez was introduced to the Horn from southern Arabia during the first millennium BC, use of Semitic speech is now widely understood to have begun there at a significantly earlier date.[5] How Aksumite Ge'ez was pronounced remains a matter for controversy, but study of names that are represented both in Ge'ez and in Greek texts can provide some clues, as can the occasional instances when a Ge'ez word was transliterated into Greek or *vice versa*. For example, the Aksumite king's name generally spelled 'Kaleb' or 'Caleb' is invariably given as ΧΑΛΗΒ – *i.e.* with an initial 'Ch' and with a long 'e' – on his Greek-inscribed coins.

Ge'ez was surely not the only vernacular language used within the Aksumite kingdom. There must have been subject populations speaking Cushitic languages, notably Agau (see Chapter 2), as has been the case in northern Ethiopia during more recent times. The presence of such Agau dialects used by people in contact with Ge'ez speakers is reflected by the incorporation of Cushitic loanwords into Ge'ez.[6] However, no ancient Cushitic-language inscriptions are known, nor is there evidence to suggest that any such languages were committed to writing prior to the nineteenth century.

Any substantial vernacular writings that may have existed were probably executed on perishable materials which, with the sole exception of the Abba Garima *Gospels* (Chapters 9 and 13), no longer survive. Other Ge'ez texts such as translations of the Greek Bible – which may be shown to date from around the sixth century (Chapter 9) – do not survive in their original form. Any Aksumite written non-religious literature has long-since perished and been forgotten.[7] *Graffiti* on pots and on rocks are rarely informative; only the former are likely to be dateable. A pot from Aksum, probably *c.* fourth-century in date, bears a Ge'ez inscription (RIE 311) that may be loosely translated 'breakage must be paid for' (see also Chapter 13).

In dealing with what seems to have been a conservative and traditional population, it is necessary to consider the likelihood of archaic linguistic forms and scripts being retained in certain circumstances, as they have been by other societies – particularly those that were experiencing rapid economic and political change. These circumstances are precisely those under which the majority of our surviving Aksumite written materials were produced; and excellent examples of archaisms are provided by the commemorative stone inscriptions dating from the fourth and sixth centuries (Fig. 16; Chapter 6).

4 *e.g.*, most recently, by Voigt 2005.

5 See Goldenberg 1977; Hudson 1977, 2000; Appleyard 1996. The linguistic history of the northern Horn during the last three millennia BC is discussed in Chapters 2 and 3.

6 Such loanwords have been evaluated by, among others, Appleyard (1978) and Ehret (1979). They are present in both Ge'ez and Tigrinya, but are more numerous in Amharic. It has been suggested (*e.g.* Ullendorff 1968: 116) that such Agau-speakers may have included adherents to a Judaic form of non-Christian monotheism, but see Chapter 9 for a reconsideration of early Ethiopian 'Judaism'.

7 It is argued in Chapter 6 that, when the *Kebra Negast* was brought into more-or-less its present form *c.* 1300, it incorporated a good deal of sixth-century material. No physical trace of this early version survives; it may have been transmitted orally rather than in writing.

Fig. 16 Inscriptions of King Ezana at Aksum: upper left – RIE 185*bis* in ASAM-derived script; lower left – RIE 271*bis* in Greek; right – RIE 185*bis* in unvocalised Ethiopic script

Ge'ez inscriptions on stone have survived in two different scripts. One, here designated 'ASAM-derived',[8] closely replicated – perhaps as a deliberate archaism – the formal script used in earlier times. It could be written either from left to right or from right to left.[9] Like all Semitic scripts at that time – and some more recent ones – it was invariably unvocalised, indicating consonants only; it provided merely an approximation of the manner in which the words were actually pronounced, and was thus of limited value to a reader who lacked any previous familiarity with the text concerned.[10] The second script was much more closely related both to that used in less-formal *graffiti*[11] and to that employed more recently in Ge'ez manuscripts: it is usually designated 'Ethiopic', and was invariably written from left to right.[12] The script used in the

[8] For ASAM [Ancient South Arabian Monumental] in this context, see Chapters 3 and 6. Alternative terms employed by some writers have included 'southern Arabian', 'pseudo-Sabaean' and 'ESA [Epigraphic South Arabian]-derived'. 'ASAM-derived' is here preferred, contrary to the practice adopted by Bernand *et al.* (1991–2000), because it carries less implication of inferiority or of an immediately foreign origin.

[9] Boustrophedon writing (*cf.* Chapter 3) was no longer practised.

[10] The difficulty is particularly apparent with numerals. In unvocalised Ge'ez, 'SR did not distinguish between *'asru* [= 12] and *'esra* [= 22], nor could SS indicate whether *sessu* [= 6] or *sessa* [= 60] was meant (Drewes 1962: 50). I am greatly indebted to Dr Laurel Phillipson for her comments on the significance of vocalisation.

[11] See Chapter 3 for discussion of earlier *graffiti*.

[12] Note that, in an Aksumite context, the designation 'Ge'ez' applies to the language, 'Ethiopic' to script.

earliest Aksumite stone inscriptions was unvocalised, but some examples – *e.g.* RIE 188 and 189 – from the fourth century onwards show signs of incipient vocalisation in the form, comprising appendages to the consonantal symbols,[13] that has continued in the modern Tigrinya and Amharic scripts. Adoption of vocalisation was slow and irregular, but became progressively more usual; resistance may have been due to conservatism, desire to restrict literacy, and/ or to the desire for simplicity; Ge'ez coin-inscriptions, regular use of which began in the early sixth century (Chapter 14), invariably employed Ethiopic script, sometimes with partial but inconsistent vocalisation.[14]

The two non-Greek scripts were associated with certain linguistic distinctions, so they should not be regarded simply as alternative ways of writing Ge'ez. For example, the word used for 'king' was MLK when written in ASAM-derived script, but NGS or *negusa* in Ethiopic script, that for 'son of' being BN and WLD or *walda* respectively, in each case the Ethiopic form being that which has been retained in the more recent Ge'ez, Tigrinya and Amharic languages. Apparent errors or inconsistencies in Ge'ez stone inscriptions suggest that the linguistic forms differed from the dialectic or other versions with which the carvers were most familiar.[15] A refinement employed in some Ethiopic inscriptions but not in Greek or ASAM-derived ones is the occasional use of dividers between words and to mark the ends of sentences.[16]

Greek

Aksumite use of Greek has received disproportionate attention, presumably because it is more readily understood by scholars from beyond the northern Horn.[17] There is no reason to suppose that it was ever more than a minority language so far as the Aksumite population was concerned. The *Periplus of the Erythraean Sea* (*q.v.* in Chapter 6) noted that Zoscales, king of the coastal region around Adulis in the mid-first century AD, had a good knowledge of Greek.[18] The account by Rufinus (Chapter 9) indicated that – at least as early as the second quarter of the fourth century – there were resident at Aksum foreign traders, some of whom were Christian. Four or five decades earlier, striking of coins had begun in the names of the kings of Aksum; initially, all these coins were inscribed in Greek (Chapter 14). Greek was primarily the language of those who were engaged in international trade, including foreigners – some of whom may have been native users of that language – as well as those Aksumites who associated with them. The latter category would almost certainly have included the kings, who would have had to establish a balance

[13] For further explanation and illustration, see Gragg 2004. Controversies about possible Indian influence on the form taken by this vocalisation (*cf.* Kobishchanov 1979: 89; Frantsouzoff 2010), and its relationship to broadly contemporaneous Armenian practice (Olderogge 1974), are not considered here. The beginning of vocalisation in Aksumite inscriptions was remarkably protracted and inconsistent, perhaps due to the archaising tendencies noted here and in Chapter 6.

[14] *e.g.* the silver coins of Gersem: type 147 of Munro-Hay & Juel-Jensen 1995, no. 51 of Hahn 2000.

[15] Examples were cited by Drewes 1991 and by Bausi 2005.

[16] See, for example, West 2001.

[17] To cite but one example, a recent account of the religious implications of Ezana's stone inscriptions (Black 2008) was based exclusively on the Greek texts, taking no account of their Ge'ez counterparts or of the not insignificant variation (*cf.* Chapter 9) between the different versions.

[18] *Periplus* 5 (Casson 1989: 2–3). See Chapters 7 and 8 for further discussion of Zoscales.

between their wish to communicate with foreigners and their need to maintain the goodwill of their native subjects.[19] It seems that Christianity was initially centred on a Greek-speaking local élite and on expatriates; this may have resulted in resentment and opposition to the new religion by those sectors of the indigenous population who did not know this language, as discussed in Chapter 9. The presence of distinct readerships is further indicated by the erection of trilingual stone inscriptions beside the two principal roads leading into Aksum. It may not be irrelevant to note that a comparable – but probably earlier – inscription (Chapter 6) erected in this position on the outskirts of Adulis seems to have been written only in Greek. Letter-forms on the stone inscriptions in Greek differ significantly from those employed on coins.[20]

During the fifth century, significant changes may be recognised. Stone inscriptions in Greek were not – so far as is currently known – erected in the names of kings who reigned after the mid-fourth century, although a simple Greek-inscribed tombstone[21] of *c.* 500 has recently been discovered near Aksum. Coin inscriptions in Greek became increasingly garbled, with letters omitted, confused or mis-ordered, indicating that the die-engravers were no longer adequately conversant with that language (Chapter 14). Under Kaleb in the first half of the sixth century, exclusive use of Greek for coinage inscriptions was discontinued: denominations in silver – now seriously debased – and in copper being inscribed in Ge'ez, while rudimentary Greek remained in use on the gold which seems to have continued to circulate internationally. It is noteworthy that, throughout this process, coin-inscriptions in Ge'ez contained significantly fewer errors than those in Greek; the problem was not one of generally incompetent or illiterate die-engravers, but of their unfamiliarity with Greek. Despite this apparent marginalisation of Greek, a distinct Greek-using Christian community may have remained in the Aksum area until at least the early sixth century (Chapter 12). As discussed in Chapter 6, Greek was probably falling out of use at this time, both at the royal court in Aksum and at Adulis.

Inter-language comparisions

It is instructive to examine the interplay and equivalence of Greek and Ge'ez. Most of the kings of the late third and early fourth centuries, as well as some later ones, bore a name or title which, in Greek, took the form BICI ... [*bisi* ...]. We are not here concerned with the meaning or significance of the word *bisi* – which is discussed in Chapter 8 – but with the fact that it is unknown in any other Greek-language context and is apparently a simple transliteration from the Ge'ez *be'seya* or *be'se* ... [= man of ...]. Conversely, a Greek-inscribed gold coin[22] of the sixth-century ruler Ella Gabaz gives his title, not in the usual Greek form based on BACIΛEYC [= king], but as NΓ which is based on a transliteration of the unvocalised Ge'ez NGS with the same meaning. This may have been a nationalist gesture, or perhaps the die-engraver could not remember the

[19] WZB, probably the third Aksumite king to issue coins around the beginning of the fourth century, employed Ge'ez in unvocalised Ethiopic script for all his coinage inscriptions (*cf.* Chapter 14). A similar practice was adopted by king MHDYS in about the third quarter of the fifth century. These temporary innovations may be interpreted as responses to the wishes of individual rulers, perhaps in response to popular nationalist sentiment.

[20] See Chapter 8 for discussion of the spelling of Ezana's name.

[21] Fiaccadori 2007b. The dating is based on stylistic comparisons with lettering employed in far-distant areas and should be regarded as approximate.

[22] Type 124 of Munro-Hay & Juel-Jensen 1995, no. 45 of Hahn 2000.

Greek word and substituted the Ge'ez, albeit employing Greek characters for the purpose.

Similar instances may be observed on the stone inscriptions. Ezana's Greek texts employed the same BICI form as do the coins. Two other words, with which the carver of the Greek inscription was evidently unfamiliar, were simply transliterated, with vowels added.[23] In both cases, the Ge'ez vocalisations were represented in the Greek versions, although the Ge'ez texts in both scripts were unvocalised. Several conclusions may be drawn: the text was first drafted in Ge'ez, then translated into Greek; it is likely that the initial draft was in vocalised Ge'ez or was read in that form; different carvers were probably responsible for the Greek texts and for the unvocalised Ge'ez ones.

Use of numerals also requires comment. No inscriptions on coins include numerals, so our information is limited to those on stone. In most early Ge'ez inscriptions, such as that from Safra (Chapter 6), numbers were spelled out as words. The Ge'ez system of numerical notation was derived from Greek; its earliest known use is on a third-century stela at Anza, described in Chapters 6 and 10. In the fourth- century Ge'ez texts of the 'trilingual' inscriptions at Aksum (Chapter 6), it is clear that spaces were left for numerals. These were subsequently added to the Ethiopic-script versions – often not completely filling the spaces that had been allowed for them. In ASAM-derived texts, by contrast, spaces were also left, but never filled in,[24] implying that the carvers responsible were uncertain how numbers should be incorporated into such a text. The earliest-known attestations of the Ge'ez system of writing numbers,[25] clearly derived from its Greek counterpart, occur on Ezana's inscriptions RIE 185/185*bis*, 188 and 189.

The Ethiopian calendar

Brief consideration of the Ethiopian calendar is appropriate here, with particular reference to its antiquity.[26] Inscriptions RIE 190 and 271, on opposite sides of the same slab but respectively in Ge'ez ASAM-derived script and in Greek, recorded that Ezana's campaign against the Noba began on the eighth day of the month Magabit.[27] The chronological implications of this statement for the exact date of the inscription are considered in Chapter 6, but it is relevant here to emphasise two points. The Greek text specified that Magabit was an Aksumite month, although no attempt was made to relate it to any other calendar; the Ge'ez version did not include a corresponding explanation. This may be taken as further support for the hypotheses that texts of these inscriptions were initially drafted in Ge'ez, and that the Greek versions were intended for a predominantly foreign readership. Secondly, at least one name for an Ethiopian month was in use as early as the mid-fourth century; this may carry significant implications for the antiquity of the calendar as a whole.

[23] This feature is preserved on both of Ezana's trilingual inscriptions (RIE 185/270 and 185*bis*/270*bis* [see Chapter 6 under 'STONE INSCRIPTIONS' for further explanation of the use of the suffix *bis*]). The words concerned are presented as SWT and BDH in both Ge'ez versions, and as COYATE and BEΔIE in Greek; their meaning in not known in either language – they may be toponyms. For the RIE, see Chapter 3, note 7.

[24] This feature may be clearly seen on the illustrations of RIE 185*bis* published by Uhlig (2001).

[25] Zitelmann 2007; Chrisomalis 2010: esp. 152–4; also Gragg 2004.

[26] For the Ethiopian calendar more generally, see Fritsch & Zanetti 2003.

[27] Magabit is a 30-day month, its first day being that designated 10 March by the Gregorian calendar. As noted in Chapter 7, mid-March would have been a good time of year to mount a raiding expedition such as that described in this inscription.

6

Some Written Sources relating to Aksumite Civilisation

To avoid repetition and encumbrance, basic information is here provided about a number of important written sources for the history of Aksumite civilisation to which frequent reference is made later in this book. Inclusion here is limited to those sources that are further considered in more than one of the thematic Chapters 7–16. Stone inscriptions are considered first, followed by manuscript material. Interpretations based on the content of these sources are discussed in these later chapters; here we are concerned primarily with such matters as their dating, provenance and integrity.

STONE INSCRIPTIONS

In reconstructions of Aksumite political and religious history, the evidence of the long monumental stone inscriptions recording the exploits of kings retains paramount importance, particularly when integrated with the recent achievements of numismatic studies and archaeological excavation. These inscriptions also yield data important in other areas of study that have so far received comparatively little attention. The published literature relating to these texts is very widely scattered, and much of it is not readily available. It is therefore appropriate that this re-evaluation should include a summary of the primary evidence, a guide to sources of more detailed information, and a commentary on some previous interpretations. The texts are in one of two languages: Greek and the local vernacular, Ge'ez. As noted in Chapter 5, two scripts were employed for writing distinct variants of Ge'ez.

The detailed *Recueil des inscriptions de l'Ethiopie des périodes axoumite et pré-axoumite* is noted in Chapter 3; its numbering system is here followed, prefixed by the abbreviation RIE.[1] The *Recueil*, as so far published, provides detailed primary data and a guide to sources; it does not attempt a critical evaluation of interpretations. It is consequently necessary for this book to make frequent reference to other publications, many of which pre-date 1991 and used different reference systems for the inscriptions. The system most frequently encountered – for inscriptions known in 1906 – is that published in the fourth volume of the report by the Deutsche Aksum-Expedition (DAE) led by Enno Littmann.[2] For ease of reference, a concordance of RIE and DAE numbers is provided here as Fig. 17.

[1] In the absence of a clear statement to the contrary, it may be assumed that a number following the prefix 'RIE' refers to an inscription and not to a page.

[2] Littmann *et al.* 1913, 4.

RIE	DAE	Ruler	Language	Script
186	8	Ella Amida ?	Ge'ez	ASAM-der., l-r
187	9	Ezana ?	Ge'ez	voc. Ethiopic
188	10	Ezana ?	Ge'ez	voc. Ethiopic
185	6	'ZN [Ezana]	Ge'ez	ASAM-der., r-l
185	7	'ZN [Ezana]	Ge'ez	unvocalised Ethiopic
270	4	AEIZANAC [Ezana]	Greek	Greek
185*bis*	-	'ZN [Ezana]	Ge'ez	ASAM-der., r-l
185*bis*	-	'ZN [Ezana]	Ge'ez	unvocalised Ethiopic
270*bis*	-	AEIZANAC [Ezana]	Greek	Greek
189	11	Ezana	Ge'ez	vocalised Ethiopic
271	-	AEIZANAC [Ezana]	Greek	Greek
190	-	'ZN [Ezana]	Ge'ez	ASAM-der., r-l
191	-	KLB [Kaleb] LSBH	Ge'ez	ASAM-der., r-l
192	-	WZB	Ge'ez	ASAM-der., r-l.
193–4	12-4	Dana'el	Ge'ez	part-vocalised Ethiopic

Fig. 17 Royal inscriptions at Aksum, correlating RIE and DAE reference-numbers, and with other details

Texts in Ge'ez employed two distinct scripts, although certain linguistic differences – discussed in Chapter 5 – are evident between them. This has resulted in controversy over the designation of those stone inscriptions that bear essentially the same text in two or more versions. The stone slabs with texts in ASAM-derived, Ethiopic and Greek scripts have often been described as 'trilingual', although there have been objections[3] that this is incorrect since three scripts are represented but only two languages. In view of the linguistic differences, this book retains the conventional 'trilingual' designation.[4]

It will be noted that RIE and DAE adopted different ways of identifying texts in these various languages and scripts. DAE allocated a separate number to each version, whether or not their content was identical or they were inscribed on the same stone. RIE gave single numbers to texts in Ge'ez, irrespective of the script employed, but different numbers to those in Greek; near-duplicate texts deemed to be in the same language were not numbered separately, but differentiated by use of the suffix '*bis*'. This complication is clearly illustrated by treatment of the two trilingual inscriptions (RIE 185/270 and 185*bis*/270*bis*), as demonstrated in Fig. 17.

Royal inscriptions at Aksum

The first of the royal stone inscriptions at Aksum to be recorded – by Henry Salt in 1805[5] – stood near the southeastern edge of the old built-up area, beside the road from Adwa. Long before this, the inscription had been visible to

[3] Notably by the late Roger Schneider (*e.g.* 1996).

[4] *cf.* also Uhlig 2001; Sima 2003–04.

[5] His account was published four years later (Salt in Valentia 1809, 3: 92–4).

travellers, several of whom had noted its presence without recording details; suggestions that it was 'discovered' by Salt are thus demonstrably incorrect. Salt did, however, clear away the earth to expose the lowest lines of the text, thus conducting the first known archaeological excavation in Ethiopia or Eritrea. The inscription's original location is marked on a sketch-plan produced by the Deutsche Aksum-Expedition in 1906,[6] and is shown in photographs that were taken at that time but not published until 1997.[7] In 1937 it was moved during Italian road-widening work and re-erected in the so-called Ezana Garden about 70 m southeast of its original position.[8] There, some four decades later, it was seen to be suffering serious deterioration and a roofed shelter was erected in order to protect it. The inscription is trilingual (*cf.* above) and bears two texts in Ge'ez – both designated RIE 185 – respectively in ASAM-derived script reading from right to left, and in unvocalised Ethiopic script, together with one in Greek – RIE 270.

Later in the nineteenth century and during the first decade of the twentieth, four further Ge'ez inscriptions came to light, all providing details of the titles and military exploits of King Ezana or his immediate predecessor. They are listed here in apparent order of discovery:

a) RIE 188. First recorded by Eduard Rüppell in the 1830s,[9] then by other nineteenth-century visitors, during which interval it suffered damage and textual loss, this slab was seen by the DAE in a private house with at least one other inscription (RIE 187). It was said – on what basis is unclear – originally to have been found in the vicinity of RIE 185/270 (*q.v.*, above). It is inscribed on one side in Ge'ez using vocalised Ethiopic script. The name of the king is only partly preserved, but *...zana* [Ezana] may be reconstructed with some confidence, and this is confirmed by later passages of the text including the patronymic 'son of Ella Amida' and the attribute '*bisi* Alene' which latter was used also on coins – exclusively those of Ezana.[10]

b) RIE 189. This also was recorded by Rüppell,[11] who did not state where it was kept, and subsequently by the DAE in 1906, by which time it was in the Cathedral Treasury.[12] The inscription is in Ge'ez, using a vocalised Ethiopic script. The name Ezana is incompletely preserved but, as on RIE 188, is confirmed by the patronymic, *bisi* name and royal titles noted in Chapter 8. This inscription's mention of the 'Lord of Heaven', formerly accepted as indicating Ezana's Christianity, is now attributed to a less specific monotheism like that also attested in southern Arabia by the mid-fourth century, as discussed in Chapter 9.

c) RIE 186 was recorded, broken in two pieces representing at least 90 per cent of the whole, in 1841;[13] subsequently the pieces became separated and only

[6] Littmann *et al.* 1913, 2: Abb. 90 (D. Phillipson 1997: fig. 174).

[7] D. Phillipson 1997: figs 208–9.

[8] Monneret de Villard 1938: 6. Unfortunately, the old Italian road was itself widened in 2009, with no prior archaeological investigation to ascertain whether any trace had survived of the inscription's original setting.

[9] Rüppell 1838–40, 1: xiii, 2: 277.

[10] For a discussion of *bisi*-names, see Chapter 8.

[11] Rüppell 1838–40, 1: xiii, 2: 277, 283.

[12] Littmann *et al.* 1913, 4: 32–42.

[13] Lefebvre 1845–51, 3: 435; Ferret & Galinier 1847, 1: 467.

one was noted by later nineteenth-century visitors. By 1906 the first piece was kept in the Cathedral Treasury, while the second was located beside the Church of the Four Animals.[14] There is no certain evidence as to the original position of this inscription although, six decades after its first record, Littmann[15] was told that it had been found close to the original site of RIE 185/270. The first line – where the king's name would have been inscribed – is damaged, but the Ge'ez words LM 'MDM [Ella Amida] may be read, implying that the missing name may have been that of Ezana, described on other inscriptions as 'son of Ella Amida', or of his immediate predecessor Ousanas Ella Amida himself.[16] The unusually elaborate script is ASAM-derived, written from right to left.

d) RIE 187. This was the one 'royal' inscription published by the DAE[17] that had not been recorded previously. It was found in 1906, together with RIE 188, hidden in a house where it was said to have been kept for several decades, there being no indication as to where it had originally been discovered. One face was inscribed in Ge'ez, using vocalised Ethiopic script. Breakage from the top of the slab had removed the first several lines of text: Littmann proposed, on the basis of formulae used in other inscriptions, that the missing section had comprised four lines, including the name and titles of Ezana, son of Ella Amida. While there seems no reason to question the implied fourth-century date, it is emphasised that this reading, including the name of Ezana, is speculative.

Three further inscribed stone slabs, bearing a total of four texts, were discovered in the late 1950s during building work in the Enda Sem'on area of Aksum, but were concealed by the land-owner/finder '*pour éviter des complications administratives*'.[18] They were not recorded until 1969.[19] All are now [2011] stored at Maryam Tsion Cathedral. One slab is inscribed in Greek (RIE 271) on one face, with a Ge'ez text in left-to-right ASAM-derived script (RIE 190) on the other face and continuing to one edge, where its termination is marked by a bold cross. The Greek text is in the name of Ezana;[20] no royal name is preserved in the Ge'ez, but there are good reasons[21] to assume that the two – which are on the same stone – were contemporaneous. Both the second and third slabs are inscribed in Ge'ez in right-to-left ASAM-derived script, one (RIE 191) in the name of Kaleb, and the other (RIE 192) in that of WZB, 'son of Kaleb'.

14 This (Littmann *et al.* 1913, 4: 18) refers to the early-twentieth-century Church of the Four Animals located west of the Old Cathedral, not to the earlier church of the same name in the southeastern area of Aksum. The two pieces of the inscription are now re-united and displayed in the Archaeological Museum at Aksum.

15 *ibid.*

16 R. Schneider 1987: 615; as Chapter 14 indicates, there are good reasons to attribute coins bearing the name of King Ousanas to Ezana's immediate predecessor. RIE 187, 188 and 189 specifically recorded that Ezana was the son of Ella Amida, The *Synaxarium* (Budge 1928a: 1164–5) named Ezana's father as 'Alameda', which is presumably to be equated with Ella Amida. For the probability that the Ella Amida of these sources and the Ousanas of the coins were one and the same person, see Chapter 14. Hahn (2006a: 262) stated firmly that RIE 186 was in the name, not of Ezana, but of his elder brother; in the present writer's opinion, this assertion is not supported by the available evidence.

17 Littmann *et al.* 1913, 4: 24–8.

18 R. Schneider 1974: 767.

19 Anfray *et al.* 1970; R. Schneider 1974.

20 Richard Pankhurst (in Huntingford 1989: 59–60) incorrectly stated that Ezana's name was not mentioned in RIE 271. He may have confused this text with RIE 190.

21 R. Schneider 1974, 1976b.

RIE 190 and 271. It has been suggested that these represent versions of the text preserved in Ethiopic Ge'ez on the previously known RIE 189. Both slabs indeed provide accounts of campaigns against the Noba and Kasu, but there are much greater differences between the texts than is observed on the two trilingual inscriptions RIE 185/270 and 185*bis*/270*bis*; furthermore, the stone slab on which RIE 189 was carved is significantly smaller in both height and width than that bearing RIE 190 and 271. Even if the inscriptions on the two slabs referred to the same campaign, it must be considered unlikely that they both formed parts of the same throne or other monument.[22] The important religious implications of RIE 190 and 271 are discussed in Chapter 9. The two texts also, and unusually, contained significant internal evidence for the date of the military campaign that they recorded and, by implication, for that of the religious situation prevailing at that time. Both texts mentioned that the campaign against the Noba and Kasu (Chapter 7) began with Ezana's departure from Aksum on the eighth day of the Aksumite month Magabit, it being specifically stated that this was a Saturday. There has been no lack of controversy concerning the precise dating,[23] but AD 349, 355 or 360, when 8 Magabit fell on a Saturday, are most widely accepted.[24]

RIE 191 and 192 are significantly younger than those discussed in the previous paragraph. The former, in the name of Kaleb, is broken at the lower left corner but the text – on one side of the slab only – is complete, albeit badly eroded.[25] The sixth-century royal titles recorded in these two inscriptions are discussed in Chapter 8. Military expeditions were conducted by Kaleb both in the northern Horn and in the southern Arabian kingdom of Himyar (see Chapter 15). The religious references are specifically and exclusively Christian, apparently including mention of church building both in Himyar and – less certainly – at Aksum.[26] The inscription of WZB (RIE 192) was divided between the two sides of a second stone slab, the first forty lines occupying the whole of one face, with ten further lines continuing on the upper part of the other. The text is poorly preserved, but it is clear that one or more military expeditions are recorded.[27] Several Old-Testament quotations are included, most of them from the Book of Psalms.

22 Arguments that most of the inscribed slabs – other than the two trilingual ones – were originally mounted as the sides and backs of thrones are presented in Chapter 11.

23 See discussion by Caquot and Nautin in Anfray *et al.* 1970.

24 Earlier and later dates are of course possible on purely calendrical grounds, but are not offered here in view of evidence (Chapter 9) that Ezana's Christianity was fully acknowledged by the sixth decade of the fourth century. Other fourth-century years when 8 Magabit fell on a Saturday were 304, 310, 321, 332, 338 ..... 366, 377, 383, 388 and 394 (I am grateful to Dr Tacye Phillipson for these computations). For further discussions of this date's significance, see Chapters 7 and 9.

25 R. Schneider (1974) translated an early reading of the poorly preserved text into French. English translations have been published by Huntingford (1989: 63–4) and by Munro-Hay (1991b: 230). Schneider's revised French version, noted as unpublished by Gajda (2009: 80), was prepared for a forthcoming fascicle of the RIE.

26 See Gajda 2009: 80. This inscription has also been interpreted as suggesting Kaleb's responsibility for the erection of Maryam Tsion Cathedral, further discussed in Chapter 11. In this context it may be noted that inscriptions bearing the name of Ella Asbeha [Kaleb] have also been reported from southern Arabia where that ruler is known to have conducted military operations (see Chapter 15). One, in Ge'ez, is included in the RIE (no. 195); for others, see Robin 2009.

27 R. Schneider 1974, 1973–79. The only attempted translation known to me is by Huntingford (1989: 65–6).

In 1981 a second trilingually inscribed stone was found by farmers near the northern edge of Aksum, beside the road that leads to the Tombs of Kaleb and Gabra Masqal.[28] Shortly after the discovery, a stone building was erected to protect the inscription which was not itself moved at that time. In 2000 the site was excavated[29] and the stone re-erected vertically, the building being retained without modification. The stone bears three texts in the name of Ezana, all of them near-duplicates of RIE 185/270; they are included in the RIE under the numbers 185*bis* [Ge'ez, in both unvocalised Ethiopic and right-to-left ASAM-derived scripts] and 270*bis* [Greek]. Being much better preserved than the trilingual inscription known previously, this new discovery permitted the elucidation of several unclear passages.

Omitting, for the moment, RIE 193 and 194 (*cf.* below), which are in the name of *hatsani* [= ruler] Dana'el and perhaps date to the eighth or early-ninth century, there are thus known from Aksum a total of nine slabs bearing royal inscriptions. All are in Ge'ez, but three of them (RIE 185, 185*bis* and 190) also have versions in Greek to which the RIE allocated separate numbers: respectively 270, 270*bis* and 271. Of the nine, seven are attributed to Ezana: three definitely, two probably, one possibly, and one (RIE 186) which belongs either to Ezana or to his immediate predecessor Ella Amida. One is in the name of Kaleb and one in that of his son WZB.

In terms of size, the inscriptions fall into two groups. The two trilingual examples (RIE 185/270 and 185*bis* /270*bis*) are relatively large and thick,[30] as befits their original free-standing situations, apparently in the open air, marking the northern and southeastern approaches to Aksum. The others are smaller and significantly thinner;[31] most show signs of further roughly executed thinning in the lowest part, immediately below the inscribed area. The measurements of these slabs match those of the slots on the throne-bases, into which they would have fitted according to the hypothesis[32] originally proposed by Daniel Krencker of the DAE (see Fig. 45). This function for the inscriptions is further discussed in Chapter 12.[33]

RIE 193 and 194 are inscribed on two components of a stone throne (*cf.* Chapter 12), lying close to the original site of the more southerly trilingual inscription of Ezana (RIE 185/270). It is clear that the monument had already become dismantled before the inscription was added. Both inscriptions are in Ge'ez, employing an incompletely vocalised Ethiopic script, but are faint and

28 Bernand 1982. A notice placed beside the inscription records the names of the original finders. For detailed discussion of the texts, see Uhlig 2001; Sima 2003–04.

29 Wendowski in Uhlig 2001: 8–10.

30 Respectively 2.47 m high x 0.98 m wide x 0.22 m thick and 2.68 x 0.92 x 0.26 m. It is only in the case of the thicker slab – discovered in 1981 – that the inscription extends onto one edge.

31 RIE 186–92 measure between 1.20 and 1.63 m high (average 1.44 m), between 0.50 and 0.64 m wide (average 0.56 m) and between 0.09 and 0.13 m thick (average 0.11 m). It is noteworthy that the widths fall into two mutually exclusive subgroups, respectively 0.50–0.54 m and 0.60–0.64 m.

32 Littmann *et al.* 1913, 2: 45, 62.

33 Of the slabs that were probably mounted as the backs or sides of thrones, all but two bear inscriptions on one face only. One exception is RIE 190/271, which is inscribed in Greek on one side, with Ge'ez in ASAM-derived script on the other side and on one edge. A. J. Drewes (in R. Schneider 1976a: 117) proposed that this slab formed the [sitter's] left side of the throne, with the Greek inscription on the inside and the Ge'ez on the outside, continuing on the front edge. The second two-sided inscription is that of the sixth-century WZB (RIE 192), where the single text has 40 lines on one face, continuing on the upper part of the other.

difficult to read. The first published record was produced by the DAE, but the readings obtained in 1906 by Littmann and those published by R. Schneider in 1991 are so divergent[34] that both should be regarded as highly tentative. Littmann's German translation of his reading has been rendered into English by both Stuart Munro-Hay and Tekle Hagos.[35] As noted by the latter author, the age of this inscription is uncertain, although it is certainly post-seventh century; Schneider's ninth-century palaeographic estimate remains plausible (see above and Chapter 16). The text, which has clear Christian connotations, appears to represent the record of one *hatsani*[36] called Dana'el who, having repelled a rival who had invaded Aksum, took command of that place himself. Both the reading and the meaning of these inscriptions are, however, uncertain; their historical significance is further considered in Chapter 16.

Inscriptions recorded at Adulis

A traveller, Cosmas, nicknamed 'Indicopleustes' [= voyager to India], visited Adulis in about 518–20, recording details in the lengthy *Christian Topography* that he compiled some 25 years later. He noted the presence, on the outskirts of the settlement, of two stone inscriptions, both in Greek.[37] It appears that King Kaleb, based in Aksum, had known of these inscriptions and asked his governor, Asbas, to obtain transcriptions of their texts. Asbas delegated this task to Cosmas and his companion Menas, with the result that a copy of their work was included in Cosmas' *Christian Topography*.[38]

It appears that there were two inscriptions, on separate monuments placed next to each other. No trace of either is known to have survived, so the *Christian Topography* is our sole source of information. This work unfortunately conflated the two texts, but it is clear that the older one (RIE 276), on basalt, was erected by Ptolemy III of Egypt; it is discussed in Chapter 3. It is only the later inscription (RIE 277), carved on a marble throne,[39] that is relevant here. It recorded military exploits of a king, whose name had not survived. There has been much controversy about the identities both of this monarch and of his kingdom, with attempts being made to attribute them to Aksum or to a kingdom on the Arabian side of the Red Sea.[40] The similarities – in textual style and in the royal titles – with inscriptions of the fourth-century Aksumite

34 Littmann *et al.* 1913, 2: 58–60, 4: 42–8; Bernand *et al.* 1991–2000, 1: 278–83.

35 Munro-Hay 1991b: 232; Tekle 2008: 13–18.

36 For discussion of this title, see Chapter 8.

37 Cosmas made no mention that either inscription was accompanied by a version in any other language. It is implied that Greek was not widely used at Adulis at the time of Cosmas' visit. I have been unable to find evidence to support the statement by McCrindle (1897: vi) that Kaleb 'could speak Greek'. The fact that transcription was – according to Cosmas – entrusted to him and Menas would seem to imply that literacy in Greek was uncommon amongst the sixth-century inhabitants of Adulis (*cf.* Chapter 5).

38 *Christian Topography* II 56–63. For the Greek text and a French translation, see Wolska-Conus 1968–73, 1: 368–79; an English version was provided by McCrindle 1897: 54–66. English renditions of the later inscription (RIE 277) were published by Kirwan 1972: 172–3 and Shitomi 1997: 84–5. Most surviving manuscripts of Cosmas' work contain a sketch-map depicting the inscriptions; this is discussed below (*cf.* Fig. 18).

39 This throne, as described by Cosmas (*Christian Topography* II 54; Wolska-Conus 1968–73, 1: 364–5) was apparently elaborately carved and completely different in form from those at Aksum (*cf.* Fig. 18).

40 Kirwan 1972, 1979; Beeston 1980; overview and additional references in Shitomi 1997 and Fauvelle-Aymar 2009.

kings are noteworthy, but geographical considerations weigh against either of these attributions. François-Xavier Fauvelle-Aymar has proposed an alternative attribution: to a ruler of an earlier kingdom with Hellenistic affinity that was located in the vicinity of Adulis itself.[41] This is fully concordant with the geography and with the suggestion made in this book (Chapters 7 and 8) that the Greek-speaking King Zoscales mentioned in the first-century *Periplus of the Erythraean Sea* (below) ruled in the coastal region rather than – as has usually been assumed – at Aksum. The similarity in titles with those of the later Aksumite kings is a further indication of the deliberate archaism for which there are several indications in the latter texts.

Inscription from Safra

This remarkable inscription (RIE 183) was discovered by a farmer, probably in the mid-1950s, at Zeban Kutur near Cohaito, Eritrea.[42] Its find-spot was not far from that of the inscribed copper-alloy figurine of a humped bovid, described in Chapter 10.[43] The Ge'ez inscription comprises four texts in unvocalised Ethiopic script, cut into a thin slab of stone that had been trimmed to a roughly square shape, 24 x 24 cm x *c.* 1 cm thick. Three of the texts are inscribed on the smoother side of the slab, with the fourth on the back. All are executed in a similar manner, arguably by the same hand, although the one text on the reverse of the slab may have been done slightly later than the others. The clearly legible and well-preserved lettering was executed freehand, cut rather than pecked, layout being clear and competent but somewhat careless in execution. It is noteworthy that numbers were here spelled out as words rather than presented as numerals. In the absence of any recorded archaeological associations, the only way in which the date of the Safra inscription may be estimated is by palaeographic comparison. The generally accepted view places it later than the GDR inscription (RIE 180; see Chapter 8) from the Addi Gelamo cache and earlier than the Matara stela (RIE 223; Chapter 9), implying a date in the second half of the third century.[44] Two factors, however, suggest the need for caution in accepting this estimate: no Aksumite inscriptions prior to the reign of Ezana are independently dated, and the differing materials and production-technologies involved make palaeographic comparisons difficult.[45]

The Safra texts, like others on similar thin slabs, appear to be relatively informal records or memoranda. The longest gave details of food and drink to be provided in circumstances that were not clearly specified but which may have involved the accommodation of a royal entourage. The authority likewise is uncertain: one reading[46] suggests reference to a kingdom called DWLY that is otherwise unknown. The stipulated provisions were modest, implying

41 Fauvelle-Aymar 2009.

42 The published information makes it difficult to pinpoint the location exactly, but it should not be confused through identity of name with the not-far-distant dam noted in Chapter 3.

43 Although the present location of the figurine is stated to be unknown (Bernand *et al.* 1991–2000, 1: 232), the inscription is in the National Museum, Addis Ababa.

44 Drewes 1962: 30.

45 For example, RIE 180 was incised into a cast object of copper alloy, RIE 183 was incised into schist and RIE 223 was pecked into trachytic rock. While inscriptions on schist are unusual, two others are known, both from Matara only 20 km from Safra (RIE 181, 182); both closely resemble that from Safra in size and lettering but are chance finds and neither is dateable on other than palaeographic grounds.

46 Drewes 1962: 38–9, 48.

that – whoever the donors or the recipients of these provisions may have been – neither party directly represented an entity that operated on the scale of the Aksumite kingdom. It is tempting to conclude that the Safra inscription dates from a time when this part of Eritrea had not yet been subsumed within Aksum's hegemony.

Inscription at Anza

First reported by Antonio Mordini in 1939, this fallen 6.5-m stela lies approximately 5 km north of Hawzien, in an area of eastern Tigray where extensive ancient remains await investigation. On one face it bears the crescent-and-disc symbol in relief; on the other – currently the underside – is an inscription (RIE 218)[47] of eight lines of Ge'ez in unvocalised Ethiopic script. Palaeographically, a third-century date is indicated. Although differing opinions have been expressed about the precise meaning of the text, it appears to record the erection of the stela at the instigation of a king of 'GB and the rations supplied to those who undertook the task (Chapters 7 and 10). As noted in Chapter 5, this inscription provides the earliest-known attestation of Ge'ez numerical notation.

MANUSCRIPTS OF ANCIENT TEXTS

The Periplus of the Erythraean Sea

This short but important work was compiled in Greek by an unknown Egyptian author who clearly had a detailed knowledge – not all of it necessarily obtained at first hand – of the coastlands of the Red Sea and Indian Ocean and of the trading conditions that prevailed there. Its style indicates that it was intended as a practical handbook rather than as a literary text. Numerous commentaries and translations have been published from the sixteenth century onwards, but that by Lionel Casson is widely accepted as definitive and is followed in this book.[48] Following considerable controversy over the date of its compilation, broad agreement was reached in the 1970s in favour of the mid-first century AD.[49] The possibility has not yet been fully considered, however, that additions or alterations may have been made to the text after its initial compilation.[50] Comparison of extant manuscripts can contribute little to resolution of these problems since the earliest surviving text – in Heidelberg – dates from the early-tenth century and has been described as containing a 'plethora of mistakes'.[51] Thus, although a mid-first-century date for the initial compilation of the *Periplus* may be accepted, it does not necessarily follow that every name or detail must be attributed to that early period.

[47] The most detailed available account of the inscription so far available is by Drewes (1962: 65–7). Professor Manfred Kropp has kindly provided me with a copy of his further study in advance of publication.

[48] Casson 1989. Other significant contributions include those by Schoff 1912, Huntingford 1980, and Seland 2007, 2010.

[49] *e.g.* Pirenne 1961; Robin 1991.

[50] This possibility was raised by J. Palmer 1947 but opposed by Fraser (1972, 2: 294) and Casson (1989: 7) who considered that the work had a unitary style. In the present writer's opinion, the latter view does not preclude a single compiler having worked from diverse materials.

[51] Casson 1989: 5.

The Kebra Negast

This Ge'ez text, of which many manuscripts – including summaries or partial versions – are extant, has accrued great – arguably undue – prominence in Ethiopian historiography. The work was originally untitled, *Kebra Negast* [= the Glory of the Kings] being the heading of its first chapter.[52] Although probably rendered in its current form in the early fourteenth century, there is good evidence that it incorporated material dating back a further seven hundred years. Together with much theological discourse on both Old- and New-Testament themes, it included a detailed account of the visit by Makeda, Queen of Sheba, to King Solomon of Israel,[53] of the birth of their son – Solomon's first – Menelik I, and of the latter's subsequent appropriation of the Ark of the Covenant which he brought to Ethiopia. A recurring theme was the seniority of the king of Ethiopia over the ruler of Rome/Constantinople. It was proposed that both these potentates could trace their descent from Solomon and had claim to 'Israelite' status, despite the strongly anti-Jewish sentiments expressed in other passages of the *Kebra Negast*. In terms of Western-style historiography, the chronology was confused and there was no effective distinction between pre-Christian and Christian periods. Notably, the brief mentions of events prior to the reign of Solomon were presented in exclusively Old-Testament terms, with no mention of Makeda's own antecedents that were recorded in other Ethiopian traditions. Likewise, Menelik's Ethiopian successors named in the Ethiopian king-lists (Chapter 8) received no notice, and there was no account of the advent of Christianity to Aksum.

Conflicting views have been expressed on the age and significance of this text. The most detailed study yet undertaken is that by David Hubbard in a doctoral dissertation which, although frequently cited by others, sadly remains unpublished.[54] Internal and external evidence strongly indicates that the fourteenth-century rendition of the *Kebra Negast* was undertaken as a prop to the so-called Solomonic dynasty[55] that had recently assumed the authority of the Ethiopian monarchy, and most accounts produced before the 1974 revolution emphasised this aspect, as formally enshrined in the 1955 Ethiopian Constitution. Subsequently, several new translations[56] of the *Kebra Negast* have appeared, some of which have been supported by Rastafarian interests.

Here, it is appropriate to emphasise the evidence for pre-fourteenth-century materials incorporated in the *Kebra Negast*. These have long been

[52] Beyond Ethiopia itself, attention was first focused on the *Kebra Negast* by James Bruce, who commissioned a copy to be made for him from a text kept at Maryam Tsion Cathedral at Aksum; this was subsequently acquired by the Bodleian Library in Oxford. Bruce (1813, 3: 411–16) also published an extensive summary of the book's contents. A copy in the Bibliothèque nationale, Paris, is probably the most ancient version extant, but not as early as the thirteenth-century date originally assigned by its cataloguer. In 1870 the passage (chapters xix–xxxii) relating to the Queen of Sheba was translated and discussed – all in Latin – by F. Praetorius of Halle; a German translation of the entire work was subsequently undertaken, with a detailed scholarly apparatus, by Carl Bezold (1905) of Munich. Bezold's work was thus the first published translation into a modern European language, contrary to the claim made by the publisher of a free English rendition – of sections relating to the Queen of Sheba – by van Vorst (1907). It was followed, in 1922 by Budge's English translation, with a comprehensive introduction. The best concise survey is by Marrassini (2007).

[53] Beylot 2004 provided a reconsideration of this aspect. In the *Kebra Negast*, the Queen of Sheba was accorded her New-Testament appellation *negasta azeb* [= the Queen of the South].

[54] D. Hubbard 1956, *The Literary Sources of the Kebra Negast*, unpublished doctoral dissertation, University of St Andrews.

[55] For the 'Solomonic' dynasty, see Chapters 1 and 17.

[56] *cf.* Wion 2009.

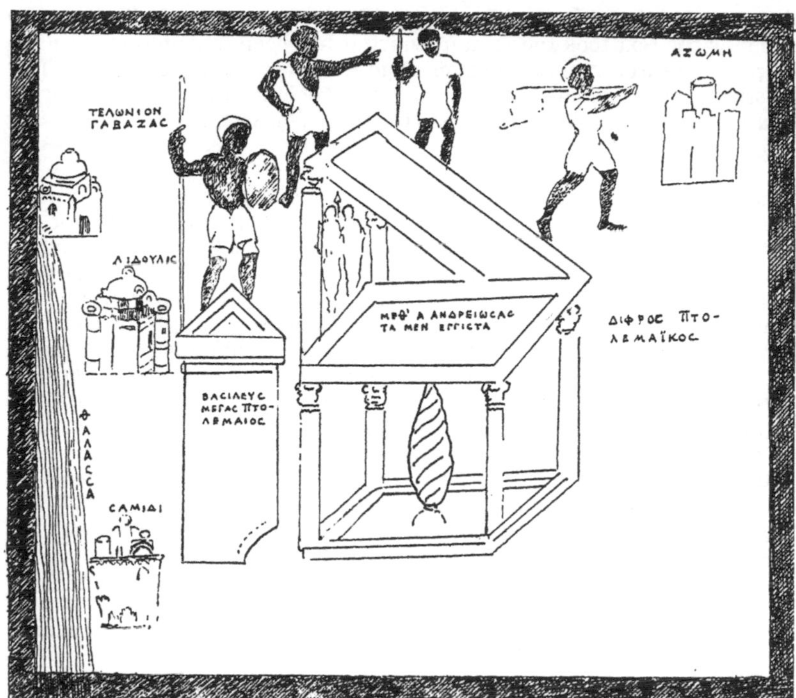

Fig. 18 Sketch-map of Adulis, Gabaza and Aksum, from a manuscript of Cosmas' *Christian Topography* (after Wolska-Conus 1968–73)

recognised[57] and, although some commentators[58] have attached little significance to them, throw considerable light on the earlier periods with which this book is primarily concerned. Some versions of the text include a colophon to the effect that the *Kebra Negast* was translated/compiled from an Arabic version by Yeshaq, known to have been *nebur'ed* of Aksum early in the fourteenth century.[59] The Arabic version seems to have been derived from Coptic about one hundred years earlier. None of this precludes the incorporation of much earlier material for which, indeed, there is strong internal evidence. In chapter cxvii of the *Kebra Negast* there is an account of the Aksumite King Kaleb and the Byzantine Emperor Justin I (518–27), both named, visiting Jerusalem together and dividing the world between them, it being recognised that Kaleb was *primus inter pares* as being descended from Solomon's first-born son, while Justin's ancestor was junior. The treatment in chapter l of the passage in Psalm 68, 31 'Ethiopia[60] shall stretch out her hands to God' has been claimed as having inspired a passage in an anonymous Syriac *Apocalypse* written during

[57] *e.g.* Budge 1922: xxiii–xc; Vasiliev 1933; Ullendorff 1960: 144; Shahid 1976; Fowden 1993: 113–4; Johnson 1995.

[58] Notably Munro-Hay 2001.

[59] The *nebur'ed* was the head of the Aksum ecclesiastical hierarchy. At least in later times, the holder of this office also exercised significant authority in non-ecclesiastical matters.

[60] The Hebrew 'Kush' was rendered 'Ethiopia' by the translators of the Greek Septuagint.

the second half of the seventh century.[61] The colophon thus indicates when and how the text took the form in which it has been transmitted since the fourteenth century, gaining great prestige and authority in the process.[62] This prestige is amply demonstrated by the request of Emperor Johannes IV for the return of the copy removed in 1868 to the British Museum.[63]

Illustrations accompanying the Christian Topography of Cosmas Indicopleustes
The *Christian Topography*, containing much valuable information for the historian of the Aksumite kingdom, was written in Greek by an author based in Alexandria or Sinai, probably during the early 540s.[64] This book makes considerable use of the exemplary edition and French translation of Wanda Wolska-Conus,[65] but there is one topic that requires further comment here. There has been much controversy over the significance of a series of illustrations that are included in several manuscripts of Cosmas' *Christian Topography*. Most significant for the present work is a map of the Aksumite port-area at Adulis (Fig. 18), showing a customs post at Gabaza and sketches of the two monuments bearing the Greek inscriptions that Cosmas transcribed at the request of the Aksumite king (see above and Chapter 3). The important question here is whether this map originated in the sixth century, perhaps even from the hand of Cosmas himself, or whether it was a subsequent addition to a manuscript, in which case its historical significance would be greatly reduced. The text of the *Christian Topography* survives in three early manuscripts,[66] one from the ninth and two from the eleventh century; the illustrations are present in all, although the text introducing the map is omitted from the earliest version. Wolska-Conus, whose knowledge of the work and illustrations is unparalleled, noted that Cosmas' text made numerous references to the illustrations and that the map was not a simple compilation of details contained in the text; she considered that it originated in the sixth century, thus endorsing the view presented earlier by Brubaker.[67] However, successive copyists clearly introduced significant differences, and the manuscripts preserve two very different versions of the map, reproduced by McCrindle and Wolska-Conus respectively.[68] These versions are clearly derived from a common source that was the work of someone who had access to information additional to that included in the *Christian Topography* text. While this observation could lend support to the attribution to Cosmas himself, the present writer feels unable to dismiss the possibility that the map is – at least in part – a later compilation.

61 See Fowden 1993: 132. The *Apocalypse* (A. Palmer *et al.* 1993) was probably written in northern Mesopotamia; its unknown author is sometimes designated 'Pseudo-Methodius'.

62 Heldman's (2007: 96) dismissal of the colophon as 'falsified' was not appropriate.

63 In 1872, it was duly 'returned to the King of Ethiopia by Order of the Trustees of the British Museum'. The book, bearing its British Museum stamps and the inscription here quoted, may still be seen in Addis Ababa. For details of this episode, see Rita Pankhurst 1989.

64 Wolska 1962.

65 Wolska-Conus 1968–73. The English translation by McCrindle 1897 is also useful.

66 Wolska-Conus *op. cit.*, 1: 44–134.

67 Brubaker 1977; Wolska-Conus 1990.

68 McCrindle 1897: pl. i; Wolska-Conus 1968–73, 1: 367.

7

The Emergence and Expansion of the Aksumite State

Definitions and chronology

The emergence of Aksumite civilisation was a gradual process, not necessarily concomitant with the extension of Aksum's political hegemony. As was shown in Chapter 3, many of its characteristics can be traced back into the period between the fourth and the second/first centuries BC at Beta Giyorgis. However, even there, no sharply defining initial stage may be recognised. Based primarily on artefact typology revealed in their important excavations, Rodolfo Fattovich and Kathryn Bard[1] placed the onset of Aksumite civilisation *c.* 400–350 BC, at the start of their 'Proto-Aksumite' period. That interpretation is not followed in this book, partly because of the conceptual difficulty of incorporating a strongly localised entity within one of hugely greater extent.[2] Instead, the defining stage is seen as concomitant with a shift in the focus of settlement from Beta Giyorgis to the lower and less circumscribed area between that hill and Mai Qoho (see Fig. 19). There, in an area that had apparently seen little previous settlement, rapidly developed the conurbation that ever since has been known as Aksum.

The time at which these developments took place cannot yet be estimated with any precision. On Beta Giyorgis, the excavators have defined the transition from their 'Proto-Aksumite' phase to their 'Early Aksumite' primarily on the basis of ceramic typology, and its date is not fully clear. The estimate of 150 BC originally published has been replaced by one of 50 BC,[3] but in neither case has its basis or justification been clearly set out. In the present writer's opinion, an age in the first half of the first century AD provides a better fit with the historical data, while taking account of archaeological evidence from Aksum as well as from Beta Giyorgis.[4] This later date has wider relevance to areas where continuity from earlier times is less apparent.

At Aksum itself, little is known about the earliest phases, such as might aid our understanding of the transition. Archaeological investigation has been restricted by the presence of the modern town, and penetration of the lowest levels is impeded by later features which merit preservation. The earliest traces have been encountered in two areas: the principal burial ground at the south-eastern foot of Beta Giyorgis and, a short distance to the south, the area now occupied by the cathedrals of Maryam Tsion. In both places, confused stratig-

[1] *e.g.* Fattovich 2010.

[2] The difficulty is exemplified by the application of the 'Proto-Aksumite' label and its dating in the Gulo Makeda area, 130 km east of Beta Giyorgis (D'Andrea *et al.* 2008a), and at Emba Derho near Asmara (Schmidt *et al.* 2008c).

[3] See, in particular, Bard *et al.* 2003; Fattovich 2010.

[4] Michels (2005: 129) also preferred a later date and placed the transfer from Beta Giyorgis in the second stage of his 'Early Aksumite' period.

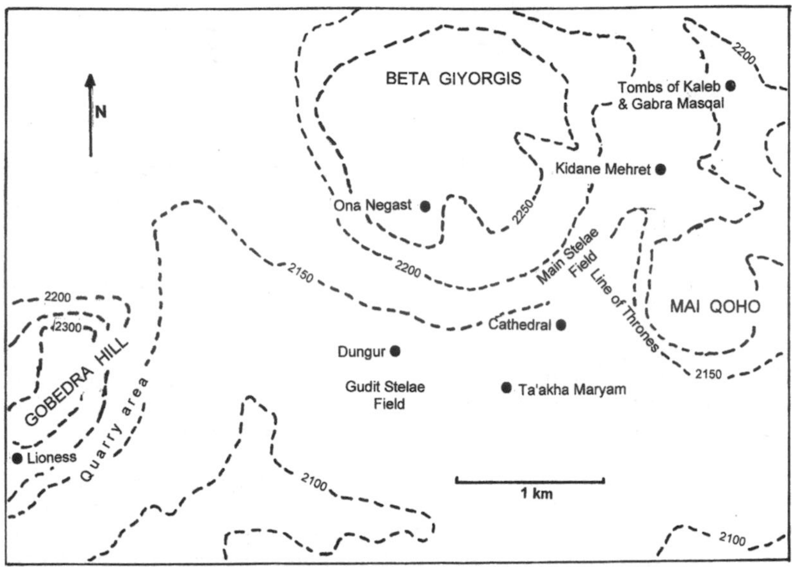

Fig. 19 The Aksum area, showing principal archaeological sites

raphy proved difficult to interpret, and it is to be hoped that future work will provide much-needed clarification. Excavations in the burial area indicated features dated – somewhat imprecisely – to the first century AD.[5] A series of platforms analogous to earlier examples at Beta Giyorgis was constructed as settings for shaft-burials marked by small stelae. Subsequently, by the late third century, these platforms were incorporated within a single huge terrace used for grandiose tombs and stelae, as described and illustrated in Chapter 12. The second area where traces of early occupation have been recognised was investigated in the 1950s during preparation for building the New Cathedral.[6] Here was revealed a series of monumental buildings, apparently of early date with some of them preceding construction of the Cathedral podium; but constraints of space and time prevented comprehensive investigation.

The reasons for the move from Beta Giyorgis are not at all clear, but may have been linked to ease of communication, both with the hinterland whose water and produce was required to support a growing population, and with tributary and trading contemporaries further afield; the need to occupy a defensible location may also have diminished. Beta Giyorgis offered only limited land for grazing and cultivation. The move to lower ground facilitated the keeping of larger herds of cattle, as indicated by the excavated faunal assemblages. It is noteworthy that, following the move to Aksum, Ona Negast and other sites on Beta Giyorgis were not abandoned, but continued as peripheral settlements lacking the grand developments that took place at the new capital.[7] As noted in Chapter 8, there is

[5] Chittick 1974: 164–9; Munro-Hay 1989a: 60–104, 150–5, 329–31.

[6] Caquot & Leclant 1956; de Contenson 1959a, 1959c, 1963a; no full report of this, nor of subsequent work nearby by Anfray (1963b), has been published. The Cathedral precinct is clearly an area of great archaeological interest and potential, but its comprehensive investigation has not yet been permitted by the ecclesiastical authorities.

[7] Bard *et al.* 1997, 2003; Fattovich *et al.* 2000, Michels 2005: 123–53.

epigraphic evidence for a king of Aksum from about AD 200, but the extent of the territory that he ruled at this early date remains unknown.

A further factor in the rise of a major polity in this region was the availability of elephant-ivory. The Aksumite heartland lay far beyond the range of the Ptolemaic hunters noted in Chapter 3; large herds of elephants were reported in central Tigray or south-central Eritrea during the sixth century, and artistic representations suggest that they were still familiar to the region's inhabitants long afterwards.[8] Further to the west, they survived even longer: during the second half of the nineteenth century, elephants were still plentiful south of the Takezze-Atbara in what is now the frontier area between Sudan and Ethiopia, while they were recorded in the late-twentieth century in the extreme southwest of Eritrea, barely 150 km west of Aksum.[9] By the third century, if not before, export of ivory contributed greatly to Aksum's prosperity, as discussed in Chapter 15.

Before proceeding further, it will be wise to clarify a possible ambiguity. The location called Aksum[10] gave its name to a kingdom that eventually achieved very great extent. There can be no doubt that the king was, first and foremost, the ruler of Aksum. In the fourth-century stone inscriptions, his title 'king of Aksum' was placed before 'king of kings' and the listing of peripheral territories over which – on whatever grounds – he claimed suzerainty.[11] Further substantial areas on the periphery of this kingdom owed enforced nominal allegiance to the Aksumite king and paid him tribute. For clarity, simple mention of 'Aksum' will, in this book, always refer to the site itself; the adjective 'Aksumite' will be employed more broadly, with the associated noun indicating whether reference is made to the capital, the kingdom, or some other feature; likewise, the noun 'Aksumites' will apply to inhabitants of the kingdom, not just to those of its capital.

Attempts to establish internal periodisations of Aksumite civilisation have tended to be based on narrow considerations, usually numismatics or ceramic typology relevant to a particular site or area.[12] For multi-disciplinary coverage, such as is attempted here, a more broadly based framework is required. Fig. 20 tabulates a selection of the schemes that have been proposed by several researchers; although a fair measure of agreement has been achieved, the overall picture is confusing. It may now be recognised that, with the increased refinement of chronologies based on radiocarbon analyses and on historical correlations, definition of phases based on artefact typology imparts a misleadingly rigid compartmentalisation and is becoming increasingly redundant; as noted in Chapter 1, wherever possible this book relies on estimates of absolute dates rather than on arbitrary periodisations.

Kingdoms immediately preceding Aksumite expansion

There is limited evidence for the existence of independent kingdoms during the first two centuries AD in areas that were subsequently made subject to Aksum. This evidence comes mainly from the coastal region centred on Adulis

[8] *e.g.* Nonnosus in Freese 1920: 17–20; Littmann *et al.* 1913, 4: 70.

[9] Baker 1867: 478–80; Mayo 1876: 157–60; Bustorf & Smidt 2005.

[10] Various etymologies have been proposed for this toponym (*e.g.* R. Schneider 1994; Tekle 2010), invoking both Cushitic and Semitic elements.

[11] In Greek, the form ΒΑCΙΛΕΥC ΑΞΩΜΙΤΩΝ [= king of the Aksumites] was employed, following common usage in that language. Inscriptions on coins used similar forms, whether in Greek or in Ge'ez.

[12] *e.g.* those proposed respectively by Munro-Hay & Juel-Jensen 1995 and by Fattovich and Bard. The latter has been published in successive revisions, most recently by Fattovich 2010.

BC / AD	Michels (2005)	Fattovich (2010)	D. Phillipson (2000b)
1000	----------		
	Late Post-Aksumite	Post-Aksumite	
900			Post-Aksumite

800	Early Post-Aksumite		
		----------	----------
700	----------		
		Late Aksumite	
600	Late Aksumite		Late Aksumite

500		Middle Aksumite	----------

400		----------	
			Classic Aksumite
300	Early Aksumite		
		Classic Aksumite	----------
200			
	----------	----------	Early Aksumite
AD 100			
		Early Aksumite	----------
0	Late Pre-Aksumite		

BC 100			
	----------	Proto-Aksumite	
200			
	Middle Pre-Aksumite	----------	
300		Late Pre-Aksumite	
400		----------	
500			
	Early Pre-Aksumite	Middle Pre-Aksumite	
600			
700	----------	----------	
800			
		Early Pre-Aksumite	
900			

1000			

Fig. 20 Some proposals of phasing for Aksumite civilisation and its predecessors

and from the adjacent highlands of south-central Eritrea and northeastern Tigray. Archaeological knowledge is derived mainly from excavations at Adulis and Matara, neither of which have been adequately published: outline details are noted here, but emphasis must also be placed on the relevant texts and inscriptions despite the chronological uncertainties that surround them.

It is frequently stated that the Zoscales named in the *Periplus of the Erythraean Sea*[13] was a king of Aksum during the mid-first century AD. However, although clear mention is made of Aksum, nowhere in the text is it explicitly stated that Zoscales reigned there. Both a careful reading of the *Periplus*' Greek text, and a more general consideration of what is known from other sources about the growth of the Aksumite state, suggest that Zoscales' rule was probably restricted to the coastal region centred on Adulis.[14] This interpretation is in accord with the attribution of RIE 277 to a ruler of a coast-centred kingdom during the first two centuries AD.[15]

While the *Periplus* mentions Zoscales in the context of Adulis-based trade, there is no indication that the port was his capital. The history of Adulis is not easy to reconstruct either from available archaeological records or from literary references; in both cases data relating to the sixth century are more comprehensive than those for earlier periods.[16] Archaeological investigation beside the Gulf of Zula has rarely penetrated levels that pre-date the period when the principal port of the Aksumite kingdom occupied the site, but it is clear that occupation began during the first millennium BC or – conceivably – earlier.[17] Recorded details about this early occupation are, however, extremely sparse.

Our knowledge of the plateau sites is somewhat more comprehensive. The period before the last century BC is discussed in Chapter 3. There are indications both at Matara and in the Gulo Makeda region that intensive settlement was effectively continuous between then and the time of the areas' respective incorporation within the Aksumite kingdom.[18] A 5-m stela at Matara bears a crescent-and-disc symbol at its apex and, lower down, an unvocalised Ge'ez inscription relating to the monument's erection but giving no information about the status or authority of those involved.[19] Although neither of these archaeologically investigated areas has yielded information relating to their political status at this time, there are two further inscriptions that contribute useful data. Some 70 km to the south, the similar-sized Anza stela (Chapters 6 and 10) likewise bears the crescent-and-disc, together with an unvocalised Ge'ez inscription (RIE 218) that is palaeographically similar to, but possibly slightly later than, that on its Matara counterpart. The Anza inscription records

13 *Periplus* 5 (Casson 1989: 53, 109–10; see also Chapter 6).

14 This point was made by Dillmann 1879 and then by Kirwan 1979 and Huntingford 1980: 147, the latter was noted with approval by Chittick 1981, but seems otherwise to have escaped consideration until revived by Fauvelle-Aymar 2009.

15 Fauvelle-Aymar 2009; Chapter 6. This attribution, following suggestions by – *e.g.* – Dillmann 1878, attributed the inscription to Zoscales or one of his successors.

16 It is not even certain that the port called Adulis was always located in the same place. While most authorities assume that it was always situated near the western shore of the Gulf of Zula (Peacock & Blue 2007), Casson's (1981, 1989: 102–6) view that – at least in earlier times – it occupied the site of the modern Massawa, some 40 km to the north, should probably not be dismissed.

17 Paribeni 1907; Anfray 1974; Fauvelle-Aymar 2009: 147–9, fig. 1.

18 Anfray 1974, 2007; Negussie 1994; Curtis & Daniel 2008; D'Andrea *et al.* 2008a.

19 Ullendorff 1951; Kropp 2006a.

that the stela was erected at the instigation of a king who ruled over a territory known as 'GB.[20] Much closer to Matara is the find-spot of the remarkable Safra inscription (RIE 183; see Chapter 6), interpreted as referring to a minor kingdom called DWLY.[21] Neither 'GB nor DWLY are otherwise known. Taken together, however, we have indications of two presumably distinct kingdoms during the first three centuries AD in territories that subsequently formed eastern parts of the Aksumite hegemony.

Expansion of the Aksumite kingdom

By the second half of the third century AD, Aksum's prosperity had vastly increased. Long-distance trade, based at least in part on the exploitation of resources over a wide area, together with control of labour on an unprecedented scale, strongly suggest that territorial expansion had already been under way for at least several decades.[22] More detailed information comes from the fourth-century royal inscriptions at Aksum (see Chapter 6) which indicate military consolidation, implying that the process of expansion had begun earlier. The expedition against the Noba and Kasu, described in RIE 190 and 271, departed on the eighth day of the month Magabit [mid-March of the Gregorian calendar], representing probably the best season of the year for such a raid, and implying that seasons for military expeditions may have been carefully chosen. Despite the difficulty of identifying the peoples and places involved, these inscriptions also provide some indication of the territorial extent of Aksumite influence at that period.

Attempts to estimate the extent of the Aksumite hegemony must recognise that this changed significantly over time. The discussion is usefully combined with a consideration of the possible mechanisms by which control was exercised. Three principal sources of evidence are available, each beset with its own problems. Since the distribution of archaeological sites and materials remains poorly recorded through most of the regions of Eritrea and northern Ethiopia with which this study is concerned,[23] their assessment remains an inconclusive guide to the fluctuating extent of Aksumite influence. Oral traditions, whether or not subsequently committed to writing, are subject to problems of transmission. As discussed in Chapter 1, very little if any of this material is demonstrably contemporary with the events to which it ostensibly relates. Thus, unless they can be linked with evidence from primary contexts, such sources must be treated with reserve. The final group of sources, and at first sight the most promising, is the series of stone inscriptions which record military campaigns and other events connected with the maintenance and/or expansion of Aksumite rule. These sources are informative despite their restricted chronological range, but their value largely depends on our ability to understand the geographical significance of ancient place-names.

[20] Drewes 1962: 65–7; Kropp in press. A word BZT, interpretation of which is uncertain, may be the king's name.

[21] Drewes 1962: 30–64.

[22] Archaeological survey (*e.g.* Michels 2005; L. Phillipson 2009a, 2009b; unpublished), despite much unrecorded evidence having been destroyed by uncontrolled modern development, continues to yield evidence with which this conclusion is not incompatible, but its dating lacks precision.

[23] This is due both to the very incomplete coverage of research, and to the difficulty of establishing a chronological framework for the chance surface finds that are, in many places, all that are available. Comprehensive records published by Godet (1977, 1983) made little attempt to distinguish materials of different periods, and have not been comprehensively updated.

Several of the fourth-century inscriptions at Aksum describe relations with neighbouring lands and peoples; RIE 186 also mentions improvements to the roads.[24] Since it seems likely that the timespan covered by these inscriptions was only a few decades, the evidence that they provide may be considered together. Also relevant – despite an apparent difference in date – is the inscription RIE 277 copied at Adulis by Cosmas Indicopleustes from a marble throne that was probably set up by a king of the coastal region in about the second century AD (see above and Chapter 6).

All six texts on Ezana's two trilingual slabs (RIE 185, 185*bis*, 270, 270*bis*) record the repression of a revolt by a people known as Bega: captives were taken and settled in Aksumite-controlled territory at a place called Matlia.[25] The unvocalised RIE 186 mentions several peoples including the kingdoms of 'GDT [Agwezat?], GBZ [Gabaz], HMS, SMN [Samen] and WYLQ. RIE 187 refers to the Agwezat and to seventeen additional place-names, including Hatsabo, which could all indicate localities relatively close to Aksum,[26] RIE 188 mentions the Afan who were on a trade-route with which they interfered. RIE 189 and 190/271 contain references to the Noba and Kasu. RIE 277 provides additional data. These names may now be considered separately:

Afan: this was Littmann's reading of RIE 188, following Rüppell, but the 'fa' is unclear in both places where the word occurs and Huntingford suggested Awan,[27] which could be the Aua/Aue of Cosmas and Nonnosus, probably somewhere north or northeast of Yeha (see Chapter 16).

Agwezat: According to the unvocalised Ge'ez (*cf.* Chapters 5 and 6) RIE 186, their king [NGS] was called SWST and paid tribute at a place called LBH. However, the vocalised Ge'ez RIE 187 gives the name of their king (*negusa*) as Aba'alke'o and the place of his meeting with the Aksumites as Angabo.[28] The older Greek inscription (RIE 277) copied from the throne at Adulis recorded war with a people called Gaze who may or may not be the same as the Agwezat.[29]

The **Bega** may confidently be identified with the Beja (or Bedja) who inhabited territory east of the Nile in what is now the northern Sudan, being thus northerly neighbours of the Aksumites.[30]

24 The attribution of this inscription to Ezana's father, Ella Amida, is uncertain (see Chapter 6) but in any event a date in the first half of the fourth century may be considered secure. For further discussion of roads, see Chapter 13 and Fig. 68.

25 Matlia is the name given in the Greek texts; its counterpart in the Ge'ez versions is MD (R. Schneider 1984; Uhlig 2001).

26 See discussion by Huntingford (1989: 53–4).

27 References are to Littmann 1950: 110, Rüppell 1838–40, 2: 277 and Huntingford 1989: 55.

28 Although generally read as referring to a military campaign or conquest, with details of tribute exacted, Kobishchanov (1979: 164) argued that in fact RIE 186 referred to an expedition for the collection of tribute from an already-subject population.

29 For this inscription, see Chapter 6. Two eleventh-century manuscripts of Cosmas' text (*Christian Topography* II 60) preserve a copyist's note – absent from the sole surviving ninth-century version – that sought to identify the Gaze with the Agazi, a name that the copyist regarded as synonymous with 'Aksumites' (Wolska-Conus 1968–73, 1: 374). This identification – probably correct (*cf.* Fauvelle-Aymar 2009: 143) – has not been taken into account by all recent commentators (*e.g.* Kirwan 1972; Shitomi 1997); it provides a strong argument against the attribution of RIE 277 to an Aksumite king.

30 See Procopius, *History of the Wars* I xix 27–37 (Dewing 1914–28, 1: 184–9). The Beja were also known, particularly in earlier times, as Blemmyes (Edwards 2004: 250–1) on whom see also Updegraff 1988 and Welsby 2002.

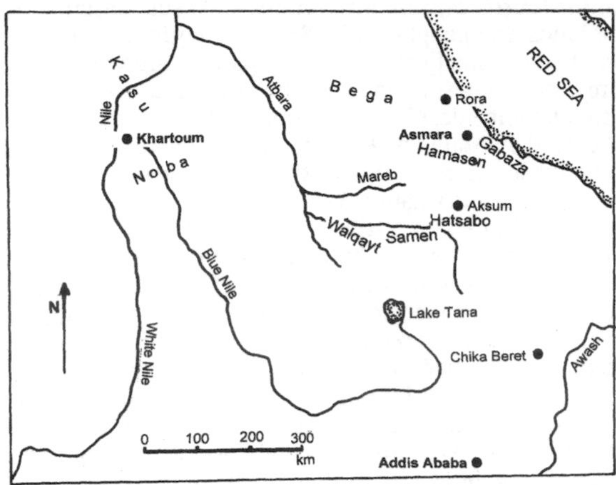

Fig. 21 Map to illustrate the expansion and conquests of the Aksumite kingdom, according to prevailing identifications of names recorded in the fourth-century royal inscriptions

Gabaz: probably refers to the region of Adulis, where a place of this name was recorded on the map (Chapter 6; Fig. 18) included in the earliest extant manuscripts of Cosmas' *Christian Topography.*[31]

Gaze: see Agwezat.

HMS: perhaps Hamasen, the plateau area around Asmara.[32]

Hatsabo is the name of the plain in the immediate vicinity of Aksum.

Kasu: almost certainly Kush, in the northern Sudanese Nile Valley.[33]

The location of **Matlia**, where the Bega were resettled, is unknown; the Greek wording of the relevant inscriptions implies that readers were not expected to be familiar with the name.[34]

The **Noba** are probably the same as the people called Nuba in Kaleb's inscription RIE 191, *i.e.* Nubians.

Samen: the stone inscription at Aksum attributed to Ella Amida (RIE 186) mentioned that the inhabitants of SMN were pacified and made tributary. The snow-covered Simien mountains were also mentioned in RIE 277 at Adulis, with a note – or subsequently inserted gloss – to the effect that this was a

[31] This map (Fig. 18) is further discussed in Chapter 6; see also Littmann 1907; Wolska-Conus 1968–73, 1: 366–7; Peacock & Blue 2007: *passim.*

[32] Smidt 2005.

[33] Lusini 2007.

[34] Both Kobishchanov (1979: 166) and Munro-Hay (1991b: 51) suggested the possibility that the Beja were resettled somewhere in Begameder, an area extending from the Takezze southwards and westwards to Lake Tana. While possible, this speculation is based on an unproven etymology.

Fig. 22 The sphinx-like carving at Chika-Beret, south of Dessie: the Christian-style cross between the paws appears to have been cut into an earlier inscription

place to which criminals or outlaws were banished by the king of Aksum.[35] It is not wholly clear from this whether the mountains were fully included within Aksum's hegemony, but the area does not appear to have been actively hostile to Aksumite interests. The name Samen, or Simien, currently signifies 'north' in Amharic, which is concordant with the mountains' geographical position relative to Amhara territory. It is, however, interesting to find them known by the same name in an Aksumite inscription, since they lie to the south of Aksum – whence they can, indeed, be seen on a clear day.[36]

WYLQ: possibly Walqayt, the area southwest of Aksum and beyond the northward bend of the Takezze.[37]

Several other regions were noted that were raided and where tribute was exacted, but they were not designated kingdoms. Manuscript copies survive of several charters that purport to record Aksumite kings' land-grants to churches and monasteries; in all cases the manuscript copies that survive are of much later date, and the authenticity of the texts is open to serious doubt.[38] These locations, in so far as they may with reasonable confidence be ascertained, are plotted on the accompanying map (Fig. 21), from which may be gleaned

[35] Cosmas, *Christian Topography* II 60 (McCrindle 1897: 61–2, 67; Wolska-Conus 1968–73, 1: 80–6, 374–9). The note about banishment is either part of Cosmas' sixth-century commentary or a – possibly – subsequent addition; it does not form part of the inscription.

[36] A. Pankhurst (1989 citing Dillmann 1865: cols 105, 334) has drawn attention to a reversal of the terms for north [now *samen*] and south [now *dabub*] respectively. Dillmann's proposed derivation of *samen* from Syriac is now considered improbable. Is it not more likely that the name originally designated the mountains, being subsequently adopted to indicate the direction in which they were located?

[37] Nosnitsin 2010. Since the nineteenth century if not before, Walqayt has been known, *inter alia*, for cotton production. Note, however, Huntingford's (1989: 52; but see Taddesse 1993) tentative suggestion that the much more southerly Walaqa region may have been meant.

[38] *cf.* Huntingford 1965a, 1989: 60–1. Claims by churches and monasteries for Aksumite royal foundation are further discussed in Chapters 16 and 17.

an approximate idea of the extent both of the Aksumite kingdom, and of those neighbouring polities from which it exacted tribute.

Aksumite presence and/or influence further afield is not easy to evaluate. There may have been a tendency in later times to assume or exaggerate Aksumite connections with peripheral areas. Coverage of archaeological survey is not yet sufficiently comprehensive to yield credible negative results. The most northerly sites currently known to have yielded materials indicative of Aksumite presence or dominant influence are located in the Rora area approximately 180 km north of Asmara.[39] To the west, such sites are known in the Shire district of Tigray.[40] To the south, in the highlands of what is now Ethiopia's Amhara Region, ruins and other remains have been reported which, although not yet dated or adequately published, could plausibly be interpreted as Aksumite in affinity.[41] Even further to the south, at Chika-Beret some 30 km south-east of Dessie, a rock outcrop carved to a sphinx-like form (Fig. 22) has been known since 1843 but has received little detailed attention.[42] Stylistic arguments for its Aksumite affinity are not wholly convincing, and its location close to a possible route between the highlands and the Red-Sea port of Assab may not be relevant in the absence of any evidence that Aksumites made use of a port so far to the south.[43] Later Aksumite connections with southerly and westerly regions are discussed in Chapter 15.

The processes through which territories were brought under Aksumite control are illuminated – albeit imperfectly – by the fourth-century stone inscriptions. The ruler of a neighbouring population was made subject to the Aksumite king and obliged by military action to pay tribute as a mark of subordination. The extent to which this resulted in other forms of control and exploitation remains unclear, but relocation of entire populations seems sometimes to have accompanied these processes. Revolt or hostility was usually cited as a pretext for annexation, but in such a way that it is often unclear whether territorial expansion or punishment for insubordination is recorded. In some cases, numerous captives and livestock were apparently brought back to Aksum, perhaps both to weaken the annexed territory and to augment the labour and other resources readily available near the capital (*cf.* the trilingual inscriptions, as noted above). Inscriptions of Kaleb and his son WZB imply similar operations, but several of their features – including their use of titles – display consciously archaic forms, and it would be unwise to conclude that 'pacification' of subordinate neighbours necessarily continued into the sixth century.

So much of our information about the expansion of the Aksumite kingdom is derived from the stone inscriptions of Ezana that it is tempting to draw the conclusion that expansion took place mainly during the middle decades of the fourth century. This might be a mistake; the concentration of inscriptions may be due to the vaguaries of preservation and/or to a predilection for self-publicity on Ezana's part. The process described probably began well before the fourth century, and may have continued for some time afterwards. Clarification must await archaeological investigations in the areas that were incorporated within the Aksumite hegemony or where conquered people were resettled.

39 Piva 1907; Manzo 2010.

40 Cossar 1945; Finneran & Phillips 2003; Finneran *et al.* 2005.

41 See, for example, Anfray 1970; Chojnacki 2005a. Kirwan 1972 also discussed possible southward extension of Aksumite authority and/or influence.

42 Lefebvre 1845–51, 3: 427 and atlas: pl. viii; also Anfray 1970: 34–5, 47.

43 Claims for Aksumite use of ports on the southern shore of the Gulf of Aden (*e.g.* Doresse 1971: 93–6) are likewise unproven (Desanges & Reddé 1993).

8

Aksumite Kingship and Politics

Since much of our information about Aksumite politics is derived from what was essentially royal propaganda, it is not surprising – although nonetheless unfortunate – that we know very little about the lower levels of administration.

The king

There can be no reasonable doubt that the prime authority in the Aksumite state was that of the king. For reasons set out in Chapter 7, the hypothesis that the Zoscales mentioned in the *Periplus of the Erythraean Sea* was a first-century king of Aksum is not accepted here. The earliest incontrovertible and dateable mention of an Aksumite king dates about 150 years later and occurs, not at Aksum itself, but on an inscribed copper-alloy object (Fig. 23) found in a cache at Addi Gelamo in the eastern highlands of Tigray.[1] The inscription (RIE 180), which seems to have been incised into the object after it had been cast, is in Ge'ez, using an early form of unvocalised Ethiopic script read from left to right; it mentions GDR NGSY KSM [= GDR, king of Aksum]. Note that, at this early period, the king of Aksum already bore the title *negus* (*cf.* below). It is tempting, but not wholly convincing, to equate this individual with an Aksumite ruler called GDRT, known from inscriptions in southern Arabia of roughly the same period.[2] Southern Arabian inscriptions name three further individuals as kings of Aksum, but give no indication that they exercised political control – as opposed to more transitory influence – over Arabian territory.[3] There is likewise no evidence that any area of the northern Horn was subject to Arabian rule at this period.

Based on the style of the lettering, the date of RIE 180 has been estimated as *c.* AD 200.[4] If this date for GDR's reign is accepted, the Aksumite kingdom must have developed by the end of the second century AD.[5] During the following two hundred years it expanded greatly through the incorporation of neighbouring polities. The extent of the territory over which GDR ruled cannot be ascertained. Since the Addi Gelamo cache comprised disparately-dated materials brought together from elsewhere, it cannot be regarded as proof that this part of the

1 Kropp 1994. The cache and its contents are discussed in Chapter 3 (see also Caquot & Drewes 1955: esp. 32–9).

2 Sima 2005.

3 For contrary views, see Robin 1989; Shitomi 1997.

4 R. Schneider 2000.

5 This conclusion agrees closely with that of Michels (2005: 123–53; see Chapter 7), based on totally independent arguments.

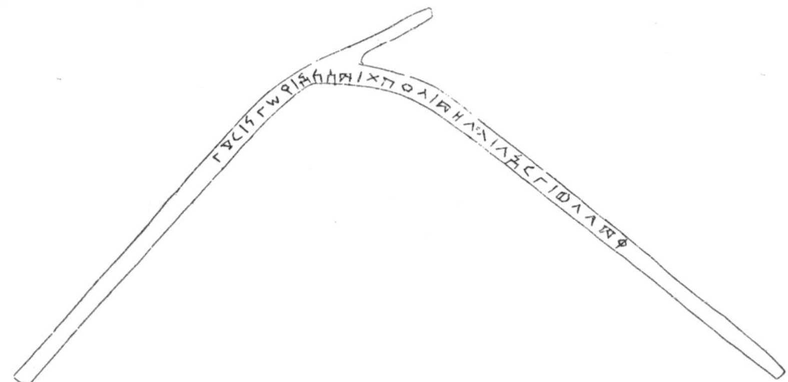

Fig. 23 The copper-alloy object from the Addi Gelamo cache (after Bernand *et al.* 1991–2000); the inscription records 'GDR, king of Aksum'

Tigray eastern highlands formed part of Aksum-controlled territory as early as AD 200.

A stone inscription in Greek (RIE 275), thought to date from the third century, was reported in 1906 as having been found at Daqqi Mahari in Eritrea, *c.* 40 km north of Asmara. It provides another name – CEMBPOYΘHC [Sembrouthes] – of an individual described as 'great king', 'king of kings of the Aksumites'.[6] However, doubt has recently been cast on the historicity of this text.[7]

Such evidence as we have suggests that succession to the Aksumite kingship was patrilineal, from father to son or – in certain circumstances – between consanguineous brothers. For example, both Ezana and Kaleb followed their fathers on the throne, while at least two of Kaleb's sons ruled successively. To what extent primogeniture was involved cannot be determined.[8] Neither do we know whether monogamy prevailed nor – if it did not – how the resultant complications were resolved. The fact that we have no clear evidence for rival claimants of the Aksumite throne does not necessarily mean that such disputes did not occur.[9] Only one instance of abdication by an Aksumite king – by Kaleb in the mid-sixth century – is recorded.[10] The controversy over whether Aksumite kings exercised individual authority, or whether some system of shared or joint rule may at times have prevailed, is discussed below. In no contemporary local source is there evidence for full royal authority being held by a woman. It seems, however, that a woman could act as regent for an under-age male, as indicated by Rufinus (Chapter 9) in a passage that is interpreted as referring to the young Ezana and his mother during the first half of the fourth century.

6 Much ingenuity has been expended on attempts to date Sembrouthes' reign and/or to identify him with one of several kings known from other sources (*e.g.* Kobishchanov 1979: 47; Hahn 1989; Pedroni 1997a; Fiaccadori 2004).

7 Kasantchis (in press) has suggested that this inscription may be a hoax of unknown age; I am grateful to Professor François-Xavier Fauvelle-Aymar for providing me with a copy of this paper (see also Fauvelle-Aymar 2009: 139) in advance of publication.

8 It could be argued that the emphasis placed in the *Kebra Negast* (see Chapter 6) on Menelik I being the first-born son of Solomon indicates early recognition of this principle.

9 Disputed succession to the throne was frequent during later periods of Ethiopian history, when potential claimants were incarcerated in order to remove them from circulation. The monastery at Debra Damo, which claims a sixth-century foundation (Chapters 11 and 16), is sometimes cited as having served such a function in later Aksumite times (Tsegay 2005: 17 and references cited).

10 Fiaccadori 2007a.

Royal names

Several sources provide sequential lists or other information relating to the identity of the kings. Broadly, they may be divided into three categories. By far the largest and most varied group of sources comprises traditional king-lists[11] which – disconcertingly – display much variation between different versions. However, for the earlier period – before the inception of the coinage in the second half of the third century – they are effectively the only currently available source of information about individual kings and the lengths of their reigns. For the later period, the coinage issues (Chapter 14) can generally be set in chronological order through study of typology, die-links, weights and metal-fineness, thus providing a reasonably firm basis for reconstructing a list of kings.[12] Such a list may, however, be incomplete: there is no reason to assume that all kings necessarily had coins struck in their own names. Many coins – particularly those in copper (Fig. 72) or silver but also occasionally some in gold – were anonymous, giving the title 'king' but not naming him; likewise, there seems to have been little if any attempt to include an individual's features in the royal portraits. So far as the coinage was concerned, the royal office rather than the individual monarch was often emphasised. Unfortunately, and remarkably, very few of the names preserved on the coins also occur in the traditional king-lists, and *vice versa*. Reasons for this are hard to determine, but may be connected with the widespread custom – also known from later times in Ethiopia – whereby a ruler assumed a new name on ascending the throne.[13] Another factor may be that the king-lists are invariably in Ge'ez, whereas several of the stone inscriptions and most of the pre-sixth-century coin inscriptions are in Greek. To cite but one example: the sixth-century Aksumite king known in Ge'ez – and in his Greek coin-inscriptions – as Kaleb was referred to by Greek writers using various transliterations of 'Ella Atsbaha'.[14]

The stone inscriptions at Aksum (Chapter 6) record the names of four pre-seventh-century kings, who may – with varying confidence – be correlated with those recognised on coins. It is noteworthy that the names on some inscriptions took forms which, while not identical to those on the coins, are significantly closer to them than to those in the traditional lists. Only two Aksumite kings, Ezana and Kaleb, were named in non-Ethiopian written sources; both were also recorded on stone inscriptions and on coins. These foreign references are

11 See, among others, Conti Rossini 1909 and Budge 1928b: 204–12. In this category may also be included mentions of individual kings – but not their sequence – in other Ethiopian traditional sources such as those relating to the foundation of religious institutions or to grants of land, as discussed in Chapter 17.

12 Anfray (1968) was one of the first to attempt an overall comparison between the numismatic evidence and that provided by the traditional king-lists. Hahn (2010) has suggested revisions to the sequence of the sixth- and seventh-century kings, as further discussed in Chapter 14. It has also been suggested that some names included in king-lists may have been derived from careless readings of Ge'ez coin inscriptions; in particular, Munro-Hay (2002: 270) proposed that the name Ramhai – otherwise unknown – may have been inspired by a poorly preserved coin of king Armah.

13 Throne-names are a potential source of confusion for the historian. Throughout the history of monarchy in Ethiopia since at least the fourth century, individuals appear to have adopted a new name on their accession to the throne, as did other people on the occasion of any major transformation in status. For example, an Aksumite king called Gabra Masqal is recorded in several traditions as the son of Kaleb and so presumably ruled around the mid-sixth century, but no king of that name is represented in the coinage series (*cf.* Hahn 2010: 7). On the other hand, several subsequent Ethiopian monarchs are known to have taken the throne-name Gabra Masqal, and it is not always easy to distinguish between them (D. Phillipson 2009a: 63, 184, 209).

14 The sole known use of 'Ella Atsbaha' in Ge'ez is on Kaleb's unvocalised inscription, RIE 191, found at Aksum. This, unusually, gives both names: LSBH and KLB.

particularly valuable in that they provide independent evidence for the dates at which these monarchs reigned. Fig. 24 tabulates the evidence currently available concerning the sequence of Aksumite kings.

At first acquaintance, the names of Aksumite kings present a highly confusing variety of forms and spellings. The name of King Ezana may be cited as an example. All his coins were inscribed in Greek, with the name spelled HZANAC [Ezanas] on all issues except his final issue of gold (Fig. 71) where the form HZANA [Ezana] was given. The stone inscriptions in Greek, on the other hand, employed the form AEIZANAC [Aeizanas], while Constantius II, in the letter discussed below,[15] omitted the E. Ge'ez renditions are known only from the stone inscriptions where they were invariably given an initial *ain* but no final S. It seems safe to conclude that the initial AEI represented an attempt to facilitate Greek rendition of Ge'ez pronunciation, and the final C to give the Greek version of his name a masculine form; the usual local version of the king's name would seem to have been Ezana, which has therefore been adopted in this book.

It seems that only comparatively rarely did Aksumite kings make public use of their fathers' names, Kaleb providing the only instance of a patronymic recorded on coins. Some of Ezana's stone inscriptions name his father, and so do the single known texts of both Kaleb and his son WZB.[16] The reasons for their doing so remain obscure, but may indicate a wish or a need to emphasise these rulers' legitimacy; alternatively, perhaps the usage simply reflected a practice that may have been widespread among the Aksumite population, as it is today.

King	Date	Coins	Internal evidence	External evidence	bisi name
GDR	c. 200	-	*	?	-
Endybis	c. 270–90	*	-	-	Daku
Aphilas		*	-	-	Dimele
WZB		*	-	-	ZGLY
Ousanas (Ella Amida)		*	*	-	Gisene
Ezana	c. 330–60	*	*	*	Alene
Wazebas		*	-	-	-
Eon		*	-	-	Anioskal ?
MHDYS		*	-	-	-
Ebana		*	-	-	-
Nezana		*	-	-	-
Nezool		*	-	-	-
Ousas		*	-	-	-
Ousana[s]		*	-	-	-
Kaleb	c. 510–40	*	*	*	LZN
WZB	after 540	-	*	-	HDFN

Fig. 24 Kings of Aksum prior to the mid-sixth century

Some kings – notably those of the earlier period when coin inscriptions were almost invariably in Greek – used an additional title or name, introduced by the

[15] In Constantius' text, as recorded by Athanasius, the names of Aizana(s) and Sazana(s) are in the dative, so the presence of a final *sigma* in the nominative cannot be determined.

[16] As indicated in Fig. 24, there appear to have been two Aksumite kings called WZB. One, known only from coins, was a pre-Christian ruler at the very beginning of the fourth century. The second, named on stone inscription RIE 190, was a son of the early-sixth-century king Kaleb.

term BICI [*bisi*]. Each of these kings, even fathers and sons, appears to have had a different *bisi* name, a total of eight being recorded. Each of the first five kings to strike coins during the pre-Christian period, up to and including Ezana, used a *bisi* name in his coin inscriptions (see Fig. 24). The gold coins of WZB B'SY ZGLY and the stone inscriptions of Kaleb and his son indicate that the Greek BICI – the meaning of which had been the subject of much speculation – was simply a transliteration from the Ge'ez *be'seya* or *be'se* ... [= man of ...]. Although Ezana's *bisi* name is given in the same form on both his pre-Christian and his Christian coins, the only later king to whom such a name is attributed on his coins was Eon in the fifth century.[17] However, evidence for *bisi* names is not restricted to the coins: that of Ezana is confirmed by stone inscriptions RIE 185, 187–9, 271, while other inscriptions (RIE 191–2, in Ge'ez: *cf.* Chapter 6) indicate that Kaleb's *bisi* name was LZN and that of his son WZB was HDFN, demonstrating continued use of such designations into the sixth century. The most plausible explanation of the *bisi* names is that they designated matrilineal clans,[18] although it fails to explain how such a system – not otherwise attested in northern Ethiopia – accommodated patrilinear transmission of royal authority.

Dual rule?

It is has been suggested that the Aksumite throne was sometimes shared between two joint rulers. The belief may have been supported, or inspired, by the tradition that Christianity was first adopted at Aksum during the reign of Abraha and Atsbaha (Chapter 9). An external suggestion of such a practice is first provided by the letter addressed by the Roman Emperor Constantius II (337–61) to Ezana and Sazana, rulers of Aksum; the text of this letter has been preserved in the writings of St Athanasius whose implication of *verbatim* reproduction is, however, open to question.[19] The latter person probably equates with the Sazana or Saizana mentioned in the pre-Christian trilingual inscriptions of Ezana (RIE 185/270 and 185*bis*/270*bis*; (see Chapter 6), where both he and Adepha are described as Ezana's 'brothers'.[20] Neither the context nor known contemporaneous usage supports an interpretation that implies consanguinity or shared political authority; it is more likely that Sazana and Adepha were Ezana's military commanders, despite Constantius' – or Athanasius' – apparently mistaken impression otherwise. The Roman emperor's misapprehension, together with attempts to interpret Ethiopian tradition (Chapter 9) that Aksum was ruled by two kings at the time of its conversion to Christianity, has contributed to a view that Aksumite kingship was not infrequently dual. In my opinion, however, this hypothesis is almost certainly incorrect; joint rule was a much more familiar concept to Romans than it was to Aksumites.[21]

17 Buttrey 1971–72; Munro-Hay 1980–81; the Greek coin-inscriptions of this king are garbled.

18 This argument (de Blois 1984) included the elaboration – unnecessary in my view – that such clans formed the basis for military units.

19 For a French translation of this letter, see Szymusiak 1958: 125–6. An English rendition has been provided by Sergew (1972: 101–2). Further discussion is offered in Chapter 9.

20 The exact nominative forms of these names are uncertain. In the inscriptions they are recorded only in the accusative forms CAIAZANA[N]/CAZANAN and AΔHΦAN/AΔIΦAN on RIE 270/270*bis*, whilst in Constantius' letter Αιζανα and Σαζανα are in the dative.

21 The strongest supporter of the view that joint kings sometimes shared the Aksumite throne has been the numismatist Wolfgang Hahn, who has cited (2010: 5) 'the obvious *imitatio imperii Romani* practised by the rulers of Aksum'. Professor Hahn has recently (*in litt.*, 4 February 2011) expressed doubts on the matter: 'the question of temporary co-regencies is vexed; there is no real proof, so I am now far from defending their adoption, but on the other hand the possibility cannot be excluded'.

Royal titles

The Aksumite kings were designated NGS [*negus*] in Ethiopic Ge'ez, with those in ASAM-derived script (*cf.* Chapters 5 and 6) taking the form MLK [*malik*]; in Greek they were termed BACIΛEYC [*basileus*]. All these terms are known in other contexts to have been applied to a single absolute ruler. All three are preserved on the monumental stone inscriptions at Aksum (Chapter 6), the first and third also on the coins (Chapter 14). The title *atse*, widely used in reference to Ethiopian monarchs during recent centuries, has sometimes been applied anachronistically to Aksumite rulers.[22]

Ezana's stone inscriptions gave his titles according to a set formula: 'king of Aksum and of [four places in southern Arabia and three in the Horn], king of kings'.[23] The kingdoms were nearly always listed in the same order: Himyar, Raydan, Saba, Salhan, Seyamo, Bega, Kasu. The trilingual inscriptions added Habasat and varied the order of the others. Huntingford made the persuasive point that 'the Arabian titles were anachronistic and had no political significance, being kept as a reminder of Ethiopia's former greatness'.[24] By the sixth century, the inscriptions of Kaleb and WZB show only slight modification of the earlier formula.

Before the adoption of Christianity, the royal inscriptions generally included mention of the monarch's divine or quasi-divine status, usually in a form such as 'son of the unconquered Mahrem'. Following the conversion, such titles were discontinued or replaced by a human patronymic. Other religious invocations in the inscriptions were more easily adjusted to accommodate the change to Christianity, as may be seen from the quotations presented in Chapter 9.

The inscriptions throw interesting light on the terminology that was employed to differentiate between the subordinate rulers of subject peoples and their overlord, the Aksumite king himself. Some difficulty seems to have been encountered, particularly in Ge'ez. It may have been for this reason that the Aksumite monarch assumed the designation 'king of kings' that continued in Ethiopian use long afterwards. The distinction was made clear in Greek, both on stone inscriptions and on coins, by the restriction of the designation BACIΛEYC [*basileus*] to the Aksumite king himself, in whose name alone coins were issued. On RIE 270 and 270*bis*, rulers made subject to Aksum were termed BACIΛICKOI [*basiliscoi*], a diminutive form that has generally been translated as 'kinglets'.[25] To a visitor from the Mediterranean world, where *basileus* applied solely to the Roman or Byzantine emperor,[26] it would have seemed

22 Kaleb, in particular, has often been so designated. In fact, no ruler prior to the fourteenth century is known to have employed the title *atse*, although the word may be derived from *hatsani* [originally = 'tutor' but subsequently used in a political sense], attestation for which (RIE 193) may be tentatively dated towards the end of the first millennium AD (Nosnitsin 2003; Chapters 6 and 16). Titles of similar meaning have often been applied to political leaders in Africa and elsewhere – *e.g. Mwalimu* [= teacher] Nyerere in mid-twentieth-century Tanzania.

23 Rahlfs (1916) was one of the first to comment on this formulaic aspect of the Aksumite royal titles.

24 Huntingford 1989: 51. Note, for comparison, how coins of British kings retained the equally anachronistic title 'King of France' as late as the mid-eighteenth century.

25 The term was otherwise used in northeastern Africa mainly in reference to pagan Nubian rulers (Hansen 1986). On the Aksumite Greek inscriptions, the word appears in the dative plural form BACIΛEICKOIC on RIE 270, but in the dative singular EKACTΩ BACIΛICKΩ on RIE 270*bis*.

26 This may, of course, have been the principal reason why the Aksumites adopted it and used it on their Greek-inscribed gold coinage even when the ruler's personal name was omitted (*cf.* Chapter 14). Note also that the *Kebra Negast* placed great emphasis on the equivalence of the kings of Aksum and Rom [*i.e.* Constantinople] (*cf.* Chapter 6; also Vasiliev 1933; Martinez 1990).

inappropriate for a foreign ruler to bear the same title. When a Roman emperor addressed his Aksumite counterpart, he pointedly accorded the latter the title [*tyrannos* = tyrant].[27] In Ezana's Ge'ez inscriptions, this distinction was not made and NGS was used both for the king of Aksum and for his apparent under-kings. Was this to avoid controversy, or because the Ge'ez language could not make the distinction? Interestingly, the ASAM-derived texts (*cf.* Chapters 5 and 6) used MLK or MLK MLKN for the Aksumite king, but NGST for his subordinate *basiliscoi*. On the other hand, RIE 186 employed a distinct form of the same script but used the term NGS for both ranks.[28]

Regalia

The coins, beginning in the late-third century (Chapter 14), provide limited representation of Aksumite regalia.[29] The kings from Aphilas onward were usually shown crowned, this headgear being apparently worn over a cloth. The headcloth was also depicted, without the crown, on the reverses of those Aksumite coins – in gold and, less frequently, other metals – which retained the royal portrait[30] on both sides. Some crowned busts of the fourth and fifth centuries were shown holding a sceptre-like object occasionally resembling a spear, while those with the headcloth held an unidentifiable object similar to a branch or fly-whisk (Fig 71).[31] From the fifth century onwards, the king was sometimes shown holding a cross (Figs 72 and 75) or an orb surmounted by a cross (Fig. 74).

Apart from the representations on the coins, the only surviving record of an Aksumite king's physical appearance is that provided by John Malalas in his account of a Byzantine embassy[32] by one Julian to a ruler designated variously as 'the emperor of the Axoumitae', 'the Indian emperor' or 'the emperor of the Indians'.[33] The date (*c.* 530) and context of this episode clearly indicate that the potentate who received this embassy was none other than Kaleb:

[27] *e.g.* Constantius II to Ezana and Saizana in 356/7, as recorded by Athanasius (*Apology to Emperor Constantius* 31; see Chapter 9). The English word 'tyrant' is derived from the Greek [= absolute ruler] which, however, did not always carry the derogatory implications that now attach to the former term.

[28] Possibly there was a refinement of terminology under Ezana.

[29] *cf.* Munro-Hay 1991b: 150–5, 1994.

[30] The term 'portrait', normally employed by numismatists, is retained in this book, even though Aksumite coins rarely – if ever – show any attempt to represent the features of individual rulers.

[31] The fly-whisk has long served in Ethiopia as a mark of prestige; by the thirteenth century a royal official was as known as 'keeper of the fly-whisks', and palm branches were used as ceremonial fly-whisks at coronation ceremonies that were still held at Aksum in the fifteenth century (Munro-Hay 1991b: 153).

[32] John Malalas, *Chronicle* 18, 56 (Jeffreys *et al.* 1986: 268–9); for the Greek text, see Thurn 2000: 384. There can be little doubt that the embassy here described is the same as that recorded by Procopius (*History of the Wars* I 9–12; Dewing 1914–28, 1: 192–5). John Malalas (Croke 1990; Beaucamp *et al.* 2004–06) has been described (Gajda 2009: 18) as 'superficial', 'lacking in rigour' and writing 'in a common language aimed at a wide readership'. His *Chronicle*, written in the third quarter of the sixth century to provide a history of the world from Adam to the death of Justinian I, is best known from a manuscript of eleventh- or twelfth-century date.

[33] For the not infrequent designation of the Aksumites as 'Indians', see Chapter 1.

Fig. 25 Gold fifth-century coin [diameter: 16.5 mm] of MHDYS, inscribed in Ge'ez and depicting an Aksumite king with his regalia (photograph by courtesy of Professor W. Hahn)

Fig. 26 The 'Stela of the Lances', now in the Cathedral precinct at Aksum but formerly part of Stela 4

> The emperor was naked, wearing from his belt to his loins gold-threaded linen clothing, and over his shoulders and stomach a tunic decorated with pearls,[34] and bracelets in groups of five and gold bangles on his arms. Around his head was wound a gold-threaded linen[35] turban[36] with four cords on either side and a gold collar around his neck. He stood on top of four elephants which had a yoke and four discs, and upon them something like a tall carriage[37] covered with gold leaf, just as the chariots of the provincial governors[38] are covered in silver. The emperor of the Indians stood on high holding a small gilt shield

[34] This may refer to beads.

[35] It has sometimes been suggested (*e.g.* Kobishchanov 1979: 133) that a linen garment must have been imported, or that this mention of linen must be an error due to a mistaken identification of a cotton garment. No such amendment is necessary: flax had been cultivated as a source of fibre for thousands of years in Egypt, and was grown at Aksum by this time (Boardman 2000: 363–8, 373, 468; Chapter 10). Linen garments are well known from Coptic Egypt between the fifth and the eighth centuries (*cf.* also Cyril of Scythopolis in Price & Binns 1991: xxxviii–xxxix). Traces of gold-threaded textile were recovered from primary contexts in the fourth-century Mausoleum at Aksum (D. Phillipson 2000b: 200–1).

[36] The Greek term used by Malalas – in the accusative – is φακιολιν. It seems probable that the description refers to the headcloth depicted on the coins.

[37] The Greek text is not wholly clear as to whether the emperor stood on a platform supported by four elephants or in a carriage pulled by them (see Oeconomos 1950). The latter, often referred to as an 'elephant quadriga' was represented on several Roman imperial coins (*e.g.* illustrations in Scullard 1974: pl. xxiv). In earlier times, similar depictions were presented on coins of the Hellenistic kings of Syria and on Egyptian Ptolemaic ones (*ibid.*: pl. xv). For the availability of elephants in Aksumite territory, see Chapter 7. This account from Aksum is thus by no means implausible, although the possibility remains that it might include exaggerations or embellishments emanating from Julian and/or John Malalas.

[38] It is not clear from the text whether Byzantine or Aksumite governors were meant. As noted below, Aksumite governors of Adulis and the Agau were recorded by Cosmas Indicopleustes (*Christian Topography* II 51, 56; Wolska-Conus 1968–73, 1: 360–1, 368–9) at approximately the time of Julian's embassy. However, the reference to the governor's 'chariot' being covered with silver implies reference to Byzantine practice, since silver was a very scarce commodity in the Aksumite kingdom (*cf.* Chapter 13).

> and two spears, also gilt, in his hands. His whole senate[39] stood likewise at arms, with flute-players[40] providing music.[41]

This description strongly suggests that the small shield and two spears served as emblems of the Aksumite kingly office. A crowned figure thus accoutred was depicted on a gold coin of the fifth-century king MHDYS (Fig. 25 and Chapter 14). The same items (two spears and one shield) were carved in relief on Stela 4 at Aksum, almost certainly fourth-century in date (Fig. 26). Also at Aksum, and of broadly the same age, is the richly furnished Tomb of the Brick Arches (Chapter 12) which yielded a remarkable waisted iron spearhead,[42] 69 cm in length but too thin to have served any purpose other than a purely symbolic one. It is noteworthy that the spears depicted on MHDYS' coin are similarly waisted, but the closest actual parallels to that from the Tomb of the Brick Arches were discovered in the fifth-century Tumulus III at el-Hobagi near Meroe in the Nile Valley.[43]

It is interesting to compare this description with archaeological and other evidence. Although clearly seen through Byzantine eyes and recorded, using Byzantine terminology, for a Byzantine readership, there are enough parallels with independent evidence to confirm its basic authenticity.[44] It was probably based on a first-hand account by Julian himself, reported by John Malalas in his third-person narrative.[45]

Church and state

Although the data are few and inconclusive, it is appropriate briefly to consider the relationship between Church and State that developed in the Aksumite kingdom from the fourth century onwards.[46] Virtually no information on this matter is available from contemporary Aksumite sources, and very little from those elsewhere; purportedly relevant Ethiopian records were all compiled long after the events concerned had taken place.

Although the subordination of the Ethiopian Church to the Patriarchate of Alexandria is widely and popularly held to have originated with the consecration of Frumentius by Athanasius, there is no convincing support for this. The legal basis for such subordination was provided by one of the so-called 'Disciplinary Canons' of the Council of Nicaea. There is, however, no evidence that

39 This mention of a 'senate' is the only clear indication known to me that the Aksumite king may have had some sort of advisory council.

40 Musicians, likewise, are not otherwise attested in Aksumite times other than in accounts – which survive only in very much later versions – of St Yared and the sixth-century king Gabra Masqal (see Taddesse 1985).

41 This translation, by Elizabeth Jeffreys, Michael Jeffreys and Roger Scott (1986: 268–9), is reproduced by kind permission of the Australian Association for Byzantine Studies.

42 D. Phillipson 2000b: 111, fig. 93.

43 Lenoble *et al.* 1994.

44 R. Schneider's (1984: 162) view that it is largely imaginary may be discounted, despite Gajda's (2009: 18) concerns noted above.

45 This supposition is strengthened by an interesting inconsistency in Malalas' text: although the passage was presented in the third person, in one place the form 'ordered me' was retained instead of 'ordered him'. Stylistic differences from the rest of Malalas' text provide further support for this view (M. Jeffreys in Jeffreys *et al.* 1990: 268–76).

46 *cf.* Sergew 1969; Taddesse 1972: 21–68; Munro-Hay 1997: 58–94; see also Chapter 9.

these regulations were ever discussed at Nicaea, which Council[47] took place in 325, some three years before Athanasius was first elevated to the patriarchate and at least eight years before the earliest possible date for Frumentius' consecration (see discussion in Chapter 9). This canon itself is now recognised as a forgery – 'apocryphal' being the politically correct euphemism – for which the first known attestation dates from the seventh century.[48] It may be significant that this reference occurred at a period when communication between Alexandria and Aksum was becoming increasingly difficult (see Chapter 16), and when the patriarchate may have sought to create justification for asserting closer control over Ethiopian Christians.

Alexandrian patriarchal records relating to the first millennium contain remarkably few references to Ethiopia, even the consecration of Frumentius having apparently escaped their compilers' attention. Few bishops of Aksum during this period are known by name,[49] neither the manner of their appointments nor their relationship with the king having been recorded. In later times, there are several accounts of the *negus* asking the Alexandrian patriarch to appoint a replacement for a recently deceased bishop, but we have no knowledge of such matters during the Aksumite period. In view of the semi-divine nature of early Aksumite kingship, discussed above and in Chapter 9, this is hardly surprising. Ezana's stone inscriptions demonstrate that his adoption of Christianity was accompanied by a weakening in his personal claim of divine status, and further trends in this direction may be indicated on coins issued later in the fourth century (Chapter 14). In these circumstances, relations between king and bishop may have been slow to develop and to become formalised.[50]

Lower-level administration

Although definitive evidence is scarce, it is not unreasonable to suggest that the quasi-independent rulers of polities that became tributary to Aksum were in due course demoted or otherwise made fully subservient to the Aksumite king. That such a process was already under way by the mid-fourth century may be inferred from the Ezana inscriptions. The mention by Cosmas Indicopleustes of an *archon* [= Governor] called Asbas at Adulis,[51] responsible to the Aksumite king, implies that some change had taken place by the early sixth century in areas that had previously been administered less directly, as discussed in Chapter 7.

A primary function of local administrators, whatever their nominal status, was probably the collection of tribute or tax. It is reasonable to assume that such payments began before Aksum adopted its own coinage, in which case they must – at least initially – have been made primarily in the form of produce and/or labour,

47 Ayres 2004.

48 Meinardus 1962: 41; Munro-Hay 1997: 15.

49 Possible exceptions noted by Munro-Hay (1997: 68–99) include Frumentius' successor, Minas, but in all cases the evidence is confused.

50 For further discussion of this trend, see Chapter 9.

51 Cosmas, *Christian Topography* II 56 (Wolska-Conus 1968–73, 1: 368–9). A similar functionary was recorded in Agau territory (Cosmas, *Christian Topography* II 51; Wolska-Conus 1968–73, 1: 360–1). Cosmas designated Asbas as αρχων [*archon*], which was the Greek term used in the Byzantine empire to designate a regional governor; the Aksumite Ge'ez equivalent is not known. Kobishchanov (1979: 220) used the form 'arhont', which has caused confusion but is explained by the fact that the original Russian edition of this work (Moscow, 1966) employed a word – derived from the Byzantine – of which 'arhont' is an acceptable transliteration (I thank Dr Tacye Phillipson for her advice on this point).

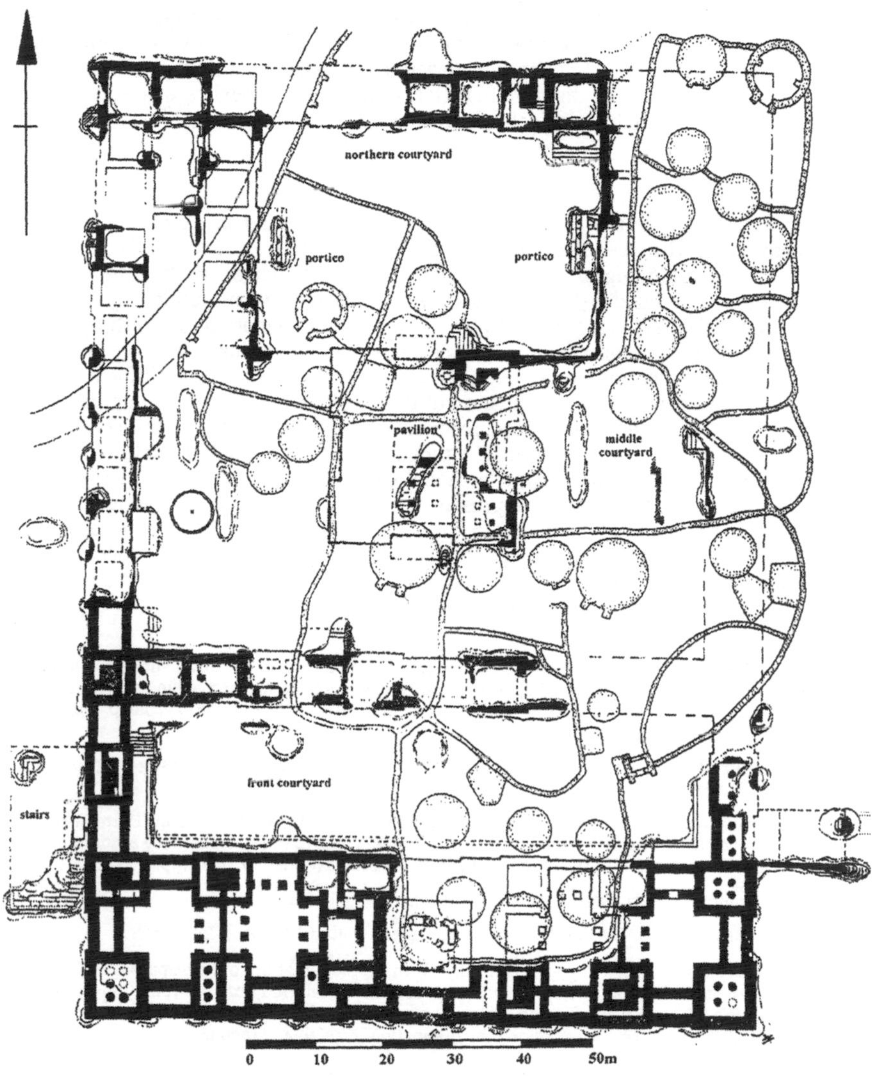

Fig. 27 Plan of Ta'akha Maryam élite structure at Aksum, as recorded by the DAE in 1906 (after D. Phillipson 1997)

with the latter apparently involving various degrees of coercion. Such tribute is recorded in Ezana's stone inscriptions, and exemplified by the abundant manpower at the disposal of the Aksumite kings for such purposes as the transport and erection of stelae (*cf.* Chapter 12). The possibility cannot be ruled out that, in later times when locally-circulating coinage was more abundant, monetary payments may also have played a part in these transactions. Population movements, involving the aggregation during the third to fifth centuries of previously scattered peoples, are also attested archaeologically, as is their subsequent dispersal.[52]

'Palaces'

No consideration of Aksumite political structure would be complete without mention of the so-called 'palaces' that have been known archaeologically since the beginning of the twentieth century.[53] These each comprised a central square building[54] standing in a court that was surrounded by a range of rooms (Fig. 27). They varied greatly in size and elaboration.[55] Although the largest and most grandiose examples are known exclusively from Aksum, analogous structures have been recognised at other sites. Unfortunately, little secure evidence is available as to their precise dates or the functions that they served. Widely reproduced reconstructions[56] of these building-complexes almost certainly exaggerate their grandeur, and the designation 'palace' implies unjustified assumptions.[57] One archaeologist[58] has gone so far as to suggest that the 'palaces' at Aksum represent a series, with a new one being built by each successive king. This interesting proposal parallels practice known for later periods in Ethiopia, but cannot yet be evaluated since no publication is available of the relevant dating evidence from Aksum. Furthermore, it takes no account of the existence of similar buildings at sites far from the capital.[59]

[52] Evidence for this is based on the distribution of pottery styles in the Aksum-Yeha area as recorded by Michels (2005: 155–99), and supported by more detailed archaeological survey and lithic-artefact studies in the more immediate vicinity of Aksum (Fattovich *et al.* 2000; Bard *et al.* 2003; L. Phillipson 2009b).

[53] The architecture of these building-complexes is discussed in Chapter 11, only their function and attribution being considered here.

[54] It was probably this feature that led the 1906 Deutsche Aksum-Expedition (Littmann *et al.* 1913) to call these features *Palast* [= palace] with reference to the sixth-century account of the 'four-towered residence of the king in Ethiopia' by Cosmas (*Christian Topography* XI 2, 4, 7).

[55] D. Phillipson 2008a: fig. 2; see also Munro-Hay 1991b: 121–3.

[56] *e.g.* those of the DAE's Daniel Krencker (Littmann *et al.* 1913, 2: Abb. 245, 251).

[57] See Cosmas, *Christian Topography* XI 2, 4, 7. In the first and third of these passages, Cosmas used the word οικος [oikos = house], but in the second he preferred παλατιον [palation = palace]. McCrindle's (1897: 358–61) English translation used 'palace' in all three instances, but Wolska-Conus (1968–73, 3: 314–27) expressed the distinction correctly in French.

[58] Wendowski & Ziegert 2006.

[59] Most notably at Matara (Anfray 1963b; Anfray & Annequin 1965).

9

Aksumite Religion

Most text-based studies of Aksumite history place considerable emphasis on religion, particularly on the king's adoption of Christianity. The account offered here lays stress on those aspects of religious development that are reflected in ancient Ethiopian sources and in the archaeological record, paying less attention to purely doctrinal or theological matters which are more rarely illustrated by contemporaneous local materials.

For hundreds of years prior to the local advent of Christianity, it seems that a form or forms of polytheistic belief-system analogous – but by no means identical – to that known to have been established in southern Arabia prevailed also in the northern Horn. Although the deities' names indicated by the known inscriptions are – with one exception – different, [1] use of the crescent-and-disc symbol – known in earlier times on altars and incense-burners in both southern Arabia and the northern Horn (*cf.* Chapter 3) – was continued in pre-Christian Aksumite times on coins and on the Anza and Matara stelae (Chapter 6 and 7 respectively), which have been dated to the third century on palaeographic grounds.[2] No detailed evidence has yet been published for pre-Christian Aksumite religious buildings, nor should it be assumed that all religious structures erected after the mid-fourth century were necessarily Christian.[3]

The coming of Christianity

Knowledge about the advent and development of Christianity in the Aksumite realm is based on varied sources: written texts originating outside Ethiopia, inscriptions, coins and other archaeological materials – including remains of church buildings – from Aksum and related sites, and Ethiopian historical tradition. The primary account of the Aksumite conversion to Christianity is

[1] Aksumite inscriptions made no mention of Almaqah, and Astar was named only in Ezana's trilingual inscriptions. The only possible exception to this statement is RIE 180 which named GDR the earliest known king of Aksum *c.* AD 200; some scholars consider (*contra* R. Schneider 1984: 152–3) that this inscription also contains a dedication to Almaqah, not otherwise recorded at this relatively late date.

[2] There is no evidence to support the portrayal of the crescent-and-disc on the reconstruction drawing of Aksum Stela 1 published by the DAE (Littmann *et al.* 1913, 2: Abb. 44) and often reproduced subsequently). It could be, however, that the failure successfully to erect this huge stela (discussed in Chapter 12) was seen as an omen favouring adoption of the new religion (D. Phillipson & L. Phillipson 2000: 252–4; L. Phillipson 2009b: 122).

[3] The structure excavated in 1958 at Wuchate Golo, some 5 km west of Aksum (de Contenson 1961b; D. Phillipson 2009a: 43), is an example of a possibly religious building sometimes assumed on chronological grounds to have been a church.

contained in the *Ecclesiastical History* by Rufinus of Aquileia;[4] the details have often been repeated, and only a summary is needed here. A certain Meropius from greater Syria,[5] accompanied by two young men – Frumentius and Aedesius – who were his relatives, had been on a journey to 'India'. At this time, as noted in Chapter 1, 'India' was a very vague term whose application was by no means restricted to the South Asian peninsula, but included also Arabia and much of Africa east of the Nile.[6] The ship on which the party was travelling – presumably on the Red Sea – was wrecked, and Meropius killed. Frumentius and Aedesius, however, were captured and taken to the king, in whose household they became employed. On the monarch's death, his widow became regent for her young son and retained the increasingly influential services of the two Syrians. At the royal capital there were already some Christians – implied to have been members of a foreign trading community – with whom they associated. When the new king assumed full authority, the younger Syrian, Aedesius, returned to his homeland, while Frumentius proceeded to Alexandria to seek the patriarch's appointment of a bishop to lead the Christian community at Aksum. Athanasius selected as the new bishop Frumentius himself, who duly returned to Aksum in that capacity and made a large number of converts.

Several aspects of this account require comment. Chronology is considered separately, below. Rufinus' treatment was marked by the absence of names: although Meropius, Frumentius, Aedesius and Athanasius were identified, the two successive kings were not, and there was no indication of the identity of their kingdom or its capital.[7] Although it has long been accepted, by historians and by the Ethiopian Church, that these developments took place at Aksum, this is not specifically stated by Rufinus.[8] However, a later document – discussed below – makes the location almost certain, and accords with the

[4] Murphy 1945; Hammond 1977. The greater part of this work comprises a translation into Latin of a Greek *Ecclesiastical History* by Eusebius of Caesarea which covered developments up to the death of Constantine the Great in 337. Rufinus extended Eusebius' account by adding two new chapters, numbered X and XI, devoted to the years 337–95; it is here (X 9–11) that is to be found the passage generally interpreted as describing the advent of Christianity to Aksum. Following much controversy (*e.g.* Honigmann 1954; Schamp 1987a, 1987b) as to their respective priority, there is now general agreement that Rufinus' chapters X and XI were largely based on a now-lost work written by Gelasius, Eusebius' successor as Bishop of Caesarea, in the 380s (Winkelmann 1966). An English translation of Rufinus' text has been provided by Amidon (1997: 18–23; see also Sergew 1972: 98–9).

[5] Rufinus employed the simple name 'Syria', but this can be confusing to the modern reader because the term was formerly applied to a much more extensive area than is occupied by the modern republic of that name.

[6] Rufinus implied that Frumentius and Aedesius were captured on their return journey from 'India'. He may not necessarily have meant that Meropius and his companions had been on a voyage to peninsular India; it is in fact perfectly possible that Aksum was their final intended destination (*cf.* Dihle 1964, 1965: 41–4; Mayerson 1993; D. Phillipson 2009b: 353).

[7] Some of the personal names recalled in Ethiopian Church tradition (*e.g.* Pétridès 1971–72; Sergew *et al.* 1997) are different from those preserved in other sources; this matter is discussed below. Other than Rufinus, the only primary source for the name Frumentius is Athanasius, quoting Constantius II, as elaborated below. The two Ethiopian texts that mentioned Frumentius by name – a homily (Getatchew 1979) and the *Synaxarium* (Budge 1928a: 1164–5) – were both significantly later compositions and so cannot be assumed to be independent of Rufinus (*cf.* Conti Rossini 1922). In other Ge'ez contexts, the first bishop of Aksum was called Abba Salama [Father Peace]. The *Synaxarium* (*loc. cit.*) added the detail that the king to whom Aedesius and Frumentius were initially brought was called 'Alameda': this is clearly a version of 'Ella Amida' who is named in several inscriptions as Ezana's father.

[8] Suggestions that the recorded exploits of Frumentius took place not at Aksum but at some unspecified location in peninsular India or in Arabia (*e.g.* Baring-Gould 1872–77, 10: 650–2; Altheim & Stiehl 1971: 393–430) are now widely regarded as untenable.

numismatic, epigraphic and archaeological evidence. Even more striking is the fact that, although Rufinus attributes numerous converts to the new bishop, he made no mention that they included the king.[9]

This brief and rather bare account was repeated by several fifth-century church historians,[10] but their narratives all appear to have been directly derived from that of Rufinus.[11] More recently, the story has been incorporated into a number of secondary narratives and has acquired embellishments,[12] including suggestions that Meropius and Frumentius were Christians before the latter's arrival at Aksum, that Frumentius and Aedesius were Meropius' sons and were sold to the Aksumite king as slaves, etc. These elaborations, while not inherently implausible or – in most cases – specifically contra-indicated, are not based on ancient sources and cannot be sustained.

The initial conversion and its context

Two additional aspects of Christianity's advent to Aksum require consideration. One is that it was no isolated phenomenon, but was part of a fourth-century trend towards monotheism that is attested also in the then-dominant southern Arabian kingdom of Himyar[13] and, indeed, elsewhere.[14] Secondly, its adoption was a tentative process, probably politically motivated,[15] presented to the king's diverse subjects with skill and selectivity. The evidence for both these features may now be set out, in which process it will be convenient to pay particular attention to the light that is thrown on so-called Jewish aspects of Ethiopian Christianity.

There is widespread agreement among historians of southern Arabia that a form of monotheism was widely adopted in Himyar during the fourth century, although it did not formally become the official religion there until the 390s; the evidence is contained both in contemporary inscriptions and in Arabic texts of later date.[16] It is largely from the latter sources that the oft-repeated

9 The Ethiopian *Synaxarium* (Budge 1928a: 1165), however, states that Frumentius and Aedesius taught 'the Faith of Christ' to their young royal charge during the regency of the latter's mother. This need not of course imply conversion, which would run counter to the evidence of the inscriptions and coins, both of which indicate that Ezana adopted Christianity during the middle years of his reign.

10 Notably Socrates Scholasticus (I 19), Theodoret of Cyrrhus (I 23) and Sozomen (II 24), all of whom wrote Greek works entitled Ecclesiastical History during the second quarter of the fifth century (Chesnut 1977). Texts and French translations of the relevant passages are available in the *Sources chrétiennes* series (Paris: Editions du Cerf), respectively vols 477 (2004): 188–93, 501 (2006): 288–93 and 306 (1983): 328–35.

11 Theodoret, however, added a new detail to the effect that Frumentius and Aedesius were Meropius' nephews. This would not, of course, imply that they were necessarily full brothers.

12 *e.g.* Trimingham 1952: 38–9; Doresse 1970: 23; Marcus 1994: 7.

13 For details of this southern Arabian monotheism see Gibb 1962; Beeston 1984; Bowersock 1997; Gajda 2009 and Robin 2009. Its supposed 'Judaic' or 'Judaising' features have given rise to much confusion, as discussed below. The evidence from the northern Horn (*cf.* Anfray *et al.* 1970; Kobishchanov 1979: 234–40; Grillmeier 1996: 324–32) comes primarily from the royal inscriptions at Aksum (Chapter 6) and – to a lesser extent – from the coins (Chapter 14). Although monotheism was not officially endorsed by the rulers of Himyar until the end of the fourth century, its more tentative beginnings in southern Arabia were broadly contemporary with the corresponding trend in the northern Horn (Gajda 2009: esp. 223–45).

14 See, for example, S. Mitchell & Van Nuffelen 2010.

15 For the possibility that broadly comparable 'conversion' events in the Caucasus at this time were also – at least in part – politically inspired, see Haas 2008. Similar developments elsewhere on the periphery of the Roman Empire are not directly relevant to this book.

16 Gajda 2009; Robin 2009; see also Bowersock 1997.

designation of this monotheism as 'Jewish' has been derived. However, it is clear that this term was sometimes employed by mid-first-millennium writers such as Cyril of Scythopolis[17] to designate non-Christian or – in later times – non-Islamic monotheists. Iwona Gajda has emphatically rejected this usage, noting that Himyaritic monotheism was *judaïsant mais pas explicitement juif*.[18]

Much confusion has resulted from attempts to connect this 'Jewish' monotheism with claimed Judaic features that have continued in Ethiopian Christianity until recent times.[19] Today, the term 'Jewish' continues to have ethnic as well as varied religious connotations,[20] the implications of which obscure historical understanding even further. Southern Arabian religious developments may be more clearly understood as part of a widely-based adoption of monotheism among South-Semitic-speaking peoples, incorporating many aspects of earlier Judaic beliefs on which foundation Judaism, Christianity – especially Ethiopian Christianity – and Islam were based. Whereas the kings of Aksum formally adopted Christianity, to the east of the Red Sea the situation is less clear, with both Christian and non-Christian monotheisms being recorded but not always clearly differentiated.[21] It is salutary to compare the different ways in which these similar processes are still recalled on the two sides of the Red Sea – by the strongly Christian communities of the Ethiopian highlands and in the equally strong Islamic traditions of what is now Yemen. The question of Judaic features in Aksumite Christianity will be considered in a later section of this chapter.

The stone inscriptions (Chapter 6) and the coins (Chapter 14) permit no doubt that the Aksumite king who first adopted Christianity was called Ezana;[22] this is confirmed by a letter of 356/7 from the Roman Emperor Constantius II (*cf.* Chapter 8), the text of which is preserved among the writings of St Athanasius of Alexandria.[23] The letter was addressed to Ezana and Sazana, in the

17 The most accessible edition of Cyril's work is that prepared by Price & Binns (1991), where the clearest example of the term 'Jewish' used in this way may be found on p. 137.

18 Gajda 2009: 239.

19 As is apparent in the work of, among others, Ullendorff 1956, 1968 and Isaac 1972. For critical evaluations, see Rodinson 1964a, 1964b, 1965.

20 A wide-ranging but controversial discussion of this point has been provided by Sand 2009.

21 Maxime Rodinson 1964a was the first to compare early monotheisms on the two sides of the Red Sea, but this review seems to have received little attention at the time of its publication.

22 The spelling and pronunciation of this name are discussed in Chapter 8. There was at one time considerable disagreement over whether the Ezana inscriptions all referred to the same monarch or whether there were two kings of Aksum called Ezana, one of whom reigned in the fourth century and the other in the fifth. Kobishchanov 1979 appears to have made hasty revisions to his text in order to accommodate this 'two Ezanas' theory. Publications relating to the controversy are numerous (*e.g.* Munro-Hay 1990) but, since the late 1980s, a general consensus has emerged, strongly supported by numismatic evidence, that there was no fifth-century Ezana II. I share this view and do not intend to repeat the arguments here, although contrary opinions are still occasionally encountered (*e.g.* Gragg 2004; Haas 2008).

23 This Athanasius was the Alexandrian patriarch who had appointed Frumentius bishop of Aksum. Szymusiak (1958: 125–6) published Athanasius' Greek text and a French translation, while noting that the text may not reproduce the original letter *verbatim*; Grillmeier (1996: 299) has drawn attention to inaccuracies in this French rendition. A partial English translation was provided by Stevenson (1966: 34–5); for discussion and a more complete English version, see Sergew 1972: 100–2. Constantius reigned from 337 until 361, so it is possible that this letter was not his first involvement with Aksumite religious affairs. The fifth-century historian Philostorgius recorded an embassy led by Theophilus, a titular bishop, to the rulers of Himyar and Aksum (Fiaccadori 1983–84; Dihle 1989), but no details of the embassy's business at Aksum appear to have been preserved. It may have been her reliance on this episode that led Gajda (2009: 35) to her unsupported statement that Ethiopia was converted to Christianity *c.* 340 through a mission sent by Constantius II. Doresse (1970: 23, 1971: 100), following Trimingham

apparent belief that they were joint rulers of Aksum.[24] After a brief attempt to justify his interference in the affairs of a region that was not part of the Roman Empire, Constantius noted that Frumentius, bishop of Aksum, had been consecrated by Athanasius, whose doctrinal suitability was – by that time – no longer accepted by the imperial authorities. This indicates Constantius' belief that Frumentius was wielding episcopal authority at Aksum in 356/7. Constantius had, a short while previously, secured Athanasius' deposition and exile – for the third time – on the grounds of his non-adherence to the Arian beliefs[25] favoured by the emperor; George of Cappadocia, an Arian, had been appointed patriarch of Alexandria in place of Athanasius. The Aksumite rulers were urged to send Frumentius back to Alexandria for examination by George, who could – if he found him acceptable – confirm his episcopacy. There is no evidence that this seemingly impertinent letter ever reached Aksum; its inclusion – whether or not *verbatim* – in Athanasius' *Apology* implies that it may have been intercepted in Alexandria. In any event, we know of no action taken at Aksum in response to it, although a delegation of 'Indians' recorded as arriving in Constantinople after Constantius' death in 361 (*cf.* Chapter 15) may indicate a belated reaction. It does not appear that Constantius – who must have recognised the weakness of his position – pressed the matter further, and Julian – his successor – would have been unlikely to do so.

The stone inscriptions tell a broadly compatible story. The exploits of the fourth-century Aksumite kings are recorded at their capital in no fewer than eleven stone-inscribed versions, some in Greek and others in Ge'ez (see Chapter 6). As has long been recognised, they provide evidence for Ezana's hesitant adoption of Christianity; their testimony in this regard significantly amplifies that provided by the historical writings and by the coinage. The fourth-century inscriptions vary significantly in their content relating to religion.

RIE 186 is generally – but not unanimously – attributed to Ezana's predecessor, Ella Amida (Chapter 6). The king is described as *son of the invincible Mahrem*, no other deities being mentioned.[26]

RIE 187 does not preserve the name of the king and most of his titles; as noted in Chapter 6, Littmann's attribution to Ezana has been widely accepted but cannot be proven. The phrase *son of the invincible Mahrem* is nonetheless preserved, but no other deities are named.

RIE 188 likewise records that the king, whose name is incompletely preserved but was probably Ezana, *son of the invincible Mahrem*, dedicated a monument to Astar, Beher and Meder, and made a thank-offering to Mahrem.

(1952: 39), believed that Theophilus was sent to Aksum specifically to replace Frumentius. Kobishchanov (1979: 72) tentatively suggested that he may have been sent there to deliver the letter of 356/7, although R. Schneider (1984: 156) cited Philostorgius as indicating that the embassy had taken place at least ten years earlier. The difficulties are compounded by that fact that Philostorgius' text (Amidon 2007) survives only in a ninth-century summary by a hostile commentator; it appears to contain lacunae and misordering.

24 The identity and status of Sazana are discussed in Chapter 8.

25 Details of Arianism are not strictly relevant to the present discussion, but the reader may be referred to accounts by Binns (2002: 63) and Ludlow (2009: 113–8); also, for greater detail, R. Williams (1987, 2004).

26 Although Mahrem was clearly a deity favoured in the Aksumite area, particularly by the kings, during pre-Christian times (Sima 2007), he appears not to be mentioned in earlier inscriptions either in the northern Horn or in southern Arabia. In Greek versions of the relevant Aksum and Adulis inscriptions, he was given the name Ares.

In the trilingual inscriptions **RIE 185/270** and **185*bis*/270*bis*,** Ezana refers to himself as *son of the unconquered Mahrem* [Ares in the Greek versions], dedicates the inscription to Mahrem, Astar, and Beher,[27] and refers to metal statues – for the possible significance of which, see Chapter 11 – erected in honour of these deities. The Greek version of the more northerly inscription (270*bis*) also includes mention of *the Lord of Heaven and Earth.*[28] The difference is strange: this phrase is absent not only from the Ge'ez versions 185*bis* but also from all texts of the southerly inscription 185/270. A chronological difference is unlikely, since both inscriptions clearly commemorate – in virtually identical detail – the same military campaign and so were presumably erected at more-or-less the same time. It seems likely, in fact, that the phrase *Lord of Heaven and Earth* in this context arose from an attempt to provide a Greek rendering for the Ge'ez names of pagan deities.

RIE 189, by contrast, refers to no deities by name but repeatedly attributes Ezana's kingship and military success to *the might of the Lord of Heaven.*[29]

RIE 190 and 271 are both interesting and problematic. The relationship between the Ge'ez (190) and Greek (271) versions is discussed in Chapter 6 – as is important internal evidence for their date. In the Greek, Ezana refers to his *faith in God* and to *the power of the Father, Son and Holy Spirit who saved for me the kingdom by the faith of his Son, Jesus Christ, who has helped me and will always help me*; he describes himself as *servant of Christ* and makes repeated reference to the *guidance* and *power* of Christ, in one instance designating Christ as *the god in whom I have believed.* This is the only one of the Ezana inscriptions which makes specific reference to the Trinity. The Ge'ez text, by contrast, does not specify Ezana's name and is less specifically religious, containing no named reference to Christ or any other divinity. In the initial publication of these inscriptions,[30] this distinction between the apparently contemporaneous Greek and Ge'ez texts was noted and attributed to different intended readerships.

Two important points immediately emerge from this discussion. First, some inscriptions[31] are couched in polytheistic and others[32] in monotheistic terms. The trilingual inscriptions are intermediate, with both beliefs indicated. Secondly, while monotheistic phraseology is present in both Greek and Ge'ez texts, it is significantly more explicitly Christian in the Greek.[33] Comparison of

[27] This last is named Meder in the Ethiopic-script version. The inconsistency may be a simple error on the part of the stone-carver, perhaps implying that the two deities were no longer clearly differentiated (*cf.* Sima 2003b). On the other hand, RIE 188 names Beher and Meder as distinct. The problem awaits adequate explanation.

[28] Uhlig 2001 drew attention to this feature of 185*bis*/270*bis*. He may have been mistaken in his interpretation that Christianity was indicated: the phrase 'Lord of Heaven and Earth' may have been due to an attempt to translate the Ge'ez names Astar and Meder, since 'STR had become the Ge'ez word for 'heaven' (Sima 2003c).

[29] In much of the pre-1970 literature, this inscription was designated 'Christian'. In fact, the term 'Lord of Heaven' occurs frequently in southern Arabian monotheistic inscriptions which notably lack any Christian references (Robin 2009). This syncretism may be another indication of uncertainty surrounding the initial adoption of Christianity at Aksum. For further examples of possible continuity in religious practice from pre-Christian to Christian times, see Chapter 3.

[30] Nautin and Caquot in Anfray *et al.* 1970; see also Kobishchanov 1979: 234–40.

[31] RIE 186, 187 and 188, only the last of which definitely names Ezana.

[32] RIE 189, 190 and 271, of which all except the second name Ezana, as do the trilingual inscriptions RIE 185/270 and 185*bis*/270*bis*.

[33] RIE 271. This conclusion is valid whether or not one accepts the hypothesis that RIE 190 and 271 refer to the same military event as RIE 189 (*cf.* Chapter 6).

Fig. 28 Greek-inscribed silver coin [diameter: 13.5 mm] of Ousanas, early fourth-century, with no religious symbol

the broadly parallel versions is beginning to yield interesting results: it appears that, in most instances, the Ge'ez rendition was primary (*cf.* Chapter 5) and that its basic form was subsequently translated into Greek with amplification to emphasise its Christian aspects. A recent claim[34] that anti-Arian tendencies are detectable in the Greek versions may have limited relevance to the doctrinal sympathies held at this time by the Christian Aksumites themselves, as opposed to those of the translator.

Study of Aksumite coinage yields fully compatible evidence. The coins of the pre-Christian kings of Aksum bore the crescent-and-disc symbol above the royal portrait (*e.g.* Fig. 69), and this practice was initially followed by Ezana, presumably before his conversion; on later coins, from Ezana onwards, this symbol was replaced by the Christian cross (Fig. 71). Those coins of Ezana and his immediate predecessor which have no religious symbol (Fig. 28) may be interpreted as reflecting uncertainty as to the popular acceptability of the new religion that was subsequently embraced by the king.

Ezana's Christianity seems to have been more openly publicised to a Greek-reading public – resident foreigners and/or users of internationally circulating currency – than to his local subjects, among whom scepticism or opposition may initially have prevailed. Only gradually did Christianity gain acceptance through the Aksumite population beyond the capital's royal, élite and foreign communities. Desire for wider acceptance of the new religion is tellingly illustrated on locally-circulating base-metal coins issued during the late fourth and/or the early fifth centuries (Chapter 14).

The date of the royal conversion

Textual, epigraphic and numismatic arguments combine to indicate that it was in or shortly after the fourth decade of the fourth century that the kings of Aksum formally adopted Christianity, which had previously been largely restricted there to members of the expatriate community. Much effort has been directed towards ascertaining precisely when this took place. Clearly, the

[34] This paper (Black 2008) was based exclusively on the Greek texts and took no account of those in Ge'ez. For Arianism, see footnote 25, above.

date must fall between 328, when Athanasius was first elevated to patriarchal status, and 356/7, when the letter from Constantius II demonstrated that Frumentius was serving as bishop in Aksum, apparently under royal support or patronage. Rufinus' account has generally been interpreted as indicating that, at the time of Frumentius' visit to Alexandria, Athanasius had but recently become patriarch.[35] Taken at face value, this would imply that Frumentius' appointment took place between 328 and 335 during which latter year Athanasius was exiled from Alexandria.[36] Ethiopian ecclesiastical tradition dates the Aksumite king's conversion to 333 EC,[37] which would correspond with AD 340; it has been argued[38] that the numismatic evidence is in good agreement with the latter date. While a royal adoption of Christianity in 340 is not incompatible with an appointment of Frumentius to the new Aksum bishopric in or before 335, it also opens the possibility that the latter event might have taken place not shortly after Athanasius' initial installation but after his return from exile in 337.[39] Although this view requires acceptance of an error or lack of clarity in Rufinus' transmitted text, additional arguments may be cited in its support. Had Frumentius' visit to Alexandria taken place before the death of Constantine the Great in 337 – effectively before 335/6 since Athanasius was exiled from Alexandria from that year until after Constantine's death – one would expect it to have been noted in the writings of Eusebius of Caesarea rather than in their supplementation by Rufinus.[40] Other authorities have

35 This is the usual interpretation of the original Latin *nam is nuper sacerdotium susceperat.* It has always been interpreted as referring to Athanasius' initial elevation to the patriarchate (*e.g.* Amidon 1997: 20) but the possibility may be considered that it was intended to refer to Frumentius becoming a priest (*cf.* Stevenson 1966: 35). However, the Ethiopian *Synaxarium* – although now surviving only in post-thirteenth-century versions – notes that, on arrival in Alexandria, Frumentius found Athanasius 'restored to his office' (Budge 1928a: 1165) or 'in his new office' (Grillmeier 1996: 299–300, translating B. Dombrowski & F. Dombrowski 1984: 116–19). This would require a more specialised meaning of *susceperat*, but one that is well attested and accepted elsewhere; it would also remove the implication that Frumentius' appointment should be placed early in the reign of Athanasius. However, the clause cited above fits uncomfortably in either context and has all the appearance of a gloss – perhaps by a later copyist – which subsequently became incorporated in the main text. This hypothesis is confirmed by the clause's absence from the Greek texts of Theodoret and Sozomen, both of which are based almost word-for-word on Rufinus: there must thus have been available a version or versions of Rufinus' work into which this particular clause had not been incorporated. Nonetheless, the clause does occur in the version of Socrates Scholasticus (see footnote 10 above). I am grateful to Dr Richard Duncan-Jones for his advice on the matters discussed in this footnote.

36 This position has been adopted by, among others, Heldman (2007). For Athanasius' chronology, see Anatolios (2004). Stevenson (1966: 1) dated the start of Athanasius' second exile to 336, but most other authorities have preferred 335.

37 For the symbolic 'triple three' date, see Sergew *et al.* 1997: 3. 'EC' designates the Ethiopian calendar, which numbers years approximately seven years behind the Gregorian (Fritsch & Zanetti 2003). Unless otherwise specified all dates cited in this book follow the Gregorian calendar.

38 This view was put forward most strongly by Hahn (1999) who subsequently (2006a) – but without clear explanation – revised his estimate of the royal conversion-date to 347–9, as previously proposed by B. Dombrowski & F. Dombrowski (1984: 131).

39 This chronological problem, and the conclusion supporting a date after 337 for Frumentius' consecration and Ezana's conversion, was already proposed by Henri de Valois [Valesius] as long ago as the third quarter of the seventeenth century. Thelamon (1981: 62) suggested that Rufinus may have wished to imply that the consecration of Frumentius took place during the reign of Constantine the Great.

40 It is also noteworthy that a detailed biography of Athanasius covering the years 328–35 (Arnold 1991) made no mention of Frumentius or of Aksum.

placed the Aksumite king's conversion even later,[41] but the evidence seems weak. The best estimate lies in the period 337–50, fully in accord with Ethiopian tradition; greater precision is not attainable pending the discovery of new evidence.

Archaeological evidence for the spread of Christianity in the northern Horn

The period between the mid-fourth and the early-seventh centuries saw Aksum's florescence under Christian rule. In considering the archaeological evidence, the first point to emphasise is that, if we omit the coins and the stone inscriptions, archaeological excavation has yielded remarkably little indication of the initial adoption of Christianity. Around the middle of the fourth century, as discussed in Chapter 12, there seems to have been a significant change in the outward trappings of the royal burial tradition at Aksum. However, explicit evidence for Aksumite Christianity was largely restricted to areas under direct royal control for 100–150 years after the king's conversion; only slowly and hesitantly was the new religion accepted by the populace at large and spread into rural areas distant from the capital. Even among the élite inhabitants of outlying urban sites, it seems that the old religion was openly followed until at least the fifth century. The stelae at Anza and Matara (Chapters 6 and 7) bear prominent crescent-and-disc symbols, together with inscriptions (RIE 218 and 223 respectively) for which a third-century date is generally considered probable.[42] At Aksum, the élite Tomb of the Brick Arches, securely dated to the late-fourth century,[43] contained funerary pottery vessels (*cf.* Chapter 13) on which a cross-motif was paired with the crescent-and-disc.[44] The best evidence for widespread acceptance of Christianity is probably the use of cross-designs in the decoration of domestic pottery. Such designs, scratched onto vessels both before and after firing,[45] did not become common until the late-fifth and early-sixth centuries. A tombstone recently discovered at Gumala, *c.* 5 km north of Aksum,[46] bears a Greek inscription headed with a cross. No grave or other associations were recorded, and the sixth-century dating is based solely on the style of lettering. The inscription, indicating the burial of a ten-year-old boy, is headed by a neatly carved cross. The name of the deceased is Greek, but one that subsequently took the local form 'Tcherqos'. This discovery may indicate the survival, perhaps in a peripheral settlement, of a distinct Greek-speaking Christian community at a time when Christianity was spread widely through the Aksumite population (Chapters 5 and 12).

41 Frend (1972: 15) dated the consecration of Frumentius *c.* 351(see also *idem* 1974: 34), which would not be incompatible with Brakmann's (1999) view that Ezana's conversion took place shortly before 356/7. Török (1987: 33–46) presented arguments for an even later date (*cf.* Munro-Hay 1991b: 205). Marcus' (1994: 7) dating of these events in the first decade of the fourth century is wholly erroneous.

42 These estimates are based on epigraphic comparisons only. It applies only to the inscription and does not preclude the possibility that the stelae themselves and the crescent-and-disc symbols could be earlier.

43 For detailed accounts of this tomb, see Chittick 1974; Munro-Hay 1989a: esp. 55–60, 273; D. Phillipson 2000b: 31–133.

44 Wilding & Munro-Hay 1989: 272–4.

45 Examples from Aksum are illustrated by J. S. Phillips (2000: figs 77, 282) and from Matara by Anfray (1963b: pls cv–cviii).

46 Fiaccadori 2007b.

Fig. 29 Leaf with portrait of an Evangelist, in the *Gospels* at Abba Garima monastery, Adwa (photograph by Jacques Mercier, supplied and reproduced by courtesy of the Ethiopian Heritage Fund)

Fig. 30 Leaf with canon table, in the *Gospels* at Abba Garima monastery, Adwa (photograph by Jacques Mercier, supplied and reproduced by courtesy of the Ethiopian Heritage Fund)

It has recently been shown[47] that the Ethiopian tradition of manuscript illumination was active by at least the sixth or seventh century (see also Chapter 13). The primary evidence is provided by two radiocarbon age-determinations on vellum fragments detached from the margins of decorated leaves bound into a gospel volume kept at the Monastery of Abba Garima near Adwa. The dated leaves bear fine portraits of evangelists (*e.g.* Fig. 29). Also bound into the same volume are canon tables (Fig. 30) for which a sixth-century date had previously been proposed on stylistic grounds.[48] Recent studies suggest that certain elements of Ethiopian ecclesiastical literature have a similar antiquity.[49] There is thus increasing evidence to support traditions that, by the sixth century, Christianity was firmly established and widespread through the Aksumite realm, already displaying many of the distinctive features that have characterised it in later times.[50] This evidence for the expansion of Christianity in the Aksumite kingdom should be viewed in conjunction with that of church buildings and burial practices, discussed in Chapters 11 and 12 respectively.

Judaism

During the sixth century, several Aksumite kings took names – *e.g.* Kaleb, Israel, Gersem – that were derived from the Old Testament.[51] This seems broadly to coincide with the time when translations of the Bible became available in Ge'ez, and when Christianity was embraced throughout the Aksumite population.[52] Widespread adoption of Old Testament practices at this period would have led to an ambivalent attitude[53] whereby Judaic traditions were respected and adopted, despite Jews themselves being reviled as responsible for the death of Christ. A large and influential part of the Aksumite population may have valued its connections with other Semitic-speaking peoples, especially with those of southern Arabia amongst whom monotheism – as at Aksum – had prevailed since the fourth century. It was probably at this time that feelings of Judaic affinity became firmly established and that Ethiopian Christianity came to emphasise many of the Judaic aspects that it has retained ever since and which have attracted attention from a wide range of commentators.[54]

[47] The evidence cited by Mercier 2000 has proved difficult for some palaeographers and art-historians to accept (*e.g.* Balicka-Witakowska 2005b), but is slowly becoming agreed more widely (see D. Phillipson 2009a: 191). For further discussion, taking no account of earlier research, see M. Bailey in *The Art Newspaper,* June 2010.

[48] Heldman 1993: 119, 129–30. Canon tables are a method of presenting a concordance of the gospels (Nordenfalk 1938; Heldman 2003) originally devised by Eusebius of Caesarea.

[49] The evidence has been summarised by Knibb 2003, Uhlig 2003b and Zuurmond 2003 for parts of the Bible, and by Bausi 2006a for other works.

[50] The traditions, primarily those relating to the 'nine saints', are discussed below. The hypothesis of strong continuity in ecclesiastical matters between ancient Aksum and so-called 'medieval' Ethiopia, has been developed by D. Phillipson (2007, 2009a).

[51] Hahn 2001. Hahn's suggestion that the name of the fifth-century king Eon should be read Noe [Noah] and regarded as the earliest example of this practice is not convincing.

[52] It was also the time when the psalms were quoted in an Aksumite royal inscription (RIE 192; *cf.* Chapter 6).

[53] This is particularly clear in many passages of the *Kebra Negast* (Chapter 6).

[54] This is not to preclude the possibility that some elements now described as 'Judaic', such as dietary practices, may be of considerably greater antiquity in the northern Horn. For further discussion, see Ullendorff 1956, 1968; Rodinson 1964a, 1965.

Abraha and Atsbaha

So far, the reconstruction offered has been based very largely on four sources of evidence: epigraphic, numismatic, archaeological, and written accounts originating outside the Aksumite realm itself. When these data are compared with Ethiopian traditions which – for the most part – were not committed to writing until later times, an inconsistency is immediately apparent. The traditions make no mention of the name 'Ezana', but clearly record that the advent of Christianity to Aksum took place during the reign of two kings named Abraha and Atsbaha. Reference is never made to either partner individually, and the impression is gained that the concept of their duality was one with which the traditions have had difficulty; it is almost as if 'Abraha-wa-Atsbaha' were recalled as a single individual.[55] It has been proposed that Abraha and Atsbaha were alternative names for Ezana and Sazana, although it has been argued that the latter's presumed status as co-ruler and biological brother of the former is due to combination of an error on the part of Constantius II with a misunderstanding of RIE 185/270 (*cf.* Chapter 8). A second, but rather more plausible, explanation takes account of the confusion that prevails in some sources – further noted in Chapter 15 – between the fourth-century Ezana and the sixth-century Kaleb as the king during whose reign Christianity was adopted at Aksum.[56] One of Kaleb's alternative names was Ella Atsbaha, and he is also closely linked with one Abraha who initially ruled in southern Arabia as his representative following that region's conquest (Chapter 15). It thus seems likely that the connection between the coming of Christianity and the linked names of Abraha and Atsbaha was largely due to this confusion.[57]

The wider political context

The conversion of the Aksumite kingdom, as described by Rufinus, shows strong similarity with that author's account of the corresponding event in the Caucasian kingdom of Iberia,[58] which took place at broadly the same time. This opens up further interesting questions as to the extent to which the fourth-century adoption of Christianity by the rulers of states peripheral to the Roman Empire was – at least in part – a reaction to political circumstances. Any perceived political advantage was, however, soon eroded by doctrinal controversy. Athanasius' relations with the Constantinople imperial authorities regularly ran into difficulty, and Aksumite Christianity was consequently regarded as suspect in the latter quarter. The efforts of Constantius II to confirm Frumentius' Arianism or to secure his deposition have already been noted.

Clearer understanding of these developments is unlikely until such time as more light can be cast on the evolving relationship between political and

[55] Significantly, neither the advent of Christianity nor Abraha and Atsbaha receive any mention in the *Kebra Negast* (Chapter 6).

[56] It was recorded by John Malalas (Jeffreys *et al.* 1986: 248, 251) that, on initiating his military invention in southern Arabia, Kaleb vowed that he would – if successful – become a Christian. This source betrays its originator's ignorance of the Aksumite kingdom's history and circumstances.

[57] This hypothesis seems first to have been proposed by Ullendorff 1949, and has subsequently been supported by others, including the present writer (D. Phillipson 1998: 142–3).

[58] Iberia, now more usually referred to as Kartli (Lang 1966: 57, 75–6, 82–96; Silogava & Shengelia 2007: 41–71), was a precursor of the modern Georgia, centred in that country's southern and central areas. Haas 2008 further explored the similarities between the Aksum and Kartli kingdoms' conversions – of which Rufinus himself was clearly aware.

religious authority at Aksum.[59] Constantius II clearly believed that Ezana – and Sazana – had supreme influence in both areas. This would have been Constantius' own preferred role in Constantinople, and that one which Ezana may have sought at Aksum if – as seems likely – his adoption of Christianity owed much to his perception of political advantage. By the fifth century, there is evidence that regional bishops may have been appointed within the Aksumite realm,[60] possibly suggesting greater delegation of authority in ecclesiastical matters than prevailed politically (*cf.* Chapter 8). There is little doubt that, other than for an interlude under Kaleb (see Chapter 15), the Aksumites maintained a low profile in their relations with Rome / Byzantium; some reflection of this is also discernible in religious affairs. The Ethiopian Orthodox Church has not accepted the decisions reached at any of the Church Councils held after that at Ephesus in 449 and this, of course, includes the Council of Chalcedon which, two years later, effectively reversed the decisions taken at Ephesus.

The Council of Chalcedon

The Ethiopian Church today is monophysite or non-Chalcedonian.[61] The argument is sometimes encountered[62] that its specifically monophysite features must post-date the Council of Chalcedon in 451. Such a view is not supported by current understanding of the monophysite / dyophysite controversy and of the semantic fudges by which the Council of Chalcedon sought to resolve it. The complexity and opacity of the Council's deliberations are unfortunately reflected in much recent literature.[63] The Council sought to address a strong disagreement that had arisen during the first half of the fifth century between those who considered that Christ's human and divine natures were distinct and those who held that both aspects were indistinguishable in a single nature. It was the compromise adopted at Chalcedon – *i.e.* the dyophysite position – that was the innovation; those who rejected it, the monophysites, simply preferred to retain their earlier beliefs. In the succinct words of Cardinal Grillmeier, '...the starting point of Ethiopian Christology is pre-Chalcedonian, not anti-Chalcedonian'.[64] It follows that evidence for monophysite doctrine, as opposed to specific rejection of Chalcedon, does not necessarily indicate a date later than 451.

Late-fifth-century developments recalled in Ethiopian traditional history are seen primarily in terms of penetration of Christianity into extra-urban areas, and linked with the arrivals of the 'nine saints' – missionaries from the 'Roman' [*i.e.* Byzantine] empire – to whose activities is attributed the foundation of monasteries and churches in several areas beyond the capital (Fig. 31).[65] Little significance need be attached to speculation – based partly on the

59 *cf.* Sergew 1969.

60 See Monneret de Villard 1947; Honigmann 1950. The sources are contested and the existence of these bishops remains to be proven. The churches of this period are discussed in Chapter 11.

61 For an outline of the preferred terminologies, the reader is referred to Binns 2002: 63–96. Monophysitism has taken varied forms and neither was nor is a unitary doctrinal category.

62 *e.g.* Trimingham 1952: 40; P. Mitchell 2005: 86.

63 Reasonably dispassionate surveys have been provided by Sellars 1953 for the Council itself and by Frend 1972 and Gray 2005 for its aftermath.

64 Grillmeier 1996: 372.

65 Convenient summaries of the relevant traditions have been provided by Doresse 1956 and by Sergew 1972: 115–21; see also Brita 2007. Munro-Hay 2005b took a more sceptical view and, while not denying the significance of individual 'saints' and their exploits, argued that their arrival and activity should not be interpreted as a single co-ordinated phenomenon.

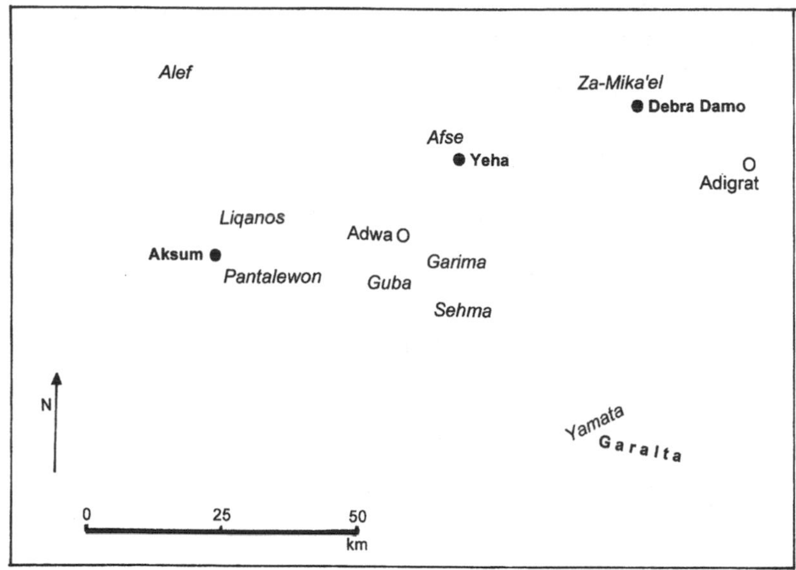

Fig. 31 The dispersal of the 'nine saints', whose names are shown in italics, relative to some modern toponyms; the area over which the saints operated was surprisingly limited (data from Sergew 1972; Belaynesh *et al.* 1975)

misunderstanding noted above – concerning the non-Chalcedonian connections of these missionaries. Pride of place among their foundations goes to the mountain-top monastery church of Debra Damo (Fig. 43), which still stands and which traces its foundation to one of the 'nine saints' – Za-Mika'el Aregawi – in the reign of the sixth-century Aksumite king Gabra Masqal.[66]

Sixth- and seventh-century developments

Between the second and fourth decades of the sixth century, the Aksumite and Byzantine Empires maintained closer contact and collaboration than at any other time, the prime reasons – at least from the Byzantine viewpoint – being political and economic.[67] A detailed account of this episode is placed elsewhere in this book (Chapter 15). Both parties – but particularly the Ethiopian – found it expedient to present the alliance in religious terms, as joint revenge on a 'Jewish' king for his persecution of a Christian community. This aspect requires brief consideration: the whole episode features far larger in Arabian and Syrian historical sources than it does in Byzantine or Ethiopian ones, where the principal record is found in Procopius' *History of the Wars*.[68] The strongly Chalcedonian Byzantine emperor, Justin, apparently had no qualms about an alliance with his non-Chalcedonian Aksumite counterpart. In Ethiopian sources, all of

[66] The church at Debra Damo is further discussed in Chapter 11. For King Gabra Masqal, see Chapter 8.

[67] An alternative view has been expressed (Gajda 2009: 102–9; *cf.* also Chapter 15), which attributes the Byzantine involvement to Justin's successor and protégé, Justinian I, the initial preparations for the invasion having been undertaken by the Aksumites alone.

[68] Procopius, *History of the Wars* I xix–xx (Dewing 1914–28, 1: 178–95).

which are significantly later in date, it is the religious aspects of the episode that appear paramount, even though Justin and Kaleb were presented to the latter's subjects as two great kings who – between them – ruled the world.[69]

Later in the sixth century, following Kaleb's abdication,[70] the principal Ethiopian events of which we have evidence are religious ones. The link with conquered southern Arabian territories rapidly weakened, and it seems likely that the Aksumite state was already feeling the effects of over-extension (see Chapter 15). As discussed in Chapters 16 and 17, a significant number of extant churches and monasteries attribute their foundation to this period, often linked with the name either of an Aksumite king or of one of the 'nine saints'. Such claims have brought considerable prestige to the institutions concerned, but they rarely merit credence unless supported by independent evidence. They may be compared with land-grants and other endowments to the Cathedral of Maryam Tsion at Aksum, notices of which are preserved only in significantly later copies of questionable authenticity.[71] These institutions were, increasingly but not exclusively, located in the eastern highlands of Tigray rather than in the vicinity of Aksum itself, and it is tempting to link this shift with the decline in Aksum's political authority and the transfer of the capital to a more easterly location (see Chapter 16 for a more detailed discussion of this process).

Two further aspects of religious development in the early seventh century require comment. First, the coinage (Chapter 14) maintained its traditional and emphatically Christian aspect to its end. It was, however, apparently at this time that exiled family and followers of the Prophet Mohammed were well received by the Ethiopian king. Muslim historians of later date are our sole source of information about this episode.[72] No reflection of these events has yet been recognised in the archaeological record or, less surprisingly, in Christian tradition. In fact, as discussed in Chapters 16 and 17, it is in the religious field – specifically Christian – that Aksum's legacy to later periods of Ethiopian history has been strongest and most pronounced.

[69] This view is preserved in the *Kebra Negast* (Chapter 6) which, although apparently brought together in its present form as late as the early-fourteenth century, incorporates much earlier material. See also Chapter 17 and Martinez 1990.

[70] Fiaccadori 2007a; see also Chapters 8 and 15.

[71] Huntingford 1965a.

[72] Trimingham 1952: 44–6 and references cited; see also Chapter 16.

10

Cultivation and Herding, Food and Drink

Settlement patterns

The territory controlled by the kingdom of Aksum was exceedingly diverse, with major topographic impediments to communication combining with highly varied productivity and carrying capacity, as discussed in Chapter 2 with reference to earlier times. When these factors are taken into account, the dominant impression given by current research is one of cultural continuity from at least the opening centuries of the first millennium BC (*cf.* Chapters 2 and 3) into Aksumite times and – with comparatively minor changes – subsequently. It is tempting to base reconstructions on circumstances and practices that have prevailed even more recently but – while such comparisons can indeed provide useful guidance to understanding ancient conditions and economies – full allowance must be made both for circumstantial changes and for limitations imposed by data-collection methodologies.

Incomplete coverage of archaeological research and publication imposes additional limitations; dated information about the farming economy is effectively restricted to the Aksum region which, because of its urban and peri-urban nature, cannot be assumed to have been typical of a wider area.[1] Archaeological survey has thrown significant light on the changing distributions of rural settlement, but has not yet been fully exploited to illustrate any coherent pattern or patterns in economic practice overall.[2] Important conclusions may nonetheless be drawn, particularly for the region around Aksum itself, although care should be exercised in extrapolating these conclusions more widely. There seems to have been steady growth in population, both within the urban centre and in peripheral settlements, during most of the first half of the first millennium AD; these localised increases reached a peak around the fifth and early-sixth centuries, and declined thereafter – with increasing rapidity during the late-sixth and early-seventh centuries.[3]

[1] The nature of Aksumite urbanism is discussed in Chapter 11. Studies of farming economy in the Asmara region (Schmidt *et al.* 2008d) relate to periods before and after the first millennium AD. Results of ongoing investigations in the northeastern Tigray highlands (D'Andrea *et al.* 2008a) are not yet fully available.

[2] The principal broad surveys have been in the Aksum-Yeha region (Michels 2005) and in the Gulo Makeda area north of Adigrat (D'Andrea *et al.* 2008a). Results of more detailed survey around Aksum are in course of publication (*cf.* Fattovich *et al.* 2000: 31–43; Bard *et al.* 2003; L. Phillipson 2009b; Fattovich 2010).

[3] Michels (1988, 1990, 1994) provided useful summaries of these trends, which were supported more fully by data presented subsequently (Michels 2005) and by radiocarbon and other dating evidence. For further discussion, see D. Phillipson 2008a; also Chapters 7, 11 and 16. L. Phillipson (2000b: 470; 2009b: esp. 128–30) discussed settlement patterns in a more narrowly defined area around Aksum.

Further information is preserved in written sources, both in Aksumite inscriptions and, occasionally, in the writings of Graeco-Roman historians. As will become apparent in the following discussion, these all present difficulties in interpretation, but an attempt is nonetheless made to integrate their data with that derived from archaeology.[4]

The subsistence economy of the Aksumite kingdom was based firmly on the exploitation of domestic plants and animals, wild species having only very minor significance. As emphasised in Chapter 2, it is inappropriate to consider cultivation and herding as a unitary phenomenon since plants and animals occupied distinct – not always interconnected – niches in economic practice. Consideration of both under the single rubric 'food-production' is even more misleading because many of the benefits derived from domestic plants and animals were in non-dietary areas.[5]

Cultivation

Contrary to earlier beliefs, it now appears that irrigation was rarely, if ever, practised by Aksumite cultivators.[6] As noted in Chapter 3, a similar situation appears to have prevailed in earlier periods also.

Much of our detailed knowledge of crops that were cultivated in Aksumite times is derived from archaeological excavations, notably at Kidane Mehret on the northern outskirts of the capital's built-up area and at K site in Aksum itself; sparse crop remains were also present in the Tomb of the Brick Arches.[7] Further information has been obtained from sites on Beta Giyorgis hill immediately northwest of Aksum,[8] although the emphasis of research there has been on the earlier periods, discussed in Chapter 3. The crops of which specimens have been recovered from stratified and dated Aksumite-period deposits are tabulated in Fig. 32; as indicated, many of these were also cultivated locally during earlier times. This section concentrates on those crops that were added to the repertoire during Aksumite times, and on a general overview of Aksumite agriculture. Continuity of cultivation since at least the first half of the last millennium BC can be demonstrated for emmer wheat, barley, lentil and flax/linseed. Oats, teff and noog, the earlier evidence for which remains doubtful,[9] all gained in popularity during the first millennium AD.

4 *cf.* Mary Harlow & W. Smith 2001.

5 For discussion of these points in a wider African context, see D. Phillipson 2005: 169.

6 Sulas *et al.* 2009.

7 These three sites were excavated in 1993–96 (D. Phillipson 2000b: 267–379, 381–418, and 31–133 respectively), the palaeobotanical research being undertaken by Sheila Boardman (2000: 363–8, 412–4, 127–8, also 468–70). Boardman's 1999 account of her work at Aksum was written before stratigraphic correlations at Kidane Mehret were finalised or radiocarbon dates obtained; it should therefore be read in conjunction with her later publications and the full excavation reports. Note that Kidane Mehret has also been designated 'D site' or 'domestic site' in some publications.

8 Details are provided by Bard *et al.* (2000 and references cited) and, somewhat more comprehensively, by D'Andrea 2008.

9 Sparse occurrences of oats in earlier times may have been derived from weeds in stands of barley. The stratigraphy at Kidane Mehret cannot rule out the possibility that teff and noog were present only in the second phase of occupation in the sixth and seventh centuries (Boardman 2000: 365). Evidence for teff on Ancient Ona sites is limited to a single seed from Mai Chiot, dated only by its apparent association (D'Andrea *et al.* 2008b; D'Andrea 2008). For further discussion, see Chapter 3.

Crop	Aksumite attestation	Earlier attestation	Comments
Emmer wheat	G2, B, G3, K, DL	DE*, A, G1	
Free-threshing wheat	G2, K*, DL	A, G1	rare at A and G1
Barley	G2, B, G3, K*, DL*	DE, A, G1	
Sorghum	B, DL		rare
Finger millet	G2, DL		rare
Teff	G2, G3, K, DL	DE?, A	DE uncertain
Oats	K, DL	DE	Perhaps weed at DE
Chick pea	K, DL		
Pea	DL		
Grass pea	K, DL		
Lentil	G2, G3, K, DL	DE?, A, G1	DE uncertain
Fava bean	DL		
Flax/linseed	G2, G3, B, K, DL*	DE, A, G1	
Cotton	B, K. DL*		
Noog	DL	DE?	DE uncertain
Grape	G2, G3, K, DL*		rare
Gourd	DL		
Cress	K, DL		

Key to sites and contexts:

DE Kidane Mehret, *c.* eighth to fifth centuries BC [219 specimens identified]

A Ancient Ona sites near Asmara, mostly *c.* eighth to fifth centuries BC [257 specimens identified]

G1 Beta Giyorgis, *c.* third century BC

G2 Beta Giyorgis, *c.* first to fourth centuries

B Tomb of the Brick Arches, fourth century

G3 Beta Giyorgis, *c.* fifth to seventh centuries

K K site, *c.* fifth to seventh centuries [420 specimens identified]

DL Kidane Mehret, *c.* sixth to seventh centuries [1418 specimens identified]

* indicates that one or more identified seeds from this occurrence have been subjected to AMS radiocarbon dating with results confirming the age specified.

Fig. 32 Archaeobotanical identifications of Aksumite crops (data from Bard *et al.* 2000; Boardman 2000; Cain 2000; D'Andrea 2008; D'Andrea *et al.* 2008b)

The plant [*Linum usitatissimum*] from which flax fibres and linseed oil may both be obtained has demonstrably been cultivated in the northern Horn through most – if not all – of the past three millennia, but its original purpose cannot yet be ascertained. In more recent times, oil has been the primary product in the region, and it has been stated that preparation of flax fibre was not locally practised; [10] it would, however, be premature to assume that this was necessarily the case during the first millennium AD. As noted in Chapter 8, a Byzantine envoy reported that the formal attire of the Aksumite king Kaleb was made of linen.

The numerous Aksumite-period introductions included sorghum, finger millet, peas, chick peas, grass peas, fava beans, cotton, gourds, cress and – perhaps – grapes. Of these, cotton was present by the fourth century, and grapes somewhat earlier, but there is no firm evidence for any of the others until the late-fifth century. These newcomers represent significant expansions. First, the earlier emphasis on cereals was reduced by the addition of a range of pulses; lentils had previously been the only representative of the latter group. Among the pulses, the grass pea [*Lathyrus sativus*] is of particular interest, being a drought-resistant crop that is widely cultivated in Ethiopia today, despite being toxic if not carefully prepared.[11] The chick pea [*Cicer arietinum*], present in fifth-to-seventh-century contexts at Kidane Mehret and K site, was a species first cultivated in southwest Asia. The specific designation of the peas from Kidane Mehret is not fully clear: either the Asian *Pisum sativum* or the indigenous *Pisum abyssinicum* could be represented.[12] Although teff may have been cultivated in small quantities previously,[13] preparation of *injera* may be indicated archaeologically by the presence of the round burnished pottery trays [*metad*] on which it was – until recently – cooked, but such artefacts have not been recognised in contexts earlier than the sixth century.[14]

Use of wheats and other cereals remains poorly understood. Before its grains can be ground, emmer requires pounding to remove the husks; in recent times, this has been done in a wooden mortar. Grinding is now done on a sub-rectangular slab of stone of a type that is also frequently preserved in archaeological deposits of the Aksumite period.[15] Adulis is the only location in the Aksumite realm where rotary querns have been recorded.[16]

Additional crops locally represented for the first time in the first millennium AD appear to have been introduced from elsewhere. It cannot yet be determined whether cotton was actually grown in the Aksum area between the fourth and the seventh centuries, or whether its fibre was imported from lower altitudes to the west for processing. Cotton has not been reported from archaeobotanical

[10] *e.g.* Simoons 1960: 121; 1965. However, precisely the opposite situation prevailed during the pharaonic period in Egypt (Vogelsang-Eastwood 2000), continuing through the first millennium AD.

[11] Butler *et al.* 1999 have provided a useful account of this crop and of its health-risks, cultivation and preparation.

[12] For a detailed discussion of these varieties, see Butler 2003.

[13] Chapter 3; also D'Andrea 2008.

[14] *Injera* is the flat, teff-flour bread cooked from fermented batter that is today the preferred and highly nutritious staple food in northern Ethiopia and much of Eritrea. For *metad*, see Wilding & Munro-Hay 1989: 268, 308–11; also D. Phillipson 1993: 354. A possible further example is illustrated by J. S. Phillips (2000: fig. 273h). *Injera* might, of course, have been made in earlier times without using *metad*.

[15] L. Phillipson 2001.

[16] Anfray 1974: 752.

research on Beta Giyorgis, although it does occur at three lower-lying sites in the immediate Aksum vicinity. This suggests the possibility that either its cultivation or the processing of imports may have been restricted to the latter area.[17] Sorghum and finger millet seem likewise to have been introduced from the west or southwest.[18] There is some evidence that cultivation of emmer may have been reduced at this time, as recently introduced free-threshing wheat gained in popularity.[19] Other crops of which cultivation apparently began during Aksumite times are cress, gourds and – less certainly (see below) – grapes. These last are of particular interest in view of the question, discussed below, as to whether the Aksumites were wine-producers as well as wine-importers. There is no evidence that coffee has ever been grown in what was formerly Aksumite territory, or that it was employed as food or beverage during Aksumite times.[20]

Herding

The following outline is based on information derived from four sources: inscriptions, rock art, figurines, and faunal remains preserved on archaeological sites. The first of these requires detailed knowledge of ancient vocabulary, and interpretation of the second is hindered – as noted in Chapter 2 – by dating uncertainties.

Few detailed studies have yet been published of animal bones from Aksumite contexts; an additional problem is that a significant proportion of the contexts selected for excavation have been funerary ones, where animal bones are rarely encountered. The faunal assemblages that have been published in detail are those of the late-fifth to early-seventh centuries from K site at Aksum and the sixth to

[17] As noted in Chapter 7, cultivation of cotton in the Takezze Valley was recorded in inscription RIE 189 of Ezana (but *cf.* Gervers 1992: 14–15), and the Walqayt area some 180 km west of Aksum was known for its cotton in more recent times (Nosnitsin 2010). Traces from sixth-century Kidane Mehret (Boardman 2000: 345–6; Chapter 14) have been identified as woven cotton. Processing of cotton, but not its cultivation, was recorded by visitors to the Tigray highlands during the seventeenth and eighteenth centuries (Barradas 1996: 35, 93; Bruce 1790, 3: 133). Most varieties of cotton do not flourish at altitudes above 1500 m (G. Nicholson 1960). Cotton was, however, mentioned as cultivated around Aksum in a fifteenth-century record (Zorzi in Crawford 1958: 143 – I am grateful to Dr Federica Sulas for this reference).

[18] It is generally accepted that sorghum was initially brought under cultivation in sahelian regions west of the Nile, although the lack of definite archaeological evidence for this has attracted much controversy (Haaland 1995; Young & Thompson 1999; Fuller *et al.* 2011). It was, however, widely distributed into Arabia and India from this source area (Fuller 2003; de Moulins *et al.* 2003) and its appearance in Aksum may be viewed as part of this latter process. Finger millet, probably first cultivated in the area now divided between southwestern Ethiopia and northeastern Uganda (Harlan 1971; Fuller *et al.* 2011), is widely cultivated in highland Ethiopia at the present time and, as noted below, is the preferred base for brewing beer. The implications of these crops' introduction into the Aksumite repertoire are further discussed in Chapter 16.

[19] D'Andrea 2008. This trend seems to have been accompanied by increased cultivation of free-threshing wheat, possible epigraphic evidence for which is discussed in footnote 36, below. For hulled and free-threshing wheat generally, see Hillman *et al.* 1996 and Nesbitt & Samuel 1996; specifically Ethiopian preferences are discussed by D'Andrea *et al.* 1999 and by D'Andrea & Mitiku 2002. For changing terminology, and the difficulty of interpreting ancient writers' references to wheat, see Jasny 1944: 12–26. Evidence from the Aksum area suggests that free-threshing wheat had been introduced during the first few centuries BC (Chapter 3), although emmer was still the dominant wheat in the archaeobotanical assemblages of the sixth and seventh centuries AD. The corresponding trend in Egypt proceeded more rapidly, beginning during the Ptolemaic period and resulting in the virtual cessation of emmer cultivation from the fourth century AD (Thompson 1999a; M. Murray 2000).

[20] My suggestion that certain *c.* sixth-century pottery vessels may have been coffee pots (D. Phillipson 1993: 354) should be discounted.

Fig. 33 Rock painting of unknown date at Amba Focada, northeastern Tigray, showing an ox-drawn plough (after Drew 1954)

early-seventh centuries at nearby Kidane Mehret. At both locations, cattle bones were by far the most numerous, with sheep, goat, chicken,[21] and an unidentified equid also present but in much smaller numbers. While the equid may have been a domestic donkey, this cannot be proven. The representation of species shows no major or significant difference from that recovered at Kidane Mehret in levels dated to the middle centuries of the last millennium BC (Chapter 3), save that chickens were not represented in the earlier assemblage. The material from K site also included rare representations of dog, cat and a single – perhaps wild – pig. Dogs were also present between the eighth and the fourth centuries BC at Kidane Mehret. The domestic cat is not otherwise attested in Aksumite Ethiopia. The pig, whether wild or domestic, is of interest since consumption of pork is avoided by Ethiopian Christians as well as by Muslims.

Preliminary study of faunal remains from Beta Giyorgis provides complementary results extending back also – as discussed in Chapter 3 – into earlier periods. Bones of domestic animals invariably represented a very high proportion of the total, but cattle were less dominant on Beta Giyorgis hill than they were in the lower, more open country around Aksum. During the last four centuries BC at Beta Giyorgis, cattle were even outnumbered by ovicaprids. Significantly, during the first millennium AD, the majority of cattle bones were from old individuals, suggesting that they may not have been kept primarily for meat but rather as embodiments of wealth, as draft animals and/or as milk producers.[22] As noted in Chapter 7, the move of the principal settlement from

[21] The domestic chicken, of southeast Asian origin, is surprisingly difficult to distinguish osteologically from African wild fowl (Macdonald 1992). Its introduction to Africa and its early spread there are as yet poorly understood (see Dueppen 2011), but the date of its presence at Aksum is broadly contemporaneous with its attestation at Qasr Ibrim in the Nubian Nile Valley (Macdonald & Edwards 1993).

[22] Data from Ona Negast on Beta Giyorgis are from Louis Chaix, quoted by Bard *et al.* 2000: 78–9; those from Kidane Mehret and K site from Cain 2000: 369–72, 414–7.

Fig. 34 Fourth-century pottery bowls from the Tomb of the Brick Arches at Aksum, with models of yoked oxen

Beta Giyorgis to the area below would have facilitated access to grazing land, and this seems to have been reflected in the larger numbers of cattle represented in faunal assemblages from sites in the latter location.[23]

Humped cattle have not been recognised in the archaeozoological assemblages, which is not surprising as few bones reflect this feature. However, a figurine cast in copper alloy, found without recorded associations at Zeban Kutur near Cohaito in Eritrea, clearly represents a humped animal; it bears an inscription (RIE 184) that has been palaeographically dated to the second or third centuries AD.[24] Clay figurines of cattle from Hawelti-Melazzo[25] include no clearly humped examples, while those from Matara, probably dating from around the sixth century, include at least one that is definitely humped.[26] Other representations of cattle, both humped and humpless, are largely restricted to rock paintings and engravings for which precise ages cannot be obtained. It thus appears that both humped and humpless cattle were present in this region during the first four centuries AD – as, indeed, is still the case today – but whether this duality extended earlier we do not yet know.[27]

[23] Cattle obtained as tribute from outlying regions, as recorded in the fourth-century inscriptions (Chapter 7), may have increased herd-numbers.

[24] Ricci 1959, 1960b. For background information on humped cattle, see Marshall 1989.

[25] de Contenson 1963a: 43–4, pls xxxv–xxxvi. See Chapter 3 for discussion of this site and the dating of its various components. The clay figurines may be later than the date usually attributed to them.

[26] Anfray 1967: 44–5. Of the two figurines illustrated, one – Anfray's fig. 7 – is more convincing than the other.

[27] See Chapter 3 for uncertainty regarding the presence of humped cattle at Ancient Ona sites.

Two domestic animals probably played fundamental roles in Aksumite agriculture: cattle for ploughing and threshing, and donkeys for transport, as discussed in greater detail below. Use of cattle for ploughing is represented in the famous – but undated – rock painting (Fig. 33) at Amba Focada in the north-eastern Tigray highlands.[28] Pottery models of pairs of yoked cattle are known from several sites, some fourth-century in date with others probably earlier; they were set in the bases of pottery bowls, the best-preserved and dated being recovered at Aksum from the fourth-century Tomb of the Brick Arches (Fig. 34).[29] The beasts represented are invariably humpless and short-horned. No Aksumite-period threshing floors have yet been identified but, if any exist and have survived subsequent cultivation, they should be easily recognisable.

The equids that are represented in small numbers in Aksumite faunal assemblages remain problematic. It has been suggested in Chapter 2 that their under-representation in such assemblages may be due to their use for traction rather than for food. The animals concerned were probably donkeys but, as none of the archaeozoological specimens has been precisely identified at the species level, wild zebra cannot be ruled out.[30] There is no convincing evidence that horses were exploited in the Aksumite kingdom,[31] although they had been known in the Nile Valley since the mid-second millennium BC.[32] It would be very surprising if domestic donkeys (*cf.* Chapter 2) were not exploited in Aksumite times, but definitive primary evidence is so far lacking. Camels, likewise, may have been employed, particularly at lower altitudes.[33]

Evidence from inscriptions

The fourth-century royal inscriptions at Aksum, notably those of Ezana, provide additional information about resources and diet, as do those at Anza and from Safra; details of these inscriptions are provided in Chapter 6. The eleven Aksum texts all include passages that present accounts of military exploits involving either bringing outlying territories under the control of the Aksumite king, or ensuring payment of tribute by peoples whose territory had already been annexed. The arrangements are recorded in meticulous and perhaps implausibly precise detail, including not only the numbers of captives taken, but also the catering and other arrangements that were made

28 This painting has been recorded by several writers (*e.g.* Mordini 1941; Graziosi 1941; Drew 1954; Leclant & Miquel 1959; Clark 1980; D. Phillipson 1993: 352; Fattovich 2003), with varying versions of the site's name. There have also been conflicting accounts of its location, whether in Eritrea or Ethiopia: it is, in fact, in the latter country. The published estimates of its date are often unjustifiably precise (*e.g.* McCann 2010) and based on circular argument; an Aksumite age is as plausible as one in the previous millennium.

29 See Wilding & Munro-Hay 1989: 261 and fig. 16.159; J. S. Phillips 2000: 63–4 and fig. 46. Comparable figurines have been discovered near Entichio between Adwa and Adigrat, at Kuhi south of Aksum (de Contenson 1961a), and at Hawelti-Melazzo (de Contenson 1963b), where they may be of Aksumite date.

30 Today, zebra are numerous in more southerly parts of Ethiopia but – like most wild ruminants – have largely disappeared from Tigray.

31 A clay figurine from an apparently late context at Beta Giyorgis has been described as representing the head of a horse (Fattovich & Bard 2003: 26 and fig. 3). While this identification is plausible, it is not conclusive and in any event would not necessarily indicate the actual presence of horses at or near Aksum.

32 Chaix & Gratien 2002.

33 Numerous donkeys flourish in the highlands at the present time, whereas camels are usually brought there only when transporting goods from the lowlands, since they will not breed in the former region.

for them. For example, the two trilingual inscriptions state – in all six texts RIE 185/185*bis* and 270/270*bis* – that suppression of a Bega revolt resulted in 4400 captives being brought back and settled at a place called Matlia, together with 3112 cattle, 6224 ovicaprids[34] and 677 beasts of burden.[35] Subsequently, the 4400 captives were provided with 22,000 loaves daily, it being expressly stated in both Greek and Ge'ez that these were of wheaten bread;[36] the daily issue of five loaves to each captive implies that the loaves were quite small.[37] For the scale of baking and supply suggested by these figures, see Chapter 18.

This last point is confirmed by the somewhat earlier inscription in unvocalised Ge'ez at Anza, near Hawzien in eastern Tigray (RIE 218, see Chapter 6). Although conflicting interpretations of the context have been proposed, there is clear mention of 15 days' rations – for an unspecified number of consumers – comprising a total of 520 jars of beer and 20,620 bread-loaves.[38] This beer/bread ratio supports the argument for the small size of the loaves.

[34] Published translations (Bernand 1982: 107; Bernand *et al.* 1991–2000, 3: 12) and Munro-Hay (1991b: 225) have respectively rendered the Greek word ΠΡΟΒΑΤΩΝ (genitive plural) as *moutons*/*ovins*/sheep, but it can in fact have wider application and there is no reason to assume that goats were not included. Note that the captured Bega herds – like those of the Noba whose conquest is recorded in RIE 189 – comprised twice as many ovicaprids as cattle, which is opposite to the proportions indicated by the archaeological faunal assemblages from Aksum, except for the material dated to the last four centuries BC at Beta Giyorgis. These figures do, of course, relate to the animals that were captured, and the composition of the total livestock holdings might have been different.

[35] The 'beasts of burden' mentioned here were presumably donkeys, not camels. RIE 187 and 189 (both in Ge'ez) make a clear distinction respectively between 'beasts of burden' on the one hand and camels/cattle on the other. Camels – probably at lower altitude – are also mentioned in Kaleb's inscription (RIE 191) although donkeys are never specifically designated. There was strong aversion to public use of the Greek word for donkey, and this may also have been the case in Ge'ez. For a comparable distinction, but apparently referring to packhorses rather than to camels, see the passage relating to the Alps in Strabo, *Geography* IV 6.6 (Jones 1917–32, 2: 274–5; also Tozer 1935: 315).

[36] Those responsible for the Aksumite texts seem to have attached importance to recording the kind of bread that was supplied to the Bega. The Greek term [accusative plural] used in both RIE 270 and 270*bis* was ΑΡΤΟΥϹ ϹΙΤΙΝΟΥϹ; strangely, Bernand (in Bernand *et al.* 1991–2000, 3: 6, 12) translated the identical Greek into French as *pains de blé* in the former case, but as *pains d'épeautre* in the latter; Uhlig's (2001: 20) translation of RIE 270*bis* was *Weizenbrote*. The corresponding term in the unvocalised Ge'ez versions – in both scripts – RIE 185 and 185*bis* represents *hebesta ʿalas*, the latter translated by Uhlig (2001: 24) as *Emmerbrot*, thus correcting Leslau's (1987: 61) tentative equation of *ʿalas* with spelt (Kropp, in press, however, suggests an alternative reading). Although σιτος was used in Ptolemaic Egypt specifically to designate free-threshing wheat as opposed to emmer (Thompson 1999a), the Ezana inscriptions provide the only use of the phrase αρτος σιτινος that is currently known (Battaglia 1989: 86). The possibility cannot be ignored that free-threshing wheat – apparently becoming more popular at Aksum around this time – was meant, but the precise meaning of the inscriptions' references to wheat remains unclear pending further research. I am very grateful to those scholars who have advised me on these matters: Professor Michael Knibb on the Ge'ez, Professor Peter Parsons on papyri, and Dr Delwen Samuel on the classification of wheat.

[37] See D. Phillipson (1993: 355) for further discussion. The suggestion (Lyons & D'Andrea 2003: 522) that inscriptions state 'that . . . wheaten bread was rationed to state workers and prisoners' is potentially misleading.

[38] The word by which these last were designated at Anza, HBST, was the same as that employed in RIE 185 and 185*bis* at Aksum, although there was no indication of the grain used in their preparation.

Beverages

The word for beer in the unvocalised Aksum, Anza and Safra inscriptions, SW, corresponds with the modern Tigrinya *sewa*, now a lightly alcoholic beverage for which finger millet [*dagussa*] is the preferred ingredient although other cereals – *e.g.* barley or sorghum – may be used if necessary. Finger millet, as noted above, was probably introduced from a southwesterly direction to the highlands of the northern Horn, where it is first attested archaeologically during the first four centuries AD.

There is also clear inscriptional evidence for a drink called MS in unvocalised Ge'ez, translated 'hydromel' in the Greek versions. This is clearly the Tigrinya *mes* [Amharic *tej*], although a weaker honey-drink – more akin to that now called *birz* in Tigrinya – is also possible. An indication of the antiquity of traditional *tej*-making in the northern Horn is provided by Strabo who, writing early in the first century AD, noted that the Trogodytes 'drink a brew of buckthorn but the tyrants mix honey and water'.[39] Buckthorn is the shrub *Rhamnus prinoides* [Tigrinya and Amharic *gesho*], leaves of which are added to both *sewa* and *mes* to improve flavour and aid fermentation.

A final point requiring consideration here is the extent to which the Aksumites made wine. There is now excellent evidence that they imported it, principally but not exclusively from the northern end of the Red Sea and from the eastern Mediterranean, as discussed in Chapter 16.[40] Its availability in fourth-century Aksum is indicated by the two trilingual inscriptions of Ezana (RIE 185/270 and 185*bis*/270*bis*) which recorded that wine [WYN, OINOC] was included amongst the rations supplied to the Bega captives (see above and Chapter 7)[41]. Indications that it may have been locally produced fall into three categories. The two groups of interconnected rock-cut tanks at Adi Tsehafi, northwest of Beta Giyorgis and some 4 km from Aksum, were originally described as fruit-presses,[42] but there are conflicting opinions as to the purpose for which they were initially intended.[43] Small numbers of grape pips have been recovered in the vicinity of Aksum from three Aksumite-period sites;[44] while grapes – possibly in the form of raisins – are thus shown to have been

[39] Strabo, *Geography* XVI 4, 17 (Jones 1917–32, 7: 338–9; see also Crane 1999: 519). The name Trogodytes (incorrectly Troglodytes) was often widely applied by classical authors with reference to the inhabitants of the Red-Sea coastal hinterland in what is now Eritrea (G. Murray 1967).

[40] Importation of wine seems to have begun in earlier times (Chapter 3) but its source then lay in more westerly Mediterranean regions and it may have reached the northern Horn by way of the Nile Valley (Manzo 1999, 2005).

[41] The drinks provided to the Bega were stated to have been wine, beer, hydromel and spring water; the full list appears only in RIE 270*bis*; of the other five versions, all specify wine but omit some of the others. It is interesting to speculate whether the Ge'ez WYN – from which the modern Tigrinya *wayni* is clearly derived – was originally taken from the Greek OINOC, which might imply that the beverage was known primarily as an import from Greek-speaking areas. The honey drink [YΔPOMEΛITI – dative] may have resembled the modern fermented *tej* or the virtually non-alcoholic *birz*. Beer in the Greek inscriptions is named in the dative form ZYTω. For a general survey of wine in Ethiopia, see Richard Pankhurst 2006.

[42] These tanks were first described by Littmann *et al.* (1913, 2: 74–7; D. Phillipson 1997: 162–5). Similar examples were subsequently recorded by Anfray 1965: 8, 31–3 near Ham in south-central Eritrea.

[43] See L. Phillipson 2006; Sutton 2008; also Chapter 13. Tanks very similar to those at Adi Tsehafi and Ham are known in Sudanese Nubia, where similar uncertainty surrounds their purpose (Vercoutter 1957; Adams 1966; Welsby 1996: 158–60).

[44] See Fig. 32. One of these pips has been directly dated to the seventh/eighth century (D. Phillipson 2000b: 373); the others may be rather earlier.

available in first-millennium Aksum, it does not necessarily follow that they were grown in the vicinity or that they were used for making wine.[45] Carvings in both stone and ivory suggest some Aksumite knowledge of grapevines, but the implications of this observation are not wholly clear as the motif was very widely distributed at this time in southern Arabia as well as in the Mediterranean world; the Aksumite representations could have been inspired from such prototypes rather than by first-hand familiarity with the plants themselves.[46] Pending further research, the evidence for local wine-production in the Aksumite kingdom remains inconclusive.

Hunting and gathering

It is striking how firmly the Aksumite economy was based on domesticated plants and animals. Wild animals, birds and fish – while present in most of the excavated assemblages that have been discovered – were remarkably few in number,[47] and the same is true for wild plants. It would, of course, be rash to assume that this situation prevailed over Aksumite territory as a whole: the sites that have been investigated are all in areas with dense human populations where wild food-resources would have become scarce. Wild resources of ivory and timber were, by contrast, abundant although probably – especially in the case of the former commodity – brought from a considerable distance (*cf.* Chapters 13 and 15). Evidence is, however, cited in Chapter 12 that timber became progressively rarer in the Aksum area during the sixth and seventh centuries.

Environmental change and changes through time

Studies of the domestic economy in the Aksumite kingdom are at a very early stage. Among many topics that await detailed investigation are those of change through time and the extent to which such developments may have been connected – whether as cause or as effect – with environmental fluctuation. Since this question relates to numerous aspects of Aksumite history and archaeology, it is more appropriately considered in Chapters 16 and 18.

45 Raisins were apparently used in later times for making sacramental wine (Barradas 1996: 98–100; Parkyns 1853, 2: 96).

46 See further discussion by Manzo 1999.

47 This is in agreement with the rarity of iron hunting-weapons recovered from Aksumite-period sites, as noted in Chapter 13.

11

Urbanism, Architecture and Non-Funerary Monuments

Urbanism

Several concentrations of Aksumite archaeological remains have been designated sites of 'cities' or 'towns', often solely on the basis of their extent.[1] Such classification of settlements can, however, be misleading. Unlike many of their contemporaries elsewhere,[2] no Aksumite settlements are known to have been surrounded by walls or other defensible means of demarcation.[3] Furthermore, the use-pattern of space and buildings within major Aksumite settlements seems to have been less formally differentiated than that commonly encountered elsewhere: our admittedly incomplete knowledge of Aksum itself suggests a loosely packed mixture of buildings and other features that were highly variable in scale, function and socio-economic status, with little formal demarcation between them.[4] Included were places where craft activities were conducted; large tracts were also reserved for funerary and religious or ceremonial uses. There were extensive areas with buildings whose functions remain unknown or poorly understood. With increased distance from the centre, features were less tightly packed. In such circumstances, it is impossible to estimate the total area that was occupied by ancient Aksum, but it was clearly significantly greater than that covered by many contemporaneous walled 'cities' elsewhere.[5] The roughly triangular tract demarcated by the lower slopes of Beta Giyorgis and Mai Qoho hills on the northwest and northeast and by the Ta'akha Maryam élite structure (Chapter 8 and Fig. 27; see also below) on the south covers approximately 110 ha (*cf.* Fig. 19). This figure may safely be regarded as a minimum for Aksum's extent, at least between the fourth and sixth centuries, but it could with equal plausibility be argued that the kingdom's capital covered an area several times as large.[6] This uncertainty serves to emphasise just how little we know about ancient Aksum, how much archaeological investigation remains to be done there, and the extent to which this is already being impeded by modern expansion and development.

[1] *e.g.* Michels 2005: 123–53. Some of Michels' conclusions are discussed below.

[2] *cf.*, for southern Arabia: Beeston 1971, Robin 1995, de Maigret 2002: 267–86; for the Nubian Nile Valley: Welsby 2002: esp. 129–33; more generally: Fletcher 1998.

[3] The 'fortification embankment' of Kobishchanov (1979: 118, citing Littmann *et al.* 1913, 1: Abb. 30) is a natural formation.

[4] D. Phillipson 2000a.

[5] Some comparative figures for walled cities of the first millennium AD may be cited. Roman London (second to fourth centuries) covered 140 ha; Jenne-Jeno in Mali (seventh to eighth centuries) covered 33 ha; pre-Islamic Damascus covered 115 ha.

[6] Fattovich (2010: 166) estimated expansion from *c.* 80–100 ha during the first four centuries AD to *c.* 180 ha in the sixth.

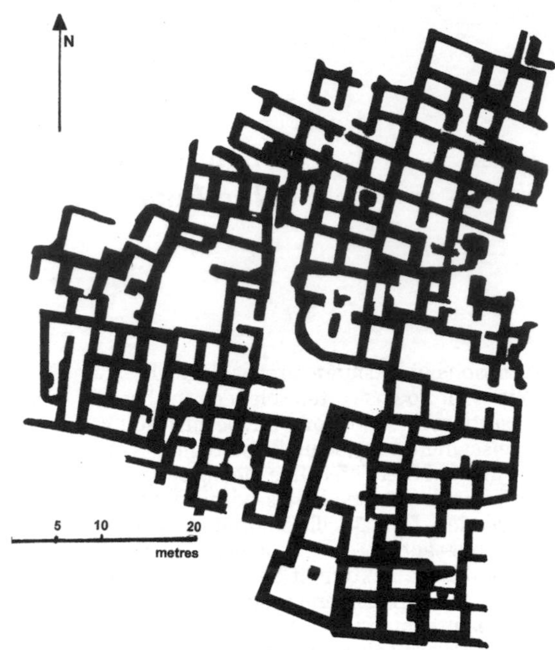

Fig. 35 Plan of close-packed Aksumite buildings at Matara (after Anfray 1974)

It is difficult to relate these data to actual populations, but an attempt should nonetheless be made to estimate the approximate numbers of people who may have been involved. So far as the kingdom of Aksum is concerned, only Michels has dared to attempt this: his calculations[7] may be accepted as hypotheses indicating the order of magnitude of ancient population levels. Michels' survey of an area of 714 sq km between Yeha and Aksum located – according to his designations and definitions – five towns, ten villages, ten hamlets and 32 élite residences or palaces; he estimated that, by the early centuries AD, the total population was about 20,000 persons. By the late-fifth and early-sixth centuries, much greater densities prevailed, with all categories of settlement more numerous and a total population in the order of 45,000. More recent survey by Rodolfo Fattovich, Laurel Phillipson and Tekle Hagos[8] has strongly suggested that these were significant under-estimates both of population numbers and of the frequency of small settlements. Perhaps more pertinent is Michels' estimate that 90 per cent of the population in his entire survey area was, by the sixth century, concentrated within the 11 per cent of that area that lay within 5 km of Mai Qoho.

These observations on the size and composition of the Aksumite capital require that the question of its correct designation be addressed. The features outlined above suggest that it may be misleading – and hence inappropriate

[7] Michels 2005: *passim*. For reservations about the underlying assumptions and presentation of Michels' estimates, see D. Phillipson 2008a.

[8] Although the full results remain unpublished, an account focused primarily on the lithics has been provided by L. Phillipson 2009b. See also Bard *et al.* 2003; Fattovich *et al.* 2000; Fattovich 2010; Sernicola & L. Phillipson 2011.

– to call it a city, since it clearly lacked many of the characteristics implied by common use of that term, particularly at this time-depth and in other parts of the world. It is noteworthy that the anonymous author of the *Periplus of the Erythraean Sea*, writing in Greek during the mid-first century AD, did not call Aksum a city but a metropolis.[9] His reasons for choosing this term are not wholly clear, but in post-classical Greek the word appears to have signified a political and/or commercial capital, particularly when viewed in the context of its offshoots or dependencies.[10] In view of this general congruence, the designation 'metropolis' is applied to Aksum in this book.[11] The capital was served by a network of roads, maintenance and security of which was a state concern.[12]

Apart from the capital, the Aksumite conurbation that has been most comprehensively investigated archaeologically is at Matara in Eritrea. Only preliminary accounts[13] have been published of the extensive investigations that were undertaken there from 1959 to 1964. The excavations took place within an area covering no more than 5 ha – less than 5 per cent of the minimal extent argued above for Aksum.[14] Several large élite buildings were exposed (see below), but extensive work revealed an area where simpler and smaller rectilinear stone buildings were tightly packed between meandering lanes (Fig. 35).

Numerous other conurbations or building-complexes of apparent Aksumite age – some very extensive – are known both from northern Ethiopia and from Eritrea. They vary considerably in size and possibly in age, but none has yet been excavated on a scale adequate to show its full extent or the nature and function of its buildings. In addition, numerous concentrations of Aksumite-type artefacts – in both rural and peri-urban situations – are not associated with remains of stone architecture.[15] The extent to which Aksum and Matara were characteristic, and how they fit in an overall picture of settlement within the kingdom of Aksum, are questions that await future research.

General features of Aksumite architecture

Before presenting detailed descriptions of various types of Aksumite building, it will be useful to make some general observations. The buildings of which physical traces survive were almost all of stone, often incorporating wooden components. Stone ranged from large, carefully dressed blocks obtained at specialist quarries, to small pieces of undressed fieldstone. Walls often

[9] *Periplus* 4 (Casson 1989: 52–3).

[10] There is no contradiction in terming the culture of the Aksumite kingdom a 'civilisation', while denying its capital designation as a 'city'. Although the two English words are ultimately connected, their common root is remote.

[11] It has also been adopted by a number of other writers, notably Michels (2005: 155–62) with particular reference to his 'Late Aksumite' period *c.* AD 450–750.

[12] Sernicola & L. Phillipson 2011. Inscription RIE 186 records maintenance of roads at royal instigation.

[13] Anfray 1963b, 1964, 1967; Anfray & Annequin 1965. Brief overviews have been provided by Anfray 1974, 1990, 2007 and by Curtis & Daniel 2008. Publications devoted specifically to artefacts, notably pottery and inscriptions, are noted elsewhere. No detailed and comprehensive account of the Matara excavations has ever been published, and its lack – more than four decades after the fieldwork was concluded – is a serious impediment to understanding. Only the Aksumite phases at Matara are considered here, the earlier ones having been discussed in Chapter 3.

[14] The original area of the Matara site could, of course, have been significantly larger than 5 ha.

[15] *e.g.* L. Phillipson 2009b: 128.

Fig. 36 Aksumite building techniques in stone and timber (after Matthews & Mordini 1959; Buxton & Matthews 1974)

comprised carefully built faces with a mud-and-rubble infill. Those not of massive dressed stone were frequently strengthened with a timber framework (Fig. 36) of horizontal beams set parallel to the line of the wall, linked with shorter ties that passed through the wall and had domed ends known as monkey-heads[16] that formed a decorative feature. Door- and window-frames were also usually of wood, fixed to horizontal beams so as to provide additional strengthening for the overall structure. By the late-fifth or early-sixth centuries, it seems that – at least in the area around Aksum – sources of heavy timber were becoming depleted, and that use of beams-and-monkey-heads construction was restricted to particularly prestigious buildings.[17]

Very little evidence is yet available as to the techniques employed for roofing or for the flooring of upper storeys. It must be assumed that the supporting framework was usually of timber and that the available lengths determined the spans between walls or pillars. No evidence has been observed that slate or tiles were used for roofing. Today, many traditional stone buildings in Tigray and the adjacent highlands of Eritrea have flat roofs of wood covered with stone slabs and/or clay; such may also have been the fashion in Aksumite times, although one house-model shows a ridged roof apparently covered with thatch. Floors were of hardened clay or stone paving; the latter generally employed dressed rectangular slabs, occasionally re-used from earlier features, but with little overall standardisation. Stone pillars were generally square in cross-section with bevelled corners and stepped bases. More elaborate column-bases show fluting, but no fluted drums are known, suggesting that most columns

[16] This is a literal translation of the Ge'ez term *re'esa habay*.

[17] As described in Chapters 16 and 17, this style of architecture continued in use for churches long after it had been abandoned for other buildings. An excellent example, dating from the mid-twentieth century, may be seen at Yeha.

Fig. 37 Iron clamp at the Tomb of the False Door, Aksum

may have been wooden. A fluted column-base of this type at Hawelti-Melazzo suggests that such refinements may not have been confined to the capital.[18]

Fired brick was employed in clearly defined circumstances, notably for arches and vaults in tombs or for domed structures such as ovens. The bricks were usually rectangular, between 4 and 8 cm thick, but otherwise unstandardised; they show signs of having been shaped in wooden moulds, but it seems that those required for individual structures were often produced separately. Although bricks were carefully set in lime-mortar, this was not used in conjunction with stone other than as a facing or render; dressed stone was usually assembled dry, or with mud-mortar – often incorporating grass or straw – employed as needed in rougher work. The fact that no use of sun-dried daub or mud-brick has been noted archaeologically does not necessarily mean that these techniques were not employed.

Metal seems to have been rarely employed in the assembly of building components. Beams and timber framing materials were jointed in such a way that nails were not required. Iron clamps (Fig. 37) were, however, sometimes used to join large dressed stones in monumental buildings, the best known examples at Aksum being at Nefas Mawcha and the Tomb of the False Door – both fourth- or fifth-century in date and described in Chapter 12 – and at the Ta'akha Maryam élite structure, discussed below.[19]

Aksumite buildings, particularly those of high status, were often set on a high foundation or plinth, the sides of which were stepped back at intervals, presumably in order to increase stability.[20] Except where construction employed large dressed-stone blocks, these steps were often capped with slabs of slate or similar rock, thus minimising penetration of water. In addition, walls were recessed at regular intervals that may have been determined by the lengths of the timbers that were available for use as beams (*cf.* Fig. 36).

[18] Leclant 1959: pl. xlv*a*, *b*. I was shown the same base – or one virtually identical – at Hawelti in 1994. The object/s were reported as surface find/s, however, so a Hawelti provenance cannot be regarded as indubitable.

[19] With two exceptions – both at the Tomb of the False Door – the clamps have long-since been removed and are only represented by the holes made to accommodate them. Three forms are known, all of which may be paralleled in Graeco-Roman architecture whence their use may have been inspired. A detailed account is in preparation.

[20] A similar feature was employed at a very much earlier date in the Great Temple at Yeha, as noted in Chapter 3.

The stelae carved to represent multi-storeyed buildings (*cf.* Chapter 12) have given rise to speculation[21] that the beams-and-monkey-heads technique was used at Aksum to erect buildings of considerable height. In fact, there is no hard evidence for this. Remains of internal stairs demonstrate that some buildings did have upper floors, but a total of two or three storeys – plus, in some cases, a basement storage facility – was probably the maximum attained. The high foundations noted above often created voids that could be used for storage below the principal entrance-level floor.

Elite structures

The best-known type of Aksumite building is that which has been misleadingly designated a palace (*cf.* Chapter 8). Examples have been recognised in both urban and peri-urban situations, so it may be that similar structures were also erected in the countryside. The term 'palace' implies that such a building served as a combined residence and operating centre for a ruler and/or overlord of some description; while plausible, there is as yet no good evidence for such a function, and the numbers in which such buildings were present at both Aksum and Matara might argue against it.[22] The less explicit term 'élite structure' is here preferred.[23]

In urban contexts, each of these complexes comprised a central building, sometimes termed a pavilion, its four sides approximately equal in length, with a projection at each corner and an entrance approached by broad steps in the recessed centre of three or four sides. The projections at the corners of these central buildings are often assumed to have formed the bases of towers, but there is no firm evidence for this other than the reference by a sixth-century visitor, Cosmas Indicopleustes, to the 'four-towered house / palace' of the king.[24] These pavilions were remarkably standardised in size, but each was set in an open court, surrounded by ranges of rooms, the whole covering an extremely variable area.[25] The largest and grandest of these complexes, Ta'akha Maryam at Aksum (Fig. 27), extended over more than one hectare, whereas Dungur, some 700 m to the west, covered – like an example at Matara – less than one third of that area. The detailed chronology of these structures is not known, so it would be premature to propose a link between this variation and changing economic fortunes. A building underlying the Cathedral podium at Aksum, noted in Chapter 7, may be the earliest known example; it is also significant as having housed a row of massive jars such as might have been used for the storage of cereals.[26] Estimates of the dates for Ta'akha Maryam and other sites investigated by the 1906 Deutsche Aksum-Expedition are based

21 *e.g.* Kobishchanov 1979: 141; Munro-Hay 1991b: 119; see also the excessively grandiose reconstructions proposed by Krencker (Littmann *et al.* 1913, 2: Abb. 245, 251; D. Phillipson 1997: figs 124, 135). Krencker's drawing has been reproduced numerous times, but Anfray's 1990: 103 reconstruction of Dungur is preferable.

22 The unproven hypothesis (noted in Chapter 8) that a new 'palace' was erected by each successive king suggests a possible answer to this objection, at least so far as the capital is concerned.

23 The term was first employed by Munro-Hay 1989a, and subsequently by Michels 2005: 51 who, however, retained 'palace' to designate the larger buildings of this type.

24 Cosmas, *Christian Topography* XI 2, 4, 7 (Wolska-Conus 1968–73, 3: 314–27); see Chapter 8 for discussion of Cosmas' inconsistent terminology.

25 See tabulation and discussion in D. Phillipson 2008a.

26 de Contenson 1963a: pls vii, xii, xiii*a*.

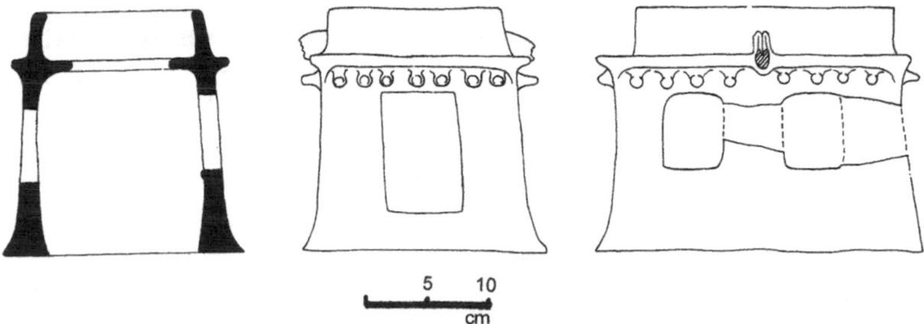

Fig. 38 Pottery house-model from Hawelti (after de Contenson 1963b): although often attributed to the first millennium BC, it is – in the present author's opinion based on comparison with dated fragments from other sites – probably later

on poorly documented artefact provenances,[27] while the detailed results of the more recent and more comprehensive Dungur excavations have not been published.[28] In non-urban situations, élite structures were smaller and simpler, although retaining many of the architectural features described above.[29] While it seems likely that the élite structures were in vogue for much of the Aksumite kingdom's duration, at least from the third century, more detailed studies of their functions and chronology are required before they can be properly understood.

Houses

The domestic buildings of lower-status Aksumites are in some ways better understood than those of the élite. Examples have been excavated at Beta Giyorgis and other sites in and around Aksum, as well as at Matara and in the northeastern highlands of Tigray. There are also informative house-models[30] from sites in the Aksum area (*e.g.* Fig. 38). The excavated buildings were rectilinear, with rooms rarely exceeding 3 m in width, sometimes surrounding open courtyards. In urban situations they were tight-packed, but intersected by narrow lanes (Fig. 35). Construction was of largely undressed mud-set fieldstone, often erected in thin skins with a rubble-filled core. Door- and window-frames were usually of wood. Only rarely is there evidence for stairs, and it may be assumed that the majority of these buildings had one storey only. The models provide the only indication of roof-form, both flat and ridged examples being represented, with the latter apparently thatched.

In both peri-urban and rural areas, archaeological survey has demonstrated the presence of numerous concentrations of Aksumite-period pottery and/or chipped stone tools, with only rare metal or glass fragments but no traces of stone buildings, although roughly piled compound- or field-walls may be

[27] *cf.* Michels 1990, 2005: 155-99. Note also, however, that the metal clamps used at Ta'akha Maryam to join stone blocks (Littmann *et al.* 1913, 3: Abb. 257; D. Phillipson 1997: fig. 153) were of the same form as those employed at the fifth-century Tomb of the False Door (Munro-Hay 1989a: pl. 6.35).

[28] A date for Dungur in the late-sixth or even early-seventh century seems, however, probable (*cf.* Anfray 1972b: 63).

[29] One example was partly excavated at Kidane Mehret, outside Aksum (J. S. Phillips *et al.* 2000: 290). Others are indicated elsewhere.

[30] These come from Aksum (de Contenson 1959b: pl. xix; Chittick 1974: fig. 21a; Munro-Hay 1989a: fig. 16.314) and from Hawelti (de Contenson 1962, 1963b: pls xxxviii–xxxix).

associated. While some of these sites may represent open-air activity-areas with no structures or only temporary shelters,[31] it also seems likely that there were other houses of wood and mud, archaeological remains of which have not yet been recognised.[32] There is one model that may represent such a structure.[33]

Churches

Although no details of non-Christian religious structures are yet published,[34] buildings have been recognised as churches at several Aksumite archaeological sites, some of which may have been deemed sacred in earlier times. It is likely that non-Christian religious buildings continued to be erected – or at least to be used – in some areas of the kingdom for a considerable time after the initial conversion. It is claimed that certain churches still in use today were founded during the Aksumite period, and some may preserve physical elements from that time.[35] Church buildings earlier than the sixth century have not yet been positively identified, but it is possible that the first manifestation of Aksum's Maryam Tsion Cathedral – of which only the podium now survives – dates from this early phase.

The Cathedral site (Fig. 39) is one of great sanctity and importance, but its chronology remains problematic, detailed archaeological excavation having not yet proved possible. Ethiopian tradition, as recorded long afterwards in the *Synaxarium* and in the fifteenth-century compilation known as the *Mashafa Aksum* [= 'Book of Aksum'],[36] clearly states that the church of Maryam Tsion was first constructed in the time of Abraha and Atsbaha – under whom Christianity first came to Ethiopia – in the mid-fourth century (*cf.* Chapter 9). On the other hand, King Kaleb – who reigned almost two centuries later than this – is also recalled as a great church-builder, and stone inscription RIE 191 (Chapter 6) contains a passage recording his work at GBZ; this may refer either to Maryam Tsion or to the magnificent sixth-century cathedral at Sanaa (*cf.* Chapter 15).[37] It must be recognised that the epigraphic evidence is open to alternative interpretations, and that there is demonstrable confusion in the traditions between events that took place during the reign of Ezana and that of Kaleb.[38] It is unclear whether a church of the size and magnificence suggested is likely to have been erected as early as the fourth century, but it seems safe to conclude that – while the first church on the Maryam Tsion site at Aksum may have been erected at

[31] L. Phillipson 2000b: 471, 2009b: 128; L. Phillipson & Sulas 2005.

[32] Inscription RIE 189 – describing Ezana's campaign against the Noba and Kasu (Chapters 6 and 7) – makes a distinction between 'towns of stone' and 'towns of straw', but this probably refers to the Sudanese lowlands (*cf.* Török 1987: 33–46).

[33] de Contenson 1963b: pl. xxxvii.

[34] For the relevance in this context of the structure at Wuchate Golo excavated by de Contenson 1961b, see Chapter 9.

[35] *e.g.* Debra Damo, discussed below. The temptation must be resisted to consider ruined churches exclusively in an archaeological context and thus distinct from those still in use. Similarly, it must not be assumed that all religious buildings erected after the mid-fourth century served as Christian churches (*cf.* Chapter 9).

[36] For the *Synaxarium*, see Budge 1928a. Conti Rossini 1909–10 published the Ge'ez text and a French translation of the *Mashafa Aksum*, further discussion being provided by Hirsch & Fauvelle-Aymar 2001: 66–9. A useful index to the *Mashafa Aksum* has been published by Bausi 2006b.

[37] R. Schneider 1974; Fiaccadori 2007a; see also Gajda 2009: 80.

[38] This confusion is also apparent in the traditions relating to Abraha and Atsbaha (Chapter 9).

that time – it was perhaps not until the early- or mid-sixth century that it was enlarged or replaced by the more elaborate structure to which the *Mashafa Aksum* refers.

The present 'Old Cathedral', which occupies the site, stands on a massive podium, 3.4 m high and covering an area 66 m by at least 41 m, with a broad flight of steps at the west end. There being no sign of it ever having been extended, it must be concluded that the podium was first created to accommodate a building significantly larger than the present one. The 'Old Cathedral' is largely mid-seventeenth-century in date, but has been shown to incorporate part of an older building.[39] It is not known how many earlier churches successively stood on this site but, by the sixth century if not before, the podium was occupied by a church that was almost certainly basilican in form, probably with two aisles on either side of a central nave; the details of its architecture remain, however, a matter for controversy.[40] The *Mashafa Aksum* lists the numbers of several architectural features such as pillars and monkey-heads, implying that the pre-sixteenth-century church may have been a stone-and-timber construction, possibly surrounded by an external colonnade (Fig. 40).[41] In the seventh century, early Muslim visitors recorded the magnificence of the church of Mary at Aksum and the paintings with which it was then adorned.[42]

By the sixth century, remains of church buildings may be recognised at Aksum, in Eritrea at Matara and Adulis, and – less certainly – elsewhere.[43] These were stone-built in characteristic Aksumite style with indented, stepped-back walls, basilican in form, with a single aisle on either side of a central nave. One church at Adulis may have had a dome.[44] Architecture is not always a sure guide to original function, and it is possible that not all these buildings actually served as churches, but orientation and associated carvings and other features are often suggestive. At least two churches at Adulis were adorned with marble screens, imported in prefabricated form from the vicinity of Constantinople;[45] a component of a similar screen has recently been recognised at Aksum (Fig. 41), but it is not known where it had originally been installed, whether at Maryam Tsion or elsewhere. Further significant features of sixth-century date at Aksum are the twin churches built over the subterranean tombs (Chapter 12) traditionally attributed to King Kaleb and his son Gabra Masqal; the basilican plans of these

39 D. Phillipson 1995: 29–36, 2009b: fig. 44.

40 The principal published sources are the *Mashafa Aksum* (Conti Rossini 1909–10: 7; also Beckingham & Huntingford 1961: 521–5) and an account by the Portuguese chaplain Francisco Alvares who visited Aksum in the 1520s (Beckingham & Huntingford 1961: 150–5). Both versions are, unfortunately, difficult to understand, but it is clear that they refer to a large and elaborate building very different from the present one. A comparison (Buxton & Matthews 1974) with the rather fanciful reconstructions of other Aksumite buildings prepared by the 1906 Deutsche Aksum-Expedition provides one plausible view of this building's appearance. For more detailed commentaries, albeit concentrating on later periods, see Munro-Hay 2002: 308–15, 2005a: 153–65.

41 See Chapter 17 for the suggestion that the architecture of the rock-hewn Madhane Alem church at Lalibela may replicate these features.

42 The accounts, discussed further in Chapter 16, have been summarised by Muir (1912: 480; see also Sergew 1972: 186 and Insoll 2003: 46–7).

43 Illustrated details, with supporting references, have recently been published (D. Phillipson 2009a: 43–50) and are not repeated here.

44 Paribeni 1907: cols 530–1, fig. 50 described a poorly preserved church at the east end of the main site. Eight pillars set in a circle *c.* 8 m in diameter were interpreted as having supported a central dome, although their apparent lack of firm foundations might argue against this.

45 Munro-Hay 1989b; Heldman 1994; Peacock & Blue 2007: 112–17, 119–24. See also Chapter 15 for more on the origin, distribution and transport of these screens.

Fig. 39 The Cathedral precinct at Aksum, photographed from the top of the 1960s bell-tower

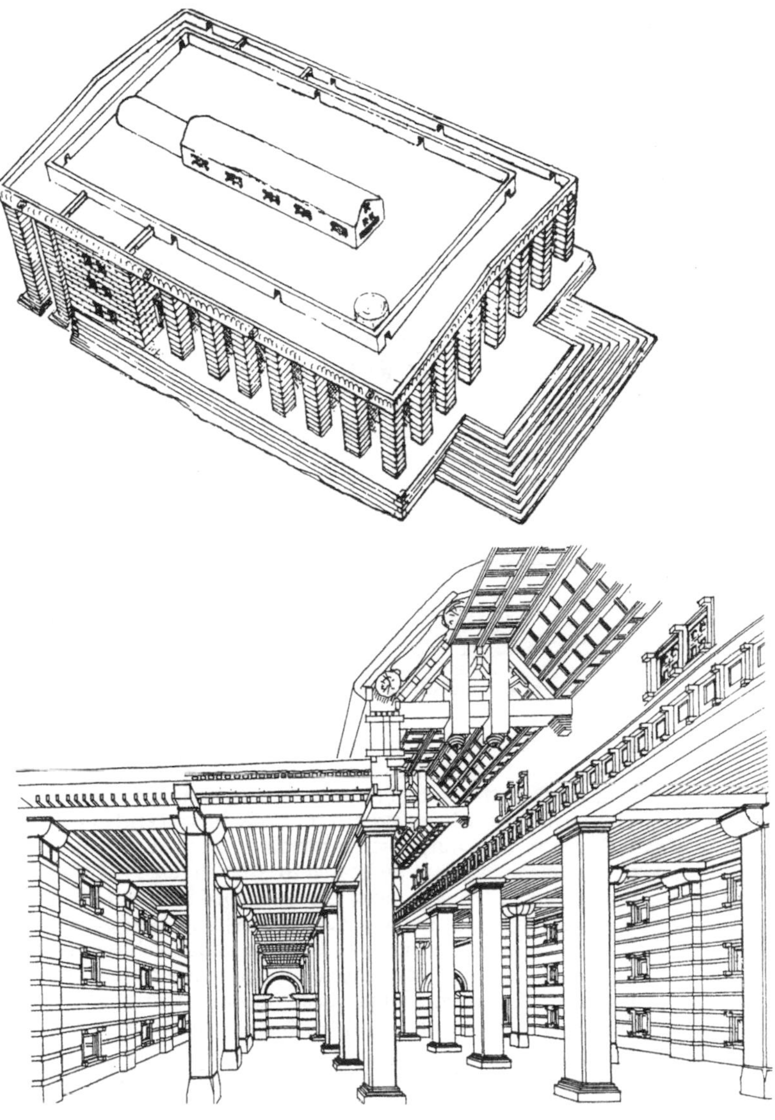

Fig. 40 Possible reconstructions of the original Maryam Tsion Cathedral at Aksum (after Buxton & Matthews 1974, not to scale)

Fig. 41 Marble slotted pillar [height: 90 cm] for a chancel screen, Aksum

funerary churches (Fig. 42) may still be traced. Other early churches at Aksum have been investigated on the southern side of Beta Giyorgis and at Mahraf on the approach to Aksum from the north, between Beta Giyorgis and Mai Qoho.[46]

A basilican church of the sixth or seventh centuries has recently been excavated by Tekle Hagos in the southeastern quadrant of Aksum:[47] measuring 26 x 13 m overall, it was apparently dedicated to *Arba'etu Ensesa* [= the 'four animals', or the supporters of the throne of God described in Ezekiel 10, subsequently interpreted as symbols of the four evangelists]. The central sanctuary had an apse embedded within the east wall;[48] the chamber at the east end of the north aisle was semi-subterranean, entered – apparently from an external door – by means of a well-constructed flight of stone stairs, and was fitted with storage niches in its east and south walls, the former framed by ornamental stone-carving.[49]

At Yeha, the ancient Great Temple (Chapter 3) was converted to a Christian church. Tradition attributes this change to Abba Afse, one of the 'nine saints' (Chapter 9). Ruins of a small building inside the Great Temple were noted by the Deutsche Aksum-Expedition in 1906[50] but were demolished without further record some four decades later. It is often assumed that this structure was of

46 Ricci & Fattovich 1987; Sernicola & L. Phillipson 2011.

47 Tekle 2008: 19–76.

48 This is the feature known as an 'inscribed apse', visible only from the church's interior.

49 This feature closely parallels that at Matara recorded by Anfray 1963b: 94–6, pls lxi and lxxi.

50 Littmann *et al.* 1913. 2: Abb. 167; D. Phillipson 2011.

Fig. 42 Plan of the churches built at Aksum over the Tombs of Kaleb and Gabra Masqal. The outlines of the tombs are also indicated (after D. Phillipson 2009a, based on Littmann *et al.* 1913)

sixth-century date, but this need not necessarily have been the case. The same applies to the baptismal tank that is still visible – but was not observed in 1906 – inside the southeast corner of the temple. Tanks of similar form and age have been recorded at Adulis, Matara and, rock-hewn, at Degum in the Hawzien Plain.[51]

In the extreme north of Tigray, some 90 km northeast of Aksum, is the mountain-top monastery of Debra Damo, where the larger of the two churches dedicated to Za-Mika'el Aregawi (Fig. 43) traces its origin to the sixth century.[52] Its basic plan is remarkably similar to that of each of the churches, noted above, forming the superstructure over the Tombs of Kaleb and Gabra Masqal at

[51] D. Phillipson 2009a: 37, 45–7, 89–91 and references cited.

[52] This church, its affinities and age have been discussed and illustrated by the present writer in some detail (D. Phillipson 2009a: 51–64, 185). Like most buildings of its type, it has been subjected to renovation and rebuilding throughout its history, so the present structure doubtless includes elements of many periods. Za-Mika'el Aregawi was one of the 'nine saints' (Chapter 9), 'Aregawi' being an honorific epithet indicating his elder status.

Fig. 43 The west front of the large church of Za-Mika'el Aregawi at Debra Damo

Aksum. This serves to strengthen the view that all these structures are broadly contemporary, *c.* sixth-century in date. As befits the lower status and more remote situation of the Debra Damo building, its masonry is less refined, while its exterior walling more closely resembles that of the capital's Church of the Four Animals, discussed above, than that of the churches associated with royal tombs. The original church at Debra Damo comprised a simple basilica with one aisle on either side of a central nave and, unless they were a subsequent addition – for which there is no evidence – a loft over each aisle. The finely carved panels of the ceiling in this part of the church are of first-millennium age, but perhaps did not belong to the original structure: their closest known parallels[53] come from the old church of Enda Maryam at Asmara, now destroyed. At the east end is a domed sanctuary flanked – as elsewhere – by further chambers, of which that on the north has at some stage been enlarged.[54]

Thrones

The massive stone 'throne-bases' are a highly characteristic form of Aksumite monument, but the only example so far recorded from sites other than the capital is that called the 'Throne of Kaleb' at Matara.[55] If one outlier (DAE no. 26)[56] is excluded, the throne-bases at Aksum occur in two groups: within the Cathedral precinct, and strung out beside the road that leads from the southeast, passing the east side of the Cathedral compound, to the central burial ground

[53] Sauter 1967; Fiaccadori 2006.

[54] Matthews & Mordini 1959.

[55] Littmann *et al.* 1913, 2: Abb. 135–6. These illustrations show a stone very similar to the slotted seat-blocks at Aksum. See also Anfray 1963b: 90.

[56] No longer visible at its reported location a short distance to the north of Aksum, this may have been abandoned at its quarry, or it may represent the sole survivor of another series of throne-bases along the road leading into Aksum from the north.

Fig. 44 Examples of throne-bases at Aksum: top and centre – Cathedral group; below – roadside group

marked by the principal stelae. In the following discussion, these are designated the Cathedral group and the roadside group respectively. Each group of thrones is homogeneous in style and workmanship, there being also strong similarities between the two groups. In basic form, each throne-base comprises a massive neatly dressed slab, between 1.8 and 2.4 m square and about 0.35 m thick; in its centre, either integral or separate, is a smaller block forming the seat (Fig. 44). At the back and sides of this block are deep slots into which vertical slabs of stone appear to have been inserted. There are good reasons[57] to believe that some of the inscribed slabs discussed in Chapter 6 had originally been fitted into these slots, each slab thus forming a side or a back of a throne. Throne-bases of the Cathedral group retain monolithic pillars at each corner, or the sockets in which such pillars must have stood; it seems safe to assume that these pillars originally supported a canopy in the manner illustrated by Daniel Krencker of the DAE (Fig. 45). There is no indication that corner-pillars were ever associated with any of the throne-bases in the roadside group. Tradition states that the thrones in the Cathedral group were used on occasion by kings, bishops or judges: in other words, that living people sat on them;[58] the sizes of the seats are in accord with this interpretation.[59] In the roadside group, however, the seats are significantly smaller, and would have been uncomfortably tight for an adult. It may therefore be concluded that the larger thrones in the Cathedral group were apparently used on ceremonial occasions, while the roadside ones were occupied, if at all, by reduced-size statues.[60] Two of the throne-bases in the roadside group have central sockets that could have served as fixings for such statues.

The seats of the throne-bases vary considerably in height, but there is little apparent difference between the two groups. Several of the throne-bases in both groups show depressions in front of the raised seat that all writers seem agreed on interpreting as settings for foot-stools.[61] Since the presence of foot-stools in this position indicates a sitting posture with the lower legs vertical, the seats might be considered to have been inconveniently low in comparison, for example, with the representation of an enthroned Aksumite monarch on seventh-century coins (see Fig. 74).[62] This interpretation receives some degree of support from the inscriptions themselves, which refer to the dedication of statues (RIE 185/270, 185*bis*/270*bis*) and to the setting up of commemorative thrones both in the area of Aksum called Sado[63] (RIE 188) and, further afield,

57 For example, the measurements of the inscribed slabs fit this suggestion, and several of their texts refer to the erection of thrones. Since most of the inscriptions date from the fourth century, a similar age for the throne-bases is implied.

58 Measurements of the throne-bases in both groups were tabulated by the DAE (Littmann *et al.* 1913, 2: 49; D. Phillipson 1997: 128). The average width between the vertical sides of the roadside-group thrones is almost 30 per cent smaller than the corresponding figure for the Cathedral group.

59 In this context, the presence in the Cathedral group of two double thrones (Littmann *et al.* 1913, 2: 51, 53-4, Taf. xiii; D. Phillipson 1997: 130-8) is of particular interest.

60 The only possible Ethiopian parallel known to me is the baldachin – so-called *naos* – from Hawelti, discussed in Chapter 3 and probably predating the Aksum throne-bases by almost a millennium, which may itself have accommodated a small sitting statue.

61 *cf.* the southern Arabian throne and foot-stool from Dar el-Beida, described by Pirenne 1965a.

62 Although the king's feet are clearly depicted, I am not aware of any examples where they were set on a foot-stool.

63 The precise location of Sado has long been uncertain, although both Kobishchanov 1979: 86 and Huntingford 1989: 55 believed it to have been in or near Aksum. Could the name have referred to the area at the foot of the southwestern slopes of Mai Qoho, where throne bases are still preserved and where several inscriptions are believed to have been found? I am grateful to Ato Tekle Hagos for his comments on this matter.

Fig. 45 Reconstructions of Aksumite thrones (after Krencker in Littmann *et al.* 1913)

Fig. 46 Base slab for a gigantic statue, discovered at Aksum by the DAE in 1906 but not seen since (after Littmann *et al.* 1913)

at the confluence of the rivers Sida and Takezze[64] (RIE 189). Such monuments may thus have been widely distributed,[65] despite the fact that almost all the surviving examples are at Aksum.

The following concluding observations about the commemorative thrones may be stressed. It is not possible to be certain whether inscriptions – as opposed to plain slabs – formed parts of thrones in both the Cathedral and the roadside groups. The inscriptions' measurements noted in Chapter 6 make it probable that some were from the latter group, but their inclusion in the former group also cannot be precluded. Next, the inscriptions associated with the thrones were predominantly in Ge'ez; the only Greek text being RIE 271 which was on the reverse of its Ge'ez counterpart, RIE 189. Lastly, the practice of erecting inscribed commemorative thrones was of long duration, the earliest example so far recognised being at Adulis and dating from around the second century (Chapter 6), and continuing at Aksum from the fourth century at least into the mid-sixth. By the time of *hatsani* Dana'el (Chapters 6 and 16) around the eighth or ninth century, the thrones had fallen into ruin, although their function commemorating Aksum's former greatness was probably still remembered.

64 It is not easy to pinpoint this place, which was where Ezana inflicted a defeat upon the Kasu. Huntingford 1989: 58, followed by Munro-Hay 1991b: 215, thought that the Sida was the Blue Nile, but this is impossible because the Blue Nile and the Takezze do not meet. The Aksumites probably regarded the lower Atbara as a continuation of the Takezze, so a location in the Sudanese lowlands, perhaps even the Atbara / Nile confluence, is possible (*cf.* Taddesse 1993).

65 *cf.* also RIE 277, recorded at Adulis by Cosmas Indicopleustes, probably dating rather earlier than the fourth century (Chapters 6 and 7).

Other[66]

Mention should be made here of the dressed stone slab discovered by the DAE in 1906 in the southwestern quarter of Aksum some 130 m north of the Ta'akha Maryam élite structure.[67] It was not in its original position when found, but traces of its apparent plinth were recorded nearby. Although clearly Aksumite, there was no more precise evidence as to its age or associations. It bore two depressions, 5 cm deep and 92 cm long in the shape of human feet, each with deep pits at the heel and ball, apparently for the fixture of a metal statue (Fig. 46). These depressions being three-and-a-half times the size of the average foot, it may be calculated that the statue – if it represented a complete upright human figure as the positioning of the feet would suggest – was between 5.5 and 6.0 m tall. No other metal statues of this age are known to have approached this size anywhere in the world, although some Greek bronze and chryselephantine figures[68] probably did so. Repeated enquiries and efforts to locate this statue-base, which appears not to have been seen since 1906, have met with no success.

66 The dressed stone slabs called *mistah werki*, thought to have been used in the processing of gold, are described in Chapter 13.

67 Littmann *et al.* 1913, 2: 44–5; D. Phillipson 1997: 155–6.

68 Lapatin 2001.

12

Aksumite Burials

In the study of Aksumite civilisation, a disproportionate emphasis has been placed by archaeologists on the burials of the élite. This is not hard to explain: such interments were marked by the most impressive of Aksum's surviving monuments, and their investigation has – despite the frequency with which such prominent tombs have long ago been robbed – yielded artefacts and information of great significance. Until recently, however, the position that the élite and their monuments occupied in ancient Aksumite society was poorly contextualised, since little attention had been paid to their less prosperous contemporaries and to the basic economic underpinning of the state. The information at our disposal is almost totally archaeological.

As noted in Chapter 7, one of the earliest recognised signs of the transfer of settlement from Beta Giyorgis hill to the site of Aksum is the series of burial platforms at the foot of the southern slope of Beta Giyorgis. These platforms, now buried beneath a considerable thickness of later accumulation, grew to constitute a terrace in the area that now forms the northern half of the Stelae Park. Archaeological investigation in 1973–74 revealed traces of a series of repeatedly extended platforms with associated graves, at least some of which had been marked by stelae; there were indications that these features dated back as early as the first century AD.[1] It was probably during the latter part of the third century that the process began of creating further tombs which – like the stelae that marked them – far exceeded in size and grandeur anything produced previously in the northern Horn. During the next hundred years, the terrace was extended some 30 m to the south, covering the new tombs, with a new retaining wall, over 120 m long, marking its final extent.[2]

Stelae

In a prominent focal position at the centre of Aksum, the huge artificial terrace noted above was gradually built up until – by the third century – it became the royal burial ground, probably replacing the analogous feature at Beta Giyorgis described in Chapter 3. It was dominated, as it still is today (Fig. 47), by the series of monolithic stelae, the largest of which – two of them weighing *c.* 160–170 tonnes each and one as much as 520 tonnes – were elaborately carved in imitation of multi-storeyed buildings. They were carved in nepheline syenite – a granite-like rock that, when freshly cut, exposes a glittering blue surface – obtained from quarries located approximately 4 km to the west of central

[1] Chittick 1974, 1976; Munro-Hay 1989a: 153–4.

[2] The terrace-wall visible today is almost entirely a mid-twentieth-century reconstruction on the original alignment, its style based on that of surviving fragments. For the original wall, see Caquot & Leclant 1956; Leclant 1959b; de Contenson 1959a.

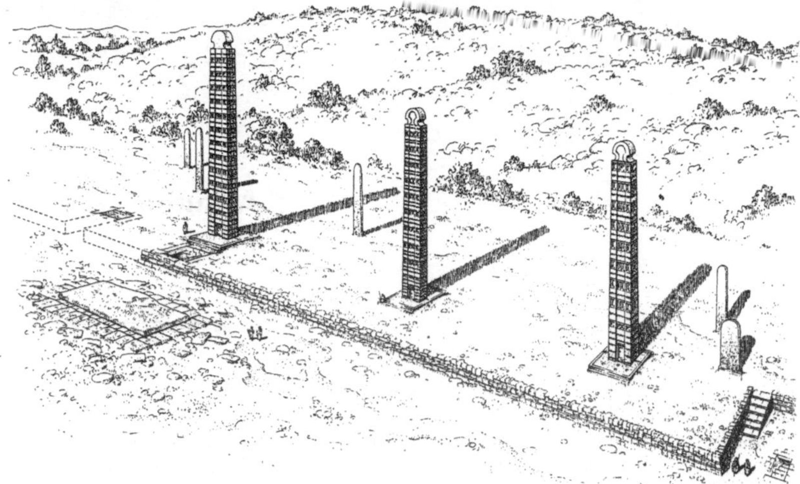

Fig. 47 Reconstruction, drawn by Eric Robson, of how the main stelae at Aksum would have appeared, had Stela I [on the left] been successfully erected (after D. Phillipson 2000b)

Aksum.[3] Window-frames and apertures, false doors, horizontal wooden beams and the projecting ends – known as monkey-heads – of transverse ties (Chapter 11) were all depicted in low-relief carving (Fig. 48).[4] Now known to date from the late-third and early-fourth centuries AD, these stelae marked elaborate tombs. It is remarkable that, although Aksumite society at this time is known to have been literate, no inscriptions have been found associated with any of these tombs or stelae to indicate the names of those who were buried there. In the absence of this information, it cannot be conclusively proven that the tombs marked by the largest and most elaborate stelae were those of Aksumite kings but, since these are the burials on which by far the most substantial resources had been expended, royal attributions seem highly probable.

Of the six stelae that are elaborately carved in representation of multi-storeyed buildings, the three largest were set – facing south – in line from east to west, each larger and more grandiose than its predecessor (Fig. 47).[5] They were also set progressively further apart, probably because the subterranean tombs that they marked likewise increased in size. Because the smallest of the three still stands approximately upright, there has been no possibility of investigating its foundations or the tomb to mark which it had presumably been erected. Designated Stela 3,[6] it is 20.6 m in height – plus *c.* 3 m buried underground – and

[3] The quarries and transport of their products are discussed in Chapter 13.

[4] As discussed in Chapter 11, this form of architecture was widely employed in the Aksumite state, and has been continued into recent times as a preferred method of church construction, especially in Tigray. An excellent recent example may be seen at Yeha. Note, however, that buildings constructed in this way seem never to have exceeded two or three storeys in height; there is absolutely no evidence that buildings with between six and thirteen storeys, as represented by the Aksum stelae, were ever erected.

[5] Detailed arguments for this sequence were set out in D. Phillipson 2000b: 478. The three smaller 'storeyed' stelae also formed part of this progression, but on a different and less precise alignment.

[6] This numbering scheme was devised by the Deutsche Aksum-Expedition (DAE) of 1906 (Littmann *et al.* 1913, 2: 1–43, Taff. i–xii) and has been followed by subsequent writers. The illustrations of the stelae in the DAE volume have never been surpassed; they were reproduced, with Rosalind Bedlow's English translation of the original German text, by D. Phillipson 1997: 11–47. For a summary tabulation showing details of the six 'storeyed' stelae, see D. Phillipson 1998: fig. 37.

Fig. 48 Stela 3, Aksum, south face

Fig. 49 The apex of Aksum Stela 3, showing iron attachments for a plaque

is estimated to weigh *c.* 160 tonnes. On the west, south and east the tapering shaft of the stela was carved to represent a building of ten storeys, the north face being dressed flat but with decoration only at the apex. Below the semicircular apex, the tapering east and west sides were interrupted by concavities, and the top of the south face was neatly recessed to accommodate some form of inlay, originally secured by iron pegs that are still clearly visible (Fig. 49). Such inlays were originally affixed to all the six 'storeyed' stelae, nos 6 and 4 having two circular inlays each, set one above the other.

Excavations in 1994–97 on the site of the next largest stela, no. 2, demonstrated that it had been intentionally undermined to make it collapse; this took place many centuries ago, perhaps towards the end of the first millennium AD.[7] When the stela collapsed, it broke into five principal pieces which were recorded and photographed, lying on the ground, by the 1906 German expedition.[8] In 1937, during the Italian occupation of Ethiopia, these pieces were transported – on the personal order of Mussolini – to Rome where they were re-assembled and erected in the Piazza di Porta Capena. Despite the stipulation of a treaty signed in 1947

[7] D. Phillipson 1995: 24–5; Watts 2000: 147–8. There are widespread traditions that this and other stelae were cast down by Queen Gudit in about the tenth century; the archaeological evidence is not incompatible with this.

[8] During the Ethiopian campaign to secure the stela's return from Rome, it was often stated that the Italians had demolished and broken it in order to facilitate its removal. This was demonstrably untrue.

that all looted Ethiopian antiquities be repatriated, it was not until more than half a century later, in 2005, that Stela 2 was returned to Aksum.[9] Measuring 24.6 m in height – including the underground section – and weighing some 170 tonnes, it was carved on all four faces to represent an eleven-storey building, doors being depicted on both the north and the south sides.

Stela 1 is by far the largest of the Aksumite stelae: carved to indicate thirteen storeys, it is probably the largest – but not the longest – single block of stone that people anywhere have ever attempted to set on end. Thirty-three metres in total length and 520 tonnes in weight, it appears that it fell and broke during the attempt to erect it.[10] The retaining wall had already been built to mark the southern edge of the terrace at this point, and twin tombs had already been created on either side of the stela's socket. The tomb on the west has now been largely excavated;[11] that on the east – less well preserved – was probably its mirror-image. The western tomb, known as the 'Mausoleum', was an elaborate stone construction, roofed with massive rough-hewn granite slabs and subsequently buried (Fig. 50). More than 250 sq m in extent, it had ten side-chambers leading off a central passage. Monolithic portals supported brick arches at either end of this passage, the eastern portal and the western arch being preserved intact and *in situ*. The interior stone-built walls of the Mausoleum, like the brick arches at either end of the central passage and at the entrance to each side-chamber, had been coated with a coarse gritty render – giving the impression that the whole structure had been carved from solid rock. Although extensively robbed in ancient times, enough remained of the original deposits to indicate that the tomb had received at least some of its intended contents – including cloth of gold and items decorated with gold leaf and engraved mother-of-pearl, perhaps also a burial or burials – before the unsuccessful attempt was made to erect the stela. Artefact typology and radiocarbon age-determination of a sample well associated with the original construction combine to support a date around the middle of the fourth century AD, indicating that this complex probably marked the tomb of the last of the Aksumite kings to be interred according to the pre-Christian tradition. Since, remarkably, no inscription was incorporated in the Stela-1 burial complex, it seems that we shall never know for certain who was buried there, but the strongest candidate would appear to be Ezana or his immediate predecessor. On this basis, and accepting the sequence of kings indicated by the coins (Fig. 24;

[9] Tragically, as a result of intense political pressure both within Ethiopia and from Italy, the decision was then taken to set the stela upright in its original location, despite the fact that this would for ever preclude archaeological investigation of the tomb that the stela had been intended to mark, and despite the danger that was foreseen of causing subsidence that could result in destabilising the still-erect Stela 3. At the time of writing [February 2011] this anticipated disaster has occurred, with results that are all-too-obvious to any visitor.

[10] This was originally proposed by Van Beek 1967 (*pace* Francaviglia 1994); for detailed arguments in support, see D. Phillipson 2000b: 222. When Stela 1 fell, its apex shattered against another megalithic tomb, known as Nefas Mawcha (see below) that was still unfinished at the time. When the stela collapsed, the false door on what had been intended to be its south face was embedded in the ground and thus hidden from view, while that on the intended north face was fully exposed. Both false doors had been elaborated with carved handles: that on the exposed face was neatly removed, the resultant scars being still visible, while the hidden one survived – excellently preserved – and may be viewed from a passage originally excavated by the DAE beneath the fallen stela (for illustrated details, see D. Phillipson 1994). Removal of the exposed handle may have been intended to cancel the stela's symbolism in some way. Other, indirect, results of the failure successfully to erect Stela 1 lack primary archaeological evidence but may nonetheless have had major historical implications (D. Phillipson & L. Phillipson 2000: 252–4; L. Phillipson 2009b: 122).

[11] For illustrated details, see D. Phillipson 2000b: 165–218.

Fig. 50 The interior of the fourth-century 'Mausoleum' at Aksum; note the coarse render at the foot of the walls

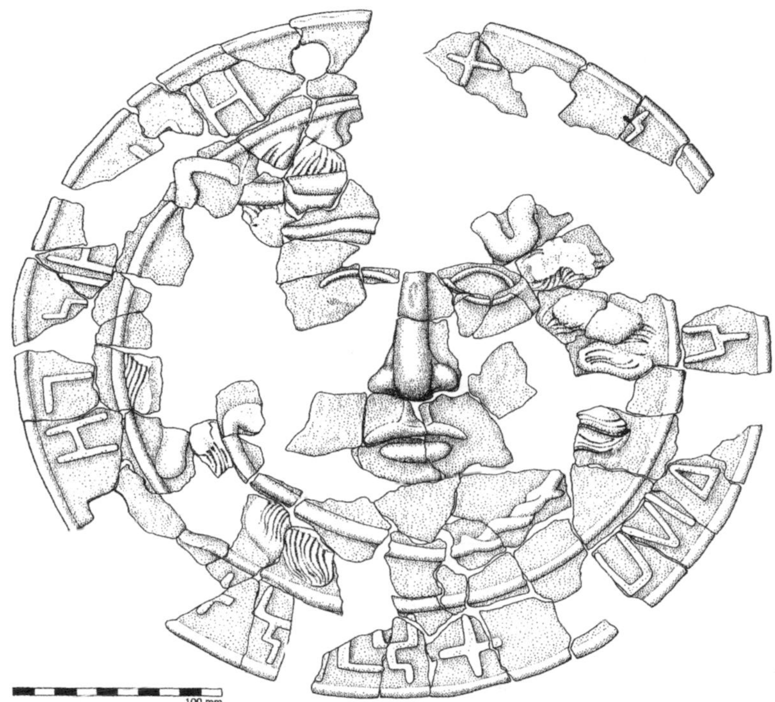

Fig. 51 Fragmentary cast brass plaque from the fourth-century Tomb of the Brick Arches at Aksum (after D. Phillipson 2000b)

Chapter 14), Stela 2 could be attributed to Ousanas / Ella Amida or to WZB, and Stela 3 to Aphilas or WZB, all within the period AD 300–70.

A circular plaque of cast brass, 38 cm in diameter, recovered from the fourth-century Tomb of the Brick Arches (discussed below) portrays a facing human head surrounded by a raised inscription in unvocalised Ethiopic letters of angular monumental style, unfortunately too incomplete to be read (Fig. 51).[12] This plaque had probably been intended for mounting on the apex of a stela; the reason for its being broken up before being deposited – with other scrap metal – in the tomb where it was found may have been due either to a casting failure or to a change in prevailing burial practice.

Before leaving the great stelae, it is appropriate here to consider how they were erected. The fallen remains of Stela 4, lying near the gateway to Enda Yesus church at the eastern end of the main Stelae Park (Fig. 52), are particularly informative and – in conjunction with features of the other monuments – have permitted the methodology to be reconstructed with some confidence, as summarised in Fig. 53.[13] The stela was placed on a ramp that often took advantage of a natural slope. A socket was excavated adjacent to the foot of the ramp,

[12] D. Phillipson 2000b: 97–100; R. Schneider 2000; *cf.* also Hirsch & Fauvelle-Aymar 2001: 84–5.

[13] D. Phillipson & L. Phillipson 2000: 251–3. This reconstruction provides explanations for several features that have sometimes given rise to controversy: notably the lack of baseplates for Stela 1, and the lean of Stela 3 despite its apparent stability (D. Phillipson & Hobbs 1996); this stability has recently been disturbed (*cf.* footnote 9 above).

Fig. 52 The fallen remains of Stela 4 at Aksum, showing how the stela had originally been set in a socket lined with vertical slabs of stone

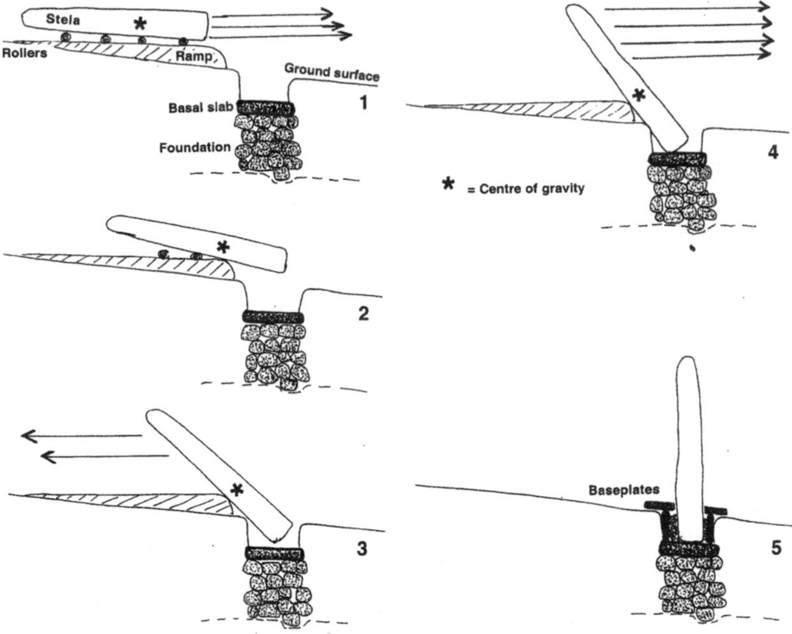

Fig. 53 Reconstruction of how the Aksum stelae were probably erected (after D. Phillipson 2000b, based on a draft by Dr Laurel Phillipson)

its base and sides being lined with slabs of stone. The stela was then raised and tipped into the socket, stones being quickly packed around its base to secure it. Finally, horizontal baseplates were added to hold everything in place. If this sequence is correct, it must follow that carving of the stelae was completed before they were erected, as is further confirmed by the carving preserved on the underside of the fallen Stela 1.

Other élite tombs

Contiguous with the royal burial ground discussed above are areas where further interments – somewhat less elaborate but nonetheless rich and grand – took place. To the north, along the west side of the Mai Hedja stream, is an extensive area with numerous stelae where little archaeological investigation has taken place.[14] At the edge of the central stelae field, a remarkable rock-cut tomb has been excavated, the rich contents of which had escaped comprehensive robbing and survived essentially intact.[15] The entrance lay outside the area demarcated by the terrace-wall but was connected by a broad well-made stone stairway to the top of the terrace, beneath which the tomb itself extended.[16] It is unclear whether this tomb was ever marked by a stela; if it were, the most likely surviving candidate is a comparatively small one, dressed but otherwise undecorated, that was designated no. 24 by the Deutsche Aksum-Expedition.[17] Unlike the tombs attributed to the kings, this tomb was cut into the soft underlying rock, its entrance and four chambers being demarcated by a series of brick arches that have given the monument its name. It is dated around the second half of the fourth century, possibly slightly later than Stela 1. Artefacts deposited in the Tomb of the Brick Arches include numerous items that attest to Aksumite technological skill, but remarkably few for which a foreign origin is indicated. Details need not concern us here, save to note the finely carved ivory that included numerous pieces interpreted as coming from an elaborate chair or throne. There was also a quantity of fine metalwork which gives an insight on the expertise that was available in ancient Aksum during the peak of its prosperity.[18]

A similar position on the edge of the royal burial ground is occupied by the remarkable monument known as Nefas Mawcha [= the place where the winds blow], which was badly damaged by the collapse of Stela 1 (Fig. 54). Successive archaeological investigations have not succeeded in fully illustrating its original form or function. A concise overview postulates a pit excavated to bedrock, where a rectangular walled chamber was constructed, 9 x 15 m internally and apparently subdivided lengthwise, the whole surrounded by a passageway that was roofed with a series of massive stone blocks joined with metal clamps.[19]

14 Anfray 1972b. The relative chronology cannot be established, although it has frequently been surmised that the smaller, undecorated stelae preceded the large 'storeyed' ones. Low on an undressed stela in this northern area, a symbol resembling the Egyptian *ankh* has been roughly incised. It has little chronological significance, since the symbol was used in Egypt from pharaonic into Coptic times, and its carving at Aksum cannot be shown to have been contemporaneous with the erection of the stela.

15 Details were published in D. Phillipson 2000b: 31–133.

16 For plans, see Munro-Hay 1989a: fig. 4.2. The entrance to the Tomb of the Brick Arches is also indicated in Fig. 47 of this book.

17 Littmann *et al.* 1913, 2: 38–9; D. Phillipson 1997: 52–3; see also plan in Munro-Hay 1989a: fig. 4.2.

18 For details of the ivory and the metalwork, see Chapter 13 and D. Phillipson 2000b: 86–116. For the dating of the tomb and its contents, see *ibid.*: 128–9.

19 Lewcock in Munro-Hay 1989a: 165–6.

Fig. 54 Nefas Mawcha, Aksum

Fig. 55 The Tomb of Bazen, Aksum

Over the central chamber but resting on the roofing slabs of the passageway was a huge capstone, 6 x 17 m in size and 1.35 m in maximum thickness, and estimated to weigh *c.* 360 tonnes; the capstone was neatly dressed on the underside and edges but left rough and incompletely finished on the upper surface, indicating either that work was still in progress when Stela 1 fell, or that Nefas Mawcha was planned to be – or had already been – covered with earth so that fine finishing of its upper surface was not considered necessary. All that may safely be concluded about the age of this monument is that it must precede – if only briefly – the collapse of Stela 1, for which event a mid-fourth-century date has been argued above.

Details of another burial area on the outskirts of Aksum remain obscure, such research as has been undertaken being inadequately recorded, while the site itself is now largely covered by recent development. This was termed the Southeastern Stelae Field by the 1906 German expedition responsible for its initial investigation.[20] In the 1950s several tombs were excavated there by Jean Doresse; they may still be seen but very little information relating to any contents, associations or age has been made available.[21] Particularly significant in the present context is the so-called 'Tomb of Bazen' (Fig. 55),[22] cut entirely from soft rock and comprising four *loculi* opening from a single chamber which is itself entered through a round-topped doorway. The approach to this doorway seems to have involved the replacement of a vertical shaft with a stepped approach.

Royal tombs of the Christian period

Following the unsuccessful attempt to erect Stela 1, major changes were adopted in royal burial practice. As discussed in Chapter 9, this was also the time of the king's conversion to Christianity, and endless speculation is possible as to the connections between these three developments.

A short distance to the west of Stela 1, a remarkable tomb was discovered in 1973. Probably royal, and later in date than its stelae-associated counterparts, this 'Tomb of the False Door'[23] clearly represents a major change in style (Fig. 56) and in quality of execution. It was never marked by a stela; instead, its superstructure was squat, 12 m square and 3 m high, incorporating at the centre of its south face a large stone slab carved to represent a false door virtually identical to those on Stelae 3 - 1. The massive coursed masonry of which it was built was dressed only on its exterior, suggesting that the superstructure had been solid – perhaps an understandable reaction to the collapse of Stela 1.[24] Beneath was a small burial chamber in which a badly damaged stone sarcophagus – without its lid – survives, approached down a flight of stone stairs

20 Littmann *et al.* 1913, 2: 33. Stelae in this area had, however, been noted long previously (map by Salt in Valentia 1809, 3: 82).

21 Kebbede & Leclant 1955; also D. Phillipson 2000b: 425–7.

22 Bazen – a name known only from the king-lists (Chapter 8) and from an undated but probably late inscription (RIE 200) now built into a wall adjacent to the Old Cathedral at Aksum – was traditionally recalled as a king of Aksum around the time of Christ's birth, some versions naming him as one of the *magi* (Belaynesh in Belaynesh *et al.* 1975: 39). His association with the tomb that now bears his name appears to date from shortly after Doresse's excavation and to be based solely on a tradition that Bazen had been buried somewhere in that vicinity.

23 Chittick 1974: 175–9; Munro-Hay 1989a: esp. 55–60.

24 Chittick (1974) and Lewcock (in Munro-Hay 1989a: 165) both made an interesting comparison between the form of this superstructure and that of the central pavilions of Aksumite élite structures (*cf.* Chapters 8 and 11), but the relevant details are not fully clear.

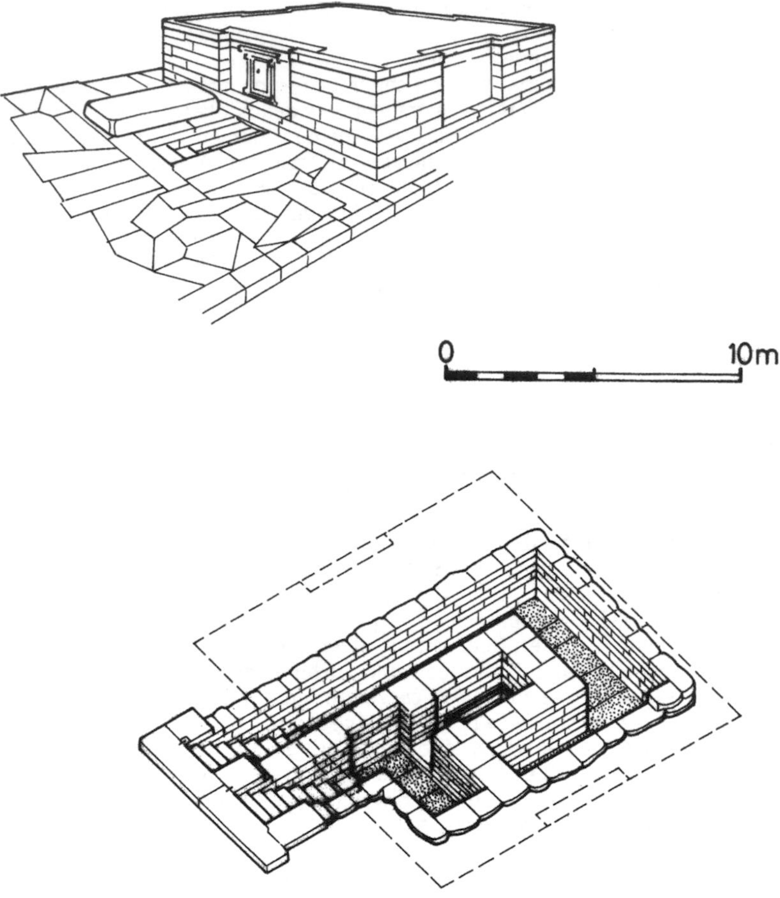

Fig. 56 Reconstructed views of superstructure and substructure, Tomb of the False Door, Aksum (after Chittick 1974)

and through a small antechamber; the whole was surrounded on three sides by – but not interconnected with – a spacious passageway that was entered by means of a separate stair.[25] Comprising massive courses of finely dressed stone, this underground complex had been built in a pit into which a huge stone slab had been set as a foundation; it thus contrasted markedly both in plan and in construction with the more ostentatious stela-marked tombs, while maintaining their tradition of a massive underground building subsequently covered. Both in its general form, and in being constructed in a previously excavated pit, this infrastructure bears some resemblance to Nefas Mawcha. In front of the tomb was an open paved courtyard, some of its blocks framing the stairs being fixed together by means of metal clamps, one of which may still be seen *in situ* (Fig. 37). An important distinction from the Stela-1 tomb is the provision of a separate burial chamber, perhaps suggesting that less importance was attached to the provision of grave goods. Unfortunately, the Tomb of the False Door had been thoroughly robbed in ancient times and, when excavated in 1973–74, retained no trace of any original contents other than the damaged remains of the sarcophagus noted above. To judge from the measures taken by the robbers to gain access to the peripheral passage, they obviously believed that this contained materials of value, but whether this was actually the case remains unknown.

Some 2 km north of Aksum, in an elevated location overlooking but beyond the ancient built-up area, a building-complex now known as the 'Tombs of Kaleb and Gabra Masqal' has been recognised since at least the early-sixteenth century.[26] Two underground tombs are located here, approximately 25 m apart,[27] the northern one being traditionally attributed to the sixth-century king Kaleb, and the other to his son, Gabra Masqal (Fig. 42).[28] The separate tombs, while far from identical, are broadly similar both in plan and in construction, that attributed to Gabra Masqal being the more elaborate as well as the better preserved (Fig. 57). Each was entered down a walled flight of steps, finely constructed from large blocks of dressed stone, leading to a transverse chamber, all closely resembling those at the Tomb of the False Door despite a difference in walling-style. Further chambers led from the transverse ones: five at the Tomb of Gabra Masqal and three at the Tomb of Kaleb. One of the chambers at the latter tomb retains three stone sarcophagi, one of which bears a neatly carved cross. Other motifs, including more crosses, may be discerned on the walls in several parts of both tombs, but they were less carefully executed and it should not be assumed that they were necessarily contemporary with the initial construction. Several of the inner chambers have portals, each hewn from a single slab – analogous to those of the Mausoleum – so as to represent a wooden doorway. Unlike the Tomb of the False Door, the massive stone blocks of which these tombs were constructed were not always coursed, but were individually dressed with great care and skill to fit extremely closely against each other at varying angles. A further underground feature, located east of Gabra

25 Each stair was covered by a massive stone slab; only that covering the stair to the outer passageway now survives, bearing clear signs of attempts to break it up (Munro-Hay 1989a: pl. 6.32). Francaviglia's (1994) suggestion that these covers had been cut from a baseplate belonging to Stela 1 is groundless speculation.

26 The main primary accounts are Littmann *et al.* 1913, 2: 127–31 (D. Phillipson 1997: 73–88); Munro-Hay 1989a: 42–7, 157–8 and D. Phillipson 2000b: 427–31. Earlier records of the site are noted below.

27 Beckingham & Huntingford (1961: 158) were mistaken in stating that they are connected by a tunnel.

28 For King Gabra Masqal and difficulties in interpreting traditions referring to that name, see Chapter 8.

Fig. 57 Inside the Tomb of Gabra Masqal, Aksum

Masqal's tomb, is under investigation at the time of writing [2011], but details are not yet available.

A further striking feature of these tombs is that their superstructure takes the form, not of a magnificent stela, nor of a simple squat monument, but of twin churches, mirror-images of each other, one set over each tomb, with the two churches linked by a colonnaded courtyard approached from the west up a broad flight of steps. The differences between the tombs contrasts with the overall homogeneity of the superstructure, the two churches showing only very minor differences between them, raising the possibility that they may have been constructed at a date contemporary with or even slightly later than that of the second tomb.[29] The plans of the churches at this site are remarkably similar to that of the large church of Za-Mikael Aregawi at the mountain-top monastery of Debra Damo (Fig. 43).[30] The churches and their significance are discussed in Chapter 11.

The Tombs of Kaleb and Gabra Masqal have been known and visited for several centuries. The first record of them is probably a reference in the *Mashafa Aksum* (Chapter 12) to their being filled with treasure, and they are almost certainly the 'two houses under the ground' seen in 1520 by the Portuguese Jesuit Francisco Alvares, with 'very large chests' that 'they say ... were the treasure chests of Queen Sheba'.[31] Whether or not these tales had any foundation in fact, no trace has survived of any materials that the tombs may originally have contained. There is, indeed, effectively no archaeological evidence that might indicate their date, other than traces of buildings erected in the late-sixth or early-seventh centuries up against the south wall of the tomb-superstructure.[32] The traditional attribution of these tombs to kings who reigned in the first half of the sixth century thus receives some degree of support.

Although it is clear that only a small proportion of the Aksumite royal tombs are now known, there is convincing evidence for their development over time in response to changing economic, political and religious circumstances. The earliest examples of which we have knowledge, dating from a period at least two hundred years after that when the kingdom originated, were elaborate underground masonry structures, the position of each being marked by a stela finely carved to represent a multi-storey building.[33] Other grand and rich tombs – of markedly different design – are known from this same period, but we do not know whether they belonged to non-ruling members of the royal family or to other élite individuals. With the collapse of Stela 1 broadly coinciding with the royal adoption of Christianity, an abrupt change seems to have been

[29] Unfortunately, the 1906 investigation was concerned more with recovery of the building's plan than with distinguishing phases of construction. Subsequent consolidation work, for the most part poorly recorded, has obscured any such evidence as may have survived. The extent of such consolidation may be recognised by comparing the present state of the stonework with that recorded photographically in 1906. Anfray 1990: 97 suggested that the linked superstructure may post-date both tombs.

[30] D. Phillipson 2009a: 63–4.

[31] Beckingham & Huntingford 1961: 158–9. It is likely that the 'chests' were the sarcophagi still visible in the Tomb of Gabra Masqal, although Alvares apparently saw – or remembered – only two of them.

[32] Munro-Hay 1989a: 42–5, 157–8.

[33] Stelae were used as grave-markers by many sections of the Aksumite community, and it is only the largest and most elaborate that can plausibly be attributed to the kings of the late-third and early-fourth centuries. As noted in Chapter 2, use of stelae as grave-markers had been practised over a wide area of northeastern Africa for several millennia prior to the rise of Aksum, and has continued subsequently.

implemented, with use of stelae being abandoned in favour of low built superstructures.[34] This development was accompanied by preference for a small burial chamber and for a reduction of the space available for grave goods. Later, in the sixth century, the superstructure took the form of a funerary church or chapel, built directly over the tomb.

Other Christian tombs

This last development is paralleled in areas distant from Aksum. At Matara in modern Eritrea, an early Christian underground tomb with stepped entrance, antechamber and burial chamber beneath a basilican church (Fig. 58) was excavated in 1961–63 by Francis Anfray on behalf of the Ethiopian Institute of Archaeology.[35] Some thirty years earlier, an apparently similar tomb had been located at Amba Focada[36] 35 km to the south of Matara and just across the border in northernmost Ethiopia. Particular interest attaches to a rock-hewn tomb at Degum in the Hawzien Plain some 40 km north of Makalle.[37] The group of church-related features cut into the low rock outcrop now occupied by the church of Degum Selassie is discussed in Chapter 16; here we are concerned only with what is probably the oldest of these – a tomb entered by means of a steep stair and comprising a lobby, an antechamber and a burial chamber with raised *loculi* on three sides. Uncertainty concerning the age of this tomb can currently be resolved only by comparison with features elsewhere, most of which are themselves poorly dated. It is, however, conceivable that the Degum tomb could be as early as the sixth or seventh century.

An apparently Christian form of burial in the late-fifth or early-sixth century is indicated by part of a Greek-inscribed tombstone found during building work at Gumala, *c.* 5 km north of Aksum.[38] As noted in Chapter 9, this suggests that a distinct Greek-speaking Christian community may have survived in that vicinity, practising a distinctive burial tradition more than a century after the initial conversion.

The Gudit Stelae Field

Burials of non-élite Aksumites are for the most part poorly recorded and have rarely received attention from archaeologists.[39] Again, most of the examples that have been fully investigated are in the vicinity of Aksum

[34] This change, it must be emphasised, relates to the royal tombs only. It has not yet been established whether or not use of stelae continued in association with lower-status burials; but it seems likely that it may have done so, at least in peripheral areas of the Aksumite polity.

[35] Although preliminary details have been published (Anfray & Annequin 1965: 65–76, pls xliii–l), no full account of these excavations is yet available. An excellent photograph of the tomb has been published by Anfray 1964: Abb. 18. At the time the field research was undertaken, what is now Eritrea was subsumed within the Empire of Ethiopia. Contrary to the statement by Rezene 2005, the artefacts recovered are currently housed at the National Museum, Addis Ababa.

[36] Only very brief details are available, with no indication of any superstructure (D. Phillipson 2009a: 47 and references cited). The area is currently subject to further investigation under the direction of Dr Catherine D'Andrea (D'Andrea *et al.* 2008a).

[37] The site was first described in detail by Lepage 1972; see also Lepage & Mercier 2005: 46–55; D. Phillipson 2009a: 89–91.

[38] Fiaccadori 2007b; for further discussion, see Chapters 5 and 9.

[39] Their wide occurrence is, however, indicated by frequent sighting of distinctive Aksumite funerary pottery found during farming or development operations in many areas and offered for sale on the antiquities market or as souvenirs.

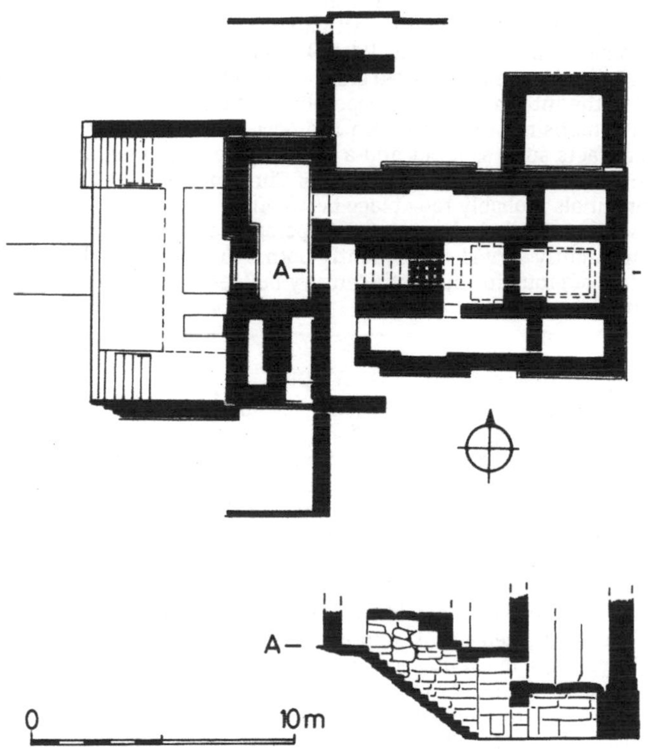

Fig. 58 Plan and section of a tomb beneath a basilica at Matara (after Anfray & Annequin 1965)

itself.[40] Many – but not necessarily all – of these burials were marked by rough-hewn stelae, typically between 1 and 3 m high. Investigations at the so-called Gudit Stelae Field on the southwestern outskirts of Aksum have proved particularly informative,[41] although most of the burials were those of middle-class Aksumites and it is probable that no graves belonging to the poorest members of the community have yet been located. The site has an extent slightly in excess of 10 ha, demarcated on its down-slope southern side by a walled revetment to create a gently sloping terrace. Within this area are preserved almost 600 stelae; with the exception of a few round-topped dressed examples near the northeast corner of the site, these are all rough-hewn and relatively small. Burials were investigated by means of small-scale excavations conducted in 1973–74 and 1994–95. One, an earth-dug tomb, contained abundant pottery, well-preserved glassware and numerous iron tools, perhaps indicating the interment of a prosperous artisan.[42] Other burials were much simpler, comprising a pit in which the deceased was accompanied only by a few artefacts such as a pot and a knife. None contained artefacts bearing decorative crosses or other indications of Christianity. Use of the Gudit Stelae Field for burials probably took place between the second and fourth centuries AD; this estimate is based on artefact typology, radiocarbon dates and the fact that it apparently served subsequently both as a carving-workshop area[43] and as a source of stone for the sixth-century builders of the nearby Dungur élite structure.

Shaft tombs

A further widely distributed type of Aksumite tomb comprised a vertical shaft, square, rectangular or cruciform in cross-section, from the bottom of which opened one or more burial chambers. Examples have been excavated in the vicinity of Aksum and at Matara, as well as at Yeha where most if not all probably originated in earlier times. Others are known at numerous localities, including Adigrat, but have not been recorded or published in detail. These shaft tombs show significant continuity, probably for about one thousand years from the fifth century BC if not earlier. (Chapter 3) until after Christianity had become widely established. As noted above, the Tomb of Bazen at Aksum may have been a shaft tomb before it was modified by creating a rock-cut stair, perhaps indicating a typological progression. Other examples are preserved below the modern Church of the Four Animals.[44] Although no shaft tombs are known to have survived unrobbed from the Aksumite period, the general lack of care and elaboration in their construction, together with their somewhat cramped accommodation, suggest that they were not themselves burial places for the élite or the most wealthy.

Overview

Although our knowledge of Aksumite burials is hampered by sparse research and publication, as well as by the frequency with which graves have been –

[40] Others have been recorded in the eastern highlands of Tigray but the details remain unpublished.

[41] Munro-Hay 1989a: 142–9; Ayele 1996; Ayele & D. Phillipson 2000.

[42] Chittick 1974; Munro-Hay 1989a: 143–6.

[43] Puglisi 1946; D. Phillipson 1990; L. Phillipson 2000b, 2000c.

[44] Anfray 1965: 5.

and are still being – robbed, a picture is emerging that emphasises enormous disparity in the resources that were expended in disposal and commemoration of the dead. There are no grounds for believing that the burials so far investigated include any examples belonging to the poorest strata of Aksumite society.[45] At several levels there are indications for significant continuity in burial practice from earlier times. Changes associated with the adoption of Christianity are well illustrated only for the richest – presumed royal – burials. A final point requiring emphasis is the extent to which Aksumite burial places, from shaft tombs to the more elaborate Tomb of the Brick Arches, were rock-hewn.[46] In cases where an underground tomb was built and then covered, an attempt could be made to disguise this fact and give the impression that the whole structure had been hewn from solid rock – as at the Mausoleum. The significance of this point is further discussed in Chapter 16. It is only to be expected, however, that future research and discovery will require significant modification to the overview offered here.

[45] *cf.* L. Phillipson 2009b: 75.

[46] The Aksumite date and identification as an unfinished 'rock-tomb' of the feature so recorded by the Deutsche Aksum-Expedition at Aksum (Littmann *et al.* 1913, 2: 69–70; D. Phillipson 1997: 71–2) are both open to question.

13

Aksumite Technology and Material Culture

This chapter does not attempt to provide a comprehensive account of Aksumite material culture. It concentrates on technology and affinities rather than on typology. For detailed descriptions and illustrations of artefacts, the reader is referred to the principal excavation reports included in the bibliography.

Aksumite material culture displays many remarkable features due to its blending of indigenous elements with those derived from external contacts, notably with the Nile Valley, southern Arabia and the circum-Mediterranean region. In the past, there has been a tendency for the external to be emphasised at the expense of the local (*cf.* Chapter 1). Correction of this imbalance being one of the aims of the present book, this chapter seeks to evaluate the extent to which different elements of Aksumite material culture and technology may be traced either to local antecedents or to indigenous innovation. It is convenient to arrange the treatment under the principal raw materials that were exploited, despite the cross-referencing that such an approach inevitably involves.

Pottery

So far as is currently known, all pottery produced within Aksumite territory was hand-made – without use of the wheel – employing technology that had been locally established long previously (Fig. 59). Such wheel-thrown pottery as has been recovered from Aksumite archaeological contexts appears to have been imported; some of its forms were, however, imitated by local potters using their own technology.[1] While some accounts place considerable emphasis on the imported pottery, locally-produced wares invariably represent a very high proportion of the total ceramic assemblages. This is not to discount pottery that was produced in Aksumite regions at some distance from the site where it was used and subsequently found. There is, for example, good evidence that some painted vessels excavated at Aksum had been produced in the eastern highlands of Tigray or, further north, around Matara.[2] Establishment of comprehensive pottery sequences has so far been hindered by a number of factors, notably the fact that several of the most informative and most firmly dated assemblages have been recovered from tombs where the vessels that were buried with the dead may have been significantly different from those in everyday use. Furthermore, regional differences in pottery traditions remain very poorly understood; inter-site correlations are therefore difficult and potentially misleading.[3] Emphasis

[1] *e.g.* J. S. Phillips 2000: 457 and *passim*.

[2] See Anfray 1966, 1973; Wilding & Munro-Hay 1989: 311–12; J. S. Phillips 2000: 326; D'Andrea *et al.* 2008a: 163.

[3] For example, the chronology proposed for the Gulo Makeda region of northeast Tigray (D'Andrea *et al.* 2008a) is largely based on ceramic comparisons with the Aksum region and must be regarded as tentative.

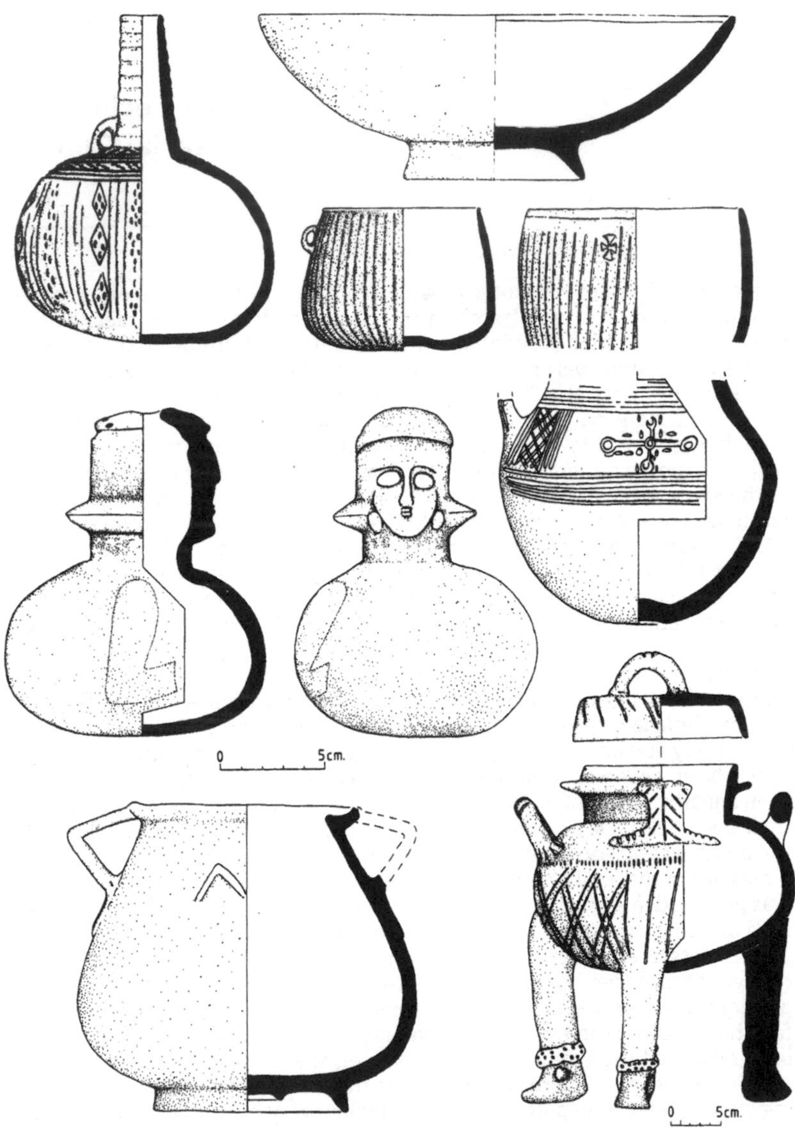

Fig. 59 Aksumite pottery (after Wilding and Munro-Hay 1989)

on fabric and colour, sometimes at the expense of form, size and decoration, has hindered understanding. Virtually no research has been undertaken on the sources of clay used for making pottery.

A pot from Aksum bears a Ge'ez inscription,[4] noted in Chapter 5, recording the name of the owner and warning that breakage must be compensated. It appears from the published photographs that the inscription was made while the clay was still soft, possibly before the handle was applied. This suggests – but does not prove – two conclusions: that the potter was literate and produced the vessel for his or her own use. At least in the early centuries AD, potting would seem to have remained a largely domestic craft, although specialisation may have gradually developed subsequently.

Aksumite-period pottery displays elements of technological and typological continuity from that of earlier periods, most clearly demonstrated at Beta Giyorgis. The overall impression is one of conservatism; development was continuous, and there seem to have been no clear discontinuities in the Aksum-area sequence.[5] Some chipped stone instruments were used for decorating pottery: examples include flakes with neatly trimmed ends for making grooved designs, and pebbles or flat flakes for burnishing.[6] Vessels that clearly originated far beyond Aksumite territory (Chapter 16) seem for the most part to have served as receptacles for the transport of consumer luxuries, notably – but not exclusively – wine. One class of pottery that may have been imported for élite use comprised small platters and bowls of wheel-thrown red-slip ware from Roman North Africa; significantly, hand-made vessels apparently imitating their forms were then produced by Aksumite potters. The local imitations produced between the late-fifth and early-seventh centuries significantly outnumber the examples of imported prototypes that have been reported from Aksum and Matara.[7] Glazed vessels, notably from the Persian Gulf and further east but also possibly from Nubia, are also present in mainly late contexts. A high proportion of the locally-produced vessels appear to have been used for domestic purposes such as carrying water and the preparation, storage and service of food or beverages. The quality and refinement of such pottery presumably depended on the taste and wealth of its owners. There seem to have been distinctive vessels that were made – but sometimes imperfectly fired – specifically as grave-goods, to accompany the élite dead.[8]

[4] RIE 311; Anfray 1972b: 69; Drewes & R. Schneider 1972: 101. The vessel was excavated on the west side of Aksum, in a trial trench to the north of Dungur. A date in about the fourth century is suggested on palaeographic grounds and is not contradicted by the context. Unfortunately, the name of the maker/owner is incomplete and could be that of a man or a woman.

[5] Bard *et al.* 1997: 397, 400; J. S. Phillips 2000: 453–8; Fattovich *et al.* 2000: 70–1, fig. 16. A somewhat wider view was provided by Michels (2005: 103–53). Similar continuity in other geographical areas cannot yet be demonstrated, and its investigation must be a priority for future research in view of its bearing on the expansion of the Aksumite polity. Until further details are published, and greater chronometric precision attained, it will not be possible to establish whether similar continuity prevailed at Matara (Anfray 1966, 1974; Curtis & Daniel 2008; Fattovich 2010) or in the Gulo Makeda region (D'Andrea *et al.* 2008a).

[6] Instruments from Hamed Gabez, in an area now largely covered by the eastward expansion of Aksum town, were illustrated by L. Phillipson (2009b: 91–5, pls 1–4). For a flake burnisher from Kidane Mehret see *eadem* 2000b: 360.

[7] See Anfray 1966: 17, 44; Wilding & Munro-Hay 1989: 314–15; J. S. Phillips 2000: 326, 394–6). The suggestion that earlier vessels may also imitate imported forms (J. S. Phillips 2000: 60) is more problematic, since they seem to pre-date the arrival in Aksumite territory of their putative prototypes.

[8] D. Phillipson 2000b: 130.

Glass

For many years it was assumed that all the glass preserved on Aksumite sites had been imported, but it is now known that this was not necessarily the case. Fragments of raw glass dating between the late-fifth and the early-seventh centuries have been recovered from K site at Aksum and from broadly contemporaneous levels at Ona Negast on Beta Giyorgis.[9] There can be virtually no doubt that, despite this evidence for local glass working, some items were nonetheless imported; a not insignificant proportion of this was likely to have been broken in the course of the long and difficult overland transport from its port of entry at – presumably, at least in most cases – Adulis.[10] There is no firm evidence that the Aksumites created their own raw glass *ab initio* from silica,[11] and it seems that their local glass industry involved the melting and reworking of imported material, doubtless including breakages. Already in the 1980s, analysis had led to the tentative conclusion that, in terms of colouring, glass from Aksum showed greater affinity with that from western Asia than with that from Egypt or the eastern Mediterranean;[12] although the possibility of local glass making – as opposed to glass-working – was already recognised, its use of broken imports seems not to have been specifically considered. Typological study of glass from Aksum has yielded broadly compatible results, emphasising the unusually extensive use of coloured material and the extent to which vessels from Aksum may be paralleled at distant Aksumite sites such as Matara – thus indicating that local taste or fashion prevailed over a wide area of the realm. Significant pieces in this connection are a set of goblets (Fig. 60) and a handled beaker from a tomb in the Gudit Stelae Field that is dated to the second or third centuries (Chapter 13): the latter closely resembles a common Aksumite pottery form, although no parallels in glass have been located.[13] There are, on the other hand, glass vessels that may confidently be regarded as imports, including a fine blue fluted tankard, a red goblet (Fig. 60) and an engraved bowl, all from the fourth-century Tomb of the Brick Arches.[14]

This reconsideration of the original sources of glass objects recovered from Aksumite sites has parallels in Meroitic Nubia, particularly those from graves at Sedeiga where local production has been proposed for items previously regarded as imports.[15] In both areas, the presence of glass earplugs,[16] similar in form to stone ones, provides a further indication of local production. It must be emphasised, however, that there is no suggestion that all Aksumite glass was

[9] Michael Harlow 2000: 401–2, 459; Manzo 2005: 59. An earlier discovery of comparable debris in a westerly area of Aksum town (Puglisi 1941: 124–5) is less securely dated. Fragments of glass vessels that appear to have been intentionally comminuted for melting were recovered from the fourth-century Mausoleum at Aksum (Michael Harlow *loc. cit.*: 198). For a similar process in a broadly contemporary British context, see Shepherd & Wardle 2009. Note also that export of raw glass from Roman Egypt to India, but not to Adulis or any other Red-Sea port was noted in the *Periplus of the Erythraean Sea* (49, 56; Casson 1989: 80–1, 84–5).

[10] J. S. Phillips 2009 has given a useful account of evidence relating to the packing and transport of glass.

[11] *cf.* L. Phillipson 2009b: 40.

[12] Kaczmarczyk 1989: 333–9.

[13] *ibid.*

[14] Michael Harlow 2000: 78–9; Morrison 1989: 194, fig. 14.71; see also below. This tallies with the evidence of the *Periplus of the Erythraean Sea* (6; Casson 1989: 52–5) for the import of glass vessels through Adulis in earlier times.

[15] For discussion, see Leclant 1973; Cool 1996; Edwards 2004: 167–8.

[16] *e.g.* Morrison 1989: 206–7.

Fig. 60 Glass goblets from Aksum: left [height: 12.5 cm] – probably a local manufacture imitating an Alexandrian product, from a third-century tomb in the Gudit Stelae Field; right [height: 25 cm] – probably an import, from the fourth-century Tomb of the Brick Arches

Fig. 61 Plaques of brass over iron from the Tomb of the Brick Arches at Aksum, the perforations in the brass being filled with coloured glass-paste: the lower example shows how plaques with different designs were juxtaposed, joined by a metal strip; the iron on the back retains traces of the wooden object to which these plaques were affixed

produced locally: a foreign origin for some pieces is highly probable. Whether they came as gifts or through formal trade,[17] the value of those that arrived in Aksumite territory unbroken must have been significantly enhanced.

Glass vessels[18] were blown, both with and without moulds, comprising goblets, beakers, bowls, bottles, flasks, phials and probably – although represented only by fragments – hanging lamps. Mosaic and layered fabrics were rare and may all have been imported; elaborations included applied handles, base-rings

[17] For stimulating discussion of this distinction, see Edwards 1996: 39–47.

[18] For illustrations, see Morrison 1989: 171, 177; Michael Harlow 2000: 82–6, 339–42, 459–60.

and other trails, as well as grinding, wheel-engraving[19] and surface-painting. Glass was also used for bracelets, ear- or lip-studs, and a large variety of beads.[20] Manufacture of glassware, unlike pottery, was clearly in the hands of specialists.

Finally, note should be taken of the extensive use of glass-inlay. A large number of small trimmed insets was recovered from primary deposits of the fourth-century Mausoleum at Aksum;[21] there was no trace of the object into which these pieces had been set, and it may have been of wood. Similar, but larger, specimens from the Tomb of the Brick Arches had been set in copper-alloy plates.[22] An analogous technique was the use of coloured glass-paste to fill patterns in iron-backed cut-out brass panels from the same tomb (Fig. 61).[23]

Metals

The Aksumites possessed highly accomplished metalwork with items in gold, silver, iron, and copper together with its various alloys including bronze, speculum and brass. As with many of the materials discussed in this chapter, most of the specimens that have been described and dated in detail come from Aksum and its immediate vicinity, those buried with the élite being better represented than those in everyday use. The sheer quantity of the surviving metalwork suggests that the majority was manufactured locally, although the lack of evidence for mines and/or quarries, smelting sites and workshops is a strange and surprising feature of the archaeological record currently available. The facts that – so far – Aksumite sources of metals remain unknown, and that no positively-identified smelting sites or forges have been located,[24] seriously impede our understanding.

Gold was used for coins and jewellery, as foil or inlay on items made of other metals, and for thread in weaving and/or embroidery.[25] Jewellery, including gold cross-pendants of clear Christian type, has been found in a hoard at Matara and at Adulis.[26] Rapid debasement of the coinage (Chapter 14) could imply that gold itself was in short supply, at least from the mid-fourth century onwards, despite continuation of its use for embellishment of base-metal issues.

19 Grinding was most frequently employed to finish the bases of vessels, notably those with foot-rings. Ground decoration was rare, but wheel-engraving was employed on a bowl with two motifs resembling widely separated letters 'A' and 'E' (Morrison 1989: 194, fig. 14.71). If these were indeed letters, they could be either Greek or Latin, but not Ge'ez.

20 Beads were also made of stone, *cf.* below. It is likely that beads of both glass and stone included locally produced as well as imported examples, but further study and analysis is needed on this question.

21 Michael Harlow 2000: 198–9.

22 D. Phillipson 2000b: 102–3.

23 Munro-Hay 1989a: 215; D. Phillipson 2000b: 105–8. No analyses of the glass paste have been undertaken.

24 See below. *Fourneaux* were noted by the excavator at Matara (Anfray 1963b: 99, pls lxxx) and at Dungur (*idem* 1972c: 65; 1990: 103). Those at the latter site were built of fired bricks but no further details or indications of their possible use are available. Ziegert 2006 made mention of materials interpreted as metal-working residues from Berik Audi on the northern side of Aksum, but his account is difficult to understand and cannot be evaluated until further details are made available. (See * note on p. 180).

25 Gold coins and the gilding of those in other metals are discussed in Chapter 14. For jewellery, see Anfray & Annequin (1965: 68–71); for foil, inlay and thread, see D. Phillipson (2000b: 200–03, 497–8). A stone mould for casting metal pendants was recovered at Adulis by Paribeni (1907: fig. 7).

26 Paribeni 1907: figs 20, 21; Anfray & Annequin 1965: 68–71. For Roman gold coins re-used as jewellery in the Matara hoard, see Chapter 14.

Sources of gold are uncertain. Several stone slabs in the vicinity of Aksum still bear the name *mistah werki* [= where gold is spread out to dry].[27] The form of these slabs is concordant with their use for washing auriferous earth in order to extract the gold, which would suggest that the material thus processed was obtained in fairly close proximity. There are indeed sixteenth-century records[28] of gold being found after rain in the Aksum vicinity: the suggestion[29] that they actually refer to the recovery of gold coins, while plausible, should be viewed as unlikely in view of the interests and statements of the original observer. In the early-seventeenth century, Barradas recorded the wide distribution of auriferous deposits in the – then – kingdom of Tigray, while a nineteenth-century prospector was noted by Bent as having discovered gold in the vicinity of Adwa.[30] Laurel Phillipson considered that areas of disturbed terrain immediately west of Aksum might have been caused by mining for alluvial gold.[31] She also raised the question whether the deep rock-cut vats at Adi Tsehafi may have been used for gold-processing rather than for the pressing of fruit – possibly for wine-making – as has more usually been suggested.[32]

Sources of silver are likewise problematic; it is often held that silver was very scarce in Ethiopia until the advent of Austro-Hungarian coins in the late-eighteenth century,[33] but the abundance of Aksumite silver coins suggests that there may have been an earlier and more local source.[34] Other than for coins, however, it seems to have been employed by the Aksumites only rarely.[35]

Although the *Periplus of the Erythraean Sea* records the import of iron tools through Adulis in the first century AD,[36] the quantity in which iron was used at Aksum by at least the fourth century[37] makes it hard to believe that the metal was not obtained locally. With one possible exception,[38] no iron artefacts have been recovered for which a foreign origin is indicated. Objects made of iron included weapons [spear- and arrow-heads], and tools such as saws, hammers and knives, nails, rivets, clasps and hooks; with the exception of the weapons and their ceremonial counterparts, these were items used for the most part by non-élite

27 Anfray 1965: 4, pl. *ib*; L. Phillipson 2000b: 421–3; Tekle 2001: 38–9; L. Phillipson 2006.

28 Alvares in Beckingham & Huntingford 1961: 159–60, 457.

29 *e.g.* Munro-Hay 1991b: 171.

30 Barradas 1996: 21–5; Bent 1893: 132.

31 L. Phillipson 2006. Tekle 2010 made further mention of gold deposits in the Aksum area.

32 See Littmann *et al.* 1913, 2: 74–7 (D. Phillipson 1997: 162–5). Further discussion and counter-arguments have been set out by Sutton 2008. Very similar tanks are known in Sudanese Nubia, where a parallel controversy surrounds their purpose (Vercoutter 1957; Adams 1966; Welsby 1996: 158–60). Aksumite wine and its sources are discussed in Chapters 10 and 15.

33 Buxton 1970: 165; Richard Pankhurst, note in Barradas 1996: 25.

34 Professor Wolfgang Hahn (*in litt.* 4 February 2011) has suggested that silver may have been separated from mined or alluvial gold.

35 Silver, usually debased, is represented only by a few small decorative items and as an inlay on objects of iron or copper alloy (*e.g.* Munro-Hay 1989a: fig. 15.58; D. Phillipson 2000b: 86-7), also as a rivet in the iron object noted below.

36 *Periplus* 6 (Casson 1989: 52–3). Little significant information has been derived from the small amount of surviving metalwork from Paribeni's excavations (Zazzaro 2006), which is currently the only such material from Adulis that has been published.

37 This is indicated both by the preserved ironwork, as in the Tomb of the Brick Arches (Munro-Hay 1989a: 225–8; D. Phillipson 2000b: 105–16) and by the evidence for large-scale stone quarrying (below) in which there is good evidence for the extensive use of iron tools.

38 The exception is an object from the Tomb of the Brick Arches (D. Phillipson 2000b: 114–6), formerly suggested (*idem* 1998: 67–8) as possibly Chinese in origin.

persons. More widespread in their use were iron items employed in carpentry, masonry or other composite objects, the bimetallic plaques of perforated brass with iron backing (noted above) being particularly noteworthy.[39] All these iron items could have been produced using forging techniques likely to have been available locally, but no sources have yet been identified where there is evidence for Aksumite extraction or smelting of iron ore.[40]

Copper and its various alloys were widely employed, but only in two locations at Aksum is there any possible evidence for its processing; neither is conclusive.[41] It was employed for a wide range of artefacts where decorative form and finish were deemed more important than strength or sharpness. Softer than iron, and with a low melting-temperature, it could be more readily worked using a greater variety of techniques. Alloys could, for example, be varied according to the finish required: bronze [copper plus tin] for hardness combined with malleability, speculum [bronze with a high tin-content] for reflective mirrors,[42] and brass [copper plus zinc] for a bright shining finish.[43] The most striking example of the use of brass at Aksum is the cast disc recovered, broken into many fragments and mixed with other pieces of scrap metal, from the fourth-century Tomb of the Brick Arches (Chapter 12 and Fig. 51); there can be little doubt that it had been designed for mounting on the apex of a stela intended to be seen at a distance, and it is easy to see why brass was chosen. In Aksumite times, unalloyed copper seems to have been used only rarely. A large and remarkable cast copper-alloy lamp in the form of a sea-shell, a dog and an ibex was recovered from Matara, where it had been hidden in about the sixth century,[44] although it had almost certainly been produced in southern Arabia several centuries earlier. A much smaller casting from Aksum[45] depicts two human figures which share stylistic features with the ivory figurine noted below, and was probably manufactured locally. A cross, bells and links of a chain from Yeha, all of copper alloy, are interpreted as coming from a censer.[46] The principal artefacts made of copper alloys, in addition to those already noted, were decorative plaques, nails, hinges, handles and other items evidently used in the fabrication or decoration of wooden constructions; and items used for personal adornment or grooming. At Aksum, and perhaps elsewhere, copper alloy was markedly more common in élite contexts than in those of lower status. Examples of Aksumite artefacts in copper alloy and iron are illustrated in Fig. 62.

Aksumite metalworking techniques display considerable sophistication and expertise, the work clearly being largely in the hands of specialists, while

39 Munro-Hay 1989a: 215; D. Phillipson 2000b: 105–08; see also below.

40 In the seventeenth century, however, Barradas 1996: 24 noted that iron ore was plentiful, although he did not mention particular localities. There are also reports of 'ancient' smelting sites near Entichio.

41 In both cases the evidence is tantalisingly inconclusive. At K site, analysis of sixth-century crucible fragments and slag revealed evidence for copper (Feuerbach, cited by D. Phillipson 2000b: 407). The report of metal-working residues from Berik Audi on the northern side of Aksum has been noted above.

42 As, likewise, from the Tomb of the Brick Arches (D. Phillipson 2000b: 94–5).

43 Brass was a comparatively recent addition to the metallurgical repertoire (Tylecote 1992). Although known earlier in China, it does not appear to have been known in Egypt until *c.* 30 BC, but it was then adopted rapidly throughout the Roman world and – as the Aksum evidence now shows – beyond.

44 Anfray 1967: 46–8.

45 Munro-Hay 1989a: 220–1, pl. 15.1.

46 Doresse 1956: 219–20.

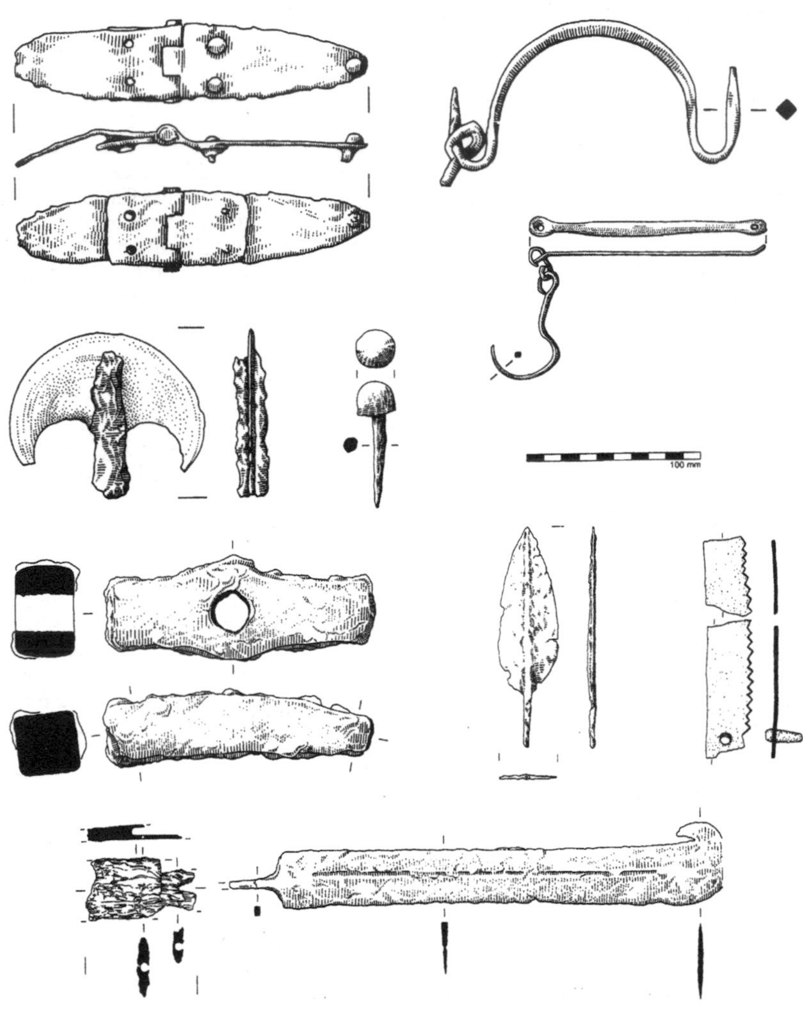

Fig. 62 Aksumite metalwork (after D. Phillipson 2000b); the specimens above the scale are of copper alloy, those below being of iron

most of their products were at the disposal of the élite. Even base metal was a valuable commodity, as is reflected both by the assiduity with which it was reworked rather than simply discarded, and its scarcity among items recovered from occupation and workshop-sites as opposed to burials. This scarcity is particularly striking at the stone-quarrying sites where no physical remains of iron tools have been recovered, despite the frequency with which they were evidently employed. Recycling of worn-out or broken iron artefacts may be attributed mainly to the extremely labour-intensive nature of its smelting. The same factor may also have a bearing on the fact that the Aksumites continued to use flaked-stone artefacts for certain operations, as discussed below. Metalworking techniques of which the products are attested in Aksumite contexts include smelting, forging, casting, purification and control of alloys, riveting, engraving, preparation of foil and thread, diffusion bonding of gold foil, amalgam (mercury) gilding, die-sinking and the striking of coins.[47]

Four metals have been noted that were clearly available in Aksumite times although we have no knowledge of how and where they were obtained. Zinc was used to produce brass, and varying proportions of tin were added to copper to yield bronze or speculum. Numerous coins were struck from silver but there is little evidence that it was put to other uses. Gilding of coins (Fig. 70 and Chapter 14) involved the use of mercury. There are several records of tin, zinc and silver being mined or otherwise obtained during the past four centuries within former Aksumite territory.[48] The source of mercury remains to be investigated: it was employed for gilding in the eastern Mediterranean area, India and China as early as the last millennium BC, some of the processes involved in obtaining it being analogous to those employed for zinc and the production of brass.[49]

Wood

Detailed knowledge about use of wood in Aksumite times is reduced by the rarity of its preservation, much information being gleaned from traces or representations in other materials. So far, such sources have rarely permitted recognition of the actual varieties of wood that were employed. Beams-and-monkey-heads building construction (Chapter 11), also door- and window-frames, are represented on stelae and by impressions in surviving stonework, rarely by charred beams etc. Surviving examples at churches may include occasional instances of actual Aksumite age, such as the fine coffered ceiling at Debra Damo; it is argued that this church may have originated as early as the sixth century although it cannot be demonstrated that any wood of this age has survived the building's repeated episodes of renovation (Chapters 11 and 16). Roofs and – in buildings of more than one storey – suspended floors must have incorporated wooden beams which may also have been used as pillars (Chapter 11). Presumably doors were made of wood.

Traces of wood are preserved in corrosion of metal objects fixed to or embedded in wood, *e.g.* nails, hinges and clasps, especially those in the Tomb of the Brick Arches, where were also found a number of elaborate plaques made of brass with apertures filled by coloured glass-paste (Fig. 61), each plaque backed by iron which showed signs of the wood to which they had originally been fixed – perhaps some sort of large box or coffer. Mortise-and-tenon joints were used in construction of the ivory chair preserved in the Tomb of the Brick

47 See, primarily, Feuerbach 2000.

48 Tekle 2010.

49 Craddock 1995: 302–5.

Fig. 63 Carved ivory from the fourth-century Tomb of the Brick Arches, Aksum (photographs by D.W. P. and Laurel Phillipson): left – one of the two carved panels, probably from the back of the chair / throne; upper right – turned plaque with brass central stud; lower right – *pyxis*;

Fig. 63 continued Details of carved ivory panels (see opposite)

Arches (below), most probably inspired by carpentry techniques for the making of jointed furniture, perhaps akin to that known from Egypt or represented in southern Arabian relief-carving.[50] Late Aksumite copper coins (Fig. 75) depict a chair of jointed – probably wooden but possibly ivory – construction.

Specific identification has proved possible of fragments of charred wood preserved in Aksumite-period archaeological deposits, including species characteristic of Afromontane forest.[51] Not incompatible evidence for former afforestation in the Aksum area is beginning to emerge,[52] but more such work is needed. It has been demonstrated by experiment that the small steeply-flaked Gudit scrapers (see below) are effective for working wood and, by implication, fresh ivory.[53]

Ivory

The principal concentration of Aksumite ivory artefacts is that recovered from the Tomb of the Brick Arches, but occasional specimens are known from elsewhere, including workshop debris at K site.[54] The export of elephant-ivory from Aksum is discussed elsewhere (Chapter 15); it seems probable that much of it was shipped in the form of unworked tusks, but clearly some was carved locally from at least the fourth century, with high levels of technological and artistic achievement. Dr Laurel Phillipson has published illustrated accounts of the techniques involved, including sawing, chiselling, fluting, drilling, turning, and carving.[55] Some pieces show signs of careful marking out before these techniques were applied, not always fully removed by subsequent polishing.

Few close stylistic parallels have been recognised for the fourth-century carved ivory from the Tomb of the Brick Arches. The elaborate chair or throne (Fig. 63) contrasts both in style and in manufacture with its counterparts elsewhere. The structural framework itself was of ivory, and its back comprised two large panels carved with representations of birds and animals intertwined with vines. Ivory chairs evidently existed in the Byzantine world since at least 432 when fourteen *cathedrae eburneae* are recorded as having been donated by Cyril, Patriarch of Alexandria, to the court in Constantinople.[56] It is noteworthy that St Cyril's gifts presumably originated – or were obtained – in Alexandria, and that the sixth-century throne of Maximian in Ravenna has often – but not unanimously – been argued to be of Alexandrian craftsmanship[57]. Such attributions, it must be emphasised, have rarely been based on comparisons with pieces that are incontrovertibly known to have originated in Alexandria.[58] Ivory-carving

50 For jointed furniture in Egypt, see Killen 1994; for Arabia, Simpson 2002: 125.

51 Chittick 1976; Gale cited by Boardman 2000: 368; Boardman & Gale 2000: 509.

52 Machado *et al.* 1998; Darbyshire *et al.* 2003; French *et al.* 2009.

53 L. Phillipson 2000c.

54 D. Phillipson 2000b: 407; L. Phillipson 2000b: 460–8.

55 L. Phillipson 2000b: 460–8, 2002.

56 Batiffol 1911: 260. Although Batiffol translated these words *des sièges ornés d'ivoire*, implying that they were decorated with ivory, he cited as comparison the sixth-century throne of Maximian in Ravenna which, like the earlier Aksum example, is largely made of ivory, not merely decorated with it. I am grateful to M. Pierre Ferrand for his advice on the precise meaning of Batiffol's text.

57 *e.g.* E. Smith 1917. For the throne of Maximian more generally, see Cecchelli 1936–44; for other examples, less securely documented, see Weitzmann 1972. Ivory chairs and thrones are further discussed in Chapter 15.

58 *e.g.* Kollwitz 1964.

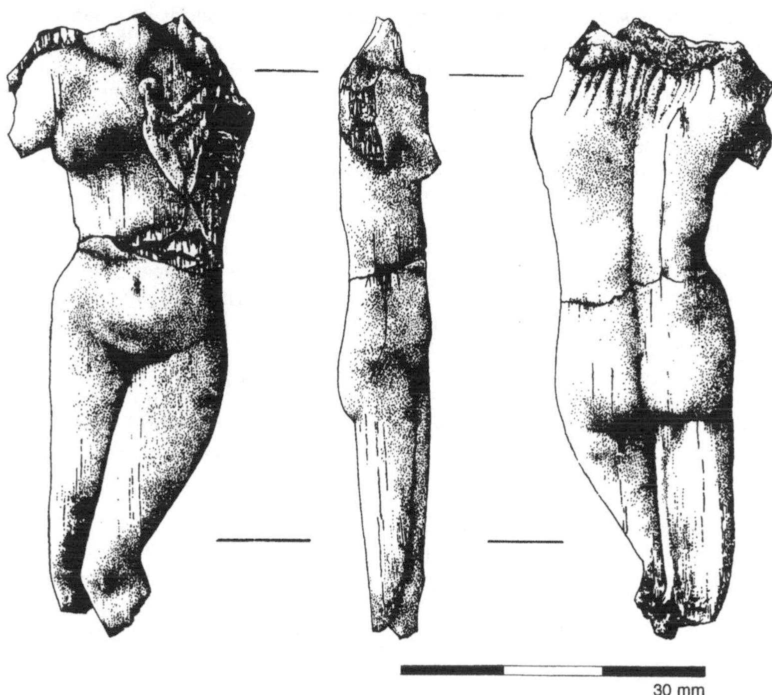

Fig. 64 Ivory figurine from the fourth-century Tomb of the Brick Arches, Aksum (drawing by Sarah Semple, after D. Phillipson 2000b)

workshops in that city have been investigated in detail – along with their products – by Dr Elizabeth Rodziewicz[59] and no close stylistic parallels with the Aksum or the Ravenna chairs are demonstrable. The chair from the Tomb of the Brick Arches may be accepted as earlier than any of its known Byzantine counterparts, and there are no good reasons for attributing it to an Alexandrian workshop. Its decoration of vines is of a type very widely employed by stone- and ivory-carvers during the early centuries AD in southern Arabia and at Aksum itself, as well as in Egypt and elsewhere in the Mediterranean world.[60]

A tiny carving of a naked woman (Fig. 64) from the Tomb of the Brick Arches shows superficial similarity to Graeco-Roman examples; it differs, however, in being not truly three-dimensional but rather a combination of two-dimensional representations of front and back in a manner seen in other Ethiopian sculptures.[61] It is best interpreted as an Aksumite copy or interpretation of a Graeco-

[59] Rodziewicz 1998, 2003, 2007, 2009.

[60] For southern Arabian parallels, see Béal 1991 [in ivory] and Simpson 2002: 108–9 [in stone]; for Aksum, see the baseplate of Stela 3 (D. Phillipson 1997: 26–32, 1998: fig. 36) and a Christian-period stone of unknown provenance now built into the vestibule wall of the Old Cathedral (Littmann *et al.* 1913, 2: Abb. 144; Manzo 1999: fig. 3a).

[61] For this piece, see D. Phillipson 2000b: 123–4; L. Phillipson 2000b: 461–2. I am grateful to Drs Laurel Phillipson and Elizabeth Rodziewicz for their observations regarding its affinities.

Roman type.[62] A similar interpretation is offered for a series of small turned cylindrical boxes, or *pyxides*; the basic form, but not the details of its interpretation, being well known in several circum-Mediterranean regions. The final major class of ivory artefacts from the Tomb of the Brick Arches comprises over one hundred plaques, the more complete ones measuring *c.* 10 cm square, carefully turned to produce concentric raised bands; most – but not all – had a brass stud in the centre, apparently turned after installation.[63] These plaques were probably fixed by means of overlying strips to some large object that may have been a chest or coffer. I have not been able to trace any parallels for these plaques.

It may be concluded that the carved ivory artefacts from the Tomb of the Brick Arches were locally produced, although several forms were apparently inspired by knowledge of contemporary practice elsewhere – principally in the Mediterranean world but also in southern Arabia. Features for which non-Aksumite parallels have not been traced are the skilled turning of the plaques and the use of chipped stone artefacts in the initial shaping of some pieces, as demonstrated by the surviving tool-marks.[64] In view of the Aksumite kingdom's prominence (Chapter 15) in the supply of raw ivory to the Mediterranean world, the export of carved ivory from the latter area to Aksum would have been unlikely.

Quarries and monumental stonework

Stone was put to such varied uses that discussion is best subdivided. Massive dressed-stone for masonry was quarried at several localities in the Aksum vicinity (see Fig. 65); it must be assumed that stone used for such purposes in other parts of the kingdom was also obtained locally, but its sources have not yet been documented, and there is no reason to believe that they would have been on anything approaching the scale attested around Aksum itself. Of the Aksum stone-quarries, those most fully investigated extend along the south-eastern slopes of Gobedra [or Gobo Dura] hill, some 3–4 km west of central Aksum.[65] Blocks of nepheline syenite, including huge ones evidently intended as stelae, were separated from the parent rock either by continuous grooves or, more usually, by creating a line of deep rectangular sockets; in both cases there is clear evidence for the extensive use of iron tools. Outward pressure from the sockets was achieved, most probably, by the insertion of wedges. This method of detaching large blocks of stone was also employed at broadly the same time in Roman Egypt, notably at Mons Claudianus and Mons Porphyrites in the

[62] The long straight hair must have been inspired by such a prototype, being – like the woman's stance – wholly un-Ethiopian.

[63] D. Phillipson 2000b: 119–22; L. Phillipson 2000b: 465–8.

[64] L. Phillipson 2000b: 460–8.

[65] The Gobedra quarries have been known to archaeologists for several decades (*cf.* Anfray 1972b: 70). Although the 1906 Deutsche Aksum-Expedition visited and recorded the relief carving of a lioness (see below; also Littmann *et al.* 1913, 2: 73–4; D. Phillipson 1997: 160–2) on the boulder-strewn hillside, they do not appear to have noted the extensive signs of ancient quarrying there, although they did draw attention to much smaller-scale traces between Mai Shum and the Tombs of Kaleb and Gabra Masqal. The more recent research is described by J. B. Phillips & Ford 2000: 229–47; L. Phillipson 2000b: 254–66. For the sudden abandonment of the quarries, see Chapter 16. Breaking and removal of stone for road- and building-construction since the 1990s has resulted in destruction of many traces of ancient quarrying.

Fig. 65 Aksumite quarrying at Gobedra Hill, Aksum

Eastern Desert.[66] Much Aksumite stone dressing seems to have involved the use of specialist iron tools: their forms may be discerned from their products, although no physical specimens are known to have survived.[67]

Flaked lithics

This section is largely based on the research of Dr Laurel Phillipson, who has undertaken extensive studies of this material (Fig. 66).[68] Tool classes have been defined on the basis of the specimens themselves, paying particular attention to the nature of the working edges and to evidence for use and resharpening, while experimentation and study of artefacts in other materials apparently shaped with stone tools have provided clear indications of their use. Two distinct types of scraping tool have been recognised, one probably used for hide-preparation and the other – the Gudit scrapers noted above – for cleaning and shaping of wood and, less certainly, ivory. Some tools were apparently made by specialists, apparently working under pressure or duress, from carefully selected raw material. Gudit scrapers were repeatedly resharpened as necessary. Backed flakes and blades, often thought to be associated with hunting by means of bows and arrows, were here generally used as small knives. Other – less intensive – uses for which there is evidence include decoration and burnishing of pottery and smoothing of vellum.[69] The skills involved in the manufacture of these tools seem directly derived from those employed in earlier times, when more than one such tradition has been recognised (*cf.* Chapter 3). A trend to increased specialisation in the mass-production of certain standardised implements may be discerned by the fifth or sixth centuries, alongside continued *ad hoc* use of informal tools. There is evidence from a lithic workshop at Mai Agam on Beta Giyorgis for the mass-production of small triangular points that may have served as arrowheads for military use.[70] Lithic assemblages from later contexts show specialisation on the production of scraping tools.[71] Although flaked-stone tools were probably used throughout Aksumite territory, their ubiquity and significance was not always recognised by earlier researchers, and detailed analyses from other areas are not yet available.[72]

Other stonework

Brief mention may be made of the wide variety of other stone artefacts that were made and used in Aksumite times. A variety of grinding and pounding

66 For accounts of Roman-period quarrying at these Egyptian sites, see Peacock & Maxfield 1997; Maxfield & Peacock 2001. At these sites, as at Aksum, iron implements must have been extensively used in the quarrying process, but it was remarkable how few were recovered during the archaeological investigation. For the value of iron tools used in the quarries of Ptolemaic Egypt, see Thompson 1999b, recording a labour dispute in which quarrymen threatened to pawn their tools.

67 For a detailed, illustrated discussion, see L. Phillipson 2000b: 254–66.

68 L. Phillipson 2000a, 2000b: 433–47, 449–53, 2002, 2009a, 2009b.

69 For lithics used in pottery decoration from the Hamed Gebez site – now largely covered by the recent eastward expansion of Aksum town, see L. Phillipson 2009b: 91–5, pls 1–4. For a small burnisher of basalt, probably used for smoothing vellum, from Gumala north of Aksum, see *ibid.*: 69–70. For an obsidian flake used as a pot-burnisher (Fig. 66i) from a *c.* sixth-century deposit at Kidane Mehret, see *eadem* 2000b: 360.

70 L. Phillipson & Sulas 2005.

71 L. Phillipson 2009b: 113–5.

72 See, however, Puglisi 1941; Michels 2005; D'Andrea *et al.* 2008a.

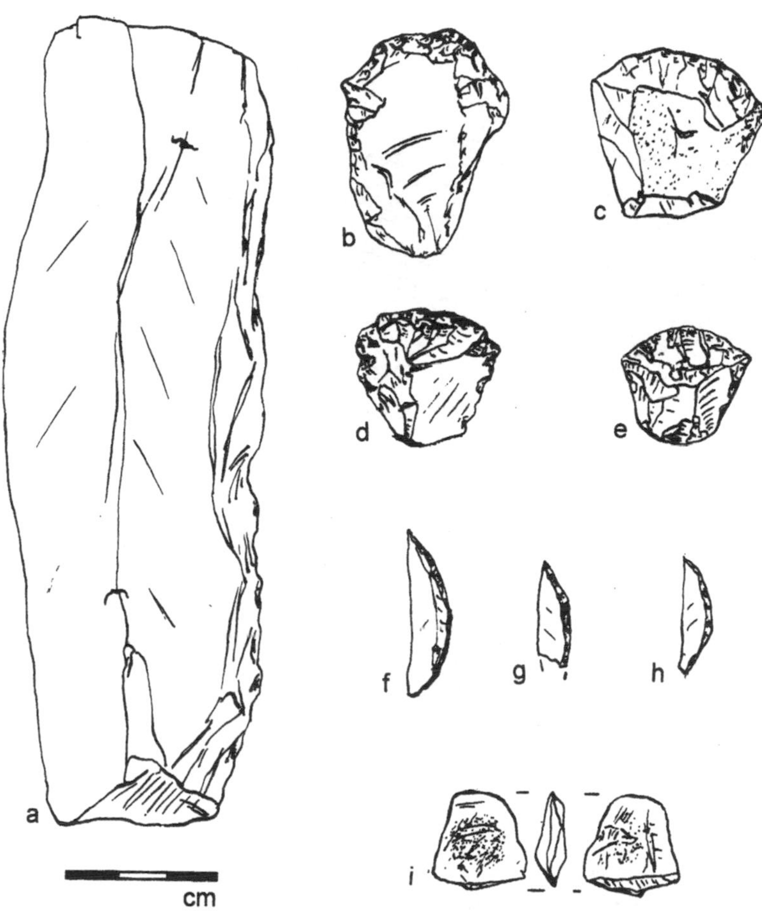

Fig. 66 Aksumite lithic artefacts (after L. Phillipson 2000b): a – casual basalt 'knife'; b-e: – Gudit scrapers in progressive stages of use and resharpening; f-h: – backed crescents with worn edges and broken tips; i – obsidian flake probably used for burnishing pottery

Fig. 67 Relief carving of uncertain age at Gobedra, probably depicting a lioness, 3.27 m long

instruments was employed in the preparation of food and, probably, other substances. Rotary querns, however, are only attested at Adulis.[73] On a smaller and finer scale are items such as inscribed seals,[74] jettons, dice, pendants and beads.[75] Intaglios were both imported from the Mediterranean region and imitated locally.[76] A group of fine lathe-turned bowls in purple-and-white breccia was recovered at Aksum from a context tentatively dated to the fifth century;[77] analogous objects are known elsewhere, some of which are probably earlier. Objects in steatite [soapstone], including a lamp carved in representation of a building,[78] should also be noted.

73 L. Phillipson 2001. Rotary querns at Adulis were noted by Anfray 1974: 752; their significance is discussed in Chapter 10.

74 As in earlier times (*cf.* Chapter 3), seals and counters have been cited (*e.g.* Fattovich *et al.* 2000: 158) as demonstrating bureaucracy, but the arguments are weak.

75 Some of the stone beads were manufactured at Aksum, as evidenced at K site (Michael Harlow 2000: 404). An unfinished carnelian bead (L. Phillipson 2009b: 37) also indicates local manufacture of a type previously regarded as an import.

76 For an imported third-century intaglio from Ona Negast, see Manzo 2005: fig. 15. A perforated example found in an undated Aksum context depicts clasped hands in a motif commonly used on Roman ring-stones during the early centuries AD, apparently continuing later in the eastern Mediterranean area. On the basis of its distinctive features, Dr Martin Henig (cited in D. Phillipson 2000b: 156) suggested that it was a local production.

77 Munro-Hay 1989a: 317–8.

78 D. Phillipson 2000b: 348–9.

Fig. 68 An ancient paved road at Aksum, photographed in 1969 but since obliterated

Miscellaneous

Other materials known to have been used, but of which few physical traces survive, include textiles,[79] leather and vellum.[80] Controversy continues over the extent to which sixth- and seventh-century manuscript illustration (Figs 29 and 30) and mural art were imports, the work of specialists from overseas, or had been incorporated into local traditions, as discussed in Chapters 9 and 15. Almost certainly local in origin, although their age is uncertain, are open-air rock carvings ranging from crude *graffiti* to the low-relief representation of a lioness at Gobedra (Fig. 67), a short distance west of Aksum.[81]

Transport

Finally, it is relevant to the general theme of this chapter to include mention of transport methods and infrastructure. Traces of Aksumite-period paved roads have been noted in several areas but not recorded in detail (*e.g.* Fig. 68). It is clear, however, that such roads must have greatly facilitated internal links

[79] For fragments of cotton textile from sixth-century deposits at Kidane Mehret, see Boardman 2000: 345–6. A fourth-century occurrence of cloth incorporating gold thread was noted above and in Chapter 12.

[80] Vellum is indicated archaeologically by the presence of stone tools (noted above) likely to have been used in its preparation, and by evidence (Chapter 9) that the Abba Garima *Gospels* date – at least in part – to around the sixth century.

[81] For examples of *graffiti*, some of which probably pre-date the rise of Aksum, see Ricci 1960a, 1988; L. Phillipson 2000b: 423-4. The Gobedra lioness was recorded by the DAE (Littmann *et al.* 1913, 2: 73–-4; D. Phillipson 1997: 160–2) and has subsequently been the subject of much speculation (*e.g.* Ricci 2002), frequently ill-informed.

between different areas and elements of the Aksumite kingdom, as well as long-distance communication.[82] The stone inscription RIE 186, attributed to Ezana's predecessor Ella Amida (Chapter 6), records improvements to a road and the granting of safe-conduct thereon. Movement along such roads and elsewhere would have been on foot, by donkey and/or camel (Chapter 10). There is no evidence for the use of wheeled transport. Survey has revealed traces of a slipway for lowering stones at the Gobedra quarries and of a level terraced route from there to the central area of Aksum, along which stelae and large building-stones could have been transported by means of rollers.[83]

Conclusion

This incomplete survey has indicated not only the complexity of Aksumite technology and material culture but also that it was rooted in local tradition and innovation to a greater extent than previously thought. Its study, which remains patchy and incomplete, requires not only descriptive precision and scientific analysis, but an awareness of the implications that may be derived for social, political and economic aspects of the Aksumite kingdom.

82 Sernicola & L. Phillipson 2011.

83 For further discussion, including an estimate of the manpower that may have been involved in such endeavours, see D. Phillipson & L. Phillipson 2000: 247–51. For stela erection, see Chapter 12.

* Since this chapter was written, analysis has demonstrated that the evidence for metal working at Berik Audi, Aksum (p. 165, above) relates, not to copper as originally suggested, but to iron (T. Severin *et al.* 2011). Early metal smelting in Aksum, Ethiopia: copper or iron? *European Journal of Mineralogy* 23: 981-92).

14

Aksumite Coinage

Study of Aksumite coinage has proved highly informative both to numismatists and to historians more generally. Although its issue did not begin until the late-third century AD, it is important to recognise that small quantities of coins were already reaching northern Ethiopia from elsewhere during earlier periods, including examples struck in the Roman Empire, southern Arabia, and the Kushan kingdom in the region now comprising northeastern Afghanistan, northern Pakistan and parts of northwestern India. With the exception of very occasional specimens from excavated contexts in the Aksum area, most examples of southern Arabian coins – including one hoard – are chance finds.[1] Despite ancient documentary evidence[2] that small quantities of Roman coinage were imported to Adulis, apparently around the mid-first century AD, for use by the foreign merchants there, it seems that no such specimens have yet been recorded from archaeological excavations other than those from contexts of significantly later date. A hoard of gold objects from Matara (Chapter 13) included fourteen second-century Roman gold coins, all but one with suspension-loops indicating their eventual use as jewellery, but the excavators considered that the hoard was deposited in the sixth century and the date when the coins were imported cannot be ascertained.[3] Even more intriguing is a hoard of 105 gold Kushan coins recorded as having been found *c.* 1940 in an ancient wooden box buried in a cavity of the cliff beneath the Debra Damo monastery in northernmost Tigray. The coins themselves form a close-dated group, apparently brought together around the beginning of the third century AD, but this does not necessarily represent the date when they were deposited at Debra Damo.[4] There is thus no evidence as to how or when these Kushan coins came to Ethiopia, although it may be significant that they were apparently assembled just a few decades before the Aksumite polity began

[1] *e.g.* those illustrated by Conti Rossini 1921, de Contenson 1963a: pl. xiv*e*, Manzo 2005: fig. 12 and Hahn 2006b: Abb. 1–5. For ancient South Arabian coinage more generally, see Munro-Hay 2003. The suggestion (Breton & Munro-Hay 2002) that certain coins of southern Arabian type may have been minted at Aksum should be dismissed as speculation pending further evidence.

[2] *Periplus of the Erythraean Sea* 6 (Casson 1989: esp. 52–3). For the *Periplus*, including observations relating to its date, see Chapter 6.

[3] Anfray & Annequin 1965: 68–71.

[4] The best account of the Kushan coins from Debra Damo is by Göbl 1970, but it should be noted that some degree of uncertainty still surrounds the precise dates of these particular issues (Alram 1999). Examination of the box in which the coins were found would seem to offer the best chance of determining the date of the hoard's deposition. However, Professor Wolfgang Hahn (*in litt.*, 27 February 2008) has kindly searched Göbl's files at the Institut für Numismatik in Vienna and informed me of correspondence from Mordini indicating that the coins had passed into private hands but that the box had apparently not been preserved. For further advice on this matter I am grateful to Dr Robert Bracey of the British Museum.

producing its own coinage. It is appropriate to end this brief introductory survey by noting that, although occasional southern Arabian coins were present in domestic circumstances, there seems to have been no regular use of money within Aksumite territory before the indigenous coinage series began. Prior familiarity with southern Arabian Himyaritic silver coins of the type most frequently reported from the Aksum area may serve to explain certain features of the first Aksumite issues, as further expounded below.

Pre-Christian coinage

Between the second half of the third century AD and the middle decades of the seventh, the kingdom of Aksum was the only polity in sub-Saharan Africa to issue its own coinage, which it did in gold, silver and copper. Representative specimens are illustrated in Figs 25, 28 and 69–75. The inscriptions on Aksumite coins preserve the names of approximately twenty kings, whose reigns provide a sequence and chronology for the series as a whole. Unfortunately, and remarkably, very few of the names preserved on the coinage also occur in the traditional king-lists noted above, and *vice versa*; a detailed discussion of the successive kings of Aksum is provided in Chapter 8. It has generally been assumed that the mint was located at Aksum itself and, indeed, the capital would have been the obvious place for it, but there is no firm evidence that such was the case in this particular instance.[5] Detailed study of the coins' typology, style, weight, metallic composition, die-links and other factors has permitted establishment of the kings' approximate chronological order (see Fig. 24), concerning most of which broad agreement now prevails.[6] Two of these kings, Ezana and Kaleb, were also recorded on stone inscriptions (Chapter 6) at Aksum itself, and references in independent historical sources permit their reigns to be dated within reasonably narrow limits in the mid-fourth and early-sixth centuries respectively. Ezana's mid-reign adoption of Christianity, discussed in greater detail elsewhere (Chapter 9), was clearly reflected in the coinage.[7]

Minor disagreements notwithstanding, it is now widely accepted that issue of Aksumite coinage began in the second half of the third century and lasted for at least 350 years. It commenced quite suddenly under King Endybis at the time when the kingdom's wealth and prosperity were rapidly increasing, and came to a more hesitant end following a period of fairly rapid decline (Chapter 16). From the start, it employed clearly defined denominations in gold,

[5] See discussion by Oddy & Munro-Hay 1980: 75. I know of no evidence to support the statement by Shitomi (1997: 9) that 'It is considered that the mint itself was probably transferred to [southern Arabia] ... between the mid-fourth and early-sixth century'.

[6] The statement by Chrisomalis (2010: 154) that Aksumite coin inscriptions record regnal years is, unfortunately, totally incorrect. Uncertainty still surrounds the sequence of the latest issues, after the sixth-century reign of Kaleb (Hahn 2010).

[7] There is extensive specialist literature devoted to Aksumite coinage. The 1995 book by Munro-Hay and Juel-Jensen includes a comprehensive bibliography and, despite its shortcomings, is widely accepted as the standard work. A regularly updated list of amendments and of more recent publications is maintained by the numismatist Vincent West and may be consulted on his website <www.vincentwest.org.uk>. Further comprehensive treatments of the series, well illustrated by photographs, include those by Hahn 1983, Pedroni 1997b and Munro-Hay 1999. Munro-Hay's first book on Aksumite coins (1984a), although greatly amplified by that author's more recent work, is illustrated with clear but slightly schematised drawings (*cf.* Fig. 72) which are a useful aid to identification of poorly preserved specimens. Godet 1986 and Hahn 2000 provided invaluable surveys of research by themselves and others. The extent to which Aksum relied on local sources of gold and silver for production of its coins has not yet been determined (see also Chapters 13 and 15).

silver and copper,[8] all of which bore legends in Greek. The first gold coins (Fig. 69)[9] were 93–97 per cent pure and weighed 2.4–2.8 g, apparently based on the standard then prevailing in the Roman Empire, being one half the weight of the contemporary Roman *aureus*.[10] The silver coins, by contrast, were rapidly debased, and both they and the copper specimens showed significantly greater variations in weight.[11] Two features of these coins, which bear the name and title of King Endybis, are unusual in the Aksumite series: their designs were in relatively high relief, analogous to that of most Roman coins prior to the closing years of the third century, and their legends employed squared forms of the Greek *epsilon* and *sigma* in contrast with the rounded forms which soon replaced them.[12]

It has frequently been stated that changes in the weights of Aksumite gold coins during the late-third and early-fourth centuries followed broadly contemporaneous reforms of the Roman gold coinage. In the Eastern Roman Empire, the *aureus* of 5.45 g was replaced in 324 by a *solidus* weighing 4.54 g. There was undoubtedly a reduction in average weights of the Aksumite gold unit from that noted above under Endybis to 1.85– 2.09 g and 1.35–1.67 g for successive Christian issues of Ezana, produced between seventy and ninety years later. However, while the earlier coins approximated in weight to half an *aureus* and the later ones to one third of a later-fourth-century *solidus*, there is no evidence in the Aksumite series for a clearly defined change from one to the other. Rather, throughout the fourth and early-fifth centuries there were repeated reductions in the weights of the Aksumite gold coins and in the fineness of the metal on which they were struck.[13] Subsequently, there was little further diminution in the weights of the coins, but both the gold and silver employed underwent progressive debasement.[14]

[8] The copper was often an alloy of that metal, quite variable in composition as analyses published by Pedroni 1997b and others indicate. The term 'bronze' has been employed by some authors, but this has the precise connotation of a copper-tin alloy and its more general use is better avoided.

[9] Hahn 1998 noted that gold coins of Endybis are today relatively common, a high proportion of the known specimens being derived from an inadequately recorded hoard discovered, apparently in Tigray, in the 1960s. Prior to this discovery, Endybis' gold was extremely rare (*cf.* Doresse 1970: 21), although Paribeni (1907: col. 468) had recovered an example at Adulis as long ago as 1907. I am grateful to Mr Vincent West for his advice in this connection.

[10] The weight of the Roman *aureus* was fixed at 5.45 g under the coinage reform of Diocletian in 286, having previously fluctuated rather wildly for several decades. The proposed link between Aksumite and Roman gold coins has been based primarily on the apparent coincidence of their weights, and then been cited as evidence for dating the Aksumite issues (*cf.* Hahn 2000: 289–92). The inferences drawn are best regarded as hypothetical pending further evidence; in the present writer's view, a date *c.* 270 for the start of the Aksumite coinage (as argued by Munro-Hay in several publications) is not precluded and allows more adequate time for the series preceding the adoption of Christianity in the mid-fourth century.

[11] The relative value of coins in the three metals remains completely unknown. A token value may have been attributed to those in copper.

[12] The square forms of *epsilon* and *sigma* made a brief reappearance on coins of Ebana in the mid-fifth century (Munro-Hay 1984b; Hahn 1994). See Chapter 5 for a comparison of Greek lettering on coins with that on stone inscriptions erected under Ezana. Aphilas' coins retained the high relief noted for those of Endybis, albeit less consistently.

[13] The silver suffered similar debasement, the fineness of Endybis' coins in that metal never being matched subsequently (Blet-Lemarquand *et al.* 2001).

[14] Data and arguments were summarised by Munro-Hay & Juel-Jensen (1995: 45–7) and by Munro-Hay (1999: 15–16). Further analyses have been recorded by Oddy & Munro-Hay 1980 and by Atkins & Juel-Jensen 1989; for a critical overview, see Barrandon *et al.* 1990.

Recognition of Aksumite coinage types has not followed a consistent methodology. The better-preserved gold has tended to be examined in greater detail than have the far more numerous copper coins, with the result that minor variants among the gold issues are sometimes listed as distinct types,[15] whereas those in base metals may be lumped together. This difficulty is compounded by the comparative scarcity of Aksumite coins available for study;[16] this probably does not mean that production was originally low and, indeed, the numbers of dies represented for an individual issue would support the view that the proportion of Aksumite coins struck that is now preserved or available for study is significantly lower than, for example, among Roman coins.[17] One result of this is that studies of die-links between Aksumite coins are still at an early stage, and the varied symbols often interpreted as mint administration- or control-marks are not adequately recorded or understood.[18]

Both the precise date of the start of the Aksumite coinage series and the circumstances surrounding it are debated. Although it was clearly inspired by knowledge of contemporary practice in the Graeco-Roman world or in southern Arabia, the extent to which its implementation was wholly local or involved specialists from elsewhere remains controversial. Aksumite coins were inscribed in Greek, albeit some words were translations or transliterations from Ge‘ez, as discussed in Chapter 5. Affinities with Himyaritic coinage (*cf.* above), examples of which are known to have reached the northern Horn and issue of which apparently ceased at approximately the same time as its Aksumite counterpart commenced, are particularly noteworthy in size, module and the practice of depicting a human head on both sides. The types, although incorporating the widespread Hellenistic and Roman use of a royal portrait,[19] name and titles, were executed in an essentially non-Roman style, with the gold coins incorporating such portraits on both obverse and reverse. Some silver and copper issues shared this feature, which was almost invariable on the gold. Endybis was depicted on both sides of all his coins wearing a sort of cap or headcloth, but his immediate successor wore a crown or tiara on the obverse while retaining the headcloth on the reverse. This pattern was retained on Aksumite gold coins until the end of the series in the early-seventh century, both portraits being framed by cereal-stalks[20] and surmounted by a centrally-placed religious symbol, initially the crescent-and-disc (Fig. 69). Striking was careful, with the

[15] The type-system proposed by Hahn 1983 (updated 2000) is less confusing in this regard than that published by Munro-Hay & Juel-Jensen 1995.

[16] Hahn (2000: 288–9) provided some figures which have, of course, been increased by more recent discoveries.

[17] The database is so small that a single new discovery can necessitate major revisions in interpretation. For example, the hoard found – probably *c.* 1980 – at al-Madhariba in Yemen more than doubled the number of Aksumite gold coins known. Note, however, that Munro-Hay's 1989c publication of this hoard may not have included all the coins originally discovered. Several important coin-types are known from only a single specimen.

[18] Munro-Hay 1989c recognised significant die-links during his study of Aksumite gold coins from the al-Madhariba hoard. From 1994 until his death in 2006, Juel-Jensen published in the *Spink Numismatic Circular* a number of notes on previously unrecorded Aksumite die varieties. See also West 2006.

[19] Following standard numismatic usage, the term 'portrait' is retained in descriptions of Aksumite coin-types, despite the fact that virtually no attempt appears to have been made to depict the rulers as recognisable individuals.

[20] Although identification as barley is possible, the usual view is that ears of wheat are represented (*cf.* D. Phillipson 1993: 354).

obverse and reverse dies – at least until the fifth century – carefully aligned.[21] It seems reasonable to conclude that the knowledge of how to prepare dies and to strike coins from them was derived from an overseas, probably Mediterranean or South Asian, area, but that the designs were essentially local, albeit sometimes interpretations of overseas concepts.[22] A few gold specimens, notably one that was formerly the property of Ras Mengesha Seyoum and is now in the Ashmolean Museum at Oxford, were struck from exceptional, finely engraved dies, and could be interpreted as early issues: [23] the weight and the purity of their metal fall firmly within the overall ranges for Endybis' gold.

The coinage of subsequent reigns shows significant variation from the rigid uniformity of the first issues under Endybis. That of his successor, Aphilas, who seems to have reigned *c.* 300, retained the high relief noted above but was unique in the Aksumite series in having more than one denomination in each metal; in gold, the half-aureus unit was accompanied by its half, quarter and eighth, following a system of subdivision for which there are stronger indications in southern Arabia[24] than in the Roman Empire. The weights of the four gold denominations were carefully controlled, and their obverse types were varied, presumably to avoid confusion between them: the half-unit had a facing head and shoulders, while the tiny eighth-unit had no obverse inscription.[25] The silver and copper coins of Aphilas likewise showed typological variety, with two denominations in each metal. All were inscribed in Greek, employing the rounded *epsilon* and *sigma*. They were the first Aksumite coins to show the highly characteristic and visually pleasing feature – unique to the Aksumite series – whereby parts of the design were selectively gilded (*cf.* Fig. 70).[26] This neat and careful gilding, evidently applied after the coins had been struck and involving the use of mercury, has not been adequately investigated but must have been exceedingly painstaking, labour-intensive and time-consuming; the reasons for its adoption are not known. Coins of Aphilas – notwithstanding their diversity – are comparatively rare, and his reign may have been brief.

For Aphilas' successor, WZB [conventionally vocalised as Wazeba], only one gold and one silver type, but no copper coins are so far known.[27] A major innovation was introduced under this ruler: all his coins were inscribed in

21 Ancient techniques of coin production have been discussed by Hill 1922. Juel-Jensen 1999 recorded evidence that flans for Aksumite copper coins were sometimes produced by multiple casting. At least some of the irregular, unofficial miniature copies of various coins noted below were also cast, and moulds – but none for Aksumite-style pieces – have been recorded by Dattari (1913: 501).

22 Similar observations based on other Aksumite artefacts are discussed in Chapters 13 and 15.

23 There appears to be no indication that this coin (illustrated by Munro-Hay & Juel-Jensen 1995: 289 bottom right) was in His Highness' possession prior to 1968, so the possibility that it came from the hoard noted above cannot be ruled out.

24 As discussed by Irvine 1964.

25 Two copper denominations of Aphilas with full-face portrait are also known. The suggestion (Hahn 1993: 318) that these full-face portraits may have been inspired by Roman gold coins issued AD 320–22 in the names of the Roman Emperors Licinius I and II is possible but not convincing; it seems likely that the Aphilas coins were issued a decade or so before those of the Licinii – who were not the only rulers of that general period to be depicted full-face on their coins and medallions. Use of variations in portraiture to indicate different denominations was common in Roman coinage from the first to the third centuries AD, but usually based on the style of headgear. With the exception of those of Aphilas, full-face portraits were not employed on Aksumite coins until the sixth century (see below).

26 F. Russo & G. Russo 1989.

27 Note that another – sixth-century – king called WZB is known from a stone inscription (RIE 192) in Ge'ez, but not from coins.

Fig. 69 The first Aksumite coinage: a Greek-inscribed gold coin [diameter: 14 mm] of the late-third-century King Endybis

Fig 70 Ge'ez-inscribed silver coin [diameter: 17.5 mm] with localised gilding, issued in the name of AGD, probably late sixth century

Fig. 71 Gold coin [diameter: 16.5 mm], issued under the fourth-century King Ezana after his conversion to Christianity, inscribed in Greek

Ge'ez instead of Greek; in fact, his name is known only from unvocalised coin-inscriptions. The gold issue of this king is represented by only two examples, each from different dies. It shows a number of unusual features as well as exceptional expertise, effectively disproving the view that craftsmanship of such quality was restricted to issues bearing Greek inscriptions. It is legitimate to speculate why this change of language was adopted and whether it was intended to promote the local acceptance of the coins, use of which may still have been viewed as a foreign practice (*cf.* Chapters 5 and 9).[28]

Coins of Ousana or Ousanas, apparently issued immediately after those of WZB, resumed the use of Greek and continued the former use of a right-facing royal portrait on both obverse and reverse, with a single denomination in gold but probably two in silver. The weights of the copper coins – as often in the Aksumite series – are so variable that it is impossible to determine whether more than one denomination is represented. A few examples are known of a silver coin of the early-fourth century which combines a Ge'ez-inscribed obverse of WZB with a Greek-inscribed reverse of Ousanas. Several specimens of this coin are known, struck from more than one set of dies, which indicates that it was indeed a formal issue rather than a mule due to an accidental confusion of dies at the mint. This has been rather unconvincingly cited as support for the joint-reign hypothesis discussed in Chapter 8. The gold coins of Ousanas continued from previous reigns the presentation of the crescent-and-disc symbol in a central position above the portrait, but on some of his silver and copper this was – for the first time in the Aksumite coinage series – omitted (*e.g.* Fig. 28);[29] the significance of this innovation is discussed in Chapter 9.

The next reign, of Ezana or Ezanas, is of exceptional interest and has attracted considerable attention. As discussed in Chapter 9, Ezana was the Aksumite ruler who first adopted Christianity. This is reflected on his gold coins and on one – currently unique – copper specimen by the replacement of the crescent-and-disc symbol with the cross (Fig. 71) although, as with his predecessor – probably his father – Ousanas, there are some silver and copper coins which have no religious symbol. Detailed study of Ezana's gold coins has shown that the portrait on the first cross-bearing issue was so similar to that on the last issue with the crescent-and-disc that their dies may have been the work of the same craftsman; [30] comparable investigation of the silver and copper has not yet been undertaken.

Errors in the inscriptions occurred from the beginning of the Aksumite coinage; under Ezana, the deterioration increased with successive issues and subsequently became even more marked. Letters were omitted, confused, or not clearly differentiated. Die-engravers were evidently less familiar with Greek than they were with Ge'ez and, after the reigns of Endybis and – perhaps – Aphilas, it seems that those engaged in this capacity were no longer competently literate in Greek.[31]

From Ezana to Kaleb

Following, and possibly partly overlapping with, Ezana's reign were a number of 'anonymous' issues in all three metals which, although retaining a royal

[28] West (1999, 2001) published useful guides to the Ge'ez inscriptions on Aksumite coins.

[29] Hahn (2000: 296) attributed the coins of Ousanas with no religious symbol to a second Ousanas who reigned after, or alongside, Ezana. Further evidence is required before this revision can be accepted.

[30] Juel-Jensen 1998.

[31] This matter, of some importance for an understanding of Aksumite literacy, is further discussed in Chapter 5.

Fig. 72 Anonymous Greek-inscribed copper coin [diameter: 15 mm] of the fifth century (after a drawing in Munro-Hay 1984a)

portrait on both sides of the gold coins and on the obverses of the others, have inscriptions simply reading 'king' or 'king of the Aksumites' without naming him (*cf.* Chapter 8). In some cases – but by no means all – the portrait is surmounted by a cross. The commonest coins of these long-lasting series, which seem to have continued until the early sixth century,[32] have a particularly interesting reverse type: the Christian cross is surrounded by the Greek inscription TOYTO APECH TH XωPA [= may this be pleasing in the countryside] (Fig. 72). The significance of the word XωPA in this context has generally escaped notice: in fourth- and fifth-century Greek, it carried the clear implication of rural as opposed to urban (*cf.* Chapter 9). [33] Coins of this type are usually struck in copper, occasionally in debased silver, but never in gold; they were clearly intended primarily for local circulation.[34] From the mid-sixth century such mottos, in Ge'ez, proliferated on the copper coinage.[35]

Following the reign of Ezana, Aksumite coinage entered a period of rather monotonous stability which lasted from the mid-fourth century until late in the fifth. Inscriptions on all denominations continued to be in Greek, with the exception of coins of a single reign late in the fifth century, all of which bore Ge'ez legends. The ruler concerned, known only from the coins, is named as MHDYS, plausibly a form of Matthias. Insistence upon Ge'ez was seen at Aksum in one earlier reign – that of WZB around 300 – and attributed above and in Chapter 5 to that king's wish to emphasise local, as opposed to Graeco-Roman, aspects of his reign. A similar explanation may be proposed in the case of MHDYS, supported by the evidence of a unique gold coin, now in the Staatsliche Münzsammlung at Munich.[36] In place of a portrait bust on the obverse, it depicts a standing figure (Fig. 25) whose accoutrements resemble Aksumite

32 Hahn 2005.

33 In the Greek versions of Ezana's trilingual inscriptions (RIE 170, 170*bis*), the word XωPA is applied to the Aksumite kingdom's subject territories. A further example is cited by Grillmeier (1996: 2), where the word referred to Egypt with the capital – Alexandria – specifically excluded.

34 However, cast, reduced-size copies in copper have been recorded from hoards in Egypt and Palestine (Noeske 1998). They are represented in several hoards alongside Byzantine and other contemporary coins, regular and irregular, which evidently circulated together (Milne 1926; Bendall 1986–87; Bijovsky 1998).

35 For a discussion, see West 1999.

36 This coin may have been found in southern Arabia. It has been described and discussed in detail by Munro-Hay 1995 and also by Hahn & Kropp 1996. I am aware of no evidence to support the statement by Hellwag 2010a, 2010b that it is 'most probably a medieval forgery'.

regalia known independently from other sources, as discussed in Chapter 8. Other features of MHDYS' coinage, however, suggest foreign inspiration. His copper coins bear a reverse inscription translated 'by this cross [MSQL] he will conquer' – clearly a reference to Constantine's vision at the Milvian bridge. The winged figure on the reverse of MHDYS' gold coin seems to be copied from the representation of Victory on contemporary late Roman and Byzantine coins, the closest parallel being a *solidus* of Theodosius II issued at Constantinople *c.* 422. Several Aksumite kings of the late-fourth and fifth centuries are known only from their gold coins; silver and copper issues at this time were often anonymous (*cf.* above and Chapter 8), successive types being struck in large numbers. The earliest copper coins of Kaleb continued the designs of the latter issues.

The sixth and seventh centuries

Significant changes took place early in the sixth century, under King Kaleb. Whereas Greek – now of a deplorable and deteriorating standard – was retained for inscriptions on the gold coins, it was replaced by Ge'ez on those of silver and copper.[37] That the change was not instituted until shortly after the start of Kaleb's reign is indicated by certain Greek-inscribed copper coins bearing his name but otherwise continuing the design of the previous anonymous issue. The practice of issuing Greek-inscribed gold with Ge'ez-inscribed silver and copper was retained until the end of the Aksumite coinage series some 120–140 years later.[38]

The final phase of the coinage, particularly the copper issues, was prolific. Standards of design and production were, with notable exceptions, poor. Although the gold coins retained the types, size and weight established previously, the fineness of their metal and the care devoted to die-engraving and to striking steadily deteriorated; the large, clumsy inscriptions on the gold led to a reduction in the space available for the royal portrait (Fig. 73). The silver and copper coins were much more varied and included several types of particular interest.

Certain copper coins of Ioel, Hataz and Gersem, struck during the second half of the sixth century and – possibly – the very beginning of the seventh, employed a full-face portrait on the obverse. In some cases, notably those of Hataz and Gersem, the crowned portrait is flanked on each side by a cross (*e.g.* Fig. 74). It is tempting to consider whether these designs were inspired by Byzantine coins, notably the – admittedly far larger – 40-*nummi* pieces introduced in 538/9 under Justinian I.[39] The facing crowned portrait was also employed – without flanking crosses – on silver coins of the late sixth century, examples being issued anonymously and in the names of kings WZN and AGD. The reverse-type of these coins is of particular interest, depicting an arch resting on pillared supports and enclosing a cross emphasised with gilding (Fig. 70). An analogous design was employed under Armah: a large cross flanked by two smaller ones in an apparent representation of Calvary. Differing opinions

[37] For non-numismatic evidence that use of Greek was declining at this time, see Chapters 5, 6, 8 and 9.

[38] The sole exceptions, issued at the end of the sixth century, were a silver issue of Ioel and its typologically identical counterpart in copper, both inscribed in Greek on the obverse and Ge'ez on the reverse.

[39] *cf.* Godet 1986; Pedroni 1997b: 6 and D. Phillipson 2009b: 364–5. For the Justinianic coinage reform, see P. Grierson 1982: 60–61.

Fig. 73 Greek-inscribed gold coin [diameter: 19 mm] of King Israel, probably late-sixth century

Fig. 74 Copper Ge'ez-inscribed coin [diameter: 16.5 mm], with facing cross-flanked portrait, of King Gersem, who probably reigned around the beginning of the seventh century

Fig. 75 Ge'ez-inscribed copper coin [diameter: 20 mm] of King Armah, shown seated and holding a processional cross: on the reverse is another cross, its centre emphasised by gilding; the age of these coins is disputed between the mid-sixth and mid-seventh centuries (*cf.* Hahn 2010)

have been put forward as to the date of this reign,[40] each supported by an interpretation of the reverse-type: it has been speculated that one or both of these types may have been inspired by Kaleb's abdication and presentation of his crown to the Holy Sepulchre in Jerusalem, by the removal of the True Cross from Jerusalem by the Persians in 614 and/or by its recovery and restitution by the Byzantine emperor Heraclius in 630.[41]

Whether or not Armah was indeed the last Aksumite king to issue coins, it is noteworthy that no gold ones bear his name and that those in both silver and copper were larger and of better quality than most of those issued under his immediate predecessors. It may be that, by the time these coins were produced, the capital of the Aksumite state had already been transferred to a more easterly part of Tigray, as discussed in Chapter 16. Armah's silver has already been noted. His copper (Fig. 75) represented a marked innovation: the obverse showed a full-length figure of the crowned king seated on a high-backed chair or throne and holding a long-handled cross; the reverse type comprised a cross with its centre gilded, the whole surrounded by a curious device which – at first sight – appears to resemble the frame of wheat ears that usually surrounds the royal portrait on Aksumite gold coins, but which closer examination reveals may rather be a wreath akin to those frequently depicted on fourth-century Roman coins.[42] The dies that were employed for striking these copper coins of Armah were even more than usually varied. The chair was sometimes represented in outline, sometimes by rows of dots. On some specimens the cross resembles a processional cross, on others it is more likely that a hand cross was intended. The king's clothing was also depicted differently: in some cases – *e.g.* that illustrated here – it seems that he was wearing baggy trousers like those represented on the gold coin of MHDYS noted above. These coins, while numerous specimens are known, seem to be comparatively rare in archaeological contexts at Aksum itself, lending support to their placement at the very end of the coinage sequence and to the suggestion that the transfer of the capital may have taken place during or before their period of issue.[43]

Discussion

Much recent research on Aksumite coinage has been undertaken from a narrowly numismatic perspective. Here, emphasis is placed on its contribution to understanding wider aspects of Aksumite civilisation. The significant differences between the gold coinage and those in base metals are fundamental to

[40] Munro-Hay (*e.g.* 1989d; Munro-Hay & Juel-Jensen 1995) regarded Armah as the last of the kings of Aksum to issue coins, probably in the second quarter of the seventh century. Hahn 2010, however, has argued that he was the successor of Kaleb around the mid-sixth century, the silver and copper coins bearing the name of Armah being issued during the same reign as a gold issue bearing the name Ella Amida. The Ella Amida so-named on these gold coins was clearly the immediate successor to Kaleb, and must not be confused with the fourth-century king named as Ella Amida on stone inscriptions and in the *Synaxarium*, but as Ousanas on his coins.

[41] The possible connection between the Holy Sepulchre and the designs of these coins was discussed by Freeman-Grenville 1992–93 and by Hahn 1994–99. As noted in Chapter 15, an Ethiopian presence in Jerusalem is independently attested by this date. Aksumite appreciation of Heraclius' recovery of the True Cross was considered by D. Phillipson 2009b: 353.

[42] Such wreaths did not subsequently form part of Byzantine coin designs, but attention should be drawn to the paired palm fronds flanking a cross on the reverse of rare silver coins of Heraclius [ruled 610–41] and his immediate successors (P. Grierson 1982: 102–3, pl. 18). The fronds are remarkably similar to Aksumite designs – both the cereals flanking the royal portait and the 'wreath' flanking the cross on the reverse of Armah's copper. Constans II was effectively a contemporary of Armah according to the sequence proposed by Munro-Hay & Juel-Jensen 1995.

[43] D. Phillipson 2000b: 485–6.

such an understanding, as are the languages with which the various issues were inscribed. Use of Greek, as discussed more generally elsewhere (Chapter 5) implies a primary target readership that was familiar with that language – principally the mercantile community. While tradition and the perceived need to maintain established forms may have contributed to the use of Greek long after literacy in that language at the Aksumite mint had declined, the predominantly international circulation of the gold coinage seems to be reflected in its recorded find-spots.[44] Gold coins of the pre-Christian period have been recovered from the northern Horn itself, with smaller numbers recorded from southern Arabia and from India.[45] Those dating between the reigns of Ezana and Kaleb have rarely – if ever – been found in the Horn, but are recorded in comparatively large numbers from southern Arabia. It is tempting to postulate, but cannot be demonstrated conclusively, that many of these coins may have reached southern Arabia during the Aksumite military campaigns and governance under Kaleb, discussed in Chapter 15. It is noteworthy that the Aksumite gold coins found in southern Arabia are all of the debased issues beginning with the second Christian issue of Ezana, and that post-Kaleb coins are not represented. The rare gold coins of Kaleb's successors (*e.g.* Fig. 73) have few recorded provenances other than Adulis. Base-metal coins of all periods are frequent site-finds in the northern Horn, but elsewhere are largely restricted to areas known to have received direct visits from there: Palestine and adjacent areas, southern Arabian ports,[46] southern India and Sri Lanka. The conclusion is inescapable that, whereas the gold coins indeed saw mainly international circulation, the base-metal issues were intended for more local use. From the reign of Ezana onwards, this distinction was increasingly reflected in the designs of the coins and in the languages of their inscriptions.

To what extent was Aksumite coinage an introduction from elsewhere? Numismatists have often tended to emphasise its foreign connections,[47] if only because many relevant *comparanda* are much more comprehensively studied and understood than are their Aksumite counterparts. As noted above, use of any coinage was extremely limited in the northern Horn prior to the start of the locally-produced issues.

Despite their apparent initial link, Aksumite and Roman gold coins soon diverged, in both weight and fineness. The types and inscriptions of each series reflected the priorities and prejudices of its issuing authority. There can be little doubt that the die-engravers responsible for the Aksumite coinage throughout its duration were themselves Aksumites. At intervals, there were indeed elements of Aksumite coin design that appear to have been inspired by contemporary Byzantine issues, but this is hardly surprising and certainly does not imply direct continuing influence. Indeed, despite the political links between Byzantium under Justin I and Justinian I on the one hand, and Aksum under Kaleb on the other (Chapter 15), it is noteworthy how little connection

44 Secure information is sadly scarce since many coins are recorded from the collectors' market, with provenances recorded – if at all – on the basis of hearsay.

45 Many gold coins recovered from India but of non-Indian – mainly Roman and Aksumite – origin are double-pierced in a manner that would have facilitated their suspension or mounting on cloth with the obverse correctly aligned (Hahn 2000: 287). This feature is so characteristic that there is a strong likelihood that unprovenanced coins so pierced were actually recovered in India, had passed through India, or had been prepared for export thither.

46 Notably Qana (Sedov 1997), but *cf.* Chapter 15 for a discussion of Aksumite-type pottery from this site.

47 For example, J. Williams 1997: 197 stated categorically that it was initiated 'under Roman influence'.

is apparent between the propaganda media represented by their respective coinages. Remarkably few non-Aksumite coins appear to have reached the northern Horn during the period that local issues were in circulation. Aksumite coinage merits study on its own terms and serves as a valuable source of information about the civilisation responsible for its issue.

The Aksumite coinage seems to have ended as suddenly as it had begun. There is no evidence, however, that any need was felt for money from elsewhere to fill the gap left by the cessation of local mintage. Although settlement sites of the late-seventh and immediately succeeding centuries have not yet been investigated, the only site where coins of this period have been discovered is Debra Damo, where dispersed finds of 'numerous Arabic coins of gold and silver' have been recorded,[48] ranging in date between the end of the seventh and the mid-tenth centuries. The presence of Arab traders in Ethiopia following the move of the capital from Aksum to Kubar is noted in Chapter 16, and it is highly likely that the monastic occupation of Debra Damo extended throughout this period.

48 Mathews & Mordini 1959: 50–51, 53.

15

Foreign Contacts of the Aksumite State

Throughout its history, the Aksumite kingdom maintained varying degrees of contact with external populations both adjacent and far-distant. These relationships have often received undue emphasis in reconstructions of Aksumite history, while being largely ignored in studies whose primary focus lay elsewhere.[1] Archaeological evidence for these contacts is derived mainly from artefacts and materials recognised as having originated far from their place of recovery. Care is, of course, needed to distinguish between transport of artefacts and that of the materials used in their production, and from the movement of people responsible for their manufacture. Likewise, extended areas of distribution may be inadequately reflected in the archaeological record as a result of uneven coverage of research. Evidence for political relations – whether military, religious or diplomatic – comes primarily from oral and written sources; these present remarkably little overlap with the archaeology, and are usually subject to varied emphasis and distortion according to the sympathies of the societies where they were created and/or transmitted. Since this book focuses primarily on the northern Horn of Africa, that area's exports will be discussed first.

Exports

As has been the pattern for thousands of years, and still continues in many circumstances today, Africa's exports to the rest of the world have mostly consisted of raw materials, while her imports have included a high proportion of manufactured items. This has created an immediate imbalance in the archaeological record and in our understanding of it, since artefacts tend to be more readily recognised than the sources of the materials from which they were made. A coin, for example, may be precisely identified as to its date and the authority under which it was issued, but it is yet rarely possible to ascertain the source of the metal from which it was struck. Likewise, an ivory carving may – with varying plausibility – be attributed to a particular workshop or school of craftsmanship, but this carries little or no implication as to where lived the elephant whose tusks were utilised. Although African and Indian elephants are classified as belonging to different Linnaean species, it is remarkable how rarely serious attempts have been made to differentiate their ivory.[2]

[1] For example, a recent account of Byzantine foreign policy (Luttwak 2009) makes no mention of support for the Aksumite invasion of southern Arabia, discussed below.

[2] *cf.* Krzyszkowska 1990.

There are clear indications that ivory was a major export from the Aksumite kingdom as early as the first century AD.[3] As noted in Chapter 3, the Egyptians had – at least in Ptolemaic times – sought both war elephants and ivory on the sections of the Red-Sea coast that now fall within Sudan and Eritrea. Indeed, it has been suggested that availability of ivory was one reason why the Aksumite capital arose in such a westerly location.[4] Ivory was an exceedingly valuable commodity in the early Roman Empire, but significant variation in its subsequent availability there can be correlated with the exigencies of Aksum's export-trade, suggesting that the kingdom was a major supplier. During the first two centuries AD, the Romans used ivory sparingly, particularly as a decorative inlay for furniture.[5] Later, coinciding with Aksum's growing prosperity in the third century, supplies to the Mediterranean world increased, and a corresponding fall in value was recorded in the price-control edict[6] issued by the Emperor Diocletian *c.* 301. This was reflected in the ivory artefacts produced in the circum-Mediterranean world at this time and during the centuries following. It seems that Aksum was – at least after the third-century extinction of the North African elephant – a major supplier of ivory to this region.[7] The sizes of some Byzantine ivory artefacts, notably *pyxides* and consular diptychs, suggest that the material of which they were made came from African elephants.[8] Aksum's international links suffered a sharp decline in about the second quarter of the seventh century, when control over the Red-Sea trade-routes passed into Arabian hands (Chapter 16). At this time, there was a marked decline in the quantity of ivory reaching the markets of the Byzantine world. These fluctuations in ivory supply were also felt in central and northern Europe.[9] Supplies of ivory from within the Aksumite kingdom and its immediate environs may, of course, have been supplemented by tusks from more southerly East African regions.[10]

Evidence for other Aksumite exports is much less clear. Suggestions that gold may have been exported on any scale may in part be due to the confusion in contemporary written sources between Kush [the Nubian Nile Valley] and the area now known as Ethiopia. By contrast, indications that gold may have been obtained in the vicinity of Aksum between the third and the fifth centuries AD are discussed in Chapter 13. In comparison with the remarkable stability both in weight and fineness of Byzantine gold coinage, the steady debasement of its Aksumite counterpart shows that gold at Aksum was – at

3 *Periplus of the Erythraean Sea* 6 (Casson 1989: 55).

4 D. Phillipson 1990; see also Chapter 7 and Tekle 2011.

5 Scullard 1974: 30–1, 261. That ivory furniture, probably including chairs, was imported to the Roman world from southern Asia by the first century AD is indicated by a piece from Pompeii (Wheeler 1954: 135, pl. xix) which closely parallels material from Begram in Afghanistan (Simpson 2011); in contrast with Roman usage at this time, ivory was employed at Begram as appliqué rather than as inlay.

6 Lauffer 1971.

7 Cutler 1999; D. Phillipson 2009b.

8 For examples, see Williamson 2010. As also in later times, considerable ingenuity was employed to make the largest possible carvings, despite the limitations imposed by the tusks themselves. It should be noted that the outermost layer [*cementum*] of a tusk is too hard to carve and had to be removed and discarded; it is not known whether this was done before or after long-distance transport.

9 Hills 2001.

10 Note, in this context, the suggestion that the outbreak of bubonic plague that spread widely through Byzantine territory in the 540s may have originated in East Africa, as further discussed below.

least in the sixth century when, according to Cosmas Indicopleustes,[11] it was actually imported by the Aksumites from a southwesterly region (see below) – a comparatively scarce commodity, with other suppliers of which that kingdom could not compete. The fourth-century inscriptions at Aksum indicate that raids – sometimes at least nominally punitive – were carried out into adjacent areas, with livestock and human captives brought back to Aksumite territory, as described in Chapter 7. The principal evidence for the export of slaves from Adulis[12] comes from references to people of that status in Arabia who were deemed Aksumite or Ethiopian in origin.[13]

Imports

For reasons set out above, imports to the kingdom of Aksum are better known both from archaeology and from documentary sources than are the exports. Again, the *Periplus of the Erythraean Sea* provides a useful baseline, although one that apparently dates before the region attained its maximum prosperity.[14] It should be emphasised also that this text records imports landed at Adulis, many of which were specifically mentioned as 'for the king', Zoscales, who – as argued in Chapter 7 – was king of the coastal region, rather than ruling at Aksum itself. Imports to Adulis listed in the *Periplus* comprised textiles, glass, brass and copper utensils, iron tools, iron for reworking, 'Roman money for the resident foreigners', wine and olive oil – the last three in limited quantities. In addition, heavy cloaks, silverware and goldware were imported 'for the king'. It should be emphasised that these items were traded at Adulis, there being no indication which – if any – were transmitted onwards to Aksum.[15] As noted in Chapter 3, some imported items probably reached the Aksum area direct from the Nile Valley during the last two or three centuries BC, but the Red-Sea route soon rose to prominence.

Glassware and beads were imported to Aksum at most – if not all – periods. Although there is now clear evidence (Chapter 13) for a local glass industry, its date of establishment is not known, nor is it yet possible to distinguish all its products from items that were imported.[16]

Pottery was also imported, both as receptacles for liquid and – perhaps – granular commodities, and as luxury utensils. In the former category, the most numerous examples were tall, elongated amphorae (Fig. 76) with horizontally ribbed bodies; many of these were produced at kilns near Ayla at the northern end of the Red Sea[17] and used for the transport of wine produced in that vicinity,

[11] *Christian Topography* II 51–2; Wolska-Conus 1968–73, 1: 360–3. See, however, fn 43, below.

[12] The *Periplus of the Erythraean Sea* (Casson 1989: 54–7, 117) did not list slaves among the exports from Adulis, but mentioned them in small numbers in connection with a more southerly port, Malao, perhaps the modern Berbera.

[13] *e.g.* summary by Richard Pankhurst 2010.

[14] See, however, Chapter 6 for the possibility that the *Periplus* text may incorporate material of different ages.

[15] *Periplus* 6 (Casson 1989: 52–5); also Munro-Hay 1991a.

[16] J. S. Phillips 2009 presented useful discussion of this problem, and of the way in which glassware may have been packed for the long and difficult overland journey from the coast.

[17] A. Melkawi *et al.* 1994. The kilns formed part of a substantial industrial installation, apparently dating to the sixth century. Pottery of this type has been recovered at Aksum in contexts that may be dated between the mid-fifth and the early seventh centuries. Aksumite coins have also been found at Ayla (Whitcomb 1994) and at Berenice (Sidebotham 2007), an intermediate port on the Egyptian coast of the Red Sea.

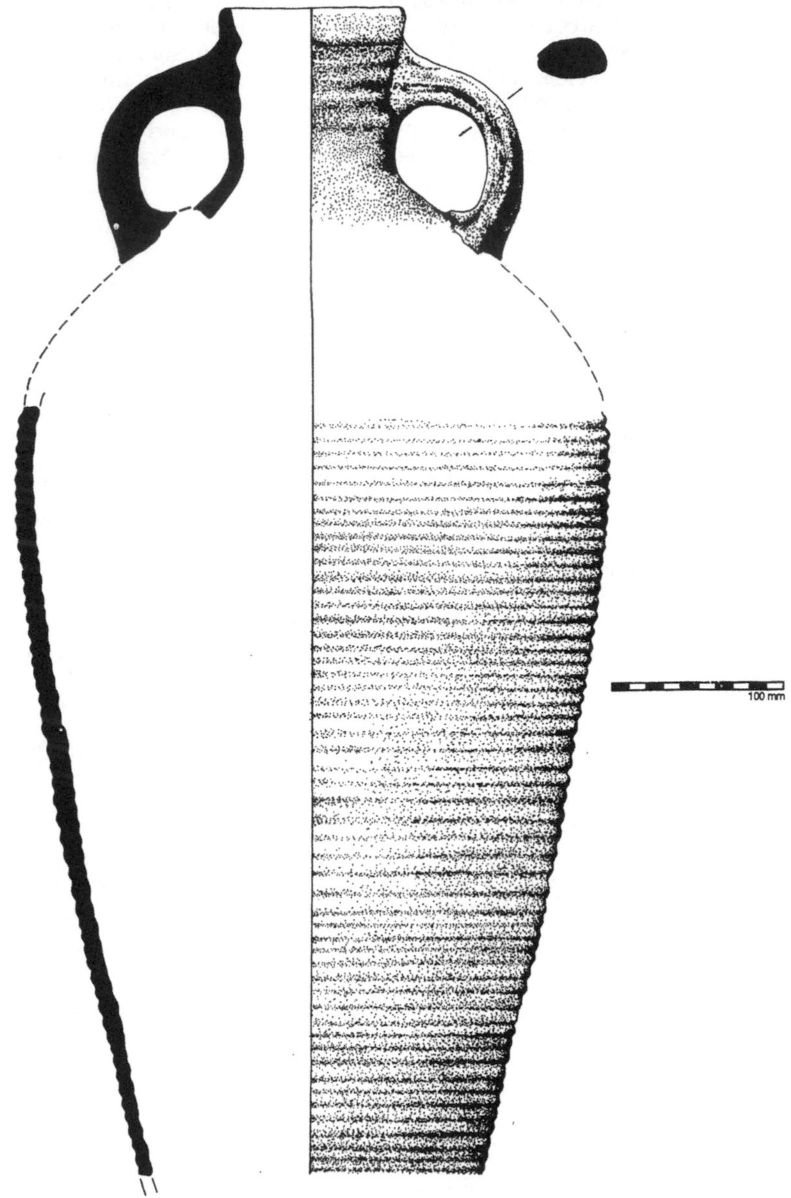

Fig. 76 Amphora from Aksum, of the type that was imported from Ayla

and perhaps other liquid commodities also. Carriage of such amphorae by ship down the Red Sea has been demonstrated by the investigation of a sixth-century wreck off Assarca island, Eritrea.[18] Red tableware,[19] mass-produced in several parts of Roman North Africa, including Egypt, was imported from at least the fourth century into the Aksumite kingdom, where local potters employed their traditional technology to copy its forms (Chapter 13). Later, in the sixth and seventh centuries, occasional glazed vessels were brought from the coastlands of the Persian Gulf, and from the Aswan area of the Egyptian Nile Valley.[20] Other sherds have occasionally been claimed as displaying distant affinities, but are for the most part differentiated by decoration or technique rather than by fabric; some may have been the work of travelling potters.[21]

The sixth/seventh centuries also saw the import of carved marble components for chancel screens in churches. Such stonework was recovered from Adulis on two separate occasions in the nineteenth and early-twentieth centuries,[22] and a single slotted post of the same type has recently been noted at Aksum (Fig. 41). Such screens are known to have been produced in prefabricated form around the sixth century in the vicinity of Constantinople,[23] and widely transported by sea around the Mediterranean coastlands;[24] numerous examples may still be seen, notably on church sites in Cyrenaica and Syria, but the Adulis and Aksum discoveries (Chapter 11) represent their most distant dispersal yet known.[25] It is likely that further items of religious paraphernalia were brought to the Aksumite kingdom at this time. Leaves bound with the Abba Garima *Gospel* texts and bearing canon tables and paintings of the Evangelists (Chapters 10 and 14; Figs 29 and 30) are in Byzantine style, and the suggestion has been made that they may have been imported.[26] Be that as it may, it is likely that Byzantine ambassadors to the court of King Kaleb at Aksum (*cf.* below and Chapter 8) would have brought diplomatic gifts of a specifically Christian nature.

Evidence is cited in Chapter 13 for the proliferation of Aksumite metalwork. It seems that the significant imports to the coastal regions noted in the *Periplus of the Erythraean Sea* (*cf.* above) were soon replaced by local products and that – by the fourth century if not before – there had been a remarkable florescence of Aksumite metalworking expertise, some aspects of which may have originated through overseas contacts.

18 Assarca island lies between the Buri peninsula, northeast of Adulis, and the much larger Dahlak island. Unfortunately, the investigation of the wreck so far undertaken (Pedersen 2008) appears to have been limited to the cargo rather than to the vessel itself.

19 This is the material designated 'African red-slip ware' (see Hayes 1972: Carandini 1981).

20 J. S. Phillips 2000: 326–9.

21 If, as seems likely, most Aksumite pottery was produced by women, research on this topic will have ramifications far beyond ceramic studies.

22 One group, now in the British Museum, was recovered at the time of the British punitive expedition to Magdala in 1868 (Munro-Hay 1989b), and the other during excavations by R. Paribeni in 1906 (Heldman 1994).

23 Stable-isotope analysis of Adulis specimens has confirmed that some – but not all – are of Proconnesian marble from an island in the Sea of Marmara (K. Matthews in Peacock & Blue 2007).

24 Detailed under-water excavations have been conducted on a ship loaded with such stonework and wrecked off Syracuse, Sicily (Kapitän 1969).

25 A possible screen fragment from Qana on the southern coast of Arabia was noted by Sedov (2007: 92).

26 For this suggestion, see Heldman 2010. No reason was given for rejecting the seemingly more plausible suggestion that they were produced within the Aksumite kingdom by a painter who was familiar with Byzantine style.

Textiles were likewise noted as imports by the author of the *Periplus*, but these seem mainly to have been high-quality materials rather than those in everyday use. Textiles are rarely preserved in Aksumite archaeological contexts, although there is evidence for the processing – if not the cultivation – of cotton and for flax/linseed (Chapter 10). It is not known whether this last crop was grown primarily for oil – as in more recent times – or for fibre, but it is noteworthy that a sixth-century Byzantine ambassador described the Aksumite king as clothed in linen (Chapter 8). Thus, although firm evidence – whether archaeological or documentary – is scant, it seems likely that imports of textiles were restricted for the greater part of the Aksumite period to luxury fabrics that could not be produced locally.

The Rome–India link

Before leaving the subject of imports to the Aksumite kingdom, it is appropriate to consider the extent to which these should be considered an adjunct to, rather than independent of, the now well-documented trade between Rome / Byzantium and peninsular India.[27] Important archaeological investigations have recently taken place at ancient ports on the Egyptian shore of the Red Sea, particularly those that operated during the first half of the first millennium AD.[28] Being situated north of Adulis, these sites were probably involved with trade both with the Aksumite kingdom and with peninsular India; indeed it would be wise to assume that the same vessels were often involved and that imports to and exports from Adulis were carried by vessels plying the route from Suez to and across the Indian Ocean. It is often tacitly assumed that such vessels were Roman – or, in later times, Byzantine – but Aksumite involvement also merits consideration. An Aksumite copper coin has been recovered from the port-settlement of Qana on the south coast of Arabia, as has pottery for which Aksumite affinity has been suggested.[29] Early in the sixth century, Cosmas Indicopleustes recorded that Aksumite ships penetrated as far east as Sri Lanka;[30] furthermore, when a fleet was being assembled for the invasion of southern Arabia (see below), a significant number of the available vessels were Aksumite ones built at Adulis itself.[31] While details of ownership and movement of individual Red-Sea trading vessels remain unknown, there can be little doubt that – by at least the beginning of the sixth century – a significant proportion was Aksumite.[32]

Balance of trade

It was shown above that ivory was exported on a substantial scale from the Aksumite kingdom to the Mediterranean world, where it was a commodity of considerable but fluctuating value. Other exports are indicated, including

27 For an up-to-date overview, with comprehensive references, see Tomber 2008.

28 See, for example, Wendrich *et al.* 2003. Aksumite pottery and a third-/fourth-century coin of Aphilas were recovered from Berenice (Sidebotham & Wendrich 2007: 201, 373).

29 Sedov 2007; Tomber 2008: 104–7. The present writer sees only generalised Aksumite affinities in this pottery (*cf.* Sedov 1992: 127–8, 1996). Identification of a sherd from Kamrej in Gujerat as Aksumite (Tomber 2005) should likewise be regarded as provisional.

30 *Christian Topography* III 65; Wolska-Conus 1968–73, 1:502–5.

31 Gajda 2009: 103, citing the *Martyrdom of St Arethas*.

32 For further relevant discussion, see Desanges 1969, 1978; P. Schneider 2004.

civet-perfume and incense,[33] but their value was probably minor. While the items that appear to have been imported in the opposite direction included a range of luxury goods, the possibility of a considerable imbalance cannot be ruled out. The Roman world is known to have bemoaned a substantial outflow of wealth – calculated in gold – to 'India', and this has usually been attributed to huge demand in the former area for spices and aromatics from the peninsula or – ultimately – further east. The possibility cannot, however, be discounted that Aksumite ivory was also a major contributor. In the late-third century, the first issues of Aksumite coinage utilised exceptionally fine gold and silver, the latter being locally an exceptionally scarce commodity (Chapters 13 and 14). The possibility that some of this metal had reached Aksum from the Roman Empire cannot be excluded. Aksumite coinage in both metals, particularly the silver, was rapidly debased thereafter, possibly in response to falling receipts from the sale of ivory following Diocletian's price-control edict. The intensity of Aksum's contacts with the circum-Mediterranean world at this time is demonstrated not so much by abundant imports as by the transfer of technology, noted above and in Chapter 13.

A further outcome of this contact was the Aksumite king's adoption of Christianity in the mid-fourth century. Discussion in Chapter 9 demonstrates that this was in part brought about through the presence at the Aksumite capital of a Greek-speaking mercantile community that included adherents to that faith, and through the king's own perception of his political advantage.[34] There can be little doubt that Aksumite Christianity was partly a manifestation of the king's wish to ally himself with, while maintaining his distance from, the dominant power in the circum-Mediterranean world.

Diplomacy

There are clear indications that the Aksumite kingdom maintained diplomatic contacts with distant polities, at least during the fourth and sixth centuries. The evidence is incomplete, much of it being derived from non-Aksumite sources; we know significantly more about contacts initiated by outsiders than about those originating at Aksum. Two incidents in the latter category may, however be noted, although in neither case is their Aksumite origin incontrovertible. In 362, an embassy was received in Constantinople by the emperor Julian who had ascended the throne the previous year on the death of Constantius II. The embassy was recorded as coming from 'India',[35] which term was used in the Roman Empire at that time to designate the area now known as Ethiopia as well as peninsular South Asia. Since it took place at a time shortly after Constantius had taken a – perhaps unwelcome – interest in Aksumite affairs, the possibility that it comprised or included emissaries from Ezana is considered in Chapter 9. Further diplomatic contacts between Constantinople and Aksum accompanied military engagement in southern Arabia, discussed below. Missions originating at the courts of Justin and Justinian have received significant attention from historians (*cf.* Chapter 8), but there is also evidence – admittedly scant and inconclusive – for embassies in the opposite direction.

[33] Von Endt 1977, 1978; Peacock & Williams 2007.

[34] Gajda's (2009: 35) view that the Aksumite king's conversion was due to missionary activity by an emissary of Constantius II is an over-simplification (*cf.* Chapter 9).

[35] Ammianus Marcellinus, *History* XXII 7, 10 (Rolfe 1935–40, 2: 210–3). Priaulx 1862–63 cited Zonaras XIII 12 to the effect that the embassy had set out to address Constantius, whose death preceded its arrival. For discussion of the possible purpose of this embassy, see Chapter 9.

The *Chronicle* of John Malalas – whose designation of the Aksumite King Kaleb as 'emperor of the Indians' was noted in Chapter 8 – mentioned the arrival at Justinian's court in Constantinople of 'Indian ambassadors' bearing gifts *c.* 532 and *c.* 549/50; in the latter case, the gifts included an elephant.[36]

As today, international diplomatic contacts were often conducted in secrecy and not publicised or admitted until long afterwards – if at all. Much diplomacy concerned religious matters: indeed, there was no clear boundary between religious and political topics, and contacts on matters that would today be regarded as strictly political were often maintained through religious connections, the majority originating in Rome / Constantinople. Episodes about which we have information include those of Constantius II in the fourth century, dealing primarily with religious matters, and those in the first half of the sixth century concerning southern Arabia and Persia (discussed below). It is noteworthy that we know of no diplomatic contacts to or from Aksum concerning the fifth-century religious controversies leading to the Council of Chalcedon (*cf.* Chapter 9).

Aksumite connections to the west and north

The highlands of the northern Horn and the Sudanese Nile Valley are almost neighbours, the straight-line distance from Aksum to the Nile being less than 650 km – virtually the same as the distance to Addis Ababa. A few imported items probably reached the Aksum area from this direction, as noted above. There is evidence that, in the fourth century, Ezana's raiding parties (Chapter 7) reached the Sudanese lowlands and defeated the Kasu, even though Aksumite political influence there was probably short-lived. By the late-sixth century, the Nubian kingdoms – like that of the Aksumites – were predominantly Christian. It is thus surprising how little evidence there is for close connections between the two areas. Occasional artefacts[37] found their way from one area to the other, but it was not until post-Aksumite times, when control of the Red Sea had passed into Arabian hands (Chapter 16), that closer connections seem to have developed.

Although the patriarch of Alexandria appears to have been influential in the Ethiopian Church through his consecration of Frumentius, the formal nature of any continuing subordination to that office is by no means clear.[38] There are indications that the patriarch's exclusive right to nominate a new head for the Ethiopian Church may date from post-Aksumite times.[39] This does not, however, negate the significance of the close and long-standing connections that prevailed between Aksum and Jerusalem. Although the details are poorly understood, there are several varied indicators that these connections date back at least to the early-sixth century. When King Kaleb abdicated (*cf.* Chapter 8), probably in the fifth decade of the sixth century, his donation of his crown to the Holy Sepulchre strongly implies an existing Ethiopian connection, although records held in Jerusalem are unclear on this point.[40] Finds of Aksumite-style

36 Jeffreys *et al.* 1986: 282, 289; Priaulx 1862–63; see also below.

37 For example, the copper-alloy bowls from the Addi Gelamo cache (Chapter 3) and an Aksumite coin found at Meroe (Zach 1996).

38 Constantius II may have been misled by his dislike of Athanasius into believing that this connection was stronger than was actually the case. For a more detailed discussion of Aksum's dependence on the Alexandrian patriarchate, see Chapter 9.

39 See Heldman 2007.

40 Cerulli 1943–47; Meinardus 1965.

coins in greater Syria – including Palestine – include only a few that appear to be regular issues, but a significant number of local miniature copies (Chapter 14), implying a wide acceptability and, presumably, some interchange of personnel. Travel by way of the Red Sea between Clysma and Ayla in the north and Adulis in the south is well attested, so little difficulty would have been encountered in the maintenance of an Ethiopian community in Jerusalem, establishment of which is much more likely to have taken place before the seventh century than afterwards.

Syrian familiarity with Aksum is also suggested by the famous mural paintings at Qusayr Amra,[41] a rural estate *c.* 100 km east of Amman with a luxuriously decorated bath-house of eighth-century date. One panel, now poorly preserved, in its principal hall depicts five rulers whom Arab expansion had recently eclipsed; all are labelled, the central figure being designated *negus*.[42]

Southern and western Ethiopia

There are tantalising indications that, during the fifth and sixth centuries, the Aksumite kingdom may have developed stronger contacts with some more southerly and westerly parts of Ethiopia than it had exercised previously (*cf.* Chapter 7). Farmers in Aksumite territory began to cultivate crops that were previously unknown there but which originated in more southerly regions (Chapter 10). Cosmas Indicopleustes recorded expeditions from Aksum to obtain gold from a place called Sasu, perhaps near the modern Sudan border southwest of Lake Tana.[43]

Southern Arabia

It is now appropriate to consider relations between the Aksumite kingdom and southern Arabia where, by the second century, the kingdom of Himyar had established paramountcy. Inscriptions in the latter area imply some degree of Aksumite involvement by the early-third century, although there can be no certainty about its extent, degree – whether commercial and/or political – or permanence.[44] This connection receives some measure of confirmation from the royal titles preserved in Aksumite inscriptions from the early- or mid-fourth century (Chapters 6 and 8), which include the possibly archaistic element 'king of Himyar'. During the following century, any political control that may have existed became significantly weaker, although parallel developments such as the adoption of monotheism continued. Contacts between the Aksumite and Himyarite kingdoms seem to have been revived at the end of the fifth century and during the first decade of the sixth, perhaps stimulating increased adherence to Christianity in the latter region. Centralised authority in Himyar was weakened, with Christian and non-Christian factions each under its own ruler, the former maintaining strong links with Ethiopia. This

41 Almagro *et al.* 2002; Fowden 2004.

42 Almagro *et al.* 2002: figs 22, 89, 92. The other figures are Rodorikos [the last Vandal king of Spain, defeated at Guadalete in 711], Cosroes of Persia, and two others who cannot be positively identified.

43 *Christian Topography* II 51 (Wolska-Conus 1968–73, 1: 360–2; see also James 2007 and A. Pankhurst 2007). Cosmas' own account of the location of Sasu (*cf.* Chapter 14) is not clear. In fact, his account of this 'silent trade' has a suspiciously mythical tone: it is strongly reminiscent of Herodotus' account (*History* IV 196; Godley 1920–25, 2: 398–9; see also Rawlinson 1862, 3: 144) of the activities of Carthaginian traders 'beyond the Pillars of Hercules'.

44 Robin 1989.

situation came to a head towards the end of the second decade of the sixth century, when the Aksumites under King Kaleb are reported to have begun military preparations for an expedition to southern Arabia.[45] On the assumption that this operation did subsequently take place, it was the first of several incursions that Kaleb made across the Red Sea, and perhaps the occasion when he set his own appointee – Ma'dikarib Ya'fur – on the throne of Himyar.[46]

Later, perhaps *c.* 522–3, the non-Christian faction led by Yusuf As'ar Yath'ar, also known as Dhu Nuwas, sought to reinforce or re-establish Himyarite authority.[47] He attacked Zafar, the old capital of Himyar in the highlands *c.* 150 km north of Aden, killed many of the Ethiopians there and burned the church. He then raided settlements in the Red-Sea coastal plain, taking steps to prevent a counter-invasion from Aksumite territory. Forces were then dispatched northwards, followed by Yusuf himself, and Najran, 400 km north of Zafar in what is now southern Saudi Arabia, was besieged; it eventually capitulated and many Christians were burned to death in their church along with their leader, the Arab chieftain Harit [Arethas in Greek].

When news of the Najran siege reached Constantinople, the emperor Justin sought the assistance of the Alexandrian patriarch in urging Kaleb to intervene on behalf of the Christian Najranites, apparently promising assistance and support.[48] A fleet was assembled at Gabaza,[49] adjacent to Adulis, from a variety of sources, several of which were ports under Byzantine and/or Egyptian control on more northerly shores of the Red Sea. Despite difficulties caused by Yusuf's defensive measures, Kaleb's army eventually landed on the Arabian shore, proceeded to Najran, and defeated Yusuf.[50]

This invasion and its aftermath have given rise to an extensive literature, proliferating in the 1920s with the discovery of a previously unknown Syriac text, the so-called *Book of the Himyarites*.[51] Neither the details nor

[45] The sole evidence for this date is provided by a passage in the *Christian Topography* of Cosmas Indicopleustes (II 56; Wolska-Conus 1968–73, 1:368–9) where it is dated to the beginning of the reign of Justin I. Justin succeeded Anastasius as Byzantine emperor in July 518. Cosmas wrote some 25 years after these events, and one should not ignore the possibility that he had mis-remembered the date and that the expedition took place around the middle of the following decade.

[46] There have been many attempts to elucidate the chronological sequence of sixth-century Aksumite operations in southern Arabia following the research of S. Smith 1954 and Shahid 1971. The account offered here is largely based on the conclusions of de Blois 1990, as refined by Beaucamp *et al.* 1999 and Gajda 2009.

[47] Arguments have been put forward that these events may have taken place somewhat earlier, perhaps beginning in 518 (Shahid 1971, 1994; de Blois 1990; Gajda 2009).

[48] The extent of Byzantine involvement remains unclear. Procopius (*History of the Wars*, I 19–20; Dewing 1914–28, 1: 178–95) mentions their desire to disrupt Persian trade in silk as being of primary importance. This seems, however, to have been a later development under Justinian I, who succeeded Justin as emperor in 527. Full consideration must also be given to the difficulties facing the Byzantine authorities in making their intentions publicly known. They, unlike the Aksumites and the Najranites, were adherents to the 'dyophysite' doctrine adopted some sixty years previously by the Council of Chalcedon (*cf.* Chapter 9), and it was thus very much in the Byzantine interest that Kaleb, rather than they, should be seen as the prime supporter of the Arabian 'heretics'.

[49] Although not named in the text of the *Christian Topography*, the map accompanying that text shows Gabaza as a customs post adjacent to Adulis (Wolska-Conus 1968–73, 1: 367; see also Chapter 6 and Fig. 18).

[50] An undated inscription cited by Gajda 2009: 108 indicates that Yusuf was killed.

[51] Moberg 1924; see also Shahid 1963, 1971.

the controversies to which they have given rise[52] require rehearsal here. Information comes from a number of sources, most of them written. Relevant archaeological discoveries in southern Arabia, apart from the Himyaritic inscriptions and two in Ge'ez ,[53] are almost totally lacking, although there is both documentary and architectural evidence for the subsequent erection of major churches, as at Sanaa.[54] Texts, other than the inscriptions, are in Syriac, Greek, and Arabic; not surprisingly, they provide markedly differing emphases. It is regrettable that no Ethiopian texts concerning this episode are known to have survived.[55] Reconstructions based on the known texts present a potentially distorted view of events that took place. A related uncertainty concerns the role of the Byzantines: the only well-attested intervention under Justin being that, noted above, in which the patriarch of Alexandria acted as intermediary. More overt contacts between Byzantines and Aksumites did not take place until after the accession of Justinian to the former throne in 527. Doctrinal differences – probably more strongly felt under Justin than under his successor – may have prevented the Byzantine authorities' open admission of support for Himyarite Christians.

In the aftermath to this successful operation, several new churches were established, whereupon Kaleb and much of the Aksumite army withdrew *c.* 529–30, leaving their own appointee, one Sumyafa Ashwa,[56] as the new ruler of Himyar paying annual tribute to Aksum. In 530, however, according to Procopius,[57] Justinian sent an embassy lead by Julian to urge both Kaleb and Sumfaya Ashwa to participate in a Byzantine invasion of Persia, in the hope that an ally in southern Arabia would serve to weaken Persian control of the silk trade. This invasion duly took place – it is not known whether Aksumite assistance was forthcoming, but the late timing of the request suggests that it was not – resulting in a Byzantine victory and the death of the Persian king later in 531.[58] Himyarite opposition to Sumfaya Ashwa continued, leading to his deposition and replacement by Abraha as the Aksumite-appointed ruler of Himyar later in the 530s.[59]

Significantly more is known about Abraha than his predecessor.[60] The titles and activities recorded in inscriptions that were erected under Abraha's own

52 The comprehensive summary and bibliography provided by Gajda 2009: 73–156 are valuable although, being based largely on southern Arabian sources, they may underestimate the extent and significance of Byzantine support.

53 All the inscriptions were found in southern Arabia. Those in Ge'ez were included in the RIE under numbers 263 and 265; for the Himyaritic ones, see Robin 2009.

54 Lewcock 1979; Serjeant & Lewcock 1983.

55 The only contemporary exception is the royal inscription of Kaleb, found at Aksum (RIE 191; see Chapter 6, also Gajda 2009: 80), which makes brief mention of an expedition to Himyar and to church-construction. The Ge'ez rendition of the *Martyrdom of St Arethas* appears to be a late translation from the Greek and Arabic versions.

56 This is the name given in the southern Arabian inscriptions. In Greek, as recorded by Procopius (*History of the Wars* I 20; Dewing 1914–28, 1: 188–9), his name took the form Esimiphaios.

57 Procopius, *History of the Wars* I 20 (Dewing 1914–28, 1: 192–3). This was the embassy that was also described by John Malalas (see Chapter 8) and in the account by Nonnosus from which extracts were preserved in Photius' later compilation noted in Chapter 8.

58 Greatrex 1998.

59 The title 'viceroy', often applied to Sumfaya Ashwa and to Abraha, is not strictly appropriate, at least for Abraha after he broke the link with Aksum and sought to make his own dynasty's position hereditary.

60 Sima 2003a.

authority in Arabia[61] emphasise his status as a king but not his subordination to Kaleb who, according to Procopius, mounted two military expeditions to Arabia in his attempts to bring Abraha to order. Abraha took credit for repairing the great Marib dam and is recalled as a builder of churches. His campaign against Mecca in 'the Year of the Elephant' has been attributed to desire that his church at Sanaa should become a premier place of pilgrimage.[62] After Kaleb's abdication, Abraha regularised his position by resuming payments of tribute to the new Aksumite king.[63] The end of Abraha's reign, probably in the late 550s, is not clearly documented. Arab historians, writing long afterwards, record that he was briefly succeeded in turn by two sons, one of whom was called Yaksum. By the 570s, much of southern Arabia was under Persian control.

Plague

In AD 541–42 a virulent outbreak of bubonic plague spread rapidly through the circum-Mediterranean lands.[64] In most accounts that focus primarily on the latter area, in order to distinguish it from earlier and later infections, it is designated the 'Justinianic plague', after the Byzantine emperor who ruled at that time.[65] Contemporary accounts clearly indicate that its first Mediterranean occurrence was in 541 at the port of Pelusium near the eastern side of the Nile Delta, whence it was apparently transmitted by sea to numerous other ports throughout the Mediterranean, including – in the spring of 542 – Constantinople.[66] It was suspected at the time, and has been repeated ever since, that the infection derived from 'Ethiopia' but, as discussed in Chapter 1, the meaning of that term in the mid-first millennium AD was ill-defined, and it cannot be assumed that it referred to the Aksumite state.[67] It is thus pertinent to consider here whether there is any evidence – primary or indirect – that this state may have suffered such infection during the first half of the sixth century.

No relevant archaeological evidence for plague itself has yet been reported from any Aksumite site. There are no indications – such as mass burials or careless interment – for sudden, large-scale mortality. Although it is now possible to recover traces of the plague virus *Yersinia pestis* from ancient skeletal material,[68] the relevant techniques have not been applied to Aksumite remains. It is, however, noteworthy that the second quarter of the sixth century was, as discussed in Chapter 16, precisely the period during which the

61 Drewes 1962; Kropp 1991; Nebes 2004.

62 This invasion (Guillaume 1967: 21–8; Fiaccadori in A. Berger 2006: 67; Gori 2007) probably took place in 547 or 552. It is thus unlikely to have coincided with the birth of the Prophet Muhammad, as some later Arab historians aver.

63 These details were recorded by Procopius, *History of the Wars* I 20 (Dewing 1914–28, 1: 190–1) who, however, refers to the reign of Kaleb / Hellestheaeus ending by death rather than abdication (*cf.* above and Chapter 8).

64 Recent overviews are provided by Horden 2005 and Little 2007. More detailed references are provided in the following discussion.

65 Justinian I [ruled AD 527–65] caught the plague himself, but recovered.

66 Procopius, *History of the Wars* II 22.6 (Dewing 1914–28, 1: 452–3. Egypt was at that time still a major supplier of cereals, and it is likely that plague-carrying rats were dispersed through the grain-shipments.

67 For discussions of the ultimate origin of the 'Justinianic plague', see Sarris 2002, 2007, also McCormick 2007. These authors do not, however, give adequate consideration to the meaning of the term 'Ethiopia' in the ancient sources (*cf.* Chapter 1).

68 See, for example, Garrelt & Wiechmann 2003, Drancourt & Raoult 2004.

beginnings of Aksumite decline may first be discerned in the archaeological record.[69] For example, this was the time when deterioration of the Aksumite coinage first became apparent (Chapter 14), and similar factors in Byzantine coinage[70] have been plausibly attributed to the economic aftermath of the 'Justinianic plague'. However, no such link is apparent in the Aksumite case, where numerous other factors are more likely to have contributed to decline at this time, notably over-extension and political instability associated with Kaleb's military exploits in southern Arabia, discussed above.

The primary vector of bubonic plague is a flea borne by the black rat, *Rattus rattus.* A major area of this rodent's distribution is in east and south-central Africa where it is attested during the first millennium in a large area extending from southern Zambia to Zanzibar.[71] It is thus perfectly plausible that the infection was brought from the latter place to Pelusium by ship. Such a voyage must have passed through the Red Sea and would have been regarded by Byzantines as having come from 'Ethiopia', whatever precise meaning may have been attached to that term.

Conclusion

This chapter attempts to pull together into a coherent narrative the very diverse evidence – much of which is also cited in chapters devoted to other themes – concerning the Aksumite kingdom's relationships with more distant territories and potentates. While such relationships were rarely directly political, they nonetheless had not infrequent major influences on the kingdom's internal affairs, technology and prosperity. Similar influences may be detected in the opposite direction, although the extent to which they were recognised by the recipients is tantalisingly unclear. It was a situation that is – or should be – familiar to twenty-first-century politicians, both in the northern Horn and elsewhere.

[69] This general argument could equally apply to the impact of a major volcanic eruption in southeast Asia which had wide repercussions *c.* AD 536 (Gunn 2000).

[70] A significant reform of Byzantine copper coinage instituted under Justinian I in 538 proved very short-lived (Metcalf 1960), and the weight of the gold *solidus* was reduced (P. Grierson 1982: 52–3). For a discussion of these developments and their connection with the economic results of the plague outbreak, see Sarris 2007.

[71] Davis & Fagan 1962; Fagan 1967: 75; Horton 1996: 386–7. I acknowledge with gratitude valuable discussions with Professor Mark Horton, and the assistance of Professor Brian Fagan on this subject.

16

Decline and Transformation of the Aksumite State

By the middle decades of the sixth century, economic decline was becoming apparent in the northern Horn, most noticeably in the area around Aksum itself. The overall population of the capital area diminished sharply.[1] Several of Aksum's grand buildings fell into disrepair and were apparently occupied by squatters.[2] Use of the Gobedra quarries to provide the materials for massive masonry came to an abrupt end, to judge from the number of blocks that were abandoned after extraction had begun.[3] The coinage suffered a marked reduction both in technical quality and in metallurgical fineness, accompanied by a proliferation of tiny base-metal issues that may indicate inflation and reduction in living standards. Detailed interpretation of this last point is hindered by continuing uncertainty surrounding the sequence of reigns and coinage issues between the mid-sixth and mid-seventh centuries, as discussed in Chapter 14, but the most likely picture appears to be that debasement of the gold accelerated during the third quarter of the sixth century, followed shortly afterwards by the proliferation of small copper coins.

The expansion of Aksum and its population during the fourth century and – perhaps to a lesser extent – the fifth is indicated by archaeological survey, results obtained by Michels in the 1970s being supported by those of more recent fieldwork based on more precise chronological indicators.[4] This concentration probably resulted in serious depletion of resources, notably timber, accompanied by environmental deterioration.[5] A rapid and pronounced depopulation followed. This may have been partly due to reduced carrying capacity of the local environment, but other factors probably contributed. The size of Kaleb's army in southern Arabia (Chapter 15) may have been exaggerated, but it was clearly substantial;[6] Procopius wrote that many of the soldiers, particularly slaves, preferred to remain in Arabia and refused to

[1] Michels 2005: 201–16.

[2] Puglisi 1941; Munro-Hay 1989a: 158, 332.

[3] J. B. Phillips & Ford 2000. Note, however, that there is no clear evidence as to when this abandonment took place, and that the possibility cannot be ruled out that it had occurred earlier than the period under consideration here.

[4] Michels 2005: 123–99; L. Phillipson 2009b; Sernicola & L. Phillipson 2011; Fattovich 2010.

[5] This was first argued by Butzer 1981, whose account should be used with care since it was based on a chronology that has since seen radical revision. Recent geoarchaeological research (French *et al.* 2009; Sulas *et al.* 2009) has raised doubts about the extent of environmental deterioration during the sixth and seventh centuries but, in the present writer's opinion, the older argument still holds good.

[6] See the *Martyrdom of St Arethas* (Detoraki & Beaucamp 2007: 262–3).

return.[7] We have no means of knowing how and where such a large army was recruited, but if it drew disproportionately on men residing in and near the capital, the effect of this episode on the population of the Aksum region could have been marked. The suddenness and scale of depopulation cannot be evaluated archaeologically: although sites vaguely designated 'post-Aksumite' are fewer and smaller than those of earlier times, with less indication of substantial structures, the duration of this period is not known, and meaningful comparisons with earlier times cannot be made.

Control of the Red-Sea waterway had, in the early-sixth century, been largely in the hands of the Aksumites and their Byzantine allies, thus guaranteeing free movement of Aksumite exports northwards. With the capture of Himyar by the Persians in the 570s and by the Arabs shortly afterwards, this movement was denied, thus depriving the Aksumite kingdom of the overseas markets on which its prosperity had for several centuries been based.[8] It is possible, indeed, that supply of these exports was already diminishing. Ivory may have been increasingly difficult to obtain in the most accessible areas, as is perhaps indicated by the elephant-protection measures that were in place by the early sixth century.[9] Gold may have been exported in earlier times, but the report that it was by this time obtained from far afield[10] implies that auriferous deposits in the vicinity of Aksum were becoming exhausted, as is confirmed by the accelerated debasement of the gold coinage at this time.

The effects of Aksum's decline may also be seen in the flaked-stone industries.[11] By the sixth century, these were largely restricted to specialist use involving standardised tools, metal implements having replaced lithics for many other purposes. With the decline of the civilisation that had nurtured these developments in the Aksum area, supplies of metal decreased markedly, but the stone-knapping skills had been lost, being replaced by production of small numbers of crude *ad hoc* implements showing little standardisation. There are indications that this collapse may have been restricted to Aksum and its immediate surroundings; more skilled stone knapping may have continued nearby. The nature of parallel developments elsewhere in the Aksumite kingdom remains unknown.

As a result of these developments, the factors that had led to the establishment of Aksum as the capital of a major kingdom no longer operated. Neither the plentiful food and materials, nor the valuable commodities for export, could be obtained in the quantities previously prevailing. The kingdom fell back on the resources available in the eastern highlands of Tigray, which were perhaps already more densely populated than the area around Aksum. It is clear from the writings of Arabic historians – admittedly produced some time after the period to which they relate – that Aksum ceased to be the political

[7] Procopius, *History of the Wars* I 20 (Dewing 1914–28, 1: 188–91).

[8] Communication with Alexandria would also have been made more difficult and contact between the patriarchate and the Ethiopian Christians would have become tenuous.

[9] Such measures were recorded by Nonnosus, an ambassador of the Byzantine emperor Justinian I who visited the court of Kaleb at Aksum *c.* 530. Nonnosus, probably a co-ambassador or near-contemporary of Julian (*cf.* Chapter 8), observed a large herd of elephants – he estimated that there were 5000 of them – at a place called Aue somewhere northeast of Yeha, and noted that the local people were not allowed to molest them. Nonnosus' full report does not survive, but a brief summary was included in his *Polybiblion* by Photius, a ninth-century Patriarch of Constantinople (Freese 1920: 19). For the location of Aue, see Chapter 7; also Munro-Hay 1991b: 31.

[10] Cosmas Indicopleustes, *Christian Topography* II 51–2 (Wolska-Conus 1968–73, 1: 360–3). However, for the perhaps mythical nature of this report, see Chapter 15.

[11] L. Phillipson 2009b: 116.

capital, its replacement being established at a place called Kubar,[12] the location of which has not yet been ascertained although it is thought to have been at some distance to the southeast of Aksum. The possibility needs to be considered that the name 'Kubar' applied not to a permanent built capital, but to one that was periodically moved as the ruler progressed through his subject territory as is known to have been the practice during much of the second millennium.[13] Such demotion of Aksum can only have accelerated its decline.

It has been argued[14] that the move of the capital took place shortly before the final cessation of Aksumite coinage-issue. Such a view was in accord with the observation that excavated assemblages from Aksum have included relatively few coins of Armah, who was believed to have been the last of the kings in whose name coins were issued. Re-evaluation of the coinage-sequence for this late period[15] requires that the matter be reconsidered, although no definitive conclusion is yet possible. A further relevant factor is the identification of Armah with the Aksumite king who granted refuge to early followers of the Prophet Mohammed, as recalled in Muslim tradition that was committed to writing some two or three centuries later.[16] The Muslim shrine at Negash in eastern Tigray incorporates a tomb that is traditionally attributed to this period. No reflection of these events has yet been recognised in the archaeological record or, less surprisingly, in Christian tradition.[17] The comments recorded by the Prophet's followers about the rich decoration of the church of Mary at Aksum require further consideration since, taken at face value, they might imply that Aksum was still the royal capital at this time. It should be noted, however, that the written record of these comments is not contemporaneous; it is possible that the details of the church's dedication and location represent a subsequent and potentially misleading gloss.

Critical evaluation of the sparse source-materials that are available for this period permits tentative conclusions to be drawn. Abandonment of the old capital at Aksum marked, not an end, but a transition. The rulers were no longer surrounded by reminders of the pre-Christian past, of great wealth and prosperity, and of international recognition. The kingdom had to rely, to a greater extent than previously, on its own material resources and spiritual strengths. This involved emphasis of its Christianity at a time when it was coming into contact with a new and actively expanding religion. In the early-seventh century, this trend was clearly reflected in the coinage (Chapter 14) which maintained its traditional and emphatically Christian aspect to its end. There is no sign here of contact with another faith. Our knowledge of developments after the mid-seventh century in eastern Tigray is restricted by the fact that virtually no relevant archaeological research has been undertaken

12 Vantini (1975: 73, 131, 448) provided a valuable series of English translations from works of later Arabic historians who made reference to Kubar, notably those of al-Yaqubi [AD 872–91], al-Masudi [mid-tenth century], and al-Harrani [*c.* 1295]. These references provide little information about Kubar, other than that it was the capital of the Christian *najashi* and that it was visited by Arab traders. Nazret, some 70 km south of Makalle (Anfray 1970: 36–8; Henze 2007), has been suggested as a possible location, but there seems to be little supporting evidence. Vantini's view that 'Kubar' was another name for Aksum is no longer supported.

13 For the latter practice, see Horvath 1969; Richard Pankhurst 1982: esp. 41–8.

14 *e.g.* by D. Phillipson 2000b: 485–6.

15 Hahn 2010.

16 Trimingham 1952: 44–6 and references cited; see also Chapter 9.

17 Arabic inscriptions from the Dahlak islands and from eastern Tigray (M. Schneider 1967, 1983; Smidt 2004; Gori 2007) are probably all somewhat later in date.

there, although a number of potentially informative sites have been located.[18] Study of the extant churches,[19] however, has revealed several that probably date back to the closing centuries of the first millennium, and it is these that provide our most direct insight to the history of this poorly understood period.

The move of the capital and the concentration of settlement in eastern Tigray had profound effects on the areas that had been the state's former heartland. At Aksum itself, non-ecclesiastical buildings and monuments were no longer maintained. The thrones lining the approach road from the southeast shared this fate: as noted in Chapter 6, the base of one of them bears a faint Ge'ez inscription, dated palaeographically to the late-eighth or the ninth century, in the name of one *hatsani* [= ruler] called Dana'el. Although this inscription's reading is unclear, it is clear that control of the Aksum area was at this time disputed. Apparently somewhat later are traditions relating to a queen – Gudit – whose depredations included the toppling of stelae.[20] Although the ecclesiastical establishments appear to have been maintained, Aksum's eclipse was otherwise almost total.

In eastern Tigray, by contrast, the density and prosperity of settlement increased. In the more northerly part of this region, around Adigrat, as in adjacent areas of Eritrea, continuity from earlier times is indicated both by ongoing archaeological investigation in the Gulo Makeda area[21] and by the church at Debra Damo[22] which was probably founded in the sixth century. In more southerly parts of the eastern Tigray highlands, however, no convincing evidence for pre-seventh-century occupation has yet been recorded and the nature of settlement remains unknown, although the Hawzien area may have formed a separate minor kingdom during the second and/or third centuries.[23] It was only some half-millennium later that the sequence of churches and allied features appears to have begun.

Funerary churches in eastern Tigray

Establishment of a chronology for the ancient churches of the northern Horn is fraught with difficulty. The churches include conventional buildings as well as those that were hewn from solid rock; these latter were for preference carved from hard sandstone,[24] in which elements such as window- and door-frames were difficult to represent, so were made of wood and set into the rock. The churches are still in regular use and under ecclesiastical control; repeated and undocumented renovation and alteration has taken place over the centuries in almost all cases. Permission for detailed structural investigation, such as would – in these circumstances – be essential to disentangle their history, is virtually impossible to obtain. Some age-estimates that have been proposed have been based on uncertain assumptions, such as the literal veracity of

[18] As noted, for example, by Smidt 2007.

[19] D. Phillipson 2009a: 51–74, 88–107 and overview below.

[20] As noted in Chapter 12, excavations on the site of Stela 2 prior to its re-erection revealed evidence for intentional demolition that are not inconsistent with this tradition. For Queen Gudit, see Sergew 1972: 225–32; Belaynesh in Belaynesh *et al.* 1975: 76–8; el-Chennafi 1976; Molvaer 1998.

[21] D'Andrea *et al.* 2008a; see also Chapters 7–13.

[22] The church at Debra Damo is discussed in Chapter 11.

[23] This is indicated by the inscription on the third-century stela at Anza, noted in Chapters 6 and 7.

[24] Asfawossen 2002a, 2002b.

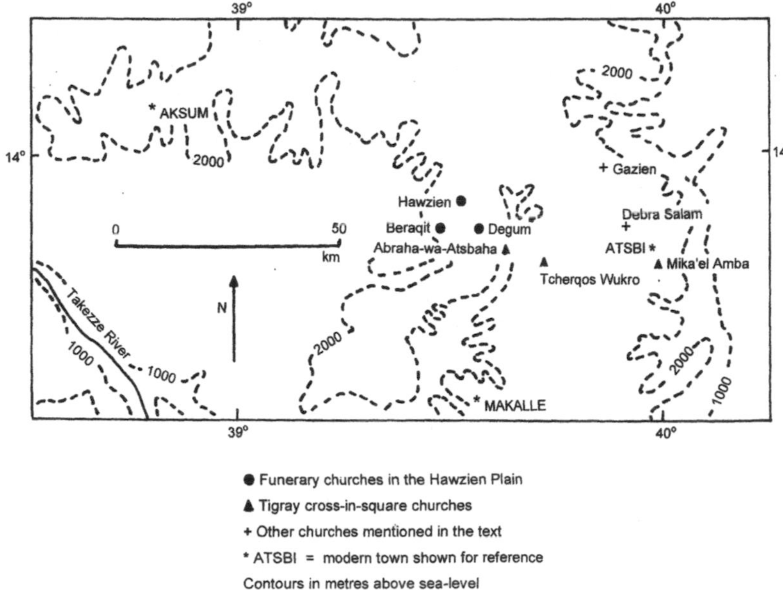

Fig. 77 Location of ancient churches and related monuments in eastern Tigray

traditions relating to foundation, the contemporaneity of foundation and existing structure, the reliability of radiocarbon dating of structural timbers, or the contemporaneity of building and mural decoration. Rock-hewn features present particular problems in this regard, because of the possibility that older elements may be completely removed. This has major implications for attempts to demonstrate connections between the form of churches and the liturgical requirements that prevailed at the time.[25] Bearing these problems in mind, we may turn to consider some historically significant churches in eastern Tigray.

The rock-hewn tomb at Degum on the Hawzien Plain is noted in Chapter 12, where the possibility of a date in about the sixth or seventh century is argued. The Degum site was further developed subsequently by the excavation of more rock-hewn features, including a baptismal tank in a form which, elsewhere, may date as far back as the sixth century.[26] Adjacent to the tomb and tank was a small rock-hewn church or chapel of a type – three examples of which are currently known, all on low rock outcrops in the Hawzien Plain (Fig. 77) within a radius of 8 km from each other – which Claude Lepage designated *églises de vallée*.[27]

All three of these monuments have been modified subsequently to accommodate their use as conventional churches, but the original form may be

[25] For general consideration of this point, see Doig 2008 and, for its relevance in Ethiopia, Fritsch & Gervers 2007; Gervers 2007, Fritsch 2008.

[26] For the Degum baptistery and its *comparanda*, see Chapter 11.

[27] Lepage 1971. This designation takes no account of the localised distribution of these monuments, nor of the fact that their original function – as argued below – was apparently funerary or reliquary. In a recent book (D. Phillipson 2009a: 88–92), I have referred to them as 'funerary hypogea in the Hawzien Plain'.

best appreciated at Beraqit (Fig. 78), close to the foot of the Garalta Mountains approximately 12 km northwest of Degum. It now combines rock-hewn and built components.[28] As at Degum, the original church was cut into the west face of the outcrop, its two eastern chambers being fully rock-hewn. Ignoring the later structures to the west, these chambers comprise a 5-m-long nave with one aisle on either side, plus an apsidal sanctuary to the east. Configuration of the nave and aisles is remarkably similar to that of the same features at Degum.

The rock ceilings are flat, carved in imitation of separate stone slabs, that of the nave being considerably higher than those of the aisles. The upper walls of the nave bear an Aksumite frieze[29] except at the east end, where it is interrupted by a narrow arch leading to the sanctuary. The frieze continues around the domed sanctuary; immediately below the frieze, a rectangular aperture – now blocked – penetrated the rock into a separate rock-cut pit immediately to the east. Both here and at Degum, the pit was formerly accessed from the north by means of a trench. These pits to the east of the sanctuaries, with the connecting apertures, are no longer maintained, and their original purpose seems to have been forgotten. Lepage[30] recognised that his *églises de vallée* probably served as reliquary chapels, the pits and apertures providing the means whereby visitors could pay respect to the relics.

The third hypogeum in this group, essentially similar to that at Beraqit, is Hawzien Tekla Haimonot where the nave is, however, significantly longer.[31] There can be little doubt that the oldest examples are those at Degum.

Three much larger churches – Abraha-wa-Atsbaha, Tcherqos Wukro, and Mika'el Amba – occur in a restricted highland area only 13 km in radius, east of the Hawzien Plain. Their distribution does not overlap with that of the small funerary monuments described above. They closely resemble each other in plan and style,[32] and retain features of funerary or reliquary use. All are extensive, 230–310 sq m in floor area, wide from north to south in proportion to their length from west to east, and further distinguished by being exposed on the west with external as well as internal features rock-carved, the eastern parts being hewn into the solid rock (Fig. 79). Buxton[33] called them 'cross-in-square churches' – an appropriate term since, although the ground-plans are roughly square, the nave and transepts form a cross which is emphasised by their greater height. However, the same term has been used by writers on Byzantine and Armenian architecture[34] with somewhat different connotations; to avoid confusion the form 'Tigray cross-in-square churches'[35] is employed here.

28 Details of its appearance prior to substantial remodelling in 1990–91 were recorded by Lepage 1972 and by Plant 1985: 68–9. For a further illustrated account, see D. Phillipson 2009a: 89–91.

29 An 'Aksumite frieze' is a distinctive architectural feature of many ancient churches in the northern Horn, originally comprising a horizontal row of windows positioned high on an external wall or, more usually, on one separating the nave of a basilica from lofts over the aisles. Each of these windows has a massive wooden frame with square beam-ends projecting at the corners. In a rock-hewn church, however, the whole frieze – with blind windows – may be carved from the rock. An example is shown in Fig. 78.

30 Lepage 1972.

31 Lepage & Mercier 2005: 58–61.

32 This was first noted by Buxton (1971: 42–8). For a more detailed account, with illustrations and comparisons, see D. Phillipson (2009a: 92–8).

33 Buxton *op. cit.*

34 *e.g.* C. Mango 1986: 104, 118; Krautheimer 1986: 520.

35 The term 'Tigray cross-in-square churches' was first proposed by D. Phillipson 2009a: 92.

Fig. 78 The church at Beraqit, looking from the nave into the sanctuary, where the *manbara tabot* obscures the blocked aperture that formerly permitted a view from the adjacent pit

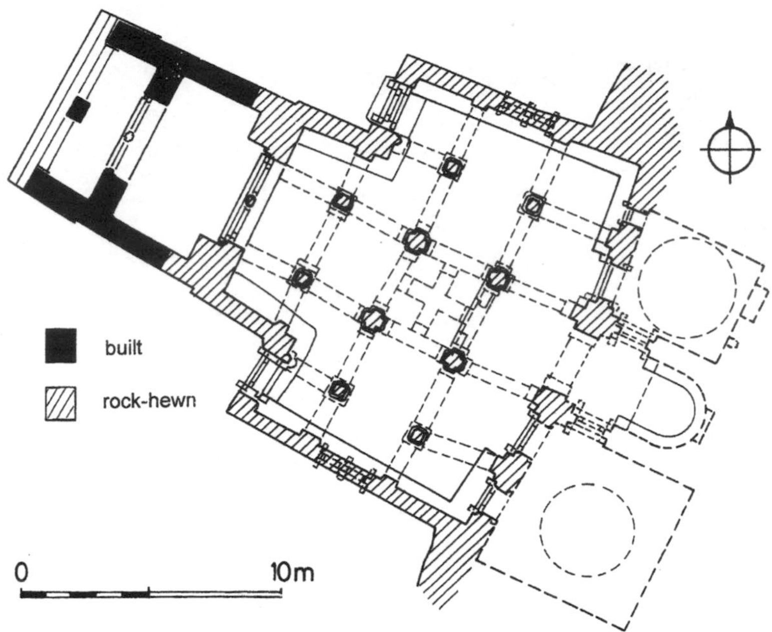

Fig. 79 Plan of the Tigray cross-in-square rock-hewn church of Abraha-wa-Atsbaha (after Lepage & Mercier 2005)

Vaulted transepts (Fig. 80) are similar at all three churches, significantly higher than the aisles – this is particularly clear at Abraha-wa-Atsbaha. All three also have prominent carvings of processional crosses identically positioned near the entrance-doors. Further elements of similarity are in the easternmost nave bay, the floor of which forms a platform level with that of the sanctuary, and the ceiling of which is domed. At Mika'el Amba this bay was formerly separated from the rest of the church by a wooden screen of post-and-panel construction (*cf.* Fig. 83) of a type clearly replicating the imported stone screens that were imported to Adulis in Aksumite times, as discussed in Chapters 11 and 15. A similar screen formerly existed at Abraha-wa-Atsbaha; although no trace of one survives at Tcherqos Wukro, its former presence cannot be discounted.

The strong similarity and connections between the three Tigray cross-in-square churches are locally recognised but not fully concordant with the traditions associated with the individual establishments. Abraha-wa-Atsbaha is regarded as the oldest hypogeum in the group, as befits its status as the supposed burial place of Aksum's rulers at the time Christianity was established. The traditions do not, however, specify whether the remains of these kings were buried here initially, or translated from elsewhere.[36] It is also unclear whether this church was a place of interment, or one where relics were preserved. The funerary or reliquary nature of all three monuments appears

[36] This is a significant point, particularly in connection with Abraha-wa-Atsbaha. Although it is not definitely known that former interments at Aksum were attributed to these rulers (*cf.* Chapter 9), it would not be surprising if their remains had been translated to eastern Tigray after the transfer of the kingdom's capital.

Fig. 80 Interior of the Tigray cross-in-square rock-hewn church of Tcherqos Wukro (from the *Illustrated London News*, 1868)

incontestable but, so far as I am aware, there is no surviving tradition of those who were interred at – or whose relics were taken to – Tcherqos Wukro or Mika'el Amba.[37]

The strong similarity between the three Tigray cross-in-square churches contrasts with the disparity in the ages traditionally ascribed to them. Buxton proposed a date in the eleventh or twelfth centuries for the group as a whole; this seems to be based on inconclusive arguments. Preference for a slightly earlier date – tenth or eleventh centuries – is hinted at by Lepage and Mercier.[38] The present writer, while recognising the problems enumerated above, has argued for an eighth-to-tenth-century bracket.[39]

The distribution of the Tigray cross-in-square churches extends as far west as the escarpment forming the eastern edge of the Tigray highlands. To the north, still bordering the escarpment, the land becomes more mountainous and less fertile. Here are found a number of ancient churches, one of which may represent an outlier to the groups of funerary churches considered above. This remote and poorly preserved rock-hewn church of Yohannes Metmek Gazien lies at an altitude of 3000 m, 33 km from Atsbi on the track leading northwards to Edaga Hamus, and presents an unusual combination of architectural elements that are recorded singly elsewhere.[40] Externally, the church is not conspicuous, being marked by two timber-framed doorways of Aksumite style set into the cliff face, behind which the basilican church, comprising an exceptionally wide nave with a narrower aisle on either side, extends 24 m eastwards. The only arches present are exceptionally wide ones that originally spanned the nave at either end. The nave is separated from the aisles on each side by rows of three octagonal-sectioned pillars with cuboid capitals. These bear paintings in an early style and support a massive architrave. Additional, higher, architraves cross the aisle ceilings to link the pillars to pilasters on the outer walls. All ceilings are flat, the rock being carved to represent separate slabs as at Maryam Beraqit. The floor of the easternmost nave bay is raised by two steps bringing it to the level of the apsidal sanctuary, but there is no visible trace of a screen. On either side of the sanctuary are additional chambers which could formerly be entered through timber-framed Aksumite-style doorways at the east ends of the aisles.

As in the Tigray cross-in-square churches, these chambers – three interconnecting ones to the southeast, and a single one on the northeast – are large and elaborate. They are now empty and show no sign of their presumed funerary function, although a finely carved lantern ceiling serves to emphasise the former prominence of the largest, southeasternmost, chamber (Fig. 81). The similarity in treatment of ceilings with the funerary chapels of the Hawzien Plain is noteworthy, and the rock-hewn nature of such monuments is reminiscent of the Aksumite tombs discussed in Chapter 12. It appears likely that the church at Gazien, like the Tigray cross-in-square churches further to the south, is comparatively early in date and funerary or reliquary in origin.

Other early churches

Elsewhere in easternmost Tigray, most notably in the area between Mika'el Amba and Gazien, are several churches, both built and rock-hewn,

[37] *cf.* Gire & R. Schneider 1970.

[38] Buxton 1971: 80; Lepage & Mercier 2005: 73.

[39] D. Phillipson 2009a: 184–7.

[40] The church has been recorded by Plant 1985: 139–40, Juel-Jensen & Rowell 1975: 40, Lepage & Mercier 2005: 90–3, and D. Phillipson 2009a: 98–9.

Fig. 81 The southeastern chamber of Yohannes Metmek Gazien church, showing the rock-hewn lantern ceiling and a wooden door-frame set into the rock

almost all of which are tiny, elaborate, and early in date, although showing little standardisation.[41] This variation need occasion no surprise, for the communities responsible for these churches may have had little contact with one another, and have varied considerably both in size and in prosperity.

Mika'el Debra Selam,[42] located in a low-roofed cave 8 km northnorthwest of Atsbi, may be taken as an example. The church was unknown to the outside world until a brief note was published by Georg Gerster in 1967. Originally complete in itself, it has more recently been treated as the sanctuary of a larger church formed by walling-in the outer part of the cave. Although some other Tigray churches combine western built sections with rock-hewn parts further east, the inner church at Debra Selam seems unique in having most of its southern and eastern lower walls built, while the upper part of its interior space was carved out of the roof of the cave. In places, the cave was also extended sideways, notably near the northeast corner, to accommodate the inner church, part of whose north wall is thus rock-hewn rather than built.

The building has a stepped foundation of Aksumite type, effectively forming the lower part of the walls which display six horizontal beams with large and prominent monkey-heads, alternating with dressed stone masonry in place of the more usual mud-mortared rubble (Fig. 82). No sign of this construction-method is visible inside the church, confirming the supposition that the external timber features were more decorative than functional. The windows have fine lattices in stone or wood. In front of the door in the middle of the south wall, a free-standing arch has been erected, joined to the inner church by low walls and high-level beams to produce a sort of open porch; this may be a later addition to the first church, following its change of status when it became the sanctuary of an enlarged structure. At the west end is a narrow anteroom with a fine wood-panelled ceiling.

The inner church is almost square, 6.7 m from west to east, forming a tiny basilica. It comprised a nave, a domed central sanctuary with an inscribed apse, and two aisles each of two bays with rooms further east flanking the sanctuary. Flat architraves are absent, arcades separating the nave from the aisles being supported by pilasters – some built, others rock-hewn – and by square-sectioned monolithic pillars, all of which have massive bracket capitals. Above the arches, the nave is surrounded by an Aksumite frieze (see above), but there are no true window-apertures at this level since the church interior from the frieze upwards has been carved from the rock, the flat ceilings of the aisles being at about the level of the original cave roof. An exceptional survival is the wooden screen (Fig. 83) between the first and second nave bays; this, of pole and panel construction like those discussed above, is in excellent condition and retains its central arch. The panels are finely carved in relief with interwoven designs, and the arch is topped by a massive cross with flared arms; the whole wooden structure is strongly reminiscent of that – perhaps broadly contemporary – noted above at Mika'el Amba and, like it, clearly inspired by the stone screens (Chapters 11 and 15) that had been imported to Adulis in earlier times.

Extensive mural paintings survive in the interior, including representations of Christ in majesty supported by the four animals (Chapter 11), of Christ's

41 Only one example can be treated here as an example. For details of some others, with illustrations and supporting references, see Lepage & Mercier 2005: 62-71; D. Phillipson 2009a: 71–4.

42 Gire & R. Schneider 1970: 73–4; Buxton 1971: 76–7; Jäger & Pearce 1974: 132–5; Juel-Jensen & Rowell 1975: 17; Plant 1985: 109–10; Lepage & Mercier 2005: 94–101; D. Phillipson 2009a: 68–71.

Fig. 82 The earliest component of the cave-set church of Mika'el Debra Selam, with decorative wooden beams-and-monkey heads construction

Fig. 83 The fine wooden screen at Mika'el Debra Selam

Date AD						
500	)					
	) Debra					
	) Damo	)				
600	)	)				
		)				
		) *Hawzien*				
700		) *Plain*				
		)	)			
		)	)			
800			) *Tigray*			
			) *cross-*	)		
			) *in-*	)		
900			) *square*	) Debra		
			)	) Selam		
			)	)		
1000						
1100						
					)	
					)	
1200					) *Maryam Wkro*	
					)	)
					)	)
1300						) *Debra Tsion*
						)
						)
1400						

Fig. 84 Proposed chronology of early Tigray churches; two later churches, not discussed in this book, are included for comparison

entry into Jerusalem on a mule, and of two people riding a prancing elephant.[43] The murals – executed on dry plaster – display several oriental aspects, although other stylistic features link them with early murals in Ethiopian churches elsewhere; explanatory Ge'ez inscriptions are notably absent. Ewa Balicka-Witakowska noted stylistic similarities with Egyptian paintings of the late twelfth century; if accepted, this correlation might suggest a *terminus ante quem* for the construction of the inner church itself.[44]

Chronology and historical implications

For reasons outlined above, age-estimates for Ethiopian churches – both built and rock-hewn – must be reviewed critically. A recent re-evaluation[45] has yielded tentative results which are summarised in Fig. 84. For Tigray, the picture that emerges has the following principal features. The church at

[43] Lepage 1976; Gerster 1970: pls 48–59; Lepage & Mercier 2005: 95–101; Chojnacki 2003: 14.

[44] Balicka-Witakowska 2005a; see also Pascher 2005; Chojnacki 2005b. There is no reason to suppose that the paintings were contemporary with the original construction.

[45] D. Phillipson 2009a: 184–7.

Debra Damo, although much altered subsequently, probably originated in the sixth century, as argued in Chapter 11. An age similar – or slightly later – may with somewhat less confidence be suggested for the earliest tomb-feature at Degum, followed – perhaps between the seventh and ninth centuries – by the funerary or reliquary churches at the same site, at Beraqit and at Hawzien. Regionally differentiated, and perhaps only slightly later again, are the grand Tigray cross-in-square churches and the almost invariably elaborate but tiny churches near the eastern escarpment. All the Tigray churches described in this chapter – with several others – appear to date no later than the end of the first millennium. The eleventh century seems to have been a time when few, if any, churches were created in Tigray. When, in the twelfth century, the process was resumed, the churches were significantly different: often larger and more elaborate than their predecessors, they were often also in high and relatively inaccessible locations; architecturally, many of them placed less emphasis on form and quality of execution, but more on elaborate mural decoration. Unlike most of their predecessors, many were monastic institutions, and the funerary or reliquary associations that had been prominent in earlier times were no longer apparent.[46]

Before considering historical correlations and implications, it is appropriate to turn briefly southwards – to what is now the eastern part of Amhara Region. There, beyond a significant gap in southernmost Tigray, ancient buildings and rock-hewn features are also known, most notably at and in the surroundings of Lalibela, discussed in Chapter 17. The oldest surviving features at Lalibela included rock-hewn and built elements, sometimes apparently combined, and were not originally created as churches, although at least some were subsequently altered and converted to ecclesiastical use. Their original use seems to have been defensive. Detailed consideration of Lalibela chronology is offered in Chapter 17; it may merely be noted here that evidence for churches appears to date principally to the tenth and eleventh centuries, with its principal florescence coinciding with the period – noted above – when church-creation virtually ceased in Tigray. The defensive features are demonstrably older; although how much older cannot yet be ascertained, an age in or around the eighth century appears likely.[47] There can thus be no doubt that churches were in regular use in several – but probably not all – parts of Tigray for hundreds of years before there is any evidence for them in Amhara Region.

Conclusion

Evidence has been presented in this chapter for the effective abandonment of Aksum as a political centre during the first half of the seventh century, and for the subsequent florescence of eastern Tigray as a more localised focus of Christian civilisation. Knowledge about the last quarter of the first millennium in the latter area is sparse, being effectively limited to a small number of ancient churches, but the picture currently emerging points to significant changes in about the eleventh century. These are discussed in Chapter 17.

46 For illustrated details of some examples, see Lepage & Mercier 2005.

47 More detailed arguments are provided in Chapter 17; see also D. Phillipson 2009a: 184–91.

Part Three

After Aksum

17

The Zagwe Dynasty

The Zagwe and their dating

Following the decline of Aksum's successor kingdom in eastern Tigray, or its rulers' loss of authority, a period of fluidity is indicated. It is not possible to estimate with any confidence when or for how long this situation prevailed, but it would be plausible to place it in or around the eleventh century when (as argued in Chapter 16) major changes seem to have taken place. Eventually, a new centralised authority was established; it was based, not in Tigray, but further to the south in what is now Amhara Region – more precisely, in the mountains of Lasta east and north of the upper Takezze river. In due course, if not initially, its political centre was at Adefa[1] near the ecclesiastical establishment called Roha[2] – subsequently renamed Lalibela after the famous king.[3] This authority was in the hands of a dynasty, recalled in historical tradition under the name Zagwe, which probably originated – as its name has been held to imply – among Cushitic-speaking Agau peoples. The Zagwe, however, soon adopted Christianity – if they had not already done so – and, at least in some contexts, the Semitic speech of Aksum. Indeed, as is argued below, the Zagwe seem to have been as keen to stress their Aksumite credentials as their opponents and successors were in later times to deny them.[4]

Historical information about the Zagwe dynasty is not plentiful, and most of what is available was not recorded in writing until long after the period to which it relates. Very few written historical records survive from the period before 1270; those that purport to refer to such events exist in copies that were

[1] For the possible location of Adefa, see Finneran 2009.

[2] The relevance of Edessa, now in Turkey but formerly a holy city of Christian greater Syria (Segal 1970: 62–109; Ball 2000: 89–96), also requires consideration, for it has been suggested that the name Roha – by which Lalibela was formerly known – may have been taken from al-Ruha, the Arabic name for Edessa, and that the present dedication of the Beta Danagel church at Lalibela refers to young women slaughtered at Edessa by order of the Roman Emperor Julian II (Heldman 1995: 33). If its similarity with al-Ruha is not derivative, the origin of the name Roha remains uncertain. Gervers (2003a: 39) suggested that use of an Arabic-derived toponym may have been based on physical characteristics rather than sacred associations. However, King Abgar of Edessa, believed to have established communication with Christ, was venerated in Ethiopia – but not demonstrably before the fifteenth century (Getatchew 1989; Heldman 1995). King Abgar notwithstanding, the argument for a link between Roha and Edessa is weak and, until further evidence is forthcoming, may be dismissed as an attempt to rationalise an apparent congruence of names.

[3] Use of 'Lalibela' as a toponym is not attested until the sixteenth or seventeenth centuries (D. Phillipson 2009a: 199–200); in formal contexts, the Ethiopian Orthodox Church still refers to the ecclesiastical establishment there as 'Debra Roha'. In this book, the word 'Lalibela' on its own is used as a toponym, the king of that name being differentiated by his royal title.

[4] For a recent overview of the Zagwe, see Tekeste 2006.

written subsequently, based either on oral traditions or on written versions no longer extant. In either case, the accounts have been subjected to adjustment in the light of changed political circumstances. Most surviving historical traditions relating to the Zagwe were thus not committed to writing until after the Zagwe themselves had been displaced, and are preserved only in forms acceptable to their rivals. It may be for this reason that accounts of their origin and rise are remarkably imprecise. For example, although the *gadl* [= biography or hagiography] of King Lalibela edited by Perruchon[5] was based on a nineteenth-century copy,[6] internal evidence suggests that the original work was compiled in the fifteenth century – under antithetical rule more than two hundred years after the events that it purported to describe.

The chronology of the Zagwe dynasty has been a subject of much contention among historians of Ethiopia.[7] Estimates of its duration – based on traditionally recounted royal genealogies – range widely between 130 and 370 years; since its termination is securely dated around 1270 (see below), these figures place its inception between 900 and 1140.[8] Although the most detailed calculations[9] have yielded figures of approximately three hundred years for its duration, many historians have followed Taddesse Tamrat[10] and accepted a 'short' chronology, placing the rise of the Zagwe in the early twelfth century. This dating was, however, based on ideas prevalent in the 1970s, when it was believed that the final decline of Aksum as a capital had taken place in the tenth century. Now that the latter event has been re-dated, there is a gap of some three centuries which needs to be taken into account. I contend that a date for the rise of the Zagwe in or even shortly before the eleventh century is more probable, and fits better with the general historical reconstructions now proposed.[11] The chronology set out in this book, with a shift of the political centre southwards from Tigray around the early-eleventh century, reopens the question of when Zagwe authority rose to prominence. If this event did indeed take place two hundred years earlier than is commonly believed, a persuasive re-interpretation of the Zagwe episode becomes possible.

A major change took place in the third quarter of the thirteenth century, around 1270. The Zagwe rulers were replaced by a dynasty that based its claim to legitimacy on direct descent from Aksumite royalty and thus, ultimately, from Solomon and the Queen of Sheba.[12] The claim for Solomonic legitimacy, formally enshrined in Ethiopian political pronouncements as recently as the 1955 Constitution, has given rise to the term 'Solomonic restoration' by which the dynastic change is still often known.[13] The propaganda that accompanied the change proved extraordinarily successful, presenting as a return to legitimacy

5 Perruchon 1892.

6 British Library Or. 718.

7 See Tekeste 2006.

8 See Sergew 1972: 239–42.

9 Godet 1988; Andersen 2000.

10 This was proposed by Taddesse (1972: 53–7, 1977) at a time when it was widely believed that the decline of Aksum did not take place until the tenth or eleventh centuries.

11 For a similar view, reached independently, see Tekeste 2006. For a thorough and dispassionate overview of controversies surrounding the Zagwe, see Derat 2010.

12 This in itself provides further evidence that the *Kebra Negast* incorporates material of pre-Zagwe age (see Chapter 6).

13 See Huntingford 1965b.

what was, in fact, a seizure of power by an ethnic group distinct from that which had ruled previously.[14]

For the purpose of this discussion, the point to be emphasised is that the 'Solomonic restoration' involved the effective transfer of political power from people of Agau descent – originally Cushitic-speaking – to Semitic-speaking Amhara; it was a further stage in the continuing southward shift of the power-centre that had begun with the decline of Aksum. It must be recognised that the areas subject to these authorities were in a state of constant flux – expanding and amalgamating as well as contracting and devolving. The dominance of Christianity continued in the highlands, being so firmly entrenched that political change had but slight direct impact on ecclesiastical affairs.

Lalibela and related sites

The rock-hewn churches of Lasta and other parts of Amhara Region show significant differences from those in Tigray. The latter, as noted in Chapter 16, were hewn from hard sandstone in which elements such as window- and door-frames could not be carved, but were made of wood set into the rock.[15] Although difficult to work, the sandstone has in most cases retained its form well, with the result that many churches hewn from it are still in remarkably good condition. In Lasta, by contrast, the location of churches was dictated by the limited distribution of the relatively soft volcanic tuff from which they were hewn.[16] Rock-hewn churches here were sometimes much larger than their counterparts further north. Wooden architectural features and finer detail could be more easily carved from this tuff but, although its cut surfaces harden when exposed to the air, it has proved much more susceptible to subsequent wear and weathering.[17] The Tigray and Lasta churches form geographically separate groups, separated by some 100 km from which no ancient churches have been recorded. As will be argued below, there are also significant differences in age between the two groups.

In establishing the relative chronology of the Lasta churches, those at Lalibela have yielded significant information. Because they form two tight complexes,[18] it has proved possible in several instances to demonstrate their relative chronology on the basis of physical inter-relationships rather than on purely stylistic grounds. Ecclesiastical tradition unequivocally attributes all the Lalibela churches to the reign of the king whose name the place now bears;[19] historians are agreed that he ruled at the end of the twelfth century and the beginning of the thirteenth. I am convinced, however, that the churches'

[14] Sergew 1972: 289–92; Taddesse 1972: 66–8; Heldman & Getatchew 1987.

[15] See, for example, D. Phillipson 2009a: fig. 145. Note, however, that Aksumite friezes were carved in their totality (*ibid*: fig. 146).

[16] It was clearly sometimes difficult to estimate the depth of tuff that was available for carving in any particular spot. At Beta Madhane Alem and Beta Giyorgis, underlying basalt was encountered that proved virtually impossible to carve.

[17] Asfawossen & Yodit 2011.

[18] For a photograph, taken from the air, that shows the inter-relationship of churches at the Eastern Complex very clearly, see Fritsch 2008: fig. 4. The most comprehensive description of the Lalibela churches is that by Bianchi Barriviera 1962–63, unfortunately illustrated by excessively reduced versions of that author's engravings, the originals of which (*idem* 1943, 1957) are very rare. Superb photographs were published by Gerster 1970 and in several subsequent picture-books on Ethiopian art and architecture. An illustrated overview, on which the present account is based, is in D. Phillipson 2009a. For complementary research, reaching not incompatible conclusions, see Fauvelle-Aymar *et al.* 2010.

[19] *cf.* Mengistu 2004.

Fig. 85 The façade of Beta Gabri'el-Rafa'el at Lalibela: behind, and not visible here, are older rock-hewn features of stages I and II, originally defensive but subsequently converted for ecclesiastical use; the visible features of the façade shown here probably date from this more recent period

creation spanned a much longer period, but I argue below that this conclusion is not incompatible with the ecclesiastical tradition.[20]

A brief account of the Lalibela churches most conveniently begins with the Eastern Complex.[21] Here are located two rock-hewn features, now known as the churches of Beta Gabri'el-Rafa'el and Beta Merkurios, both of which clearly saw several developmental phases before attaining their present forms (Fig. 85). Their earlier phases lacked both ecclesiastical elements and architectural features of Aksumite inspiration. Detailed examination of Beta Merkurios[22] has been particularly informative: its extension and conversion for use as a church clearly predated creation of the adjacent Beta Emmanuel (Fig. 86), which is one – arguably the most refined – of the so-called 'monolithic' basilican churches which each stand isolated in their own great pit, being fully and elaborately carved externally as well as internally.[23] The whole of the Eastern Complex is surrounded by a deep rock-cut trench, in a wall of which was hewn Beta Abba Libanos, traditionally believed to have been one of the last of the Lalibela churches to be created.

The nearby Northern Complex likewise shows several successive phases, although the earliest ones are not represented. Beta Danagel seems to have been the first church hewn here. It was followed by two 'monolithic' basilican churches, Beta Madhane Alem and Beta Maryam (Fig. 87), both of which were probably broadly contemporary with Beta Emmanuel, noted above at the Eastern Complex. Beta Madhane Alem is unique both for its large size and for being surrounded by an external colonnade, now extensively restored.[24] Beta Maryam is exceptional for its fine interior decoration, both carved and painted, which is without parallel elsewhere at Lalibela. The original western entrance to Beta Maryam was subsequently rendered impassable by the excavation of further churches at a lower level.[25] These include Beta Mika'el and Beta Golgotha in which is a tomb traditionally ascribed to King Lalibela himself; some of their windows have distinctive decoration of a type only attested in the most recent churches at Lalibela. Such windows are also seen at the outlying Beta Giyorgis (Fig. 88), separate from the two principal complexes.

When the results outlined above are combined, five successive developmental stages may be recognised at Lalibela (Fig. 89). It seems that the most ancient examples – created in stages I and II – did not begin as churches at all, but as defensive features of some sort, protected by massive above-ground stone-built walls, entered by an elaborately protected route, and linked to one another by an underground tunnel (Fig. 90). Architectural features in the Aksumite style are markedly absent. Although these earliest features may readily be discerned, they were subsequently subjected to major modification on several occasions, one of which – stage III – involved the excavation of

[20] D. Phillipson 2009a: 177–81.

[21] This is contrary to the order in which most guides recommend that visitors should proceed.

[22] Beta [= House of ...] is the term adopted at Lalibela to designate a church according to the dedication of its principal *tabot* (*cf.* footnote 30, below). In Tigray, Enda [= Place of ...] may be used in the same way.

[23] In some churches, most notably Beta Madhane Alem and Beta Emmanuel, the internal and external carving were lined up with truly remarkable precision. Elsewhere, as at Beta Abba Libanos, this process was less successful.

[24] The replacements may be distinguished by being built with blocks of tuff; the originals are integral to the rock from which the church was hewn.

[25] Cutting down to create Beta Golgotha and Beta Mika'el proceeded directly below the portal that gave access to this entrance. The portal may still be seen (D. Phillipson 2009a: fig. 268) but is now totally inaccessible from the west.

Fig. 86 The west façade of the 'monolithic' Beta Emanuel, Lalibela

Fig. 87 Beta Maryam, Lalibela

Fig. 88 Window with arabesque decoration, Beta Giyorgis, Lalibela

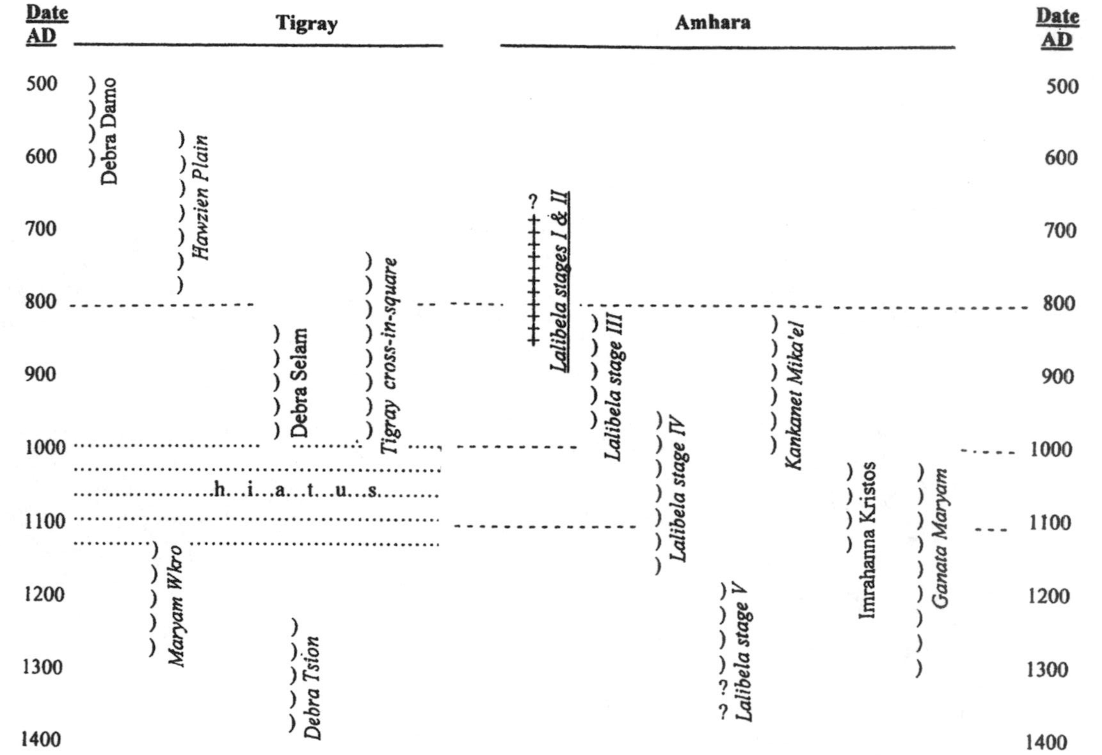

Fig. 89 Proposed chronology of the churches and other features at Lalibela, with those in eastern Tigray included for comparison (after D. Phillipson 2009a)

extensions – stylistically very different – which now serve as sanctuaries and which mark their conversion to ecclesiastical use (*cf.* Figs 90 and 85). Beta Danagel, also, was probably created at this time. It is only at this third stage that Aksumite-style features may first be recognised.

In the fourth stage, a major and very striking change took place. This is the stage to which belong the great 'monolithic' basilican churches for which Lalibela is justly famous. Architectural features of Aksumite origin now predominated but, in contrast with the practice in Tigray, door- and window-frames were not wooden inserts but were carved integrally from the rock, and horizontal wooden beams – but not monkey-heads – were represented on their walls (*cf.* Fig. 86).

To the final stage – V – at Lalibela may be attributed the remarkable sub-complex incorporating the churches of Mika'el and Golgotha, where King Lalibela himself is traditionally believed to have been buried. These churches were excavated below features associated with one of the 'monolithic' basilicas and, being so deep in the rock, necessitated major alterations to the drainage system. Beta Abba Libanos and Beta Giyorgis also belong here.

Five stages having been recognised in the development of the church complex at Lalibela, the next step is the attempt to estimate their absolute ages and to consider their historical contexts. Stages I and II were clearly the oldest, but are not otherwise easy to pinpoint: they could have begun as long ago as the eighth century, or even the seventh. Significantly, as noted above and in Chapter 16, rock-hewn features attributed to these stages were defensive, not ecclesiastical, in function, and they do not display Aksumite-style elements. Stage III, which saw the first demonstrably Christian innovations, must be significantly later, perhaps tenth century. It was at this time that the earlier, defensive, structures were apparently converted to ecclesiastical use.

Before the tenth century, rock-hewn features were created in many areas of what is now northern Ethiopia, including the place subsequently known as Lalibela. In Tigray, most of these rock-hewn features were churches, displaying many architectural features of Aksumite inspiration. At Lalibela, on the other hand, the earliest ones were defensive, with no affinities to Aksumite architecture. The stage-I rock-hewn features at Lalibela, and the massive masonry structures that appear to have been associated or contemporary with them, may represent the non-ecclesiastical importance of the place in pre-Zagwe times. This last suggestion is wholly incompatible with the interpretation and chronology proposed by Lepage who, on the strength of references in the *History of the Patriarchs of the Egyptian Church*, attributed these features to the activities of Mika'el, an early thirteenth-century Egyptian metropolitan, during the reign of King Lalibela.[26] As the arguments here presented make clear, Lalibela stage I must pre-date Mika'el and King Lalibela by at least three centuries – perhaps even as many as five.

Lalibela stage IV, by contrast, was firmly Christian and its basilican architecture owed much to inspiration that originated in Aksum. It has been suggested that the largest of the Lalibela churches, Beta Madhane Alem with its external colonnade, may replicate the original Maryam Tsion Cathedral at Aksum.[27] If that were so, it would be a clear indication of a desire to emphasise Lalibela's status as a successor to Aksum. This fits well with what little is known about the transfer of political power southwards from Tigray to Lasta, epitomised in the Zagwe 'usurpation'. A date centred on the eleventh century would best accommodate this scenario.

[26] Lepage 2002; *cf.* Munro-Hay 1997.

[27] Dabbert 1938: 70–1; Buxton 1947: 28; Buxton & Matthews 1974.

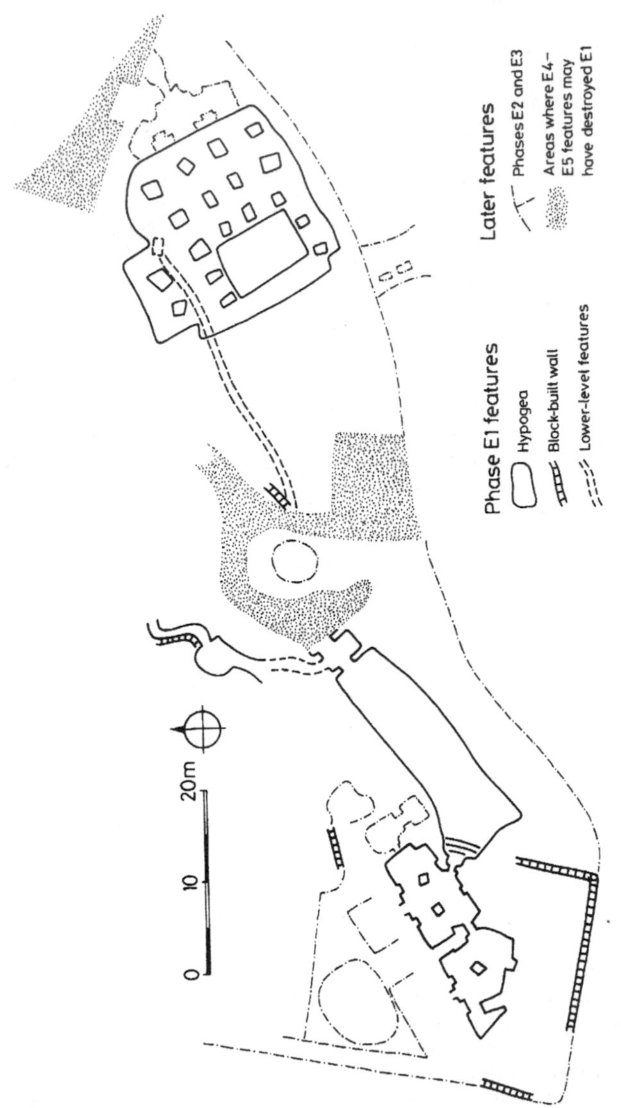

Fig. 90 Sketch-pan of the earliest features at Lalibela (after D. Phillipson 2009a)

The rock-hewn features specifically linked by tradition with King Lalibela himself, either by attribution or by virtue of his burial there, were created in stage V.[28] That stage subsumes locations central to the view of Lalibela replicating the topography of Jerusalem and its environs. The early years of King Lalibela's reign coincided with the fall of Jerusalem to Salah ed-Din in 1187, which event may have given rise to fears which stimulated development of a local counterpart.[29] Only stage V should be attributed to the late twelfth and early thirteenth centuries, when King Lalibela reigned at or close to the place that subsequently bore his name. It was during this stage that the earlier rock-hewn features were incorporated within a symbolic recreation of Jerusalem and its surroundings.

Persistent traditions attributing all the churches to King Lalibela's reign should thus be interpreted as indicating the time when the most recent ones were added, and when the complex as a whole received its present form and symbolism. This would explain the traditional attribution of the whole to King Lalibela, and also the presence in several of the churches of *manabert tabot* with inscriptions naming that potentate,[30] whether or not they are actually as ancient as their inscriptions imply.

Symbolism

There can be little doubt that symbolic values have long been attached to the churches and other features at the place now known as Lalibela, but these have clearly changed as the site itself has developed.[31] Some suggestions, notably that of pre-Christian nature-worship advocated by Irmgard Bidder, no longer merit serious consideration.[32] Jacqueline Pirenne saw numerous reflections of the Apocalypse.[33] It is now widely accepted, however, not least by the ecclesiastical community at Lalibela itself, that the complex as a whole symbolically represents Jerusalem and places that would have been visited by Ethiopian pilgrims travelling thither. This is reflected in the names currently attached to a number of prominent features in the immediate landscape, including the hills Debra Tabor and Debra Zeit [= Mount of Olives] and the Yordanos torrent. Similar names refer to rock-hewn features, notably Beta Golgotha and the Tomb of Adam; the adjacent church of Mika'el sometimes retains its former designation of Beta Debra Sina [= Mount Sinai]. Significantly, these particular features are here attributed to the latest stage, V, in the Lalibela sequence. The legend that the ensemble as a whole

[28] Gervers (2003a, 2003b) argued that these features were not created until about the fifteenth century. Had that been the case, one would have expected Francisco Alvares, who visited Lalibela – including Beta Golgotha – early in the next century (Beckingham & Huntingford 1961: 205–27), to have recognised it as a recent creation and to have mentioned that fact.

[29] Sergew 1972: 262, 273; Richard Pankhurst 1998: 52; but see van Donzel 1998.

[30] Strelcyn 1979; Gigar 1984, 1987, Lepage 2002; Bosc-Tiessé 2010. A *manbara tabot* [plural: *manabert tabot*] is a cupboard-like receptacle, usually of carved wood but occasionally of stone, in which a *tabot* is housed. A functioning *manbara tabot* stands centrally in the sanctuary of an Ethiopian church. A *tabot* [plural: *tabotat*] is correctly a wooden or stone plaque that symbolically represents the Mosaic Tablets of the Law. It is the physical presence of a *tabot* that gives a church its sanctity, and a church derives its name from the dedication of its principal *tabot*. The term is also more loosely applied to the receptacle in which a *tabot* is housed, in which case it is sometimes informally translated 'Ark of the Covenant'.

[31] Heldman 1995.

[32] Bidder 1958; *cf*. Gervers 2003a: 26.

[33] Pirenne 1989.

was created by or under King Lalibela following a vision has every aspect of *post facto* rationale. Links between Ethiopia and Jerusalem probably go back to Aksumite times and the subsequent presence there of an Ethiopian community, at the Church of the Holy Sepulchre and elsewhere, is well documented.[34] Attachment to Jerusalem on the part of Ethiopians has long been noteworthy.[35]

There are, however, other aspects to the symbolism of Lalibela.[36] The suggestion, plausible but unproven, that Beta Madhane Alem might have intentionally replicated features, or even the whole, of the ancient cathedral at Aksum has already been noted, and this would accord with the self-conscious proliferation of Aksumite architectural features in the Lalibela churches, especially those attributed to stage IV. Such a view would conform with what is known about the southward movement of the political 'centre of gravity' following the decline of Aksum, and with the implication by Abu al-Makarim that the Ark of the Covenant may have been at Lalibela during the late twelfth century.[37]

The culmination, but only the culmination, of this process came in the reign of King Lalibela, when the whole complex of hypogea received near-final additions and took its overall symbolism as an Ethiopian counterpart of Jerusalem and its environs. This was surely regarded by the Zagwe as stressing their status as the true heirs of Christian Aksum. However, only half a century after the death of King Lalibela, the Zagwe were themselves displaced by rulers from even further south, who successfully presented themselves as the rightful 'Solomonic' successors to the Aksumite kings.

Some other churches

There are other ancient churches – built as well as rock-hewn – in this part of Amhara Region which supplement and support the argument outlined above. Among the built ones, that of Imrahanna Kristos (Figs 91 and 92), standing in a huge cave to the north of Lalibela, is particularly significant.[38] It is a totally homogeneous design and construction, with no evidence for subsequent modification, incorporating many elements of Aksumite architecture, with wall and ceiling decoration in which some Egyptian influences may perhaps be detected. Tradition indicates that it was erected at the instigation of one of King Lalibela's predecessors, the priest-king from whom the church has taken its name; the early twelfth-century date conventionally ascribed to him may be somewhat too recent.[39]

High above Lalibela is the rarely visited rock-hewn church of Kankanet Mika'el, which may be one of the earliest in the region.[40] Another outlier is

34 See Chapter 15; also Cerulli 1943–47; Meinardus 1965.

35 *e.g.* Bruce 1790; see also R. Grierson 1993: 5–17.

36 Heldman 1992.

37 Abu al-Makarim is now recognised as author – *c.* 1200 – of the work formerly attributed to Abu Salih (Evetts 1895: 105–7; Zanetti 1995; but see R. Grierson & Munro-Hay 1999: 240–57; Munro-Hay 2005a: 76–80).

38 Balicka-Witakowska & Gervers 2001; Girma *et al.* 2001; D. Phillipson 2009a: 74–80.

39 For a recent and comprehensive evaluation of the evidence relating to King Imrahanna Kristos, see Derat 2010.

40 D. Phillipson 2009a: 110–2.

Fig. 91 The cave-built church of Imrahanna Kristos, north of Lalibela

Fig. 92 Wooden construction of the nave at Imrahanna Kristos

Fig. 93 Ganata Maryam: the external colonnade on the south side

Ganata Maryam,[41] a monolithic basilica with an external colonnade (Fig. 93) like that at the much larger Lalibela Madhane Alem. The interior of Ganata Maryam preserves fine paintings (Fig. 94) with extensive explanatory inscriptions.[42] These have often been cited as indicating the original late-thirteenth-century age of the church but – in my opinion – this cannot be proven, and Ganata Maryam may have been hewn from the rock somewhat earlier.

Historical correlations

Ethiopian history provides little evidence for close linkage between political and ecclesiastical developments.[43] This has so far been particularly true of the late-first millennium before the assumption of political power by the Zagwe dynasty. Noteworthy also is the contrast between the still-respected sanctity of several Zagwe rulers and their political status, at least in the eyes of their successors, as usurpers. Three Zagwe kings are now regarded as saints by the Ethiopian Orthodox Church, but none of the succeeding 'Solomonic' kings has been thus canonised.[44] Although the dynastic affiliation of rulers might seem of little relevance to popular and religious history, the ethnic connotations of the Zagwe ascendancy suggest that further consideration may well improve understanding of this period.

41 D. Phillipson 2009a: 112–8.

42 On the paintings, see principally Lepage 1975; Balicka-Witakowska 1998–99. On the dating, see Sergew 1972: 291; Heldman & Getatchew 1987: 3–4).

43 Shahid 1976; Munro-Hay 1997.

44 Sergew 1972: 251.

Fig. 94 The painted interior of Ganata Maryam: the south aisle seen from the east

Study of the architecture and chronology of early Ethiopian churches, particularly when geographical considerations are taken into account, permits several aspects of post-Aksumite history to be clarified. As noted above, evidence for late Aksumite Christianity is more abundant in eastern Tigray than in the west, location of the capital in the latter area notwithstanding. Although it was at one time believed that Aksum continued to serve as a capital as late as the tenth century, by the early 1980s it had been recognised on archaeological and numismatic grounds that its terminal decline had taken place some three hundred years earlier.[45] While this revision has not been seriously disputed, not all historians of Ethiopia have yet taken it fully into account.

It has long been recognised that, with the seventh-century decline of Aksum, the capital was transferred to a more southeasterly location (see Chapter 16). This may now be recognised as being in accord with the evidence for a florescence of funerary hypogea and churches in and around the Hawzien Plain in the immediately post-Aksumite centuries. The prominence of eastern Tigray, however, seems to have lasted for little more than three hundred years: by the end of the tenth century, creation of churches there seems to have diminished or ceased and the centre of gravity again to have moved further to the south, into the Lasta area of what is now Amhara Region. This model is in keeping with the chronology proposed in this book, and serves to explain the discontinuity between the Tigray and Amhara sequences. It also allows a new interpretation of the Lalibela site which is in keeping both with the visible archaeological features and with current historical understanding.

How closely King Lalibela combined his political and religious centres is not known, but he certainly bestowed – or was later purported to have bestowed – much economic influence on his ecclesiastical foundations through grants of land.[46] Political ambition may have contributed to the Zagwe desire to emphasise their Christian and Aksumite credentials; the attitude of their 'Solomonic' successors certainly indicates that this was the case. At Lalibela and elsewhere in the Zagwe domain, built and rock-hewn churches were created between the eleventh and twelfth centuries with a seemingly self-conscious emphasis on Aksumite connections.

Now let us look at the overall picture that emerges from this study of the ancient built and rock-hewn churches of Amhara Region.[47] The earliest rock-hewn features – created at Lalibela perhaps as early as the eighth century – were not initially churches, being only subsequently converted to that use. There is some evidence, which requires further investigation, for the creation of churches in Amhara Region during the tenth century. Their great florescence, however, came in the eleventh and early-twelfth centuries, when Imrahanna Kristos was built and the great 'monolithic' basilicas at Lalibela were excavated. Rather later, the church-complexes at the latter place were extended, including creation of the burial-place for King Lalibela himself, and the site took the aspect and symbolism that has ensured its eminence as a place of pilgrimage ever since.

This picture offers a major contrast with that proposed above for eastern Tigray. Churches were being created in Tigray for hundreds of years before they are attested in Amhara. The architecture of the two regions may be paralleled, but only in general ways. In Tigray, Aksumite elements were noticeable throughout, but in Amhara they were initially absent. In the eleventh century, there was a

45 Munro-Hay 1989a: 12–26, 1989d.

46 *e.g.* Perruchon 1892.

47 D. Phillipson 2009a: 74–85, 107–18, 123–81.

marked hiatus in church-creation in Tigray, but a major florescence in Amhara, with Aksumite features being strongly – even self-consciously – emphasised.

As has been noted, Lalibela has also become a focus for Agau pride and nationalism,[48] perhaps intensified since the old Lasta province was incorporated within Amhara Region. Nevertheless, it is from the inexorable growth of tourism and the lack – so far – of effective visitor management that Lalibela's religious eminence is most seriously threatened.

[48] *cf.* Mengistu 2004; for a contrary argument that this development began several centuries ago, see Gervers 2003a, 2003b.

18

Epilogue
The Future of the Past in the Northern Horn

Writing this book has emphasised not only what we know but what we do not. In this epilogue I shall attempt to offer some guidelines that future researchers and administrators may find useful. I hope that these suggestions may be of particular interest to the increasing numbers of Ethiopian and Eritrean scholars who are embarking on careers involving the study of their countries' past and the preservation of its remains. Of course, what cannot be taken into account is the chance unanticipated discovery such as the Almaqah temple at Maqaber Ga'ewa near Wukro, described in Chapter 3. Situations such as that emphasise the need for trained, locally-based archaeologists who can undertake rescue investigations, as the Tigray Tourism and Culture Commission was fortunately able to do at Wukro. How many other important discoveries are being lost without record as the range and scale of development increases? The cost of a local archaeological service would be minute in comparison with that of the development works whose impact it could serve to mitigate – or even to exploit. In many countries, the cost of such mitigation is regarded as an integral part of the development budget, but one that has far-reaching benefits for tourism.

Tourism is a topic that merits further thought in this context. In the northern Horn, it should no longer be regarded exclusively as a means of attracting overseas visitors and the hard currency that they bring with them. As the local middle class grows in size and prosperity, becoming in the process increasingly urbanised and separated from its cultural roots, locally-based tourism becomes all the more important, not only in spreading prosperity from towns to rural areas, but also in nurturing citizens' well-being and sense of identity. In this area, growth and dissemination of knowledge about the past, and preservation of what remains from that past, both have important roles. Conservation – clearly – must be selective, but selection should be based on knowledge and the research that generates it; conservation and research cannot be separated.

All too often – as demonstrated by recent examples in both Ethiopia and Eritrea – archaeological excavation has contributed to destruction, through failure of investigators either to conserve their sites or to backfill their excavations. It would be invidious to cite examples, but responsibility for such problems must be shared by the excavators and by the governmental authorities who do not routinely insist on appropriate measures being taken. Allied to this is the long-lasting difficulty – that has been noted repeatedly in this book – caused by non-publication of full research results. Such publication, to be effective and to reflect the needs both of scholarship and of the interested public in the northern Horn itself, must be appropriate and accessible to both audiences.

A vital foundation for future research is accessible knowledge about what has already been discovered. Between 1977 and 1983, Eric Godet published two invaluable papers summarising archaeological discoveries in the northern

Horn relating to the Aksumite and earlier periods. This work urgently needs to be brought up-to-date, not only by adding the large number of discoveries that have been made since Godet's initial compilation, but also by re-evaluating all this material in the light of greatly increased knowledge and understanding. This important task is one that can only be undertaken effectively by locally-based scholars with access to museum collections as well as to publications. An allied project, perhaps even more valuable, would involve preparation of a handbook to identification and dating of locally-produced artefacts, notably pottery and lithic industries.

In writing the present book, three major points have emerged, all of which provide pointers for future research: the diversity of the northern Horn's population during the last millennium BC, the scale and complexity of the Aksumite state's organisation, and the strong locally-based continuity that may be traced throughout – and beyond – the timespan considered here. In the concluding section of this intentionally brief chapter, I develop the implications raised by each of these points.

Pioneering archaeological research almost inevitably emphasised the sites that were already known and those that were most prominent in the landscape. This led – and still leads – to work on monumental buildings, elaborate tombs, sculpture and inscriptions, in other words, on the élite elements of the ancient population. Only recently has it been recognised that there were other, more numerous, elements who did not possess these luxuries and who effectively continued the lifestyles of their predecessors. These non-élite populations who inhabited the northern Horn during the last millennium BC require much more detailed investigation, set against the diverse and changing environments in which they lived. Gradually, and eventually, this will lead to the development of a far more comprehensive understanding than has been offered in this book.

The study of Aksumite civilisation has likewise seen an emphasis on its élite aspects, to some extent mitigated by investigation of the base provided by its subsistence economy. The present study has indicated that the geographical area directly subject to Aksumite rule – as opposed to influence – may have been somewhat smaller than has sometimes been claimed. This makes all the more remarkable its organisational achievements, for which two examples must suffice. First, manpower: the numbers of people who were organised to participate in works such as the quarrying, transport and erection of stelae cannot yet be estimated in any meaningful way, but must have totalled several thousand. As argued in this book, the capture and resettlement of subject peoples and their livestock doubtless contributed not only to the labour-force that was available, but also to the eventual over-exploitation and exhaustion of the Aksum hinterland. The second point arises directly from the first: the logistics of the resettlement process itself, if we are to believe that the precise figures recorded in Ezana's inscriptions give at least a realistic approximation of the numbers and quantities involved, would have been daunting. The daily provision of 22,000 loaves of bread – even small ones (Chapter 10) – would have involved not only resources but organisation. Our ignorance – so far – about Aksumite record-keeping on materials less durable than stone slabs represents a very serious loss, as comparison with Ptolemaic and Roman Egypt makes clear. A clearer picture could, however, be obtained from archaeological investigation of surviving materials: subject peoples would have differed in economy – the Bega, for example, were predominantly herders rather than cultivators – and in material culture from the Aksumites amongst whom they were resettled. Archaeological investigation, particularly emphasising non-élite sites, should indicate diversity of population and, ultimately, resettlement areas: our knowledge of the Aksumite kingdom would be transformed.

Appreciation of continuity is hampered by the fact that, whereas Aksumite-period sites have seen a fair amount of archaeological investigation, this is not yet true for those of subsequent times which have been primarily investigated by historians, including art-historians. This book has repeatedly argued for the breaking down of such disciplinary divisions; and it is for the period that followed the decline of Aksum and the eastward transfer of the state's capital (Chapter 16) that the difficulty is most acute and essential continuity obscured. In eastern Tigray and further to the south, virtually the only ancient sites that have been investigated in any detail are churches. We have effectively no knowledge of the domestic settlements, material culture, or economic practices of the people who made these churches; remedy of this deficiency is perhaps the most urgent need of all.

In making these observations and suggestions, I do not wish to be seen as seeking to dictate how research into the past of the northern Horn should proceed. New scholars, and an interested public that is both wider and better informed, will bring new approaches, emphases and paradigms. That is one of the reasons why the title of this book, which seeks to summarise and interpret what has already been discovered, begins with the word 'Foundations'.

Bibliographic References

Y. Abul-Haggag 1961. *A Contribution to the Physiography of Northern Ethiopia.* London: Athlone Press.

W. Y. Adams 1966. The Vintage of Nubia. *Kush* 14: 262–83.

W. Y. Adams 1993. The Invention of Nubia. C. Berger *et al.* 1993, 2: 17–22.

Admassou Shiferaou 1955. Rapport sur la découverte d'antiquités trouvées dans les locaux du Gouvernement général de Maqallé. *Annales d'Ethiopie* 1: 11–16.

Agatharchides of Cnidus: see Burstein 1989.

Agazi Negash 1997. Temben's place in the Neolithic of northern Ethiopia. pp. 389–98 in K. Fukui *et al.* (eds) *Ethiopia in Broader Perspective* (3 vols). Tokyo: Shoka.

Agazi Negash *et al.* 2011. Varieties and sources of artefactual obsidian in the Middle Stone Age of the Middle Awash, Ethiopia. *Archaeometry* 53: 661–73.

M. Almagro *et al.* 2002. *Qusayr 'Amra: Residencia y Baños Omeyas en el Desierto de Jordania* (2nd edn). Granada: Junta de Andalucia.

M. de Almeida, *Historia (geral) de Ethiopia a Alta ou Abassia*: see Beckingham & Huntingford 1954.

M. Alram 1999. Indo-Parthian and early Kushan chronology: the numismatic evidence. pp. 19–48 in M. Alram & D. E. Klimburg-Salter (eds) *Coins, Art and Chronology: essays on the pre-Islamic history of the Indo-Iranian borderlands.* Vienna: Österreichischen Akademie der Wissenschaften (*Philosophisch-Historische Klasse, Denkschriften* 280).

F. Altheim & R. Stiehl 1971. *Christentum am Roten Meer, vol. 1.* Berlin: de Gruyter.

F. Alvares. *Ho Preste Joam das Indias: verdadera informaçam das terras do Preste Joam*: see Beckingham & Huntingford 1961.

Amanuel Beyin & J. Shea 2008. Evidence for Middle and Later Stone Age cultures on the Buri Peninsula and Gulf of Zula, Red Sea coast of Eritrea. Schmidt *et al.* 2008d: 21–31.

P. R. Amidon (trans.) 1997. *The Church History of Rufinus of Aquileia, books 10 & 11.* New York NY: Oxford University Press.

P. R. Amidon (ed. & trans.) 2007. *Philostorgius: Church History.* Atlanta GA: Society of Biblical Literature (Writings from the Greco-Roman World 23).

Ammianus Marcellinus, *History*: see Rolfe 1935–40.

K. Anatolios 2004. *Athanasius.* Abingdon: Routledge.

K. T. Andersen 2000. The Queen of the Habasha in Ethiopian history, tradition and chronology. *Bulletin of the School of Oriental and African Studies [London]* 63: 31–63.

F. Anfray 1963a. Une campagne de fouilles à Yéha (Février–Mars 1960). *Annales d'Ethiopie* 5: 171–92.

F. Anfray 1963b. Première campagne de fouilles à Matara (Nov. 1959 – Jan 1960). *Annales d'Ethiopie* 5: 87–166.

F. Anfray 1964. Campagnes de fouilles à Matara. pp. 35–42 in K. Wessel (ed.) *Christentum am Nil*. Recklinghausen: Bongers.
F. Anfray 1965. Chronique archéologique 1960–1964. *Annales d'Ethiopie* 6: 3–48.
F. Anfray 1966. La poterie de Matara. *Rassegna di Studi Etiopici* 22: 5–74.
F. Anfray 1967. Matara. *Annales d'Ethiopie* 7: 33–88.
F. Anfray 1968. Les rois d'Axoum d'après la numismatique. *Journal of Ethiopian Studies* 6, 2: 1–5.
F. Anfray 1970. Notes archéologiques. *Annales d'Ethiopie* 8: 31–56.
F. Anfray 1972a. Fouilles de Yéha. *Annales d'Ethiopie* 9: 45–56.
F. Anfray 1972b. L'archéologie d'Axoum en 1972. *Paideuma* 18: 60–78.
F. Anfray 1973. Nouveaux sites antiques. *Journal of Ethiopian Studies* 11, 2: 13–27.
F. Anfray 1974. Deux villes axoumites: Adoulis et Matara. pp. 745–65 in *IV Congresso Internazionale di Studi Etiopici*. Rome: Accademia Nazionale dei Lincei.
F. Anfray 1990. *Les Anciens Éthiopiens*. Paris: Armand Colin.
F. Anfray 1996. Erythrée antique: entre période initiale et période axoumite un intervalle problématique. *Rassegna di Studi Etiopici* 38: 7–12.
F. Anfray 1997. Yéha, les ruines de Grat Be'al Gebri: recherches archéologiques. *Rassegna di Studi Etiopici* 39: 5–23.
F. Anfray 2007. Entry under 'Matara'. Uhlig 2007: 864–5.
F. Anfray & G. Annequin 1965. Matara: deuxième, troisième et quatrième campagnes de fouilles. *Annales d'Ethiopie* 6: 49–142.
F. Anfray *et al.* 1970. Une nouvelle inscription grecque d'Ezana, roi d'Axoum. *Journal des Savants* 1970: 260–74. [Reprinted 1971 in *Documents pour Servir à l'Histoire des Civilisations éthiopiennes 2*: 45–60.]
S. Antonini 2004. *I Motivi Figurative delle Banat 'Ad nei Templi Sudarabici.* Paris: Académie des Inscriptions et Belles-Lettres; Rome: Istituto Italiano per l'Africa e l'Oriente.
D. Appleyard 1978. Linguistic evidence of non-Semitic influence in the history of Ethiopian Semitic: lexical borrowing in Ge'ez and other Ethiopian Semitic languages. *Abbay* 9: 49–56.
D. Appleyard 1996. Ethiopian Semitic and South Arabian. *Israel Oriental Studies* 16: 201–28.
A. J. Arkell 1954. Four occupation sites at Agordat. *Kush* 2: 33–62.
D. W-H. Arnold 1991. *The Early Episcopal Career of Athanasius of Alexandria.* Notre Dame IN: University of Notre Dame Press.
Asfawossen Asrat 2002a. The rock-hewn churches of Tigray: why there? – a geological perspective. Baye *et al.* 2002: 1–12.
Asfawossen Asrat 2002b. The rock-hewn churches of Tigrai, northern Ethiopia: a geological perspective. *Geoarchaeology* 17: 649–63.
Asfawossen Asrat & Yodit Ayallew 2011. Geological and geotechnical properties of the medieval rock hewn churches of Lalibela, northern Ethiopia. *Journal of African Earth Sciences* 59: 61–73.
Athanasius, *Apology to Emperor Constantius*: see Szymusiak 1958.
F. B. Atkins & B. Juel-Jensen 1988. The gold coinage of Aksum: further analyses of specific gravity as a contribution to chronology. *Numismatic Chronicle* 148: 175–80.
R. Audouin 1996. Étude du décor des temples des Banât 'Ad. pp. 121–42 in C. Robin & I. Gajda (eds) *Arabia Antiqua: early origins of South Arabian states*. Rome: Istituto Italiano per il Medio ed Estremo Oriente.
Ayele Tarekegn 1996. Aksumite burial practices: the 'Gudit Stelae Field', Aksum. Pwiti & Soper 1996: 611–19.

Ayele Tarekegn & D. W. Phillipson 2000. The Gudit Stelae Field. D. Phillipson 2000b: 225–8.

L. Ayres 2004. *Nicaea and its Legacy*. Oxford: Oxford University Press.

Sir S. W. Baker 1867. *The Nile Tributaries of Abyssinia, and the Sword Hunters of the Hamran Arabs*. London: Macmillan.

S. Balanda 2005–06. The so-called 'Mine of Punt' and its location. *Journal of the American Research Center in Egypt* 42: 33–44.

E. Balicka-Witakowska 1998–99. Les peintures murales de l'église rupestre éthiopienne Gannata Maryam près Lalibela. *Arte medievale* 12–13: 193–209.

E. Balicka-Witakowska 2005a. Entry under 'Dabra Salam, Mika'el'. Uhlig 2005: 37–9.

E. Balicka-Witakowska 2005b. Entry under 'Gospel illustration'. Uhlig 2005: 859–60.

E. Balicka-Witakowska & M. Gervers 2001. The church of Yemrehanna Krestos and its wall-paintings: a preliminary report. *Africana Bulletin [Warsaw]* 49: 9–47.

W. Ball 2000. *Rome in the East: the transformation of an empire*. London: Routledge.

E. Battaglia 1989. *Artos: il lessico della panificazione nei papiri Greci*. Milan: Istituto di Filologia Classica e di Papirologia.

K. A. Bard & R. Fattovich (eds) 2007. *Harbor of the Pharaohs to the Land of Punt: archaeological investigations at Mersa/Wadi Gawasis, Egypt, 2001–2005*. Naples: Universita 'L'Orientale'.

K. A. Bard *et al.* 1997. Archaeological investigations at Bieta Giyorgis, Aksum, Ethiopia, 1993–95 field seasons. *Journal of Field Archaeology* 24: 387–404.

K. A. Bard *et al.* 2000. The environmental history of Tigray (northern Ethiopia) in the Middle and Late Holocene: a preliminary outline. *African Archaeological Review* 17: 65–86.

K. A. Bard *et al.* 2002. Aksum origins, Kassala and Upper Nubia: new evidence from Bieta Giyorgis, Aksum. *Archéologie du Nil moyen* 9: 31–42.

K. A. Bard *et al.* 2003. The Joint Archaeological Project at Bieta Giyorgis (Aksum, Ethiopia) of the Istituto Universitario Orientale and Boston University: results, research procedures and preliminary computer applications. pp. 1–13 in M. Forte & P. R. Williams (eds) *The Reconstruction of Landscapes through Digital Technologies*. Oxford: Archaeopress (British Archaeological Reports S. 1151).

K. A. Bard *et al.* 2007. Sea port to Punt: new evidence from Marsa Gawasis, Red Sea (Egypt). Starkey *et al.* 2007: 143–8.

S. Baring-Gould 1872–77. *Lives of the Saints* (12 vols). London: Hodges.

G. Barker 2006. *The Agricultural Revolution in Prehistory: why did foragers become farmers?* Oxford: Oxford University Press.

T. Barnett 1999a. Quiha rock-shelter, Ethiopia: implications for domestication. *Azania* 34: 11–24.

T. Barnett 1999b. *The Emergence of Food-Production in Ethiopia*. Oxford: Archaeopress (British Archaeological Reports S. 763).

M. Barradas (trans. E. Filleul, ed. R. Pankhurst) 1996. *Tractatus tres historico-geographici, 1634: a seventeenth-century historical and geographical account of Tigray, Ethiopia*. Wiesbaden: Harrassowitz.

J-N. Barrandon *et al.* 1990. Le monnayage d'or axoumite: une altération particulière. *Revue numismatique* 32: 186–211.

P. Batiffol 1911. Les présents de Saint Cyrille à la cour de Constantinople. *Bulletin d'ancienne Littérature et d'Archéologie chrétiennes* 1: 247–64.

A. Bausi 2005. Ancient features of ancient Ethiopic. *Aethiopica* 8: 149–69.

A. Bausi 2006a. The Aksumite background of the Ethiopic 'Corpus Canonum'. Uhlig 2006: 532–41.

A Bausi 2006b. Un indice del *Liber Axumae*. *Aethiopica* 9: 102–46.
Baye Yimam *et al.* (eds) 2002. *Ethiopian Studies at the End of the Second Millennium* (3 vols). Addis Ababa: Institiute of Ethiopian Studies, Addis Ababa University.
J. C. Béal 1991. Un coffret(?) d'ivoire du 'château royal' de Shabwa. *Syria* 68: 187–208.
J. Beaucamp *et al.* 1999. La persécution des chrétiens de Nagran et la chronologie himyarite. *ARAM* 11: 15–83.
J. Beaucamp *et al.* (eds) 2004–06. *Recherches sur la Chronique de Jean Malalas*. Paris: Collège de France - CNRS Centre de Recherches d'Histoire et Civilisation de Byzance (*Monographies* 15, 24).
C. F. Beckingham & G. W. B. Huntingford 1954. *Some Records of Ethiopia, 1593–1646*. London: Hakluyt Society.
C. F. Beckingham & G. W. B. Huntingford 1961. *The Prester John of the Indies, a true relation of the lands of the Prester John, being the narrative of the Portuguese Embassy to Ethiopia in 1520 written by Father Francisco Alvares*. London: Hakluyt Society.
A. F. L. Beeston 1971. Functional significance of the old South Arabian 'town'. *Proceedings of the Seminar for Arabian Studies 1970*: 26–8.
A. F. L. Beeston 1980. The authorship of the Adulis throne text. *Bulletin of the School of Oriental and African Studies [London]* 43: 453–8.
A. F. L. Beeston 1984. Himyarite monotheism. pp. 149–54 in A. T. al-Ansary *et al.* (eds) *Studies in the History of Arabia*, vol. 2. Riyadh: King Saud University Press.
Belaynesh Mikael *et al.* (eds) 1975. *The Dictionary of Ethiopian Biography, vol. 1: from early times to the end of the Zagwe dynasty, c. 1270 AD*. Addis Ababa: Institute of Ethiopian Studies, Addis Ababa University.
P. Bellwood & A. C. Renfrew (eds) 2002. *Examining the Farming/Language Dispersal Hypothesis*. Cambridge: McDonald Institute for Archaeological Research.
S. Bendall 1986–87. A note on 'An Axumite coin from Jerusalem'. *Israel Numismatic Journal* 9: 91, pl. 32.
M. L. Bender *et al.* (eds) 1976. *Language in Ethiopia*. London: Oxford University Press.
J. T. Bent 1893. *The Sacred City of the Ethiopians, Being a Record of Travel and Research in Abyssinia in 1893*. London: Longmans, Green & Co.
A. Berger (ed.) 2006. *Life and Works of Saint Gregentios, Archbishop of Taphar*. Berlin: de Gruyter.
C. Berger *et al.* (eds) 1993. *Hommages à Jean Leclant* (3 vols). Cairo: Institut français d'Archéologie orientale.
E. Bernand 1982. Nouvelles versions de la campagne du roi Ezana contre les Bedja. *Zeitschrift für Papyrologie und Epigraphik* 45: 105–14.
E. Bernand *et al.* 1991–2000. *Recueil des inscriptions de l'Ethiopie des périodes pré-axoumite et axoumite* (3 vols). Paris: Académie des Inscriptions et Belles-Lettres.
R. Beylot 2004. Du *Kebra Negast*. *Aethiopica* 7: 74–83.
C. Bezold 1905. *Kebra Nagast: die Herrlichkeit der Könige, nach den Handschriften in Berlin, London, Oxford und Paris*. Munich: Bayerischen Akademie der Wissenchaften (*Abhandlungen der philosophische-philologische Klasse* 23, 1).
L. Bianchi Barriviera 1943. *Le chiese monolitiche di Lalibelà*. Rome: published privately.
L. Bianchi Barriviera 1957. *Le chiese in roccia di Lalibelà e altre nel Lasta-Uagh in Etiopia*. Rome: Calografia Nazionale.

L. Bianchi Barriviera 1962–63. Le chiese in roccia di Lalibelà e di altri luoghi del Lasta. *Rassegna di Studi Etiopici* 18: 5–76 and 19: 5–94.

I. Bidder 1958. *Lalibela: the monolithic churches of Ethiopia*. Cologne: DuMont Schauberg.

G. Bijovsky 1998. The Gush Halav hoard reconsidered [with a postscript by E. M. Meyers]. *'Atiqot* 35: 77–108.

J. Binns 2002. *An Introduction to the Christian Orthodox Churches*. Cambridge: Cambridge University Press.

S. L. Black 2008. In the power of God Christ: inscriptional evidence for the anti-Arian theology of Ethiopia's first Christian king. *Bulletin of the School of Oriental and African Studies [London]* 71: 93–110.

R. M. Blench 2006. *Archaeology, Language and the African Past*. Lanham MD: Altamira.

R. M. Blench & K. C. Macdonald (eds) 2000. *The Origins and Development of African Livestock: archaeology, genetics, linguistics and ethnography*. London: UCL Press.

M. Blet-Lemarquand *et al.* 2001. Les monnaies axoumites d'argent: premières résultats d'analyse. *Bulletin de la Société française de Numismatique* 56: 86–8.

F. de Blois 1984. Clan names in ancient Ethiopia. *Die Welt des Orients* 15: 123–5.

F. de Blois 1990. The date of the 'Martyrs of Nagran'. *Arabian Archaeology and Epigraphy* 1: 110–28.

S. Boardman 1999. The agricultural foundation of the Aksumite Empire, Ethiopia: an interim report. van der Veen 1999: 137–47.

S. Boardman 2000. Contributions on archaeobotany. D. Phillipson 2000b: 127–8, 363–8, 412–14.

S. Boardman & R. Gale 2000. Appendix VII: Archaeobotanical methodology. D. Phillipson 2000b: 507–9.

C. Bosc-Tiessé 2010. Catalogue des autels et meubles d'autel en bois (*tabot* et *manbara tabot*) des églises de Lalibala: jalons pour une histoire des objets et des motifs. *Annales d'Ethiopie* 25: 55–101.

G. W. Bowersock 1997. Polytheism and monotheism in Arabia and the three Palestines. *Dumbarton Oaks Papers* 51: 1–10.

A. K. Bowman & E. Rogan (eds) 1999. *Agriculture in Egypt from Pharaonic to Modern Times*. Oxford: Oxford University Press for the British Academy (Proceedings of the British Academy 96).

H. Brakmann 1999. Religionsgeschichte Aksums in der Spätantike. *Nubica et Aethiopica* 4–5: 401–30.

S. A. Brandt 1984. New perspectives on the origins of food production in Ethiopia. pp. 173–90 in J. D. Clark & S. A. Brandt (eds) *From Hunters to Farmers: the causes and consequences of food-production in Africa*. Berkeley CA: University of California Press.

S. A. Brandt 1996. A model for the origins and evolution of Enset food production. pp. 36–46 in T. Abate *et al.* (eds), *Enset-based Sustainable Agriculture in Ethiopia*. Addis Ababa: Institute of Agricultural Research.

S. A. Brandt *et al.* 2008. Linking the highlands and lowlands: implications of a test excavation at Kokan rockshelter, Agordat, Eritrea. Schmidt *et al.* 2008d: 33–47.

J-F. Breton & S. Munro-Hay 2002. New Himyaritic coins from Aksum (Ethiopia). *Arabian Archaeology and Epigraphy* 13: 255–8.

A. Brita 2007. Article under 'Nine Saints'. Uhlig 2007: 1188–91.

L. Brubaker 1977. The relationship of text and image in the Byzantine MSS of Cosmas Indicopleustes. *Byzantinische Zeitschrift* 70: 42–57.

J. Bruce 1790. *Travels to Discover the Source of the Nile in the Years 1768, 1769, 1770, 1771, 1772 and 1773* (5 vols). Edinburgh: Robinson.

J. Bruce 1813. *Travels to Discover the Source of the Nile in the Years 1768, 1769, 1770, 1771, 1772 and 1773* (3rd edn, 8 vols). Edinburgh: Constable.
U. Brunner 2006. Die Zisterne von Safra. Wenig 2006a: 381–7.
E. A. W. Budge 1922. *The Queen of Sheba and her only son Menyelek ... a complete translation of the* Kebra Negast. London: Medici Society.
E. A. W. Budge 1928a. *The Book of the Saints of the Ethiopian Church* (4 vols). Cambridge: Cambridge University Press.
E. A. W. Budge 1928b. *A History of Ethiopia: Nubia and Abyssinia* (2 vols). London: Methuen.
S. M. Burstein (trans. & ed.) 1989. *Agatharchides of Cnidus: On the Erythraean Sea*. London: Hakluyt Society.
S. M. Burstein 1996. Ivory and Ptolemaic exploration of the Red Sea. *Topoi* 6: 799–807.
S. M. Burstein (ed.) 1998. *Ancient African Civilizations: Kush and Axum*. Princeton NJ: Markus Wiener.
D. Bustorf & W. Smidt 2005. Entry under 'Elephants'. Uhlig 2005: 254–9.
A. C. Butler 2003. The Ethiopian pea: seeking the evidence for separate domestication. Neumann *et al.* 2003: 37–47.
A. C. Butler *et al.* 1999. The ethnobotany of *Lathyrus sativus L.* in the highlands of Ethiopia. van der Veen 1999: 123–36.
T. Buttrey 1971–72 [published 1974]. Axumite addenda. *Rassegna di Studi Etiopici* 25: 44–52.
K. W. Butzer 1981. Rise and fall of Axum, Ethiopia: a geo-archaeological interpretation. *American Antiquity* 46: 471–95.
D. R. Buxton 1947. The Christian antiquities of northern Ethiopia. *Archaeologia* 92: 1–42.
D. R. Buxton 1970. *The Abyssinians*. London: Thames & Hudson.
D. R. Buxton 1971. The rock-hewn and other medieval churches of Tigré Province, Ethiopia. *Archaeologia* 103: 33–100.
D. Buxton & D. Matthews 1974. The reconstruction of vanished Aksumite buildings. *Rassegna di Studi Etiopici* 25: 53–77.
C. R. Cain 2000. Contributions on archaeozoology. D. Phillipson 2000b: 369–72, 414–17, 510–11.
G. Calegari 1999. *L'arte rupestre dell'Eritrea: repertorio ragionato ed esegesi iconografica*. Milan: Società Italiana di Scienze Naturali e Museo Civico di Storia Naturale di Milano.
A. Caquot & A. J. Drewes 1955. Les monuments receuillis à Maqallé. *Annales d'Ethiopie* 1: 17–41.
A. Caquot & J. Leclant 1956. Rapport sur les récents travaux de la section d'archéologie de l'institut éthiopien d'études et de recherches. *Comptes rendus des séances de l'Académie des Inscriptions et Belles-Lettres 1956*: 226–35.
A. Carandini (ed.) 1981. *Atlante delle Forme Ceramiche. I. Ceramica fine Romana nel Bacino Mediterraneo (Medio e Tardo Impero).* Rome: Instituto della Enciclopedia Italiana.
L. Casson 1981. The location of Adulis. pp. 113–22 in L. Casson & M. Price (eds), *Coins, Culture and History in the Ancient World.* Detroit MI: Wayne State University Press.
L. Casson 1989. *The Periplus Maris Erythraei.* Princeton NJ; Princeton University Press.
L. Casson 1993. Ptolemy II and the hunting of African elephants. *Transactions of the American Philological Association* 123: 247–60.
J. Cauliez *et al.* 2008. Première caractérisation des faciès céramiques néolithiques de la région du Gobaad en République de Djibouti: les sites

d'Hara-Idé 2 et d'Asa-Koma (As-Eyla, district de Dikhil). *L'Anthropologie* 112: 691–715.

C. Cecchelli 1936–44. *La Cattedra di Massimiano ed altri Avorii Romano-Orientali.* Rome: La Libreria dello Stato.

E. Cerulli 1943–47. *Etiopi in Palestina: storia della comunità etiopica in Gerusalemm* (2 vols). Rome: Libreria dello Stato and Topografia Pio X.

L. Chaix & B. Gratien 2002. Un cheval du Nouvel-Empire à Saï (Soudan). *Archéologie du Nil moyen* 9: 53–64.

M. el-Chennafi 1976. Mention nouvelle d'une 'reine éthiopienne' au IVè siècle de Hégire / Xè siècle aprés J-C. *Annales d'Ethiopie* 10: 119–21.

G. F. Chesnut 1977. *The First Christian Histories: Eusebius, Socrates, Sozomen, Theodoret and Evagrius.* Paris: Editions Beauchesne (*Théologie historique* 46).

H. N. Chittick 1974. Excavations at Aksum: a preliminary report. *Azania* 9: 159–205.

H. N. Chittick 1976. Radiocarbon dates from Aksum. *Azania* 11: 179–81.

H. N. Chittick 1981. The *Periplus* and the spice trade [Review of Huntingford 1980 and of *Frankincense and Myrrh* by N. Groom]. *Azania* 16: 185–90.

S. Chojnacki 2003. New aspects of India's influence on the art and culture of Ethiopia. *Rassegna di Studi Etiopici* n.s. 2: 5–21.

S. Chojnacki 2005a. New discoveries in Ethiopian archaeology: Dabr Takla Haymonot in Dawnt and Enso Gabre'el in Lasta. Raunig & Wenig 2005: 44–59.

S. Chojnacki 2005b. Peinture pariétale, icons, manuscrits, croix et autres objets liturgiques. Raunig 2005: 171–249.

S. Chrisomalis 2010. *Numerical Notation: a comparative history.* Cambridge: Cambridge University Press.

J. D. Clark 1980. The origins of domestication in Ethiopia. pp. 268–70 in R. E. Leakey & B. A. Ogot (eds) *Proceedings of the 8th Panafrican Congress of Prehistory and Quaternary Studies, Nairobi, September 1977.* Nairobi: International Louis Leakey Memorial Institute for African Prehistory.

H. de Contenson 1959a. Les fouilles archéologiques en Ethiopie de 1956 à 1959. *Comptes rendus de l'Académie des Inscriptions et Belles-Lettres 1959*: 250–55.

H. de Contenson 1959b. Les fouilles à Axoum en 1957. *Annales d'Ethiopie* 3: 25–42.

H. de Contenson 1959c. Aperçus sur les fouilles à Axoum et dans la région d'Axoum en 1958 et 1959. *Annales d'Ethiopie* 3: 101–6.

H. de Contenson 1961a. Trouvailles fortuites aux environs d'Axoum (1957–1959). *Annales d'Ethiopie* 4: 17–38.

H. de Contenson 1961b. Les fouilles à Ouchatei Golo près d'Axoum en 1958. *Annales d'Ethiopie* 4: 3–16.

H. de Contenson 1962. Les monuments d'art sudarabe découverts sur le site de Haoulti (Ethiopie) en 1959. *Syria* 39: 64–87.

H. de Contenson 1963a. Les fouilles à Axoum en 1958 – rapport préliminaire. *Annales d'Ethiopie* 5: 3–40.

H. de Contenson 1963b. Les fouilles à Haoulti en 1959 – rapport préliminaire. *Annales d'Ethiopie* 5: 41–86.

C. Conti Rossini 1900. Ricerche e studi sull'Etiopia. *Bollettino della Regia Società Geografica Italiana,* ser. 4 1: 104–20.

C. Conti Rossini 1909. Les listes des rois d'Axoum. *Journal Asiatique* série 10, 14: 263–320.

C. Conti Rossini 1909–10. *Liber Axumae.* Paris: e Typographeo Reipublicae (*Corpus scriptorum christianorum orientalium* 54, 58).

C. Conti Rossini 1921. Monete sud-Arabiche. *Rendiconti della Reale Accademia dei Lincei* 30: 293–55.

C. Conti Rossini 1922. A propos des textes éthiopiens concernant Salama (Frumentius). *Aethiops* 1: 2–4, 17–18.
C. Conti Rossini 1928. *Storia d'Etiopia*. Bergamo: Istituto Italiano d'Arti Grafiche.
H. E. M. Cool 1996. Sedeinga and the glass vessels of the kingdom of Meroe. pp. 201–12 in *Annales du 13e Congrès de l'Association Internationale pour l'Histoire du Verre*. Lochem: Association Internationale pour l'Histoire du Verre.
Cosmas Indicopleustes, *Christian Topography*: see McCrindle 1897; Wolska-Conus 1968–73.
B. Cossar 1945. Necropoli precristiana di Selaclaca, pp. 7–16 in C. Conti Rossini, *Studi Etiopici*. Rome: Istituto per l'Oriente.
P. Costa 1992. South Arabian jar sealings. *Proceedings of the Seminar for Arabian Studies* 21: 41–8.
P. T. Craddock 1995. *Early Metal Mining and Production*. Edinburgh: Edinburgh University Press.
E. Crane 1999. *World History of Bee-keeping and Honey-hunting*. London: Duckworth.
O. G. S. Crawford 1958. *Ethiopian Itineraries, circa 1400–1524*. London: Hakluyt Society.
B. Croke 1990. Malalas, the man and his work. Jeffreys *et al.* 1990: 1–25.
P. Crone 1987. *Meccan Trade and the Rise of Islam*. Oxford: Blackwell; Princeton NJ: Princeton University Press.
M. C. Curtis & Daniel Habtemichael 2008. Matara, Keskese, and the 'Classical Period' archaeology of the Akele Guzay highlands: a brief overview. Schmidt *et al.* 2008d: 311–27.
A. C. Cutler 1999. Ivory. pp. 521–9 in G. W. Bowersock *et al.* (eds), *Late Antiquity: a guide to the post-Classical world*. Cambridge MA: Harvard University Press.
Cyril of Scythopolis, *Lives of the Monks of Palestine*: see Price & Binns 1991; also Garitte 1962.
H. Dabbert 1938. *Die monolithenen Kirchen Lalibelas in Aethiopien*. Berlin: Triltsch & Huther.
DAE: see Littmann *et al.* 1913 or, for an English translation by Rosalind Bedlow of the sections relating to Aksum itself, D. Phillipson 1997.
A. C. D'Andrea 2008. Tef (*Eragrostis tef*) in ancient agricultural systems of highland Ethiopia. *Economic Botany* 62: 547–66.
A. C. D'Andrea & Mitiku Haile 2002. Traditional emmer processing in highland Ethiopia. *Journal of Ethnobiology* 22 (2): 179–217.
A. C. D'Andrea *et al.* 1999. Ethnoarchaeological approaches to the study of prehistoric agriculture in the highlands of Ethiopia. van der Veen 1999: 101–22.
A. C. D'Andrea *et al.* 2008a. The Pre-Aksumite and Aksumite settlement of northeast Tigray, Ethiopia. *Journal of Field Archaeology* 33: 151–76.
A. C. D'Andrea *et al.* 2008b. Paleoethnobotanical analysis and agricultural economy in early first millennium BCE sites around Asmara. Schmidt *et al.* 2008d: 207–16.
I. Darbyshire *et al.* 2003. Forest clearance and regrowth in northern Ethiopia during the last 3000 years. *The Holocene* 13: 537–46.
M. Daszkiewicz *et al.* 2010. The application of down-up sampling classification by MGR-analysis in the classification of raw materials used for pottery making near the site of Meqaber Ga'ewa (Ethiopia). Wolf & Nowotnick 2010b: 193–203.
G. Dattari 1913. Intorno alle forme da fondere monete imperiale romane. *Rivista Italiana di Numismatica*: 351–75, 447–510.

D. H. S. Davis & B. M. Fagan 1962. Sub-fossil house rats (*Rattus rattus*) from Iron Age sites in Northern Rhodesia. *News Bulletin of the Zoological Society of South Africa* 3, 3: 13–15.

T. Denham *et al.* (eds) 2007. *Rethinking Agriculture: archaeological and ethnoarchaeological perspectives.* Walnut Creek CA: Left Coast Press.

M-L. Derat 2010. The Zagwe dynasty (10th–13th centuries) and king Yemrehanna Krestos. *Annales d'Ethiopie* 25: 157–96.

J. Desanges 1969. D'Axoum à l'Assam, aux portes de la Chine: le voyage du 'scholasticus de Thèbes' (entre 360 et 500 après J-C.). *Historia* 18: 627–39.

J. Desanges 1978. *Recherches sur l'activité des Méditerranéens aux confins de l'Afrique.* Rome: Ecole français de Rome.

J. Desanges & M. Reddé 1993. La côte africaine du Bab al-Mandeb dans l'antiquité. C. Berger *et al.* 1993, 3: 161–94.

M. Detoraki & J. Beaucamp 2007. *Le Martyre de saint Aréthas et de ses compagnons (BHG 166).* Paris: Collège de France, Centre de recherche d'histoire et civilisation de Byzance (*Monographies* 27).

H. B. Dewing (ed. & trans.) 1914–28. *Procopius: History of the Wars.* London: Heinemann (Loeb Classical Library).

M. DiBlasi 2005. Foreword. Michels 2005: ix–xvii.

A. Dihle 1964. The conception of India in Hellenistic and Roman literature. *Proceedings of the Cambridge Philological Society* 190: 15–23.

A. Dihle 1965. *'Umstrittene Daten': Untersuchungen zum Auftreten der Griechen am Roten Meer.* Cologne: Westdeutscher Verlag (*Wissenschaftliche Abhandlungen der Arbeitsgemeinschaft für Forschung des Landes Nordrhein-Westfalen* 32).

A. Dihle 1989. L'Ambassade de Théophile l'Indien ré-examinée. vol. 2, pp. 461–8 in T. Fahd (ed.) *L'Arabie préislamique et son environnement historique et culturel: Actes du Colloque de Strasbourg, juin 1987.* Leiden: Brill.

C. F. A. Dillmann 1865. *Lexicon linguae aethiopicae.* Leipsig: Weigel.

C. F. A. Dillmann 1879. Uber die Anfänge des Aksumitischen Reiches. *Abhandlungen der Königlichen Akademie der Wissenschaften zu Berlin, 1878* (*Philosophisch-Historische Klasse*): 177–238.

A. Doig 2008. *Liturgy and Architecture: from the Early Church to the Middle Ages.* Farnham: Ashgate.

B. Dombrowski & F. Dombrowski 1984. Frumentius / Abba Salama: zu den Nachrichten über die Anfänge des Christentums in Äthiopien. *Oriens Christianus* 68: 114–69.

J. Dombrowski 1970. Preliminary report on excavations at Lalibela and Natchabiet caves, Begemeder. *Annales d'Ethiopie* 8: 21–9.

E. van Donzel 1998. Ethiopia's Lalibala and the fall of Jerusalem, 1187. *Aethiopica* 1: 27–49.

J. Doresse 1956. Les premiers monuments chrétiens de l'Ethiopie et l'église archaïque de Yéha. *Novum Testamentum* 1: 209–24.

J. Doresse 1960. La découverte d'Asbi-Dera: nouveaux documents sur les rapports de l'Egypte et l'Ethiopie à l'époque axoumite. pp. 411–34 in *Atti del Convegno Internazionale di Studi Etiopici.* Rome: Accademia Nazionale dei Lincei.

J. Doresse 1970. *Histoire de l'Ethiopie.* Paris: Presses Universitaires de France (*Que sais-je?* 1393).

J. Doresse 1971. *Histoire sommaire de la Corne orientale de l'Afrique.* Paris: Geuthner.

M. Drancourt & D. Raoult 2004. Molecular detection of *Yersinia pestis* in dental pulp. *Microbiology* 150: 263–4.

S. F. Drew 1954. Notes from the Red Sea Hills. *South African Archaeological Bulletin* 9: 101–2.
A. J. Drewes 1959. Les inscriptions de Melazo. *Annales d'Ethiopie* 3: 83–99.
A. J. Drewes 1962. *Inscriptions de l'Ethiopie Antique*. Leiden: Brill.
A. J. Drewes 1991. Some features of epigraphical Ethiopic. vol. 1, pp. 382–91 in A. S. Kaye (ed.) *Semitic Studies in Honor of Wolf Leslau on the Occasion of his Eighty-Fifth Birthday*. Wiesbaden: Harrassowitz.
A. J. Drewes 1998–99. Noms propres dans les documents épigraphiques de l'Ethiopie. *Semitica* 48: 127–43, (part 2) 50 (1999): 199–210.
A. J. Drewes 2001. The meaning of Sabaean MKRB, facts and fiction. *Semitica* 51: 93–125.
A. J. Drewes & R. Schneider 1972. Documents épigraphiques de l'Ethiopie – III. *Annales d'Ethiopie* 9: 87–102.
A. J. Drewes & R. Schneider 1976. Origine et développement de l'écriture éthiopienne jusqu'à l'époque des inscriptions royales d'Axoum. *Annales d'Ethiopie* 10: 95–107.
S. A. Dueppen 2011. Early evidence for chickens at Iron Age Kirikongo (*c.* AD 100–1450), Burkina Faso. *Antiquity* 85: 142–57.
N. Durrani 2005. *The Tihamah Coastal Plain of Southwest Arabia in Its Regional Context c. 6000 BC–AD 600*. Oxford: Archaeopress (British Archaeological Reports S. 1456).
D. N. Edwards 1996. *The Archaeology of the Meroitic State: new perspectives on its social and political organisation.* Oxford: Tempus Reparatum (British Archaeological Reports S. 640).
D. N. Edwards 2004. *The Nubian Past*. London: Routledge.
C. Ehret 1979. On the antiquity of agriculture in Ethiopia. *Journal of African History* 20: 161–77.
C. Ehret 2000. Language and History. Heine & Nurse 2000: 272–97.
C. Ehret 2002. Language family expansions: broadening our understanding of cause from an African perspective. Bellwood & Renfrew 2002: 163–76.
J. M. M. Engels *et al.* (eds) 1991. *Plant Genetic Resources of Ethiopia*. Cambridge: Cambridge University Press.
Eusebius of Caesarea, *Ecclesiastical History*; see Lake 1926; Oulton 1932.
B. Evetts (ed. & trans.) 1895. *The Churches and Monasteries of Egypt and some Neighbouring Countries, attributed to Abu Salih, the Armenian*. Oxford: Clarendon Press. [reprinted in 1969 by Oxford University Press.]
B. M. Fagan 1967. *Iron Age Cultures in Zambia, vol. 1: Kalomo and Kangila*. London: Chatto & Windus.
R. Fattovich 1972a. Sondaggi stratigrafici, Yeha 1971. *Annales d'Ethiopie* 9: 65–86.
R. Fattovich 1972b. Yeha 1972, sondaggi stratigrafici. *Documents pour servir à l'histoire des civilisations éthiopiennes* 3: 65–75.
R. Fattovich 1976. Osservazioni sulla ceramica preaksumita di Yeha, Etiopia. *Africa [Rome]* 31: 587–95.
R. Fattovich 1978a. Traces of a possible African component in the Pre-Aksumite culture of northern Ethiopia. *Abbay* 9: 25–30.
R. Fattovich 1978b. Introduzione alla ceramica preaksumita di Grat Be'al Guebri (Yeha). *Annales d'Ethiopie* 11: 105–22.
R. Fattovich 1980. *Materiali per lo Studio della Ceramica pre-Aksumita Etiopica*. Naples: Istituto Orientale (*Supplemento agli Annali*).
R. Fattovich 1989. The stelae of Kassala: a new type of funerary monuments in the eastern Sudan. *Archéologie du Nil moyen* 3: 55–69.
R. Fattovich 1990. Remarks on the Pre-Aksumite period in northern Ethiopia. *Journal of Ethiopian Studies* 23: 1–33.

R. Fattovich 1991. The problem of Punt in the light of recent fieldwork in eastern Sudan. vol. 4, pp. 257–72 in S. Schoske (ed.) *Akten des vierten internationalen Ägyptologen Kongresses* (4 vols). Hamburg: Buske.

R. Fattovich 1993a. Evidence of possible administrative devices in the Gash delta (Kassala). pp. 439–48 in L. Krzyzaniak *et al.* (eds), *Environmental Change and Human Culture in the Nile Basin and Northern Africa until the Second Millennium BC.* Poznan: Poznan Archaeological Museum.

R. Fattovich 1993b. Meroe ed Aksum: alcune riflessioni. C. Berger *et al.* 1993, 2: 117–33.

R. Fattovich 1996a. The Afro-Arabian circuit: contacts between the Horn of Africa and southern Arabia in the third-second millennia BC. pp. 395–402 in L. Krzyzaniak *et al.* (eds) *Inter-regional Contacts in the later Prehistory of Northeastern Africa.* Poznan: Poznan Archaeological Museum.

R. Fattovich 1996b. Punt: the archaeological perspective. *Beiträge zur Sudanforschung [Vienna]* 6: 15–29.

R. Fattovich 2003. Entry under 'Amba Foqada'. Uhlig 2003a: 219–20.

R. Fattovich 2007. Entry under 'Kaskase'. Uhlig 2007: 352–3.

R. Fattovich 2009. Reconsidering Yeha, *c.* 800–400 BC. *African Archaeological Review* 26: 275–90.

R. Fattovich 2010. The development of ancient states in the northern Horn of Africa, *c.* 3000 BC – AD 1000: an archaeological outline. *Journal of World Prehistory* 23: 145–75.

R. Fattovich & K. A. Bard 2001. The Proto-Aksumite period: an overview. *Annales d'Ethiopie* 17: 3–24.

R. Fattovich & K. A. Bard 2003. Scavi archeologici nella zona di Aksum, K – Bieta Giyorgis. *Rassegna di Studi Etiopici* n. s. 2: 23–36.

R. Fattovich *et al.* 1998. Meroe and Aksum: new elements of comparison. *Archéologie du Nil moyen* 8: 43–53.

R. Fattovich *et al.* 2000. *The Aksum Archaeological Area: a preliminary assessment.* Naples: Istituto Universitario Orientale.

F-X. Fauvelle-Aymar 2009. Les inscriptions d'Adoulis (Erythrée): fragments d'un royaume d'influence hellénistique et gréco-romaine sur la côte africaine de la mer Rouge. *Bulletin de l'Institut français d'Archéologie orientale* 109: 135–60.

F-X. Fauvelle-Aymar *et al.* 2010. Rock-cut stratigraphy: sequencing the Lalibela churches. *Antiquity* 84: 1135–50.

V. M. Fernandez *et al.* 2007. A Late Stone Age sequence from West Ethiopia: the sites of K'aaba and Bel K'urk'umu (Assossa, Benishangul-Gumuz Regional State). *Journal of African Archaeology* 5: 91–126.

P. Ferret & J. Galinier 1847–8. *Voyage en Abyssinie, dans les Provinces du Tigré, du Samen et de l'Amhara* (3 vols). Paris: Paulin.

A. Feuerbach 2000. Appendix IV: Metallurgical examination and analysis. D. Phillipson 2000b: 497–9.

G. Fiaccadori 1983-84. Teofilo Indiano. *Studi Classici e Orientali* 33: 295–331 and 34: 271–308.

G. Fiaccadori 2004. Sembrouthes 'gran re' (DAE IV 3 = RIE 275): per la storia del primo ellenismo aksumita. *La Parola del Passato* 59: 103–57.

G. Fiaccadori 2006. Die alte Kirche in Asmara. Wenig 2006: 297–310.

G. Fiaccadori 2007a. Entry under 'Kaleb'. Uhlig 2007: 329–32.

G. Fiaccadori 2007b. Nuova iscrizione greca da Aksum. *La Parola del Passato* 62: 70–6.

N. Finneran 2000a. A new perspective on the Late Stone Age of the Northern Ethiopian highlands: excavations at Anqqer Baahti, Aksum, Ethiopia. *Azania* 35: 21–51.

N. Finneran 2000b. Excavations at the Late Stone Age site of Baahti Nebait, Aksum, northern Ethiopia, 1997. *Azania* 35: 53–73.
N. Finneran 2007. *The Archaeology of Ethiopia*. London: Routledge.
N. Finneran 2009. Settlement archaeology and oral history in Lasta, Ethiopia: some preliminary observations from a landscape study of Lalibela. *Azania* 44: 281–91.
N. Finneran & J. S. Phillips 2003. The Shire region archaeological landscape survey 2001: a preliminary report. *Azania* 37: 139–47.
N. Finneran *et al.* 2005. The archaeological landscape of the Shire region, western Tigray, Ethiopia. *Annales d'Ethiopie* 21: 7–29.
R. Fletcher 1998. African urbanism: scale, mobility and transformations. pp. 104–38 in G. Connah (ed.) *Transformations in Africa: essays on Africa's later past*. Leicester: Leicester University Press.
G. Fowden 1993. *Empire to Commonwealth: consequences of monotheism in Late Antiquity*. Princeton NJ: Princeton University Press.
G. Fowden 2004. *Qusayr 'Amra: art and the Umayyad elite in Late Antique Syria*. Berkeley CA: University of California Press.
V. M. Francaviglia 1994. Rise and fall of obelisks at Aksum. vol. 1, pp. 26–35 in H. G. Marcus (ed.) *New Trends in Ethiopian Studies*. Lawrenceville NJ: Red Sea Press.
S. A. Frantsouzoff 2010. Entry under 'Script, Ethiopic'. Uhlig & Bausi 2010: 580–5.
P. M. Fraser 1972. *Ptolemaic Alexandria* (2 vols). Oxford: Clarendon Press.
G. S. P. Freeman-Grenville 1992–93. Jerusalem, Aksum and Aachen. *Israel Numismatic Journal* 12: 80–6, pls 18–19.
J. H. Freese (trans.) 1920. *The Library of Photius*, vol. 1 (only one published). London: Society for Promoting Christian Knowledge.
C. A. I. French *et al.* 2009. New geoarchaeological investigations of the valley- systems in the Aksum area of northern Ethiopia. *Catena* 78: 218–33.
W. H. C. Frend 1972. *The Rise of the Monophysite Movement*. Cambridge: Cambridge University Press.
W. H. C. Frend 1974. Athanasius as an Egyptian Christian leader in the fourth century. *New College Bulletin [Edinburgh]* 8, 1: 20–37. [Reprinted 1976 in *idem, Religion Popular and Unpopular in the Early Christian Centuries*. London: Variorum.]
E. Fritsch 2008. The churches of Lalibala (Ethiopia) witnesses of liturgical change. *Bollettino della Badia Greca di Grottaferrata* 5: 69–112.
E. Fritsch & M. Gervers 2007. *Pastophoria* and altars: interaction in Ethiopian liturgy and church architecture. *Aethiopica* 10: 7–51.
E. Fritsch & U. Zanetti 2003. Entry under 'Calendar'. Uhlig 2003a: 668–72.
D. Q. Fuller 2003. African crops in prehistoric south Asia: a critical review. Neumann *et al.* 2003: 239–71.
D. Q. Fuller *et al.* 2011. Across the Indian Ocean: the prehistoric movement of plants and animals. *Antiquity* 85: 544–58.
I. Gajda 2009. *Le royaume de Himyar à l'époque monothéiste*. Paris: de Boccard (*Mémoires de l'Académie des Inscriptions et Belles-Lettres* 40).
I. Gajda & Yohannes Gebre-Selassie 2009. A Pre-Aksumite inscribed incense burner and some architectural ornaments from Addi Akaweh (Tigrai, Ethiopia). *Annales d'Ethiopie* 24: 49–61.
I. Gajda *et al.* 2009. Pre-Aksumite inscriptions from Maqaber Ga'ewa (Tigrai, Ethiopia). *Annales d'Ethiopie* 24: 33–48.
G. Garitte 1962. La version géorgienne de la *Vie de Cyriaque* par Cyrille de Scythopolis. *Le Muséon* 75: 399–440.

C. Garrelt & I. Wiechmann 2003. Detection of *Yersinia pestis* DNA in early and late medieval Bavarian burials. pp. 247–54 in G. Grupe & J. Peters (eds) *Decyphering Ancient Bones: the research potential of bioarchaeological collections.* Rahden: Leidorf.

G. Gerster 1970. *Churches in Rock: early Christian art in Ethiopia*. London: Phaidon.

M. Gervers 1992. Cotton and cotton weaving in Meroitic Nubia and medieval Ethiopia. pp. 13–29 in P. Scholz (ed.) *Orbis Aethiopicus: studia in honorem Stanislaus Chojnacki.* Albstadt: Schuler.

M. Gervers 2003a. The rehabilitation of the Zague kings and the building of the Dabra Sina – Golgotha – Sellassie complex in Lalibala. *Africana Bulletin [Warsaw]* 51: 23–49.

M. Gervers 2003b. The Dabra Sina – Golgotha – Sellassie complex in Lalibala. pp. 388–414 in Birhanu Teffera & Richard Pankhurst (eds) *Proceedings of the Sixth International Conference on the History of Ethiopian Art.* Addis Ababa: Institute of Ethiopian Studies.

M. Gervers 2007. Quand la liturgie modèle les églises. *Religions et histoire* 17: 50–9.

Getatchew Haile 1979. The homily in honour of St Frumentius, Bishop of Axum. *Analecta Bollandiana* 97: 309–18.

Getatchew Haile 1989. The legend of Abgar in Ethiopic tradition. *Orientalia Christiana Periodica* 55: 375–410.

H. A. R. Gibb 1962. Pre-Islamic monotheism in Arabia. *Harvard Theological Review* 55: 269–80.

Gigar Tesfaye 1984. Inscriptions sur bois de trois églises de Lalibala. *Journal of Ethiopian Studies* 17: 107–26.

Gigar Tesfaye 1987. Découverte d'inscriptions guèzes à Lalibela. *Annales d'Ethiopie* 14: 75–80.

J. Gire & R. Schneider 1970. Etude des églises rupestres du Tigré: premiers résultats de la mission 1970. *Documents pour Servir à l'Histoire des Civilisations éthiopiennes* 1: 73–9.

Girma Elias *et al.* 2001. Peintures murales du XIIe siècle découvertes dans l'église Yemrehana Krestos en Ethiopie. *Comptes rendus des séances de l'Académie des Inscriptions et Belles-Lettres 2001*: 311–34.

W. D. Glanzman 2002. Arts, crafts and industries. Simpson 2002: 110–41.

R. Göbl 1970. Der kusanische Goldmünzschatz von Debra Damo (Äthiopien) 1940. *Central Asiatic Journal* 14: 241–52.

E. Godet 1977. Répertoire des sites pré-axoumites et axoumites de Tigré (Ethiopie) *Abbay* 8: 19–58.

E. Godet 1983. Répertoire des sites pré-axoumites et axoumites d'Ethiopie du Nord, IIe partie: Erythrée. *Abbay* 11: 73–113.

E. Godet 1986. Bilan de recherches récentes en numismatique axoumite. *Revue numismatique* 28: 174–209.

E. Godet 1988. Considérations nouvelles sur les rois d'Axoum. *Abbay* 13: 11–57.

A. D. Godley (ed. & trans.) 1920–25. *The History of Herodotus, with an English translation* (4 vols). London: Heinemann; Cambridge MA: Harvard University Press (Loeb Classical Library).

G. Goldenberg 1977. The Semitic languages of Ethiopia and their classification. *Bulletin of the School of Oriental and African Studies [London]* 40: 461–507.

A. Gori 2007. Entry under 'Arabic inscriptions in the Ethiopian regions'. Uhlig 2007: 165–7.

G. Gragg 2004. Ge'ez (Aksum). pp. 427–53 in R. D. Woodward (ed.) *The Cambridge Encyclopedia of the World's Ancient Languages.* Cambridge: Cambridge University Press.

P. T. R. Gray 2005. The legacy of Chalcedon: Christological problems and their significance. pp. 215–38 in M. Maas (ed.) *The Cambridge Companion to the Age of Justinian*. Cambridge: Cambridge University Press.

P. Graziosi 1941. Le pitture rupestri dell'Amba Focada, Eritrea. *Rassegna di Studi Etiopici* 1: 61–70.

G. Greatrex 1998. *Rome and Persia at War, 502–532*. Leeds: Cairns.

P. Grierson 1982. *Byzantine Coins*. London: Methuen.

R. Grierson (ed.) 1993. *African Zion: the sacred art of Ethiopia*. New Haven CT & London: Yale University Press.

R. Grierson & S. C. Munro-Hay 1999. *The Ark of the Covenant*. London: Weidenfeld & Nicolson.

A. Grillmeier (trans. O. C. Dean) 1996. *The Church of Alexandria with Nubia and Ethiopia after 451* (Vol. 2, part 4 of *Christ in Christian Tradition*). London: Mowbray. [German original, Freiburg: Herder, 1990.]

C. Guérin & M. Faure 1996. Chasse au chacal et domestication du boeuf dans le site néolithique d'Asa-Koma (République de Djibouti). *Journal des Africanistes* 66: 299–311.

A. Guillaume (trans.) 1967. *The Life of Muhammad: a translation of ibn Ishaq's Sirat Rasul Allah*. Karachi: Oxford University Press.

J. D. Gunn (ed.) 2000. *The Years without Summer: tracing AD 536 and its aftermath*. Oxford: Archaeopress (British Archaeological Reports S. 872).

X. Gutherz *et al.* 1996. Le site d'Asa Koma (République de Djibouti) et les premiers producteurs dans la Corne de l'Afrique. *Journal des Africanistes* 66: 255–97.

R. Haaland 1995. Sedentism, cultivation, and plant domestication in the Holocene Middle Nile region. *Journal of Field Archaeology* 22: 157–74.

C. Haas 2008. Mountain Constantines: the Christianization of Aksum and Iberia. *Journal of Late Antiquity* 1: 101–26.

W. Hahn 1983. Die Münzprägung des axumitischen Reiches. *Litterae Numismaticae Vindobonenses* 2: 113–80.

W. Hahn 1989. A numismatic contribution to the dating of the Aksumite king Sembrouthes. Taddese 1989: 11–13.

W. Hahn 1993. Review of Munro-Hay 1991b. *Numismatic Chronicle* 153: 316–9.

W. Hahn 1994. Déclinaison et orthographe des légendes grecques sur les monnaies d'Axoum. *Bulletin de la Société française de Numismatique* 49: 944–8.

W. Hahn 1994–99. *Touto Arese Te Chora* – St Cyril's Holy Cross cult in Jerusalem and Aksumite coin typology. *Israel Numismatic Journal* 13: 103–17, pl. xvi.

W. Hahn 1998. Statistisches zur Goldprägung des Endubis. *Mitteilungsblatt des Institut für Numismatik der Universität Wien* 17: 5–10.

W. Hahn 1999. Symbols of Pagan and Christian worship on Aksumite coins: remarks to [*sic*] the history of religions in Ethiopia as documented by its coinage. *Nubica et Aethiopica* 4/5: 431–54.

W. Hahn 2000. Aksumite numismatics: a critical survey of recent research. *Revue numismatique* 155: 281–311.

W. Hahn 2001. Noe, Israel und andere Könige mit biblischen Namen auf aksumitischen Münzen. *Money Trend* 33: 124–8.

W. Hahn 2005. The 'Anonymous' coinage of Aksum: typological concept and religious significance. *Oriental Numismatic Society Newsletter* 184: 6–8.

W. Hahn 2006a. Ezanas and Caleb: the pair of saintly kings. Uhlig 2006: 260–5.

W. Hahn 2006b. Auf den Spuren des spätantiken Münzverkehrs in Aksum. *Money Trend* 38: 192–5.

W. Hahn 2010. The sequence and chronology of the late Aksumite coin types reconsidered. *Journal of the Oriental Numismatic Society* 205: 5–10.

W. Hahn & M. Kropp 1996. Eine axumitische Typenkopie als Dokument zur spätantiken Religionsgeschichte. *Jahrbuch für Numismatik und Geldgeschichte* 46: 85–99.

S. J. G. Hall 2000. Characterizations of African cattle, sheep and goats and their contributions to archaeological understanding. Blench & Macdonald 2000: 269–79.

C. Hammond 1977. The last ten years of Rufinus' life and the date of his move south from Aquileia. *Journal of Theological Studies* n.s. 28: 372–429.

O. Hansen 1986. The king-title *Basiliskos* in Nubia in the fourth to sixth century AD. *Journal of Egyptian Archaeology* 72: 205.

J. R. Harlan 1971. Agricultural origins: centers and noncenters. *Science* 174: 468–74.

Mary Harlow & W. Smith 2001. Between fasting and feasting: the literary and archaeobotanical evidence for monastic diet in Late Antique Egypt. *Antiquity* 75: 758–68.

Michael Harlow 2000. Contributions on glass and beads. D. Phillipson 2000b: 77–86, 197–200, 400–4.

S. P. Harvey 2003. Interpreting Punt: geographic, cultural and artistic landscapes. O'Connor & Quirke 2003: 81–91.

F. A. Hassan 1988. The Predynastic of Egypt. *Journal of World Prehistory* 2: 135–85.

F. A. Hassan 2002. Archaeology and linguistic diversity in North Africa. Bellwood & Renfrew 2002: 127–33.

J. W. Hayes 1972. *Late Roman Pottery*. London: British School at Rome.

R. J. Hayward 2000. Afroasiatic. Heine & Nurse 2000: 74–98.

R. J. Hayward 2003. Entry under 'Cushitic'. Uhlig 2003a: 832–9.

B. Heine & D. Nurse (eds) 2000. *African Languages: an introduction*. Cambridge: Cambridge University Press.

M. E. Heldman 1992. Architectural symbolism, sacred geography and the Ethiopian church. *Journal of Religion in Africa* 22: 222–41.

M. E. Heldman 1993. The heritage of Late Antiquity. pp. 117–32 in R. Grierson (ed.) *African Zion: the sacred art of Ethiopia*. New Haven CT: Yale University Press.

M. E. Heldman 1994. Early Byzantine sculptural fragments from Adulis. *Etudes éthiopiennes* 1: 239–52.

M. E. Heldman 1995. Legends of Lalibela: the development of an Ethiopian pilgrimage site. *Res* 27: 25–38.

M. E. Heldman 2003. Entry under 'Canon tables'. Uhlig 2003a: 680–1.

M. E. Heldman 2007. Metropolitan bishops as agents of artistic interaction between Egypt and Ethiopia during the thirteenth and fourteenth centuries. pp. 84–105 in C. Hourihane (ed.) *Interactions: artistic interchange between the eastern and western worlds in the medieval period*. Princeton NJ: Department of Art and Archaeology.

M. E. Heldman 2010. Entry under 'Miniature painting'. Uhlig & Bausi 2010: 94–7.

M. E. Heldman & Getatchew Haile 1987. Who is who in Ethiopia's past, III: founders of Ethiopia's Solomonic dynasty. *Northeast African Studies* 9: 1–11.

U. Hellwag 2010a. Entry under 'Shields'. Uhlig & Bausi 2010: 650–2.

U. Hellwag 2010b. Entry under 'Spears and lances'. Uhlig & Bausi 2010: 719–21.

P. Henze 2007. Entry under 'Nazret'. Uhlig 2007: 1158–9.

Herodotus, *History*: see Rawlinson 1862; Godley 1920–25.

E. A. Hildebrand 2007. A tale of two tuber crops: how attributes of enset and yams may have shaped prehistoric human-plant interactions in southwest Ethiopia. Denham *et al.* 2007: 273–98.
G. F. Hill 1922. Ancient methods of coining. *Numismatic Chronicle* ser. 5 2: 21–43.
G. C. Hillman *et al.* 1996. Identification of archaeological remains of wheat: the 1992 London workshop. *Circaea* 12: 195–209.
C. M. Hills 2001. From Isidore to isotopes: ivory rings in early medieval graves. pp. 131–46 in H. Hamerow & A. McGregor (eds) *Image and Power in the Archaeology of Early Medieval Britain: essays in honour of Rosemary Cramp*. Oxford: Oxbow.
Hiluf Berhe 2009. Preliminary report on the archaeological excavation of Maqaber Ga'ewa at Addi Akaweh (Tigrai, Ethiopia). *Annales d'Ethiopie* 24: 15–31.
B. Hirsch & F-X. Fauvelle-Aymar 2001. Aksum après Aksum: royauté, archéologie et herméneutique chrétienne de Ménélik II (r. 1865–1913) à Zara Yaqob (r. 1434–1468). *Annales d'Ethiopie* 17: 59–109.
E. Honigmann 1950. Un évêque d'Adoulis au Concile de Chalcédoine. *Byzantion* 20: 296–301.
E. Honigmann 1954. Gélase de Caesarée et Rufin d'Aquilée. *Académie royale de Belgique, Bulletin de la Classe des Lettres et des Sciences morales et politiques* 40: 122–61.
P. Horden 2005. Mediterranean plague in the age of Justinian. pp. 134–60 in M. Maas (ed.) *The Cambridge Companion to the Age of Justinian*. Cambridge: Cambridge University Press.
M. Horton 1996. *Shanga: the archaeology of a Muslim trading community on the Coast of East Africa*. London: British Institute in Eastern Africa.
R. J. Horvath 1969. The wandering capitals of Ethiopia. *Journal of African History* 10: 205–19.
G. Hudson 1977. Language classification and the Semitic prehistory of Ethiopia. *Folia Orientalia* 18: 119–66.
G. Hudson 2000. Ethiopian Semitic overview. *Journal of Ethiopian Studies* 33, 2: 75–86.
G. W. B. Huntingford 1965a. *The Land Charters of Northern Ethiopia*. Addis Ababa: Institute of Ethiopian Studies, Haile Sellassie I University.
G. W. B. Huntingford 1965b. The wealth of kings and the end of the Zagwe dynasty. *Bulletin of the School of Oriental and African Studies [London]* 28: 1–23.
G. W. B. Huntingford (trans. & ed.) 1980. *The Periplus of the Erythraean Sea*. London: Hakluyt Society.
G. W. B. Huntingford (ed. R. Pankhurst) 1989. *The Historical Geography of Ethiopia*. Oxford: Oxford University Press for the British Academy.
T. Insoll 2003. *The Archaeology of Islam in sub-Saharan Africa*. Cambridge: Cambridge University Press.
A. K. Irvine 1964. Some notes on old South Arabian monetary terminology. *Journal of the Royal Asiatic Society* 1964: 18–36.
E. Isaac 1972. An obscure component in Ethiopian Church history. *Le Muséon* 85: 225–58.
E. Isaac & C. Felder 1988. Reflections on the origins of Ethiopian civilisation. pp. 71–83 in Taddese Beyene (ed.) *Proceedings of the Eighth International Conference of Ethiopian Studies*, vol. 1. Addis Ababa: Institute of Ethiopian Studies, Addis Ababa University.
ibn Ishaq, *Sirat Rasul Allah*: see Guillaume 1967.

O. A. Jäger & I. Pearce 1974. *Antiquities of North Ethiopia: a guide* (2nd edn). Stuttgart: Brockhaus.

W. James 2007 [issued 2011]. A 'frontier mosaic': Ethiopia's western edge. *Journal of Ethiopian Studies* 40: 277–91.

S. Japp *et al.* 2011. Yeha and Hawelti: cultural contacts between Saba and D'mt. *Proceedings of the Seminar for Arabian Studies* 41: 145–60.

N. Jasny 1944. *The Wheats of Classical Antiquity*. Baltimore MD: Johns Hopkins Press.

E. Jeffreys *et al.* (trans.) 1986. *The Chronicle of John Malalas*. Melbourne: Australian Association for Byzantine Studies (*Byzantina Australiensia* 4).

E. Jeffreys *et al.* (eds) 1990. *Studies in John Malalas*. Sydney: Australian Association for Byzantine Studies (*Byzantina Australiensia* 6).

John of Antioch = John Malalas.

John Malalas [also known as John of Antioch], *Chronicle*: see Thurn 2000; English translation in Jeffreys *et al.* 1986.

D. W. Johnson 1995. Dating the *Kebra Negast*: another look. pp. 197–208 in T. S. Miller & J. Nesbitt (eds) *Peace and War in Byzantium*. Washington DC: Catholic University of America Press.

H. L. Jones (ed. & trans.) 1917–32. *The Geography of Strabo with an English translation* (8 vols). London: Heinemann; Cambridge MA: Harvard University Press (Loeb Classical Library).

R. Joussaume 1981. L'art rupestre de l'Ethiopie. pp. 159–75 in C. Roubet *et al.* (eds) *Préhistoire Africaine: mélanges offerts au Doyen Lionel Balout*. Paris: ADPF.

R. Joussaume 2007. *Tuto Fela et les stèles du sud de l'Ethiopie*. Paris: Editions Recherches sur les Civilisations.

B. Juel-Jensen 1998. The first Christian gold coin of King 'Ezanas of Aksum. *Spink Numismatic Circular* 106: 206–8.

B. Juel-Jensen 1999. Chapelet casting in Aksum. *Spink Numismatic Circular* 107: 8.

B. Juel-Jensen & G. Rowell (eds) 1975. *Rock-hewn Churches of Eastern Tigray*. Oxford: Oxford University Exploration Club.

A. Kaczmarczyk 1989. Appendix 1: The composition of glass vessels and beads from Aksum. Munro-Hay 1989a: 333–9.

G. Kapitän 1969. The church wreck off Marzamemi. *Archaeology* 22: 122–33.

J. Kasantchis in press. L'Inscription dite de Sembrouthes, pseudo-roi d'Aksoum. In F-X. Fauvelle-Aymar & B. Hirsch (eds), *Hommage à Jean Boulègue*. Paris: Publications de la Sorbonne [2011/2].

Kebbede Mikael & J. Leclant 1955. La Section d'Archéologie (1952–1955). *Annales d'Ethiopie* 1: 1–8.

Kebra Negast: see Bezold 1905; Budge 1922.

G. Killen 1994. *Egyptian Woodworking and Furniture*. Princes Risborough: Shire Publications.

D. Killick 2004. Review essay: what do we know about African iron working? *Journal of African Archaeology* 2: 97–112.

L. P. Kirwan 1972. The *Christian Topography* and the kingdom of Axum. *Geographical Journal* 138: 166–77.

L. P. Kirwan 1979. The Arabian background to one of the 'Cosmas' inscriptions from Adulis (Ethiopia). pp. 93–9 in A. T. al-Ansary *et al.* (eds) *Studies in the History of Arabia*, vol. 1, 1. Riyadh: King Saud University Press.

K. A. Kitchen 2004. The elusive Land of Punt revisited. Lunde & Porter 2004: 25–31.

M. A. Knibb 2003. Entry under 'Bible'. Uhlig 2003a: 565.

Y. Kobishchanov 1979. *Axum*. (ed. J. Michels). University Park PA: Penn State University Press.
J. Kollwitz 1964. Alexandrinische Elfenbeine. pp. 207–20 in K. Wessel (ed.) *Christentum am Nil*. Recklinghausen: Bongers.
R. Krautheimer 1986. *Early Christian and Byzantine Architecture* (4th edn). New Haven & London: Yale University Press.
M. Kropp 1991. Abreha's names and titles: CIH 541, 4–9 reconsidered. *Proceedings of the Seminar for Arabian Studies* 21: 135–45.
M. Kropp 1994. Ein Gegenstand und seine Aufschrift (RIE 180 = JE 5). pp. 129–44 in Yaqob Beyene *et al.* (eds) *Etiopia e Oltre: studi in onore di Lanfranco Ricci*. Naples: Istituto Universitario Orientale.
M. Kropp 2006a. Die Stele von Matara. Wenig 2006a: 321–8.
M. Kropp 2006b. Stelenstumpf mit sabäischer Aufschrift aus Kaskase. Wenig 2006a: 333–42.
M. Kropp in press. Monumentalised accountancy from ancient Ethiopia: the stela of Maryam Anza.
O. Krzyszkowska 1990. *Ivory and Related Materials: an illustrated guide*. London: Institute of Classical Studies (*Bulletin Supplement* 59).
K. Lake (ed. & trans.) 1926. *Eusebius: Ecclesiastical History,* vol. 1. London: Heinemann; Cambridge MA: Harvard University Press (Loeb Classical Library).
D. M. Lang 1966. *The Georgians*. London: Thames & Hudson.
K. D. S. Lapatin 2001. *Chryselephantine Statuary in the Ancient Mediterranean World*. Oxford: Oxford University Press.
S. Lauffer 1971. *Diokletians Preisedikt: Texte und Kommentare*. Berlin: de Gruyter.
J. Leclant 1959a. Haoulti-Melazo (1955–1956). *Annales d'Ethiopie* 3: 43–82.
J. Leclant 1959b. Les fouilles a Axoum en 1955–1956: rapport préliminaire. *Annales d'Ethiopie* 3: 3–23.
J. Leclant 1964. Frühäthiopische Kultur. pp. 9–34 in K. Wessel (ed.) *Christentum am Nil*. Recklinghausen: Bongers.
J. Leclant 1973. Glass from the Meroitic necropolis of Sedeinga, Sudanese Nubia. *Journal of Glass Studies* 15: 52–68.
J. Leclant 2007. Rapport sur l'état des publications de l'Académie pendant l'année 2006. *Comptes rendus des séances de l'Académie des Inscriptions et Belles- Lettres 2007*: 429–42.
J. Leclant 2008. Rapport sur l'état des publications de l'Académie pendant l'année 2007. *Comptes rendus des séances de l'Académie des Inscriptions et Belles- Lettres 2008*: 320–32.
J. Leclant & A. Miquel 1959. Reconnaissances dans l'Agamé: Goulo-Makéda et Sabéa. *Annales d'Ethiopie* 3: 107–30.
T. Lefebvre 1845–51. *Voyage en Abyssinie executé pendant les années 1839–1843* (6 vols & atlas). Paris: Bertrand.
P. Lenoble *et al.* 1994. La fouille du tumulus à enceinte el Hobagi III. *Meroitic Newsletter* 25: 53–8.
C. Lepage 1971. Les monuments rupestres de Degum et les églises de vallée. *Documents pour Servir à l'Histoire des Civilisations éthiopiennes* 2: 61–72.
C. Lepage 1972. Les monuments chrétiens rupestres de Degum en Ethiopie (rapport préliminaire). *Cahiers archéologiques* 22: 168–200.
C. Lepage 1975. Peintures murales de Ganata Maryam (rapport préliminaire). *Documents pour Servir à l'Histoire des Civilisations éthiopiennes* 6: 59–84.
C. Lepage 1976. Dieu et les quatre animaux célestes dans l'ancienne peinture éthiopienne. *Documents pour Servir à l'Histoire des Civilisations éthiopiennes* 7: 67–112.

C. Lepage & J. Mercier 2005. *Les églises historiques du Tigray / The Ancient Churches of Tigrai*. Paris: ADPF.

W. Leslau 1987. *Comparative Dictionary of Ge'ez (Classical Ethiopic)*. Wiesbaden: Harrassowitz.

J. Lesur 2007. *Chasse et élevage dans la Corne de l'Afrique entre le Néolithique et les temps historiques*. Oxford: Archaeopress (British Archaeological Reports S. 1602).

J. Lesur-Gebremariam 2009. Origine et diffusion de l'élevage dans la Corne de l'Afrique: un état de la question. *Annales d'Ethiopie* 24: 173–208.

R. Lewcock 1979. La cathédrale de Sanaa, foyer de christianisme en Arabie au vie siècle. *Les Dossiers de l'Archéologie* 33: 80–3.

L. K. Little (ed.) 2007. *Plague and the End of Antiquity*. Cambridge: Cambridge University Press.

E. Littmann 1907. Preliminary report of the Princeton University Expedition to Abyssinia. *Zeitschrift für Assyriologie und Verwandte Gebiete* 20: 151–82.

E. Littmann 1950. Aethiopische Inschriften. *Miscellanea Academica Berolinensis* 2, 2: 97–117.

E. Littmann *et al.* 1913. *Deutsche Aksum-Expedition: Herausgegeben von der Generalverwaltung der Königlichen Museen zu Berlin* (4 vols). Berlin: Reimer.

M. Ludlow 2009. *The Early Church*. London: I. B. Tauris.

P. Lunde & A. Porter (eds) 2004. *Trade and Travel in the Red Sea Region*. Oxford: Archaeopress (British Archaeological Reports S. 1269).

G. Lusini 2007. Entry under 'Kasu'. Uhlig 2007: 355.

E. Luttwak 2009. *The Grand Strategy of the Byzantine Empire*. Cambridge MA: Belknap Press of Harvard University.

D. E. Lyons 2007a. Building power in rural hinterlands: an ethnoarchaeological study of vernacular architecture in Tigrai, Ethiopia. *Journal of Archaeological Method and Theory* 14: 179–207.

D. E. Lyons 2007b. Integrating African cuisine: rural cuisine and identity in Tigrai, highland Ethiopia. *Journal of Social Archaeology* 7: 346–71.

D. E. Lyons & A. C. D'Andrea 2003. Griddles, ovens and agricultural origins: an ethnoarchaeological study of bread baking in highland Ethiopia. *American Anthropologist* 105: 515–30.

K. C. Macdonald 1992. The domestic chicken (*Gallus gallus*) in sub-Saharan Africa: a background to its introduction and its osteological differentiation from indigenous fowls. *Journal of Archaeological Science* 19: 303–18.

K. C. Macdonald & D. N. Edwards 1993. Chickens in Africa: the importance of Qasr Ibrim. *Antiquity* 67: 584–90.

M. J. Machado *et al.* 1998. Palaeoenvironmental changes during the last 4000 years in the Tigray, northern Ethiopia. *Quaternary Research* 49: 312–21.

A. de Maigret 2002. *Arabia Felix: an exploration of the archaeological history of Yemen*. London: Stacey International.

C. Mango 1986. *Byzantine Architecture*. London: Faber.

M. M. Mango (ed.) 2009. *Byzantine Trade, 4th–12th centuries*. Farnham: Ashgate.

A. Manzo 1999. Vines, Wine ... some sculptured Aksumite decorations and their ideological meaning. *Annali dell'Istituto Universitario Orientale [Napoli]* 59: 347–67.

A. Manzo 2002. Note su alcuni oggetti sudarabici rinvenuti in Etiopia. *Rassegna di Studi Etiopici* n.s. 1: 45–61.

A. Manzo 2005. Aksumite trade and the Red Sea exchange network: a view from Bieta Giyorgis (Aksum). pp. 51–66 in J. C. M. Starkey (ed.) *People of the Red Sea*. Oxford: Archaeopress (British Archaeological Reports S. 1395).

A. Manzo 2009. *Capra nubiana* in berbere sauce? – Pre-Aksumite art and identity building. *African Archaeological Review* 26: 291–303.
A. Manzo 2010. Entry under 'Rora'. Uhlig & Bausi 2010: 410–1.
H. G. Marcus 1994. *A History of Ethiopia*. Berkeley CA: University of California Press.
P. Marrassini 2007. Entry under 'Kebra Nagast'. Uhlig 2007: 364–8.
F. Marshall 1989. Rethinking the role of *Bos indicus* in sub-Saharan Africa. *Current Anthropology* 30: 235–40.
F. Marshall 2007. African pastoral perspectives on domestication of the donkey: a first synthesis. Denham *et al.* 2007: 371–407.
F. Marshall & E. Hildebrand 2002. Cattle before crops: the beginnings of food production in Africa. *Journal of World Prehistory* 16: 99–143.
F. J. Martinez 1990. The king of Rum and the king of Ethiopia in medieval apocalyptic texts from Egypt. pp. 247–59 in W. Godlewski (ed.) *Acts of the Third International Congress of Coptic Studies, Warsaw 1984*. Warsaw: Panstwowe Wydnawnictwo Naukowe.
Mashafa Aksum: see Conti Rossini 1909–10.
D. H. Matthews & A. Mordini 1959. The monastery of Debra Damo, Ethiopia. *Archaeologia* 97: 1–58.
V. A. Maxfield & D. P. S. Peacock 2001. *The Imperial Quarries. Survey and Excavation at Mons Porphyrites, 1994–1998*. vol. 1: *Topography and Quarries*. London: Egypt Exploration Society.
P. Mayerson 1993. A confusion of Indias. *Journal of the American Oriental Society* 113: 169–74.
The Earl of Mayo 1876. *Sport in Abyssinia; or, the Mareb and Tackazzee*. London: Murray.
J. C. McCann 2010. Entry under 'Plough'. Uhlig & Bausi 2010: 163–4.
M. McCormick 2007. Toward a molecular history of the Justinianic pandemic. Little 2007: 290–312.
J. W. McCrindle 1897. *The Christian Topography of Cosmas, an Egyptian Monk*. London: Hakluyt Society.
D. Meeks 2003. Locating Punt. O'Connor & Quirke 2003: 53–80.
O. F. A. Meinardus 1962. A brief history of the Abunate of Ethiopia. *Wiener Zeitschrift für die Kunde des Morgenländes* 58: 39–65.
O. F. A. Meinardus 1965. The Ethiopians in Jerusalem. *Zeitschrift für Kirchengeschichte* ser. 4 14: 117–47, 217–32.
A. Melkawi *et al.* 1994. The excavation of two seventh-century pottery kilns at Aqaba. *Annual of the Department of Antiquities of Jordan* 38: 447–68.
Mengistu Gobezie 2004. *Lalibela and Yimrehane Kirstos: the living witnesses of Zagwe dynasty*. Addis Ababa: Gebre Egziabher Baye.
J. Mercier 2000. La peinture éthiopienne à l'époque axoumite et au XVIIIe siècle. *Comptes rendus des séances de l'Académie des Inscriptions et Belles-Lettres 2000*: 35–71.
D. M. Metcalf 1960. The metrology of Justinian's follis. *Numismatic Chronicle* ser. 6 20: 210–19.
J. W. Michels 1979. Aksumite archaeology: an introductory essay. Kobishchanov 1979: 1–34.
J. W. Michels 1988. The Aksumite kingdom: a settlement archaeological perspective. vol. 5, pp. 173–83 in A. Gromyko (ed.) *Proceedings of the Ninth International Conference on Ethiopian Studies*. Moscow: Nauka.
J. W. Michels 1990. Excavations at Aksum: review article [on Munro-Hay 1989a]. *African Archaeological Review* 8: 177–88.
J. W. Michels 1994. Regional political organisation in the Axum-Yeha area during the pre-Axumite and Axumite eras. *Etudes éthiopiennes* 1: 61–80.

J. W. Michels 2005. *Changing Settlement Patterns in the Aksum-Yeha Region of Ethiopia, 700 BC – AD 850*. Oxford: Archaeopress (British Archaeological Reports S. 1446).

J. G. Milne 1926. The currency of Egypt in the fifth century. *Numismatic Chronicle* 1926: 43–92.

P. Mitchell 2005. *African Connections: archaeological perspectives on Africa and the wider World*. Walnut Creek CA: Altamira.

S. Mitchell & P. Van Nuffelen (eds) 2010. *One God: pagan monotheism in the Roman Empire*. Cambridge: Cambridge University Press.

A. Moberg (ed. & trans.) 1924. *The Book of the Himyarites*. Lund: *Acta regiae Societatis humaniorum litterarum Lundensis* 7.

R. K. Molvaer 1998. The defiance of the tenth century: empress Yodit (Judith) of Ethiopia, from an unpublished manuscript by Aleqa Tekle (Tekle Iyesus of Gojjam). *Northeast African Studies* 5: 47–58.

U. Monneret de Villard 1938. *Aksum: ricerche di topografia generale*. Rome: Pontificium Institutum Biblicum.

U. Monneret de Villard 1947. Mosè, vescovo di Adulis. *Orientalia Christiana Periodica* 13: 613–23.

A. Mordini 1941. Un riparosotto roccia con pitture rupestri nell'Amba Focada. *Rassegna di Studi Etiopici* 1: 54–60.

H. M. Morrison 1989. Chapters on beads and glass. Munro-Hay 1989a: 168–78, 188–209.

D. de Moulins *et al.* 2003. The archaeobotanical record of Yemen and the question of Afro-Asian contacts. Neumann *et al.* 2003: 213–28.

Sir W. Muir 1912. *The Life of Mohammad*. Edinburgh: Grant.

S. C. Munro-Hay 1980–81. Aksumite addenda: the existence of 'Bisi Anioskal'. *Rassegna di Studi Etiopici* 28: 57–60.

S. C. Munro-Hay 1984a. *The Coinage of Aksum*. New Delhi: Manohar; Butleigh: Senior.

S. C. Munro-Hay 1984b. The Ge'ez and Greek palaeography of the coinage of Aksum. *Azania* 19: 134–44.

S. C. Munro-Hay 1989a. *Excavations at Aksum: an account of research at the ancient Ethiopian capital directed in 1972–74 by the late Dr Neville Chittick*. London: British Institute in Eastern Africa.

S. C. Munro-Hay 1989b. The British Museum excavations at Adulis, 1868. *Antiquaries Journal* 69: 43–52 & pls iii–vi.

S. C. Munro-Hay 1989c. The al-Madhariba hoard of gold Aksumite and late Roman coins. *Numismatic Chronicle* 149: 83–100, pls 22–9.

S. C. Munro-Hay 1989d. Aksumite chronology: some reconsiderations. Taddese 1989: 27–40.

S. C. Munro-Hay 1990. The dating of Ezana and Frumentius. *Rassegna di Studi Etiopici* 32: 111–27.

S. Munro-Hay 1991a. Aksumite overseas interests. *Northeast African Studies* 13: 127–40. [Reprinted *verbatim* as pp. 403–16 in J. Reade (ed.) 1996, *The Indian Ocean in Antiquity*. London: Routledge.]

S. C. Munro-Hay 1991b. *Aksum: an African civilisation of Late Antiquity*. Edinburgh: Edinburgh University Press.

S. C. Munro-Hay 1993. State development and urbanism in northern Ethiopia. Shaw *et al.* 1993: 609–21.

S. C. Munro-Hay 1994. The iconography of Aksumite coinage. pp. 28–32 in P. Henze (ed.) *Aspects of Ethiopian Art from Ancient Axum to the 20th Century*. London: Ashgate.

S. C. Munro-Hay 1995. A new gold coin of King MHDYS of Aksum. *Numismatic Chronicle* 155: 275–7.

S. C. Munro-Hay 1997. *Ethiopia and Alexandria: the metropolitan episcopacy of Ethiopia*. Warsaw and Wiesbaden: *Bibliotheca nubica et aethiopica* 5.
S. C. Munro-Hay 1999. *Catalogue of the Aksumite Coins in the British Museum*. London: British Museum Press.
S. C. Munro-Hay 2001. A sixth-century *Kebra Negast*? *Annales d'Ethiopie* 17: 43–58.
S. C. Munro-Hay 2002. *Ethiopia, the Unknown Land: a cultural and historical guide*. London: I. B. Tauris.
S. C. Munro-Hay 2003. *Coinage of Arabia Felix: the pre-Islamic coinage of the Yemen*. (*Mare Erythraeum* 6)
S. C. Munro-Hay 2005a. *The Quest for the Ark of the Covenant*. London: I. B. Tauris.
S. C. Munro-Hay 2005b. Saintly shadows. Raunig & Wenig 2005: 137–68.
S. C. Munro-Hay & B. Juel-Jensen 1995. *Aksumite Coinage*. London: Spink.
S. C. Munro-Hay & G. Tringali 1991. The Ona sites of Asmara and Hamasien. *Rassegna di Studi Etiopici* 35: 135–70.
F-X. Murphy 1945. *Rufinus of Aquileia (345–411): his life and works*. Washington DC: Catholic University of America Press.
G. W. Murray 1967. Trogodytica: the Red Sea littoral in Ptolemaic times. *Geographical Journal* 133: 24–33.
M. A. Murray 2000. Cereal production and processing. P. Nicholson & Shaw 2000: 505–36.
N. Nebes 2004. A new Abraha inscription from the Great Dam of Marib. *Proceedings of the Seminar for Arabian Studies* 34: 221–30.
N. Nebes 2010. Die Inschriften aus dem Almaqah-Tempel in Addi Akaweh (Tigray). *Zeitschrift für Orient-Archäologie* 3: 214–37.
C. Negussie 1994. *Aksum and Matara: a stratigraphic comparison of two Aksumite towns*. Uppsala: Institut for Arkeologi, Uppsala Universitet.
M. Nesbitt & D. Samuel 1996. From staple crop to extinction? the archaeology and history of the hulled wheats. vol. 4, pp. 41–100 in S. Padulosi *et al.* (eds) *Proceedings of the First International Workshop on Hulled Wheats*. Rome: International Plant Genetic Resources Institute.
K. Neumann *et al.* (eds) 2003. *Food, Fuel and Fields: progress in African archaeobotany*. Cologne: Heinrich-Barth-Institut.
G. E. Nicholson 1960. The production, history, uses and relationships of cotton (*Gossypium spp.*) in Ethiopia. *Economic Botany* 14: 3–36.
P. T. Nicholson & I. Shaw (eds) 2000. *Ancient Egyptian Materials and Technology*. Cambridge: Cambridge University Press.
M. Nicolotti & C. Guérin 1992. Le zébu (*Bos indicus*) dans l'Egypte ancienne. *Archaeozoologica* 5: 87–107.
H-C. Noeske 1998. Zu den gussimitationen axumitischer Bronzemünzen in Ägypten und Palästina. pp. 249–65 in M. Krause & S. Schaten (eds) *Themelia: spätantike und koptologische Studien: Peter Grossmann zum 65 Geburtstag*. Wiesbaden: Reichert Verlag.
C. A. J. Nordenfalk 1938. *Die Spätantiken Kanontafeln: kunstgeschichtliche Studien über die eusebianische Evangelien-Konkordanz in der vier ersten Jahrhunderten ihrer Geschichte*. Gothenburg: Isacson.
D. Nosnitsin 2003. Entry under 'Ase'. Uhlig 2003a: 364–5.
D. Nosnitsin 2010. Entry under 'Walqayt'. Uhlig & Bausi 2010: 1122–3.
D. O'Connor & S. Quirke (eds) 2003. *Mysterious Lands*. London: University College London.
A. Oddy & S. C. Munro-Hay 1980. The specific gravity analysis of the gold coins of Aksum. pp. 73–82, pls 2–4 in D. M. Metcalf & W. A. Oddy (eds) *Metallurgy in Numismatics*, vol. 1. London: Royal Numismatic Society.

L. Oeconomos 1950. Remarques sur trois passages de trois historiens grecs du moyen âge. *Byzantion* 20: 177–83.

D. A. Olderogge 1974. L'Arménie et l'Ethiopie au IV siècle (à propos des sources de l'alphabet arménien). pp. 195–203 in *IV Congresso Internazionale di Studi Etiopici*. Rome: Accademia Nazionale dei Lincei.

J. E. L. Oulton (ed. & trans.) 1932. *Eusebius: Ecclesiastical History*, vol. 2. London: Heinemann; Cambridge MA: Harvard University Press (Loeb Classical Library).

M. Pallottino 1938. Monumenti sud-arabici del Museo Nazionale Romano. pp. 651–7 in *Atti del XIX Congresso Internazionale degli Orientalisti*. Rome: Tipografia del Senato.

A. Palmer *et al.* 1993. *The Seventh Century in the West-Syrian Chronicles: including two seventh-century Syriac apocalyptic texts*. Liverpool: Liverpool University Press.

J. A. B. Palmer 1947. The *Periplus Maris Erythraei*: the Indian evidence as to the date. *Classical Quarterly* 41: 136–40.

A. Pankhurst 1989. An early Ethiopian MS map of Tigray. Taddese 1989: 73–88.

A. Pankhurst 2007. The logic of barter in Ethiopian history and its resilience in contemporary society. *Journal of Ethiopian Studies* 40: 155–79.

Richard Pankhurst 1982. *History of Ethiopian Towns from the Middle Ages to the early Nineteenth Century*. Wiesbaden: Steiner.

Richard Pankhurst 1998. *The Ethiopians*. Oxford: Blackwell.

Richard Pankhurst 2006. The history of grapes, vineyards and wine in Ethiopia, prior to the Italian invasion. *Journal of Ethiopian Studies* 39: 35–54.

Richard Pankhurst 2010. Entry under 'Slave trade from ancient times to 19th century'. Uhlig & Bausi 2010: 673–4.

Rita Pankhurst 1989. The legacy of the Magdala collection: the impact on Western scholarship of Ethiopian manuscripts from Maqdala acquired by the British Museum. Taddese 1989: 111–28.

R. Paribeni 1907. Ricerche nel luogo dell'antica Adulis. *Monumenti antichi* 18: cols 437–572, tavv. i–xi.

M. Parkyns 1853. *Life in Abyssinia, being notes collected during three years' residence and travels in that country* (2 vols). London: Murray.

L. Pascher 2005. Vingt-cinq siècles d'architecture: les monuments les plus importants. Raunig 2005: 45–257.

D. P. S. Peacock & L. Blue (eds) 2007. *The Ancient Red Sea Port of Adulis, Eritrea*. Oxford: Oxbow.

D. P. S. Peacock & V.A. Maxfield 1997. *Survey and Excavation, Mons Claudianus: Topography and Quarries*. Cairo: Institut français d'Archéologie orientale.

D. P. S. Peacock & D. Williams (eds) 2007. *Food for the Gods: new light on the ancient incense trade*. Oxford: Oxbow.

R. K. Pedersen 2008. The Byzantine-Aksumite period shipwreck at Black Assarca Island, Eritrea. *Azania* 43: 77–94.

L. Pedroni 1997a. Sembrouthes 'il re grande': un bilancio critico. *Rassegna di Studi Etiopici* 41: 89–106.

L. Pedroni 1997b. Una collezione di monete aksumite. *Bollettino di Numismatica* 28–9: 7–147. [Although dated 1997, this work appears to have been written *c.* 1993. It was not actually issued until 2000.]

Periplus of the Erythraean Sea: see Casson 1989; Huntingford 1980; Schoff 1912.

J. Perruchon 1892. *Vie de Lalibala, roi d'Ethiopie*. Paris: Leroux (*Publications de l'Ecole des Lettres d'Alger* 10).

S. P. Pétridès 1971–72. Essai sur l'évangelisation de l'Ethiopie, sa date et son protagoniste. *Abba Salama* 2: 77–104, 3: 208–232.

J. B. Phillips & J. P. Ford 2000. The Aksumite quarries at Gobedra Hill and Adi Tsehafi. D. Phillipson 2000b: 229–46.

J. S. Phillips 1995. Egyptian and Nubian material from Ethiopia and Eritrea. *Sudan Archaeological Research Society Newsletter* 9: 2–10.

J. S. Phillips 1996. A note on Puntite housing. *Journal of Egyptian Archaeology* 82: 206–7, pl. xxiii.

J. S. Phillips 1999. Punt and Aksum: Egypt and the Horn of Africa. *Journal of African History* 38: 423–57.

J. S. Phillips 2000. Contributions on pottery. D. Phillipson 2000b: 57–77, 303–37, 389–99, 435–8, 453–8.

J. S. Phillips 2004. Pre-Aksumite Aksum and its neighbours. Lunde & Porter 2004: 79–85.

J. S. Phillips 2009. Glass, glassworking and glass transportation in Aksum. pp. 37–47 in L. Blue *et al.* (eds) *Connected Hinterlands*. Oxford: Archaeopress (British Archaeological Reports S. 2052).

J. S. Phillips *et al.* 2000. Structures and stratigraphy [at Kidane Mehret]. D. Phillipson 2000b: 280–301.

D. W. Phillipson 1977a. The excavation of Gobedra rockshelter, Axum. *Azania* 12: 53–82.

D. W. Phillipson 1977b. *The Later Prehistory of Eastern and Southern Africa.* London: Heinemann.

D. W. Phillipson 1990. Aksum in Africa. *Journal of Ethiopian Studies* 23: 55–65.

D. W. Phillipson 1993. The antiquity of cultivation and herding in Ethiopia. Shaw *et al.* 1993: 344–57.

D. W. Phillipson 1994. The significance and symbolism of Aksumite stelae. *Cambridge Archaeological Journal* 4: 189–210.

D. W. Phillipson 1995. Excavations at Aksum, Ethiopia, 1993–4. *Antiquaries Journal* 75: 1–41.

D. W. Phillipson 1997. *The Monuments of Aksum.* Addis Ababa: Addis Ababa University Press; London: British Institute in Eastern Africa.

D. W. Phillipson 1998. *Ancient Ethiopia: Aksum, its antecedents and successors.* London: British Museum Press.

D. W. Phillipson 2000a. Aksumite urbanism. pp. 52–65 in D. M. Anderson & R. Rathbone (eds) *Africa's Urban Past.* Oxford: James Currey.

D. W. Phillipson 2000b. *Archaeology at Aksum, Ethiopia, 1993–97* (2 vols). London: British Institute in Eastern Africa & Society of Antiquaries.

D. W. Phillipson 2005. *African Archaeology* (3rd edn). Cambridge: Cambridge University Press.

D. W. Phillipson 2007 [issued 2011]. From Yeha to Lalibela: an essay in cultural continuity. *Journal of Ethiopian Studies* 40: 1–19.

D. W. Phillipson 2008a. Changing settlement patterns in northern Ethiopia: an archaeological survey evaluated. *Azania* 43: 133–45.

D. W. Phillipson 2008b. [Review of Schmidt *et al.* 2008d]. *Azania* 43: 148–54.

D. W. Phillipson 2009a. *Ancient Churches of Ethiopia: fourth–fourteenth centuries*. New Haven CT and London: Yale University Press. [Ethiopian reprint, 2010, Addis Ababa: Arada].

D. W. Phillipson 2009b. Aksum, the entrepot, and highland Ethiopia, 3rd–12th centuries. M. Mango 2009: 353–68.

D. W. Phillipson 2009c. The first millennium BC in the highlands of northern Ethiopia and south-central Eritrea: a reassessment of cultural and political development. *African Archaeological Review* 26: 257–74.

D. W. Phillipson 2010. Entry under 'Stelae'. Uhlig & Bausi 2010: 742–5.
D. W. Phillipson 2011. An evaluation of the archaeological and ethnographic work of the 1906 Deutsche Aksum-Expedition at Aksum and Yeha. pp. 81–95 in S. Wenig (ed.) *In kaiserlichem Auftrag: die Deutsche Aksum-Expedition 1906 unter Enno Littmann,* vol. 2. Aichwald: Linden Soft.
D. W. Phillipson & D. Hobbs 1996. Is the Aksum standing stela in danger? *Journal of Ethiopian Studies* 29, 1: 1–18.
D. W. Phillipson & L. Phillipson 2000. Transport and stela-erection. D. Phillipson 2000b: 247–54.
D. W. Phillipson & P. R. Schmidt (eds) 2009. *Re-evaluating the Archaeology of the First Millennium BC in the Northern Horn (African Archaeological Review* 26, 4).
L. Phillipson 2000a. Aksumite lithic industries. *African Archaeological Review* 17: 49–63.
L. Phillipson 2000b. Contributions on stone dressing, lithics, *Mestaha Werki*, rock engravings, ivory-working techniques and site distributions. D. Phillipson 2000b: 254–66, 352–63, 408–11, 421–3, 433–47, 449–53, 460–8, 470–1.
L. Phillipson 2000c. A functional consideration of Gudit scrapers from Aksum. pp. 259–76 in L. Krzyzaniak *et al.* (eds), *Recent Research into the Stone Age of Northeastern Africa.* Poznan: Poznan Archaeological Museum.
L. Phillipson 2001. Grindstones and related artefacts from Aksum, Ethiopia. *Lithics* 22: 13–21.
L. Phillipson 2002. New evidence for the autochthonous foundations of Aksumite material culture. Baye *et al.* 2002: 42–57.
L. Phillipson 2006. Ancient gold working at Aksum. *Azania* 41: 27–40.
L. Phillipson 2009a. Lithic artefacts as a source of cultural, social and economic information: the evidence from Aksum, Ethiopia. *African Archaeological Review* 26: 45–54.
L. Phillipson 2009b. *Using Stone Tools: the evidence from Aksum, Ethiopia.* Oxford: Archaeopress (British Archaeological Reports S. 1926).
L. Phillipson & Sulas 2005. Cultural continuity in Aksumite lithic tool production: the evidence from Mai Agam. *Azania* 40: 1–18.
Philostorgius, *Church History*: see Amidon 2007.
Photius, *Polybiblion*: see Freese 1920.
J. Pirenne 1956. *Paléographie des inscriptions sud-arabes.* Brussels: Koninklijke Vlaamse Academie voor Wetenschappen (*Verhandelingen, Klasse der Letteren* 26).
J. Pirenne 1961. La date du *Périple de la Mer Érythrée. Journal Asiatique* 249: 441–59.
J. Pirenne 1965a. Le trône de Dar el-Beida (Marib). *Syria* 42: 311–41.
J. Pirenne 1965b. Entry under 'Sabea d'Etiopia, arte'. *Enciclopedia dell'Arte Antica, Classica e Orientale* 6: 1044–8. Rome: Istituto dell'Enciclopedia Italiana.
J. Pirenne 1967. Haoulti et ses monuments: nouvelle interpretation. *Annales d'Ethiopie* 7: 125–40.
J. Pirenne 1970. Haoulti, Gobochéla (Mélazo) et le site antique. *Annales d'Ethiopie* 8: 117–27.
J. Pirenne 1987. The chronology of ancient South Arabia: diversity of opinion. pp. 116–22 in W. Daum (ed.) *Yemen: 3,000 years of art and civilisation in Arabia Felix*. Insbruck: Pinguin.
J. Pirenne 1989. La signification symbolique des églises de Lalibéla. Taddese 1989: 137–45.

A. Piva 1907. Una civiltà scomparsa dell'Eritrea e gli scavi archeologici nella regione di Cheren. *Nuova Antologia* ser. v, 128: 323–35.
R. Plant 1985. *Architecture of the Tigre, Ethiopia*. Worcester: Ravens Educational and Development Services.
A. Porter 2004. Amphora trade between South Arabia and East Africa in the first millennium BC: a re-examination of the evidence. *Proceedings of the Seminar for Arabian Studies* 34: 261–75.
A. Porter 2010. A Sabaean-related ceramic jar from the Almaqah temple, Meqaber Ga'ewa. Wolf & Nowotnick 2010b: 203–8.
A. Porter *et al.* 2009. The function of ceramic jar type 4100: a preliminary organic residue analysis. *Proceedings of the Seminar for Arabian Studies* 39: 337–50.
F. Praetorius [1870]. *Fabula de Regina Sabaea apud Aethiopes: dissertatio inauguralis*. Halle: Typis Orphanotrophei.
O. de B. Priaulx 1862–63. On the Indian embassies to Rome from the reign of Claudius to the death of Justinian. *Journal of the Royal Asiatic Society of Great Britain and Ireland* 19: 274–98, 20: 269–312.
R. M. Price (trans.) & J. Binns (ed.) 1991. *Lives of the Monks of Palestine* [by Cyril of Scythopolis]. Kalamazoo MI: Cistercian Publications.
Procopius, *History of the Wars*: see Dewing 1914–28.
S. Puglisi 1941. Primi risultati delle indagini compiute dalla Missione Archaeologica di Aksum. *Africa Italiana* 8: 95–153.
S. Puglisi 1946. Industria litica di Aksum nel Tigrai occidentale. *Rivista di Scienze Preistoriche 1*: 284–90.
G. Pwiti & R. Soper (eds) 1996. *Aspects of African Archaeology: papers from the 10th Congress of the PanAfrican Association for Prehistory and Related Studies*. Harare: University of Harare Publications.
A. Rahlfs 1916. Zu den alt abessinischen Königsinschriften. *Oriens Christianus* n.s. 6: 282–313.
W. Raunig (ed.) 2005. *L'Art en Ethiopie*. Paris: Hazan.
W. Raunig & S. Wenig (eds) 2005. *Afrikas Horn: Akten der Ersten Internationalen Littmann-Konferenz Mai 2002 in München*. Wiesbaden: Harrassowitz.
G. Rawlinson 1862. *History of Herodotus* (4 vols). London: Murray.
Rezene Russom 2005. The archaeological sites of Adulis and Metara. Raunig & Wenig 2005: 87.
L. Ricci 1959. Ritrovamenti archeologici in Eritrea. *Rassegna di Studi Etiopici* 14: 48–68.
L. Ricci 1960a. Iscrizioni rupestri dell'Eritrea. *Rassegna di Studi Etiopici* 15: 55–95 and 16: 77–119.
L. Ricci 1960b. La statuetta di bovino in bronzo da Zeban Kutur. *Rassegna di Studi Etiopici* 15: 112–3.
L. Ricci 1988 [but issued 1990]. Appunti archeologici. *Rassegna di Studi Etiopici* 32: 129–65.
L. Ricci 2002. Gobedra e la 'leonessa', ovverosia il leopardo. *Rassegna di Studi Etiopici* n. s. 1: 24–7.
L. Ricci & R. Fattovich 1986. Scavi archeologici nella zona di Aksum, A – Seglamien. *Rassegna di Studi Etiopici* 30: 117–69 & pls. x–xv.
L. Ricci & R. Fattovich 1987. Scavi archeologici nella zona di Aksum, B – Bieta Giyorgis. *Rassegna di Studi Etiopici* 31: 123–97 & pls. i–li.
RIE = Bernand *et al.* 1991–2000.
C. Robin 1989. La première intervention abyssine en Arabie méridionale (de 200 à 270 de l'ère chrétienne environ). Taddese 1989: 147–62.
C. Robin 1991. L'Arabie du Sud et la date du *Périple de la Mer Erythrée*. *Journal Asiatique* 279: 1–30.

C. Robin 2009. Inventaire des documents épigraphiques provenant du royaume de Himyar aux ive–vie siècles, pp. 165–216 in J. Schiettecatte (ed.) *L'Arabie à la veille de l'Islam: bilan clinique*. Paris: de Boccard.

C. Robin & A. de Maigret 1998. Le grand temple de Yéha (Tigray, Ethiopie), après la première campagne de fouilles de la mission française. *Comptes rendus des séances de l'Académie des Inscriptions et Belles-Lettres 1998*: 737–98.

C. Robin & A. de Maigret 2009. Le royaume sudarabique de Ma'in: nouvelles données grâce aux fouilles italiennes de Barâqish (l'antique Yathill). *Comptes rendus des séances de l'Académie des Inscriptions et Belles-Lettres 2008*: 57–96.

M. Rodinson 1964a. Sur la question des influences juives en Ethiopie. *Journal of Semitic Studies* 9: 11–19.

M. Rodinson 1964b. [Review of Ullendorff 1960]. *Bibliotheca Orientalis* 21: 238–45.

M. Rodinson 1965. Le problème du christianisme éthiopien: substrat juif ou christianisme judaïsant? *Revue de l'Histoire des Religions* 167: 113–7.

E. Rodziewicz 1998. Archaeological evidence for bone and ivory carvings in Alexandria. pp. 135–58 in J. Y. Empereur (ed.) *Commerce et artisanat dans l'Alexandrie hellénistique et romaine.* (*Bulletin de Correspondance Hellénique, Supplément* 33).

E. Rodziewicz 2003. On the Alexandrian School of ivory carvings in Late Antiquity. *Bulletin de la Société Archéologique d'Alexandrie*: 47: 49–69.

E. Rodziewicz 2007. *Bone and ivory carvings from Alexandria.* Cairo: Institut français d'Archéologie orientale (*Etudes Alexandrines 12).*

E. Rodziewicz 2009. Ivory, bone, glass and other production at Alexandria, 5th–9th centuries. M. Mango 2009: 83–95.

J. C. Rolfe (ed. & trans.) 1935–40. *The History of Ammianus Marcellinus, with an English translation* (3 vols). London: Heinemann; Cambridge MA: Harvard University Press (Loeb Classical Library).

Rufinus of Aquileia, *Ecclesiastical History*: see Amidon 1997.

E. Rüppell 1838–40. *Reise in Abyssinien* (2 vols & atlas). Frankfurt-am-Main: Schmerber.

F. Russo & G. Russo 1989. Sugli intarsi in oro nella monetazione aksumite. *Bollettino di Numismatica* 13: 144–60.

A. Sackho-Autissier 2002. Les sceaux et les jetons du site du Mahal Teglinos-Kassala (Delta du Gash, Soudan): aperçus du système administratif local. *Archéologie du Nil moyen* 9: 159–62.

S. Sand 2009. *The Invention of the Jewish People.* London: Verso.

P. Sarris 2002. The Justinianic plague: origins and effects. *Continuity and Change* 17: 169–82.

P. Sarris 2007. Bubonic plague in Byzantium: the evidence of non-literary sources. Little 2007: 119–32.

R. Sauter 1967. L'arc et les panneaux sculptés de la vieille église d'Asmara. *Rassegna di Studi Etiopici* 23: 220–31.

J. Schamp 1987a. Gélase ou Rufin: un fait nouveau. *Byzantion* 57: 360–90.

J. Schamp 1987b. The lost *Ecclesiastical History* of Gelasius of Caesarea. *Patristic and Byzantine Review* 6, 2: 146–52.

P. R. Schmidt 2010. [Review of Finneran 2007]. *Journal of African Archaeology* 8: 153–5.

P. R. Schmidt & M. C. Curtis 2001. Urban precursors in the Horn: early 1st millennium BC communities in Eritrea. *Antiquity* 75: 849–59.

P. R. Schmidt & A. Naty 2008. Bulls' heads and enigmas: strong inference and interpretative puzzles in Eritrea. Schmidt *et al.* 2008d: 235–45.

P. R. Schmidt *et al.* 2008a. The Ancient Ona communities of the first millennium BCE: urban precursors and independent development on the Asmara Plateau. Schmidt *et al.* 2008d: 109–61.

P. R. Schmidt *et al.* 2008b. Ancient gold mining north of Asmara: a focus on Hara Hot. Schmidt *et al.* 2008d: 179–87.

P. R. Schmidt *et al.* 2008c. The Emba Derho site: an Aksumite-period tomb north of Asmara, Eritrea. Schmidt *et al.* 2008d: 247–64.

P. R. Schmidt *et al.* (eds) 2008d. *The Archaeology of Ancient Eritrea*. Trenton NJ: Red Sea Press.

P. R. Schmidt 2009. Variability in Eritrea and the archaeology of the northern Horn during the first millennium BC: subsistence, ritual, and gold production. *African Archaeological Review* 26: 305–25.

M. Schneider 1967. Stèles funéraires arabes de Quiha. *Annales d'Ethiopie* 7: 107–122.

M. Schneider 1983. *Steles funéraires musulmanes des Iles Dahlak (Mer Rouge)*. Cairo: Institut français d'Archéologie orientale.

P. Schneider 2004. *L'Ethiopie et l'Inde: interférences et confusions aux extrémités du monde antique*. Rome: Ecole française de Rome.

R. Schneider 1973. Deux inscriptions sudarabiques de Tigré. *Bibliotheca Orientalis* 30: 385–9.

R. Schneider 1973–79. Quelques remarques linguistiques sur l'inscription de W'ZB, fils de Kaleb. *Comptes-rendus du Groupe Linguistique d'Etudes Chamito-Sémitiques* 16: 23–5. (Paris: Geuthner).

R. Schneider 1974. Trois nouvelles inscriptions royales d'Axoum. pp. 767–86 in *IV Congresso Internazionale di Studi Etiopici*. Rome: Accademia Nazionale dei Lincei.

R. Schneider 1976a. L'inscription chrétienne d'Ezana en écriture sudarabe. *Annales d'Ethiopie* 10: 109–17.

R. Schneider 1976b. Documents épigraphiques de l'Ethiopie – V. *Annales d'Ethiopie* 10: 81–93.

R. Schneider 1976c. Les débuts de l'histoire éthiopienne. *Documents pour servir à l'histoire des civilisations éthiopiennes* 7: 47–54.

R. Schneider 1984. Review article [of Kobishchanov 1979]. *Journal of Ethiopian Studies* 17: 148–74.

R. Schneider 1987. Notes sur les inscriptions royales aksumites. *Bibliotheca Orientalis* 44: cols 599–616.

R. Schneider 1994 [but issued 1996]. Remarques sur le nom 'Aksum'. *Rassegna di Studi Etiopici* 38: 183–90.

R. Schneider 1996. L'inscription 'trilingue' et l'inscription en 'pseudo-sabéen' d'Ezana. *Journal of Ethiopian Studies* 29, 2: 1–3.

R. Schneider 2000. Appendix IX: Inscriptions. D. Phillipson 2000b: 512–4.

R. Schneider 2003. Remarques sur les inscriptions sabéennes de l'Ethiopie pré-aksumite. pp. 609–14 in J. Lentin & A. Lonnet (eds) *Mélanges David Cohen: études ... présentées à l'occasion de son 85e anniversaire*. Paris: Maisonneuve & Larose.

W. H. Schoff 1912. *The* Periplus of the Erythraean Sea*: travel and trade in the Indian Ocean by a merchant of the first century*. New York NY: Longmans, Green.

H. H. Scullard 1974. *The Elephant in the Greek and Roman World*. New York NY: Cornell University Press.

A. Sedov 1992. New archaeological and epigraphic material from Qana' (South Arabia). *Arabian Archaeology and Epigraphy* 3: 110–37.

A. Sedov 1996. Qana' (Yemen) and the Indian Ocean: the archaeological evidence. pp. 11–36 in H. P. Ray & J-F. Salles (eds) *Tradition and Archaeology: Early Maritime Contacts in the Indian Ocean*. New Delhi: Manohar.

A. Sedov 1997. Sea-trade of the Hadramawt kingdom from the first to the sixth centuries AD. pp. 365–83 in A. Avanzini (ed.) *Profumi d'Arabia: atti del convegno 1997*. Rome: L'Erma di Bretschneider.

A. Sedov 2007. The port of Qana' and the incense trade. Peacock & Williams 2007: 71–111.

J. B. Segal 1970. *Edessa: the blessed city*. Oxford: Clarendon Press.

E. H. Seland 2007. Red Sea and Indian Ocean: ports and their hinterland. Starkey *et al.* 2007: 211–8.

E. H. Seland 2010. *Ports and Political Power in the* Periplus. Oxford: Archaeopress (British Archaeological Reports S. 2102).

R. V. Sellers 1953. *The Council of Chalcedon: a historical and doctrinal survey*. London: Society for the Promotion of Christian Knowledge.

Sergew Hable Selassie 1969. Church and State in the Aksumite period. pp. 5–8 in *Proceedings of the Third International Conference of Ethiopian Studies*, vol. 1. Addis Ababa: Institute of Ethiopian Studies, Haile Selassie I University.

Sergew Hable Selassie 1972. *Ancient and Medieval Ethiopian History to 1270*. Addis Ababa: United Printers.

Sergew Hable Selassie *et al.* 1997. *The Church of Ethiopia: a panorama of history and spiritual life* (2nd edn). Addis Ababa: The Ethiopian Orthodox Church.

R. B. Serjeant & R. Lewcock (eds) 1983. *San'a: an Arabian Islamic city*. London: World of Islam Festival Trust.

L. Sernicola & L. Phillipson 2011. Aksum's regional trade: new evidence from archaeological survey. *Azania* 46: 190–204.

I. Shahid 1963. The *Book of the Himyarites*: authorship and authenticity. *Le Muséon* 76: 349–62.

I. Shahid 1971. *The Martyrs of Najran: new documents*. Brussels: Société des Bollandistes (*Subsidia Hagiographica* 49).

I. Shahid 1976. The *Kebra Negast* in the light of recent research. *Le Muséon* 89: 133–78.

I. Shahid 1994. On the chronology of the South Arabian martyrdoms. *Arabian Archaeology and Epigraphy* 5: 66–9.

C. T. Shaw 1977. Hunters, gatherers and first farmers in West Africa. pp. 69–125 in J. V. S. Megaw (ed.), *Hunters, Gatherers and First Farmers beyond Europe*. Leicester: Leicester University Press.

C. T. Shaw *et al.* (eds) 1993. *The Archaeology of Africa: food, metals and towns*. London: Routledge.

J. Shepherd & A. Wardle 2009. *The Glass Workers of Roman London*. London: Museum of London.

Y. Shitomi 1997. A new interpretation of the *Monumentum Adulitanum*. *Memoirs of the Research Department of the Toyo Bunko* 55: 81–102.

J. Shoshani *et al.* 2008. Interpretations of faunal remains from archaeological sites on the Asmara plateau of Eritrea. Schmidt *et al.* 2008d: 217–33.

S. E. Sidebotham 2007. Coins. Sidebotham & Wendrich 2007: 200–10.

S. E. Sidebotham & W. Wendrich (eds) 2007. *Berenike 1999/2000*. Los Angeles CA: Cotsen Institute, University of California.

V. Silogava & K. Shengelia 2007. *History of Georgia*. Tbilisi: Caucasus University Publishing House.

A. Sima 2003a. Entry under 'Abraha'. Uhlig 2003a: 42–3.

A. Sima 2003b. Entry under 'Beher'. Uhlig 2003a: 522.

A. Sima 2003–04. Die sabäische Version von König ‘Ezanas Trilingue RIE 185 und RIE 185*bis*. *Archiv für Orientforschung* 50: 269–84.
A. Sima 2005. Entry under ‘GDR(T)’. Uhlig 2005: 718–9.
A. Sima 2007. Entry under ‘Mahrem’. Uhlig 2007: 661–2.
F. J. Simoons 1960. *Northwest Ethiopia: peoples and economy*. Madison WI: University of Wisconsin Press.
F. J. Simoons 1965. Some questions on the economic prehistory of Ethiopia. *Journal of African History* 6: 1–13.
St J. Simpson (ed.) 2002. *Queen of Sheba: treasures from ancient Yemen*. London: British Museum Press.
St J. Simpson 2011. *The Begram Hoard: Indian ivories from Afghanistan*. London: British Museum Press.
W. G. C. Smidt 2004. Eine arabische Inschrift aus Kwiha, Tigray. pp. 259–68 in V. Boll *et al.* (eds) *Studia Aethiopica in Honour of Siegbert Uhlig on the Occasion of his 65th Birthday*. Wiesbaden: Harrassowitz.
W. G. C. Smidt 2005. Entry under ‘Hamasen’. Uhlig 2005: 987–90.
W. G. C. Smidt 2007. Ein wenig erforschter aksumitischer Platz in Dabra Gargis, ‘Addi Da‘ero, Tegray. *Aethiopica* 10: 106–14.
E. B. Smith 1917. The Alexandrian origin of the Chair of Maximianus. *American Journal of Archaeology* 21: 22–37.
S. Smith 1954. Events in Arabia in the 6th century AD. *Bulletin of the School of Oriental and African Studies [London]* 16: 425–68.
T. R. Soderstrom 1969. Impressions of cereals and other plants in the pottery of Hajar bin Humeid. Van Beek 1969: 399–407.
J. Starkey *et al.* (eds) 2007. *Natural Resources and Cultural Connections of the Red Sea*. Oxford: Archaeopress (British Archaeological Reports S. 1661).
H. Sternberg-el Hotabi 1994. Die verschollene Horusstele aus Aksum. pp. 189–91 in H. Behlmer (ed.) *Quaerentes Scientiam: Festgabe für Wolfhart Westendorf zu seinen 70*. Göttingen: Seminar für Ägyptologie und Koptologie.
J. Stevenson (ed.) 1966. *Creeds, Councils and Controversies: documents illustrative of the history of the Church AD 337-46*. London: Society for the Promotion of Christian Knowledge.
Strabo, *Geography*: see Jones 1917–32.
S. Strelcyn 1979. Quelques inscriptions éthiopiennes sur des ‘manabert’ des églises de Lalibala et de sa région. *Bibliotheca Orientalis* 36: 137–56.
F. Sulas *et al.* 2009. State formation and water resources management in the Horn of Africa. *World Archaeology* 41: 2–15.
J. E. G. Sutton 2008. Aksum: goldfield or vineyards? *Azania* 43: 18–35.
J-M. Szymusiak (ed. & trans.) 1958. *Athanase d'Alexandrie: Apologie à l'Empereur Constance*. Paris: Editions du Cerf (*Sources chrétiennes* 56).
Taddesse Tamrat 1972. *Church and State in Ethiopia, 1270–1527*. Oxford: Clarendon Press.
Taddesse Tamrat 1977. Ethiopia, the Red Sea and the Horn. pp. 98–182 in R. Oliver (ed.) *Cambridge History of Africa: from c. 1050 to c. 1600* (vol. 3 of 8). Cambridge: Cambridge University Press.
Taddesse Tamrat 1985. A short note on the Ethiopian church music. *Annales d'Ethiopie* 13: 137–43.
Taddesse Tamrat 1988. Processes of ethnic interaction and integration in Ethiopian history: the case of the Agaw. *Journal of African History* 29: 5–18.
Taddesse Tamrat 1993. Lost in Ethiopia [review of Huntingford 1989]. *Journal of African History* 33: 135–7.
Taddese Beyene (ed.) 1989. *Proceedings of the Eighth International Conference on Ethiopian Studies*, vol. 2. Addis Ababa: Institute of Ethiopian Studies, Addis Ababa University.

P. Tallet 2009. Les Egyptiens et le littoral de la Mer Rouge à l'époque pharaonique. *Comptes rendus des séances de l'Académie des Inscriptions et Belles-Lettres 2009*: 687–719.

Tekeste Negash 2006. The Zagwe period and the zenith of urban culture in Ethiopia *ca.* 930 – 1270 AD. *Africa [Rome]* 61: 120–37.

Tekle Hagos 2001. New megalithic sites in the vicinity of Aksum, Ethiopia. *Annales d'Ethiopie* 17: 35–41.

Tekle Hagos 2008. *Archaeological Rescue Excavation at Aksum, 2005–07*. Addis Ababa: Ethiopian Cultural Heritage Project.

Tekle Hagos 2010. The choice of Aksum as a metropolis. *Annales d'Ethiopie* 25: 139–56.

Tekle Hagos 2011. *The Ethiopian Rock Arts: the fragile resources.* Addis Abba: Authority for Research and Conservation of Cultural Heritage.

F. Thelamon 1981. *Païens et chrétiens au IVe siècle: l'apport de* l'Histoire ecclésiastique *de Rufin d'Aquilée*. Paris: Etudes augustiniennes.

D. J. Thompson 1999a. New and old in the Ptolemaic Fayyum. Bowman & Rogan 1999: 123–38.

D. J. Thompson 1999b. Irrigation and drainage in the early Ptolemaic Fayyum. Bowman & Rogan 1999: 107–22.

I. Thurn 2000. *Ioannis Malalae* Chronographia. Berlin: de Gruyter (*Corpus Fontium Historiae Byzantinae* 35).

R. S. Tomber 2005. Aksumite and other imported pottery from Kamrej, Gujarat. *Journal of Indian Ocean Archaeology* 2: 99–102.

R. S. Tomber 2008. *Indo-Roman Trade: from pots to pepper*. London: Duckworth.

L. Török 1987. *Late Antique Nubia: history and archaeology of the southern neighbour of Egypt in the 4th–6th century AD*. Budapest: Hungarian Academy of Sciences, Archaeological Institute (*Antaeus* 16).

H. F. Tozer 1935. *A History of Ancient Geography* (2nd edn). Cambridge: Cambridge University Press.

J. S. Trimingham 1952. *Islam in Ethiopia*. London: Oxford University Press.

G. Tringali 1965. Cenni sulle 'ona di Asmara e dintorni. *Annales d'Ethiopie* 6: 143–61.

G. Tringali 1978. Necropoli di Cascassè e oggetti sudarabici dalla regione di Asmara (Eritrea). *Rassegna di Studi Etiopici* 26: 47–98.

G. Tringali 1987. Reperti antichi di scultura minore e di ornamenti dall'Eritrea e da Aksum. *Rassegna di Studi Etiopici* 31: 213–8, tavv. i–xii.

Tsegay Berhe Gebre Libanos 2005. Entry under 'Dabra Damo'. Uhlig 2005: 17–20.

R. F. Tylecote 1992. *A History of Metallurgy* (2nd edn). London: Institute of Materials.

S. Uhlig 2001. Eine trilinguale 'Ezana-Inschrift. *Aethiopica* 4: 7–31.

S. Uhlig (ed.) 2003a. *Encyclopaedia Aethiopica, vol. 1*. Wiesbaden: Harrassowitz.

S. Uhlig 2003b. Entry under 'Bible'. Uhlig 2003a: 563–4.

S. Uhlig (ed.) 2005. *Encyclopaedia Aethiopica, vol. 2*. Wiesbaden: Harrassowitz.

S. Uhlig (ed.) 2006. *Proceedings XV International Conference of Ethiopian Studies*. Wiesbaden: Harrassowitz.

S. Uhlig (ed.) 2007. *Encyclopaedia Aethiopica, vol. 3*. Wiesbaden: Harrassowitz.

S. Uhlig & A. Bausi (eds) 2010. *Encyclopaedia Aethiopica, vol. 4*. Wiesbaden: Harrassowitz.

E. Ullendorff 1949. A note on the introduction of Christianity into Ethiopia. *Africa* 19: 61–2.

E. Ullendorff 1951. The obelisk of Matara. *Journal of the Royal Asiatic Society*: 26–32, pl. 3.

E. Ullendorff 1956. Hebraic-Jewish elements in Abyssinian (monophysite) Christianity. *Journal of Semitic Studies* 1: 216–56.

E. Ullendorff 1960. *The Ethiopians*. Oxford: Oxford University Press.

E. Ullendorff 1968. *Ethiopia and the Bible*. London: Oxford University Press for the British Academy.

R. T. Updegraff 1988. The Blemmyes I: the rise of the Blemmyes and the Roman withdrawal from Nubia under Diocletian. vol. 2, part 10.1, pp. 44–106 in H. Temporini (ed.) *Aufstieg und Niedergang der römischen Welt*, Berlin: de Gruyter.

D. Usai 1997. Early Axumite lithic workshop evidences from Beta Giyorgis, Axum, Ethiopia. *Rivista di Archeologia* 21: 7–12.

Viscount Valentia [George Annesley] 1809. *Voyages and Travels to India, Ceylon, the Red Sea, Abyssinia and Egypt in the Years 1802, 1803, 1804, 1805 and 1806*. London: Miller.

G. W. Van Beek 1967. Monuments of Axum in the light of South Arabian archaeology. *Journal of the American Oriental Society* 87: 113–22.

G. W. Van Beek 1969. *Hajar bin Humeid: investigations at a pre-Islamic site in South Arabia*. Baltimore MD: Johns Hopkins University Press.

J. Vansina 1985. *Oral Tradition as History*. London: James Currey.

G. Vantini 1975. *Oriental Sources Concerning Nubia*. Warsaw: Polish Academy of Sciences; Heidelberg: Heidelberger Akademie der Wissenshaften.

A. A. Vasiliev 1933. Justin I (518–27) and Abyssinia. *Byzantinische Zeitschrift* 33: 67–77.

M. van der Veen (ed.) 1999. *The Exploitation of Plant Resources in Ancient Africa*. New York NY: Kluwer / Plenum.

J. Vercoutter 1957. The gold of Kush. *Kush* 7: 120–53.

P. M. Vermeersch *et al.* 1994. Sodmein cave, Red Sea Mountains (Egypt). *Sahara* 6: 31–40.

P. M. Vermeersch *et al.* 1996. Neolithic occupation of the Sodmein area, Red Sea Mountains, Egypt. Pwiti & Soper 1996: 411–9.

G. Vogelsang-Eastwood 2000. Textiles. P. Nicholson & Shaw 2000: 268–98.

R. Voigt 2005. Article under 'Ethio-Semitic'. Uhlig 2005: 440–4.

D. W. Von Endt 1977. Amino acid analysis of the contents of a vial excavated at Axum, Ethiopia. *Journal of Archaeological Science* 4: 367–76.

D. W. Von Endt 1978. Was civet used as a perfume in Aksum? *Azania* 13: 186–8.

J. van Vorst (trans. from the French of H. le Roux) 1907. *Magda, Queen of Sheba, from the ancient Royal Abyssinian manuscript* Kebra Negast. New York NY: Funk & Wagnalls.

M. Watts 2000. The 1997 excavation [at the Stela-2 site]. D. Phillipson 2000b: 141–54.

K. Weitzmann 1972. The ivories of the so-called Grado Chair. *Dumbarton Oaks Papers* 26: 43–91.

D. A. Welsby 1996. *The Kingdom of Kush*. London: British Museum Press.

D. A. Welsby 2002. *The Medieval Kingdoms of Nubia*. London: British Museum Press.

F. Wendorf & R. Schild 2003. [Review of *Droughts, Food and Culture: ecological change and food security in Africa's later prehistory*, ed. F. Hassan]. *African Archaeological Review* 20: 121-33.

M. Wendowski & H. Ziegert 2006. State-building and Christianity at Aksum. Uhlig 2006: 387–95.

W. Z. Wendrich *et al.* 2003. Berenike crossroads: the integration of information. *Journal of the Economic and Social History of the Orient* 46: 46–87.

S. Wenig (ed.) 2006a. *In Kaiserlichem Auftrag: die Deutsche Aksum-Expedition 1906 unter Enno Littmann*, vol. 1. Aichwald: Linden Soft.
S. Wenig 2006b. Der archäologische Platz von Kaskase. Wenig 2006a: 329–32.
S. Weninger 2005. Entry under 'Ge'ez'. Uhlig 2005: 732–5.
S. Weninger 2007. Aethiosabaeica minora. *Aethiopica* 10: 52–7.
V. West 1999. Ge'ez legends on Aksumite coins. *Oriental Numismatic Society Newsletter* 159: 5–6.
V. West 2001. Ge'ez punctuation marks on Aksumite coins. *Oriental Numismatic Society Newsletter* 166: 4–5.
V. West 2006. Recent research on Aksumite coinage. *London Numismatic Club Newsletter* 8, 9: 15–24.
R. E. M. Wheeler 1954. *Rome beyond the Imperial Frontiers*. London: Bell.
D. Whitcomb 1994. *Ayla: Art and Industry in the Islamic port of Aqaba*. Chicago IL: Oriental Institute.
R. F. Wilding & S. C. Munro-Hay 1989. The pottery. Munro-Hay 1989a: 235–316.
J. Williams (ed.) 1997. *Money: a history*. London: British Museum Press.
R. Williams 1987. *Arius: Heresy and Tradition*. London: Darton, Longman & Todd.
R. Williams 2004. Athanasius and the Arian crisis. pp. 157–67 in G. R. Evans (ed.) *The First Christian Theologians*. Oxford: Blackwell.
P. Williamson 2010. *Medieval Ivory Carvings: Early Christian to Romanesque*. London: Victoria and Albert Museum.
F. Winkelmann 1966. *Untersuchungen zur Kirchengeschichte des Gelasios von Kaisareia*. Berlin: Akademie Verlag (*Sitzungsberichte der Deutschen Akademie der Wissenschaften zu Berlin, Klasse für Sprachen, Literatur und Kunst* 1965, 3).
A. Wion 2009. Le *Kebra Nagast*, 'La Gloire des Rois', compte rendu critique de quatre traductions récentes. *Annales d'Ethiopie* 24: 317–23.
P. Wolf & U. Nowotnick 2010a. The Almaqah temple of Mekaber Ga'ewa near Wuqro (Tigray / Ethiopia). *Proceedings of the Seminar for Arabian Studies* 40: 367–80.
P. Wolf & U. Nowotnick 2010b. Das Heiligtum des Almaqah von Meqaber Ga'ewa in Tigray / Äthiopien. *Zeitschrift für Orient-Archäologie* 3: 164–213.
W. Wolska 1962. *La topographie chrétienne de Cosmas Indicopleustès*. Paris: Presses Universitaires de France (*Bibliothèque byzantine* Vol. 3).
W. Wolska-Conus 1968–73. *Cosmas Indicopleustès: Topographie Chrétienne* (3 vols). Paris: Editions du Cerf (*Sources chrétiennes* 141, 159, 197).
W. Wolska-Conus 1990. La 'Topographie Chrétienne' de Cosmas Indicopleustès: hypotheses sur quelques thèmes de son illustration. *Revue des Etudes Byzantines* 48: 155–91.
Workneh Ayalew *et al.* 2000. The characterization of indigenous goat types of Ethiopia and Eritrea. Blench & Macdonald 2000: 280–9.
R. Young & G. Thompson 1999. Missing plant foods: where is the archaeobotanical evidence for sorghum and finger millet in East Africa? van der Veen 1999: 63–73.
M. H. Zach 1996. Varia meroitica I. *Beiträge zur Sudanforschung [Vienna]* 6: 115–27.
U. Zanetti 1995. Abu al-Makarim et Abu Salih. *Bulletin de la Société d'Archéologie copte* 34: 85–138.
J. Zarins 1990. Obsidian and the Red Sea trade: prehistoric aspects. pp. 507–42 in M. Taddei & P. Callieri (eds) *South Asian Archaeology 1987*. Rome: Istituto Italiano per il Medio ed Estremo Oriente.

C. Zazzaro 2006. Oggetti in metallo da Adulis (Eritrea) nella collezione archeologica del Museo Africano di Roma. *Africa [Rome]* 61: 454–82.

Zelalem Teka 2008. Distribution and significance of ancient rock-art sites in Eritrea. Schmidt *et al.* 2008d: 49–61.

H. Ziegert 2006. Aksum: quarries and copper processing. Uhlig 2006: 396–400.

T. Zitelmann 2007. Entry under 'Numbers, numerals, numeric systems'. Uhlig 2007: 1201–4.

A. Zorzi, *Itineraries*: see Crawford 1958.

R. Zuurmond 2003. Entry under 'Bible'. Uhlig 2003a: 564–5.

Index

Please note: round brackets indicate the modern state in which a site or feature is located; other glosses or translations are indicated by square brackets.

EASTERN AFRICAN STUDIES

These titles published in the United States and Canada by Ohio University Press

Revealing Prophets
Edited by DAVID M. ANDERSON & DOUGLAS H. JOHNSON

East African Expressions of Chistianity
Edited by THOMAS SPEAR & ISARIA N. KIMAMBO

The Poor Are Not Us
Edited by DAVID M. ANDERSON & VIGDIS BROCH-DUE

Potent Brews
JUSTIN WILLIS

Swahili Origins
JAMES DE VERE ALLEN

Being Maasai
Edited by THOMAS SPEAR & RICHARD WALLER

Jua Kali Kerya
KENNETH KING

Control & Crisis in Colonial Kenya
BRUCE BERMAN

Unhappy Valley
Book One: State & Class
Book Two: Violence & Ethnicity
BRUCE BERMAN & JOHN LONSDALE

Mau Mau from Below
GREET KERSHAW

The Mau Mau War in Perspective
FRANK FUREDI

Squatters & the Roots of Mau Mau 1905-63
TABITHA KANOGO

Economic & Social Origins of Mau Mau 1945-53
DAVID W. THROUP

Multi-Party Politics in Kenya
DAVID W. THROUP & CHARLES HORNSBY

Empire State-Building
JOANNA LEWIS

Decolonization & Independence in Kenya 1940-93
Edited by B.A. OGOT & WILLIAM R. OCHIENG'

Eroding the Commons
DAVID ANDERSON

Penetration & Protest in Tanzania
ISARIA N. KIMAMBO

Custodians of the Land
Edited by GREGORY MADDOX, JAMES L. GIBLIN & ISARIA N. KIMAMBO

Education in the Development of Tanzania 1919-1990
LENE BUCHERT

The Second Economy in Tanzania
T.L. MALIYAMKONO & M.S.D. BAGACHWA

Ecology Control & Economic Development in East African History
HELGE KJEKSHUS

Siaya
DAVID WILLIAM COHEN & E.S. ATIENO ODHIAMBO

Uganda Now • Changing Uganda Developing Uganda • From Chaos to Order • Religion & Politics in East Africa
Edited by HOLGER BERNT HANSEN & MICHAEL TWADDLE

Kakungulu & the Creation of Uganda 1868-1928
MICHAEL TWADDLE

Controlling Anger
SUZETTE HEALD

Kampala Women Getting By
SANDRA WALLMAN

Political Power in Pre-Colonial Buganda
RICHARD J. REID

Alice Lakwena & the Holy Spirits
HEIKE BEHREND

Slaves, Spices & Ivory in Zanzibar
ABDUL SHERIFF

Zanzibar Under Colonial Rule
Edited by ABDUL SHERIFF & ED FERGUSON

The History & Conservation of Zanzibar Stone Town
Edited by ABDUL SHERIFF

Pastimes & Politics
LAURA FAIR

Ethnicity & Conflict in the Horn of Africa
Edited by KATSUYOSHI FUKUI & JOHN MARKAKIS

Conflict, Age & Power in North East Africa
Edited by EISEI KURIMOTO & SIMON SIMONSE

Propery Rights & Political Development in Ethiopia & Eritrea
SANDRA FULLERTON JOIREMAN

Revolution & Religion in Ethiopia
ØYVIND M. EIDE

Brothers at War
TEKESTE NEGASH & KJETIL TRONVOLL

From Guerrillas to Government
DAVID POOL

Mau Mau & Nationhood
Edited by E.S. ATIENO ODHIAMBO & JOHN LONSDALE

A History of Modern Ethiopia, 1855-1991(2nd edn)
BAHRU ZEWDE

Pioneers of Change in Ethiopia
BAHRU ZEWDE

Remapping Ethiopia
Edited by W. JAMES, D. DONHAM, E. KURIMOTO & A. TRIULZI

Southern Marches of Imperial Ethiopia
Edited by DONALD L. DONHAM & WENDY JAMES

A Modern History of the Somali (4th edn)
I.M. LEWIS

Islands of Intensive Agriculture in East Africa
Edited by MATS WIDGREN & JOHN E.G. SUTTON

Leaf of Allah
EZEKIEL GEBISSA

Dhows & the Colonial Economy of Zanzibar 1860-1970
ERIK GILBERT

African Womanhood in Colonial Kerya
TABITHA KANOGO

African Underclass
ANDREW BURTON

In Search of a Nation
Edited by GREGORY H. MADDOX & JAMES L. GIBLIN

A History of the Excluded
JAMES L. GIBLIN

Black Poachers, White Hunters
EDWARD I. STEINHART

Ethnic Federalism
DAVID TURTON

Crisis & Decline in Bunyoro
SHANE DOYLE

Emancipation without Abolition in German East Africa
JAN-GEORG DEUTSCH

Women, Work & Domestic Virtue in Uganda 1900-2003
GRACE BANTEBYA KYOMUHENDO & MARJORIE KENISTON McINTOSH

Cultivating Success in Uganda
GRACE CARSWELL

War *in Pre-Colonial Eastern Africa*
RICHARD REID

Slavery in the Great Lakes Region of East Africa
Edited by HENRI MÉDARD & SHANE DOYLE

The Benefits of Famine
DAVID KEEN